The forces that shaped the actions of the Board of Deputies of British Jews and the British Section of the World Jewish Congress are brought forth in detail in Sompolinsky's erudite study of the response of British Jewry to the Holocaust. In particular his depiction of the valiant, yet mostly futile, actions of the Chief Rabbi of Britain, Joseph Herman Hertz and those of the lesser known figures, Rabbi Solomon Schonfeld and Harry Goodman, illustrates the basic political weakness that underscored the response of British Jewry to the destruction of their brethren on the continent.

Dr. Robert Rozett
Director of the Library, Yad Vashem

Little has been written on the rescue activities by British Jewry. Sompolinsky reveals hitherto unknown events and facts, such as *The Ten Million Dollar* relief fund for the Jews of occupied Europe, which actually never existed. The chapter "Ireland and the Jews of Europe" is the first comprehensive account of the subject.

Nathaniel Katzburg
Professor Emeritus of Jewish History
Bar-Ilan University

The reader of Dr. Sompolinsky's book is struck by the weakness of a divided Jewish leadership in London during the Holocaust. The feeble attempts to negotiate changes in Britain's strict policy of refusing aid and refuge to the doomed Jews of the continent were futile. The book adds significantly to our understanding of the tragic failure of the Anglo-Jewish community and its leaders to influence the British policy of blockading the Jews of the continent during the Holocaust.

Dr. Sompolinsky's book is based on first-hand sources and constitutes an important contribution to Holocaust research. It explains the British government's reasons for turning down the Jews' intercessions and illuminates the heart-breaking helplessness of the Anglo-Jewish community during the Holocaust. This well-written book is highly recommended for anyone, professional researcher and layman, wishing to understand this truly tragic chapter of Anglo-Jewish history.

Professor Leif Danziger
York University, Canada

The enormity of the Holocaust has attracted scholars to research and analyze its various aspects and dimensions almost from the very moment of the downfall of the Third Reich in 1945. Over the decades, three major – even though loosely defined – categories of participants in the historical theatre have been discerned: "perpetrators" (Nazis and collaborators), "victims" (Jews) and "bystanders" (non-Nazi Gentiles both in occupied and outside Europe). The Jews outside the area of Nazi rule – in Britain, the United States, the non-occupied Soviet Union, in Palestine (the so-called *Yishuv*) and elsewhere were both part of the persecuted group and "bystanders". Their reactions to the Nazi horrors, and especially their rescue and aid efforts, have become a major issue of research especially during the last decades; because of its touching upon the sensitive issues of Jewish self-perception and solidarity, much of this research has been colored by accusations within Jewish circles, even causing heated political and social debates and having aftereffects.

Sompolinsky's detailed study of the reactions to and activities of the Anglo-Jewish community *vis-à-vis* the Holocaust (1942–1945) and the British government's doings in this domain is a most valuable contribution to former well-known contributions such as Bernard Wasserstein's, Martin Gilbert's and Tony Kushner's. The author skillfully depicts a segmented but nevertheless involved Jewish community and the problems it faced in governmental corridors, and explores hitherto entirely unknown aspects – such as the activities undertaken by the Chief Rabbi through his "Religious Emergency Council" and by Harry Goodman in Ireland – thus providing us not only with valuable additional information, but also with innovative insights. Every scholar interested in the Holocaust, wartime Britain and Jewish history will find this study a must.

Professor Dan Michman
Chairman, Finkler Institute of Holocaust Research
Bar-Ilan University

Dr Meir Sompolinsky's book paints a vivid picture of the competing and clashing forces within the Jewish community of London during the Second World War.

Dr Yehuda Eloni, The Levinsky Academic College, Tel Aviv

An absorbing study, well researched and presented, which brings to the fore new facts of the tragedy. This book is essential reading for all students of the Holocaust.

Professor Elie Wiesel

BRITAIN AND THE HOLOCAUST
The Failure of Anglo-Jewish Leadership?

BRITAIN AND THE HOLOCAUST

The Failure of Anglo-Jewish Leadership?

———

Meier Sompolinsky

sussex
ACADEMIC
PRESS

BRIGHTON • PORTLAND

2 4 6 8 10 9 7 5 3
First published 1999 in Great Britain by
SUSSEX ACADEMIC PRESS
Box 2950
Brighton BN2 5SP

and in the United States of America by
SUSSEX ACADEMIC PRESS
5804 N.E. Hassalo St.
Portland, Oregon 97213-3644

British Library Cataloguing in Publication Data
A CIP catalogue record for this book is available from the British Library.

Library of Congress Cataloging-in-Publication Data
Sompolinsky, Meier.
Britain and the Holocaust : the failure of Anglo-Jewish leadership? / Meier Sompolinsky.
p.   cm.
Includes bibliographical references and index.
ISBN 1–902210–09–3 (h/c: alk. paper).— ISBN 1–902210–24–7 (p/b: alk. paper)
1. Jews—Great Britain—Politics and government.   2. Great Britain—Politics and government—1936–1945.   3. Holocaust, Jewish (1939–1945)—Foreign public opinion, British.   4. Great Britain—Ethnic relations.   I. Title.
DS 135.E5S56   1999
940.53´18—dc21   98–41178
CIP

Printed by Biddles Ltd, Guildford and King's Lynn
This book is printed on acid-free paper

Contents

Acknowledgments

This research is based on a doctoral dissertation. I am indebted to Professor Nathaniel Katzburg, Bar-Ilan University, Israel, for his guidance. The translation from Hebrew is by Dr David Strassler. Chapter 14 was first published in *Yad Vashem Studies* XIII. I am grateful to the editor for permission to reproduce the material here. The jacket design is by Adina Edel Sompolinsky.

Abbreviations

AJA	Anglo-Jewish Association
AJAA	Anglo-Jewish Association Archives
BD	Board of Deputies of British Jews
BSA	Archives of the British Section of World Jewish Congress
BSWJC	British Section of the World Jewish Congress
CEC	Consultative Emergency Committee
CZA	Central Zionist Archives
FAC	Foreign Affairs Committee
ICRC	International Committee of the Red Cross
IGRC	Inter-Governmental Refugee Committee
JC	*Jewish Chronicle*
JFC	Joint Foreign Committee
Joint	American Jewish Joint Distribution Committee
JTA	Jewish Telegraphic Agency
MEW	Ministry of Economic Warfare
NCRNT	National Committee for Rescue from Nazi Terror
PCR	Parliamentary Committee for Refugees
REC	Chief Rabbi's Religious Emergency Council
WJC	World Jewish Congress
WRB	World Refugee Board

To My Wife Adina
With Love

In memory of my parents Shimshon and Devora Sompolinsky, and my wife's parents Jerucham and Sara Solbirk, whose homes in Copenhagen were havens for Jewish refugees who escaped the Nazis. They extended help and comfort to hundreds of refugees. Moreover, they initiated and carried out various, often dangerous, ventures to save Jewish lives. This outstanding chapter will shortly be unveiled in print. These first-hand experiences inspired me to devote years to the study and teaching of the Holocaust.

Introduction

As a response to international pressure resulting from the restriction of Jewish immigration to Palestine at the end of the 1930s, the British government sanctioned a liberal policy of emigration to the British Isles for the Jews of Germany and Czechoslovakia.

Jewish organizations and philanthropic foundations succeeded in absorbing, in those same years, thousands of Jewish refugees in England. On the day World War II broke out, the government, taking advantage of the new situation, decreed that the gates of England were now hermetically sealed to Jewish refugees. At the same time, the "idyllic" atmosphere that had dominated the Anglo-Jewish leadership deteriorated due to a number of events and phenomena that led to a radical change in the foreign relations of British Jewry.

The central Jewish organization, the Board of Deputies of British Jews, elected, for the first time, a Zionist president, Zelig Brodetsky, a prominent member of the World Zionist Executive Committee. Thus ended the hegemony of the scions of the veteran, non-Zionist families. Some of the Jewish refugees, who recently had arrived, sank roots in their adopted homeland. As a result, new representative organizations were established according to their countries of origin.

Against the background of the swelling in ranks of Orthodox refugees, the Chief Rabbi's Religious Emergency Council was reinvigorated. This was a political-humanitarian organization founded by and operated under the patronage of Chief Rabbi Herman Hertz, and under the independent leadership of Ultraorthodox Rabbi Solomon Schonfeld. The *raison d'être* of the organization was to act on behalf of the Orthodox public in all spheres, distinct from the Board of Deputies.

Jewish leaders from occupied Europe who had fled to London set up contacts for cooperation with, and in conjunction with, various foreign governments.

Moreover, the new Jewish international organization, called the World Jewish Congress, established a strong London branch (known as the British Section of the WJC) whose objectives were diplomatic and political – to aid Jews in crisis situations. The British Section was headed by two charismatic individuals - Lady Reading and Sidney Silverman MP.

According to long-standing tradition, the Board of Deputies alone worked for their brethren in distress by relying on government connections. This status quo was violated with the advent in the British Jewish community of the aforementioned multiple bodies all battling to win the authority to conduct foreign policy that affected the fate of the Jews. It proved impossible to prevent this struggle.

The joint goal of all the groups was to search, via negotiations with the government, for ways to succor and to save their suffering brethren. The duplication and disputes among the organizations, however, weakened the Jews' standing in their confrontations *vis-à-vis* the authorities. The numerous Jewish delegations that roamed the length of government corridors only served to aggravate state officials. These annoyances caused antipathy and ultimately eroded the Jewish organizations' relations with the government.

In the archives one can find volumes of letters attesting to correspondence between Jewish organizations pleading for intercession and the government's replies. Reams of protocols give testimony to the many meetings conducted by the two sides. These efforts produced meager, if any, results. In contrast to the dispersion of forces among the Jews, the government concentrated its attention to the matter via only a few senior Foreign Office officials. The entire matter of European Jewry was shunted off to this one ministry. Ministerial responsibility for the "Jewish Subject" was put solely on the shoulders of a very strong Cabinet personality, Foreign Secretary Anthony Eden.

To reiterate – from the war's outbreak the government's policy was to enforce a closure of Britain's gates to European Jewry. This policy had general government approval and Eden received full backing even from Cabinet members thought to be pro-Jewish.   Eden's boss, Winston Churchill, considered a supporter of Jewish and Zionist causes, refused to intercede on behalf of the Jews with his Foreign Secretary. At critical times, Churchill, without hesitation, supported Eden's callousness regarding the fate of the Jews. The PM's sole "positive" contributions were warm words of sympathy over the Jews' plight and harsh condemnation of their murderers. Martin Gilbert, Churchill's biographer, presented the PM's contribution to the wartime rescue effort in an article in *The Times* on June 7, 1996: "From the first to the last days of the war, the fate of the Jews was something on which Churchill took immediate and positive action wherever he was asked to do so." In this statement, Gilbert misrepresents his own facts. The previous sentence is out of sync with the rest of his article in which he summarizes "all the deeds" of Churchill for the Jews as just words.

Not only did Churchill not initiate action to save the Jews, he unhesitatingly supported Eden on the issue of upholding the closure, knowing full well the results. This situation developed due to the convergence of monolithic aspects of the British anti-escape policy. The problematic situation confronting the Anglo-Jewish leaders is understandable, especially when juxtaposed with their internal arguments and disarray.

Two central reasons buttressed the British government's policy of occlusion which prevented the escape of European Jewry: The fear that "the Middle East would be flooded by Jews" attempting to reach the shores of Palestine. This expectation, it was felt, would nullify the immigration policy anchored in the White Paper of 1939. London's policymakers determined that only the actualization of the White Paper would appease the Arabs and thereby calm the strategic Middle East region.

In the government's opinion, the flow of Jews to the British Isles was undesirable at a time when war was being waged with an enemy for whom anti-Semitism was at the core of its ideology. Aiding the stream of Jews to England was likely, they opined, to strengthen domestic anti-Semitism and validate German propaganda which claimed that the British were fighting a Jewish war. The British feared that internalization of this propaganda would hurt morale.

Nevertheless, the British fulfilled their blockade/closure policy with unnecessary fanatical obsession. Any movement of Jews hoping to escape Europe – in any number, in any direction – was corralled by officials who worked energetically to prevent the Jews' deliverance. The discriminatory prohibitions that were enforced only on Jews seeking to escape to British territory give rise to suspicions that anti-Semitism was not foreign to the British upper echelons.

Zionist policy of that period was to use the specter of Jewish annihilation in Europe as pressure to open the gates of Palestine. The Board of Deputies and the Jewish Congress presented petitions to that effect to the government. From the beginning this act engendered hostility. In contrast, Rabbis Hertz and Schonfeld, who were opposed to this tack, submitted appeals which deleted any reference to Palestine. They based their requests for relief solely on humanitarian grounds – in every way and in any territory. This difference in approach led to a pitched battle among the Jews which Rabbi Shonfeld lost. Thereafter, no petitions were issued regarding rescue efforts which did not mention Palestine. After a time, though, other organizations, which opposed Rabbi Schonfeld's view, did sever to a great degree their proposals from Zionist policy.

The Zionist emphasis was certainly not favorable to the refugee cause. On the other hand, awareness of the government's attitude towards non-Palestinian solutions illustrates that in all likelihood no substantial change would have occurred in its policy, even if the Rabbis' line had been followed. Paradoxically, at a later stage in the war, the British were prepared to absorb Jews specifically in Palestine. The number of candidates for *aliya* had decreased due to their deaths, and therefore permits remained for refugees within the framework and under the quota of the White Paper. Thus the British could proclaim their contribution to the rescue of the Jews without deviating from their policies. This was a method of appeasing both America and the Jews.

It rapidly became apparent that even this British step was minimal. The British made no effort to open the exit gates from Europe. When apprehensive of an exodus too large, in their opinion, as from Hungary in 1944, for example, they spared no effort in preventing or at least restricting it. Their aim was to regulate the flow of Jews to Palestine.

Documented confirmation of the destruction of the Jews was received by the Allied Powers in 1942–3 as the tide of the war was turning in their favor. Optimism wafted through Britain's populace regarding the war's outcome and anti-Semitic feelings dissipated. At this stage Jewish organizations proffered to the policymakers plans for assistance and rescue, but they were repeatedly deferred with different excuses. Despite this the groups never dared to publicly attack the government, lest they be accused of "insufficient loyalty" to the state. It was easier for them to let another element demonstrate the militant approach – an inter-religious organization called the National Committee for Rescue from Nazi Terror, led by Eleanor Rathbone, a Christian parliamentarian.

As it happens, sensitivity to the plight of European Jewry was increasing at the time and more encompassing. Many parliamentarians, church leaders and members of the elite gravitated to the subject of saving the Jews. Public opinion was supportive and indicated a noble readiness on the part of the British to absorb refugees for the war's duration. Government members, noting these strong manifestations of support for Jewish rescue, became alarmed that they would be coerced into capitulating to public opinion against their will. A special War Cabinet Committee was established to contest the new trend and deliver follow-up. They chalked up an impressive victory for themselves on this front.

The Jewish groups missed the opportunity to take advantage of the supportive mood in Britain. They were unreceptive to and failed to create new initiatives, but did not hesitate to arouse internal, purposeless commotion. After a while the activities of the inter-religious committee languished and the Jews did not reactivate it. Jewish public figures were not shaped from leadership material and were not powerful and enterprising movers and shakers, and therefore could not cope in those abnormal circumstances.

Only the rabbis occasionally dared to deviate, by degrees, in words and actions from the "norm." At a certain stage they urged the Jewish leaders to abandon their routine. The chief rabbi, Herman Hertz, beseeched them to unite and invite Lord Samuel to head the rescue effort. This step would have demonstrated unity at a critical hour and impacted strongly on the public. This personage would have raised the level of the rescue and assistance campaign. However the rabbi's proposal was rejected unanimously by the other Jewish leaders. The government was thus saved from dealing with the problem on a different level.

For the disappointed Jewish activists, what remained as a result of all their efforts was only to grasp onto the statement repeated again and again by government members: "Only victory in the war will bring redemption to the Jews." Those who relayed and those who heard the statement knew quite well that meanwhile the extermination machine was operating at full steam, with the goal of completing its work before the artillery was silenced.

Nonetheless, among the Jewish activists there remained those who even now were not pacified or reconciled to the Death Sentence. They grasped at straws and wove fantasies involving various countries which would open their gates to those Jews approaching death.

The question is not whether there was ever a chance to motivate the British government to adopt a more humane approach *vis-à-vis* European Jewry, in light of its rigid adherence to implementation of its policy. Research is needed to ascertain whether the Anglo-Jewish leadership did all that was required and feasible in their attempts to breach the government's wall of recalcitrance. This book is a first step on this path.

1

London Learns of the Final Solution

Corroborative information came from a non-Jewish source of unequivocal reliability: The Polish Government-in-Exile, which verified that the Germans were indeed carrying out the systematic destruction of European Jewry.

On August 17, 1942, British Deputy Foreign Secretary Richard Law wrote to Sydney Silverman MP, chairman of the British Section of the World Jewish Congress (BSWJC), informing him of the ominous contents of a cable sent via the British consul by Dr Gerhart Riegner, WJC representative in Geneva.

Riegner wrote that Hitler's headquarters had prepared a plan for transferring all the Jews under Nazi occupation – between three and a half to four million souls – to East Europe, and exterminating them "at one blow" in autumn 1942. The exact methods of destruction had not yet been determined, Riegner wrote, "as exactitude cannot be confirmed," but the Nazis were considering the use of prussic acid. Riegner stressed that his informant had close ties with the Nazi leadership and was usually reliable. He asked Silverman to relay the information to WJC headquarters in New York and confer with them about an appropriate response. In the margins of Riegner's cable Law wrote: "We have no information bearing on or confirming this story."[1]

This is how knowledge of the Final Solution reached Britain.

Law's letter reached Silverman at his home in Liverpool. He cabled New York on August 24[2] and four days later instructed Alex Easterman, political secretary of the British Section of the World Jewish Congress in London, not to act before a response came from New York and after he returned to London and obtained more information from the Foreign Office. Silverman added his hope that Law would be candid with him.[3]

Silverman's cable to New York broke the State Department's conspiracy of silence over European Jewry, a policy which had led them to suppress a similar message Riegner had sent to WJC headquarters in New York via the American consul in Geneva.[4] Silverman's cable expressed the BSWJC's great anxiety about the Final Solution and proposed adopting certain measures: an unequivocal condemnation by the political and religious leaders of the free world; press conferences; and, as was customary in times of distress, a plea for Vatican intervention. Now, Silverman insisted, was the time to invoke the dictum of "an eye for an eye": the torture of Nazis in the hands of the Allies and the seizure of German property in retribution for that stolen from Jews.[5]

The BSWJC's leaders' initial reaction was to make public the Riegner cable, a decision the Foreign Office was willing to leave to Silverman.[6] However, they soon changed their minds and decided to proceed with the utmost caution. Hesitation and confusion reigned both in London and New York. Rabbi Maurice Perlzweig, of the New York office, wrote that Silverman's telegram was undoubtedly accurate and a great shock, but that the WJC did not know exactly how to respond. New York, too, had initially thought of releasing the information, but then feared that if knowledge of the Nazi plan spread through Europe it would lead the Jews there to despair. Rabbi Stephen S. Wise, the president of the WJC, sought his government's advice, but it was in no hurry to respond.[7]

BSWJC leaders sought confirmation of the Riegner message, but the Foreign Office, as mentioned, claimed it had no supporting evidence. They then turned to Dr Eduard Benes, the Czechoslovak president-in-exile, who was known as a political and intelligence "oracle." Benes sought to allay Silverman and Easterman's fears. Claiming to have the best intelligence apparatus in Europe, he expressed surprise at the Riegner report and advised against making it public without further evidence. He suggested that the Germans might purposely be sowing misinformation in order to react angrily at the "lie" spread by the Western powers.[8]

Benes promised to have his secret service investigate. After waiting a considerable time the BSWJC approached him again in November 1942.[9] Benes responded that at long last the information had arrived, but it did not corroborate Riegner. On the contrary. There was no indication, Benes claimed, that the Germans "should be preparing a plan for a wholesale extermination of all Jews. Such a plan does not exist."[10] He did not stop with a presentation of his "findings," but offered an assessment of the situation: The Germans might be stepping up their anti-Jewish actions, especially as they sensed defeat. But they were no more cruel to the Jews than to any other occupied people. He went so far as to claim that the Jews were living in their homes "even almost unhindered."[11]

Benes, whose credibility the British doubted,[12] was apparently engaged in a maneuver to pacify the Jewish leaders. He did not want the Riegner information to be made public because it would violate the sacred principle that Jews and non-Jews were suffering equally under the Nazi yoke. We shall examine that principle in detail later in this work. Riegner's cable proved it to be a broken reed and therein lies its importance. If information about a definite plan to destroy all Europe's Jews within a set period of time could be verified, demands could be made for implementing drastic rescue procedures. Events in Czechoslovakia had already confirmed the true fate of the Jews, as Benes undoubtedly knew. Hence his emphasis on Nazi cruelty as Germany's defeat grew nigh. He even warned the WJC leaders that publicizing the Riegner cable would make matters even worse for the Jews.

At the beginning of September, the Swiss branch of the ultraorthodox Jewish organization, Agudat Israel, sent a shocking cable to London and New York reporting the evacuation of masses of Warsaw Ghetto Jews. It also claimed that the corpses of the victims were being used for the manufacture of fertilizer and soap. Agudat Israel officials insisted that their sources were reliable. They pleaded for intervention by Rabbi Stephen S. Wise, Rabbi Eliezer Silver, the president of American Agudat Israel, Albert Einstein, the author Thomas Mann, and other public figures. "Only energetic action from America," they argued, could "stop the persecutions."[13] Moreover, a cable arrived two weeks later from WJC headquarters in New York stating that negotiations were being held with the US government about ways to react to the information about the annihilation of the Jews. American officials tried to assuage the Jewish leaders. According to them Jews were being shipped from Warsaw not to their death, but to work on construction sites. In the first two weeks of October, WJC leaders in New York sought to delay publication of Riegner's message. They were waiting for "important guidance" from the "highest authorities," the return to Washington of the American envoy at the Vatican, and the appropriate time to make the information public: "until right effect producable entire American press."[14]

Meanwhile, the Jewish Agency office in Switzerland sent messages to Jewish organizations that echoed Agudat Israel's plea. All this activity could no longer be ignored. On September 26, Myron Taylor, US envoy at the Holy See, asked the Vatican Secretary of State to inquire into the accuracy of the Jewish Agency reports.[15]

Corroborative information came from a non-Jewish source of unequivocal reliability: The Polish Government-in-Exile, which verified that the Germans were indeed carrying out the systematic destruction of European Jewry. Only then did the BSWJC act. Easterman, the secretary, sent identical letters, based on the Polish government's information, to the prime ministers of the governments-in-exile of Belgium, Yugoslavia, Norway, Holland, Luxembourg, Czechoslovakia, and the Committee of the Free French. For some reason neither Silverman, the MP and BSWJC chairman, nor Eva, Marchioness of Reading, its president, acted. Easterman implored them to take concerted action to stop the expulsions of Jews to the death camps in Poland. He suggested broadcasting instructions to their countrymen and women that they physically resist the expulsions and grant the Jews, especially the children, shelter. The letter was sent on November 27, 1942,[16] three months after Richard Law's letter to Silverman.

Meanwhile, more verification of the Riegner cable was emerging.[17] On December 5, 1942, the two BSWJC secretaries, Easterman and Dr Noah Barou, circulated a letter classified as "private and secret," but meant for eventual publication, to the heads of the Jewish organizations in London. They wrote that a cable sent by Stephen Wise and Chaim Weizmann, the president of the World Zionist Organization who was then in the United States, confirmed that Hitler had ordered the destruction of European Jewry by December 1942.[18]

Can the British Section of the WJC be held responsible for the loss of three irretrievable months before publicizing the plan for the annihilation of European Jewry? For only after such knowledge was made public could pressure be brought upon the government to act. Before casting the onus of such a burden on the leaders of the BSWJC it is necessary to thoroughly examine the circumstances surrounding the cable.

Riegner himself was cautious and reserved about the information. Nonetheless, he considered it his duty to release it. Therefore, could pressure on the government be based on information from a Jewish source without corroboration from elsewhere? The Foreign Office claimed that it could not authenticate Riegner and it could have dismissed his information as unreliable. It was crucially important to explore informative non-Jewish sources. Thus the approach to Benes. The Czechoslovak president, however, was more concerned with furthering his own policies than with exposing the truth. What the Foreign Office never revealed to the leaders of the WJC was that it did not consider the Czechoslovak president reliable.

There was also much logic in the need to coordinate positions with the leaders of the WJC in New York. Wise had contacts in the highest echelons of the American administration and access to President Roosevelt himself. However, he was a victim of the State Department's delaying tactics.[19]

The BSWJC went into action after an impeccable non-Jewish source confirmed Riegner. This source, the Polish Government-in-Exile, upon whose soil the slaughter was being perpetrated, could not be suspected of harboring a pro-Jewish bias.

Beyond a doubt, Riegner's action was of extraordinary importance. Prior to his cable there had been reports of cruel persecutions, mass starvation, disease and expulsions. The cable, however, was the first time that the persecutions in occupied Europe were presented as a plan stemming from "the Fuhrer's headquarters" to totally destroy the Jews. The appalling communique demanded specific attention, both on the part of the Jews and the Western governments. It was necessary to examine its accuracy. After it was verified a new period opened in the relations between the Jewish and non-Jewish advocates of the oppressed Jews and with the democratic governments. Riegner's cable signalled the turn.

The great efforts to motivate the governments to take steps to stop the killing and extend relief date from then. The first achievement was the Allies' declaration on December 17, 1942, dedicated solely to the persecution of Jews. It signalled an abandonment, at least for the time being, of the principle of the "equality" of suffering. However, no practical rescue action was instituted in its wake.

2

The Changing Balance of Power in British Jewry

The prevalent feeling was that the war would soon be over and British Jewish leaders, believing that at least four million European Jews would survive, were preoccupied with preparations for a postwar peace conference, such as formulating political demands and gathering information for individual and community claims.

The Board of Deputies of British Jews

Information about the worsening condition of the Jews in Nazi-occupied Europe and Greater Germany was available in London from the beginning of the war. It was available not only within the British government; the general and Jewish press published reports of discriminatory legislation, expulsions, starvation and murder.

As early as October 31, 1939, the Ministry of Information issued a White Paper about the persecution of the Jews in Germany.[1] *The Jewish Chronicle* consistently published reports of persecutions and the White Paper was a victory against the Jewish leadership which had criticized it for exaggeration. The government would later regret its publication.[2] (*The Jewish Chronicle* is an independent weekly read by virtually every Jew in the country. Its publisher was Ivan Greenberg, a Zionist Revisionist [follower of Vladimir Jabotinsky]; the paper was managed by Neville Lasky and Leonard Stein. As we shall see, none of them, each from his own perspective, accepted the Zionist policy line of the central Jewish institutions.)

As soon as the White Paper was issued, *The Jewish Chronicle* claimed that the Jews in occupied Europe were facing annihilation. As to the Jewish "reservation" of Lublin, for instance, the paper wrote that it was nothing other than a ploy to kill Jews.[3] On December 1, 1939, it expressed the view that the destruction of the Jews was becoming ever more imminent, and on January 12, 1940, claimed that even a superficial perusal of the Nazi press showed that the intention was to kill all the five million Jews of occupied

Europe. Only a miracle, according to its prescient editors, would save the two and a half million in Poland.

The paper was consistent. In March 1940 it claimed that the arch-murderers charged with carrying out the annihilation of Polish Jewry were Reinhold Heydrich and Adolph Eichmann: "the final aim is the annihilation of the Jews, the methods of the oppression employed by the Nazi Chieftains vary . . . "[4] Nonetheless, *The Jewish Chronicle* did not call for rescue attempts perhaps because this was the time of the "Phony War" – a period of relative calm in the winter of 1939–1940 when after much preparation for war nothing much happened except for occasional clashes along the Maginot Line. It ended on April 9, 1940 with the invasion of Denmark and Norway, and Western Europe soon after.

The prevalent feeling was that the war would soon be over and British Jewish leaders, believing that at least four million European Jews would survive,[5] were preoccupied with preparations for a postwar peace conference, such as formulating political demands and gathering information for individual and community claims.[6] Unlike the Jewish leaders, the Polish Government-in-Exile, then based in France, feared that the Germans were planning to destroy the entire Polish nation including the Jews, and in April 1940 the Polish, British and French governments issued an official warning that included them.[7]

Remarkably, this public declaration elicited no specific Jewish response. Neither did the Jewish leadership and press demand any rescue action. They believed that because the United States was neutral and maintained diplomatic and other ties with Germany, it was the task of the American Jewish organizations such as the American Jewish Joint Distribution Committee (generally referred to as the Joint) and others, to extend aid to Central and East European Jews.[8]

What spurred the Anglo-Jewish leadership into action and led to a basic change in the community's central institution, the Board of Deputies (BD), was not the deteriorating condition of European Jewry, but the prospect of an imminent end to the war through American mediation.[9] The Zionists then made a successful attempt to win the BD presidency. Their main goal was to steer a British Jewish representation along Zionist lines in the negotiations leading to the peace conference and at that conference itself.

The Board of Deputies of British Jews, founded in 1760, is the central secular institution of British Jewry. The BD deals with all internal and external civil concerns of the community. Internally the Board deals with education, social welfare and registration of members of the community. Its external concerns include fighting anti-Semitism and defending Jewish interests in British society. It was also preoccupied with problems besetting Jews outside Britain, such as in Palestine even when the *Yishuv* was struggling against Mandate policies. For that reason Zionist leaders struggled to gain control of the organization as part of a strategy which indeed included all Jewish communities.

Selig Brodetsky, professor of mathematics and aeronautics at Leeds University and a prominent member of the Zionist Executive, was the sole candidate in the December 17, 1939 BD presidency elections[10] and the first Zionist ever to fill that office. Neville Lasky, who had recently left the post,[11] had enjoyed the support of the non-Zionists, especially the Rothschilds of New Court (the residence of the Rothschild bank). Anthony de Rothschild, the Jewish community activist of the family also known as The Cousinhood and the New Court's candidate to head the BD, had sought Weizmann's endorsement, but was turned down because of his opposition to Zionism and Jewish statehood in Palestine. Despite the rebuff, Lavi Bakstansky, the leading activist of British Zionism, aware of the belief that a non-Zionist president could be of benefit to current Zionist policy, feared that Weizmann might endorse Rothschild's candidacy if Brodetsky dropped out of the race.[12]

Bakstansky was co-secretary of the Zionist Federation of Great Britain and Ireland and a member of the Jewish Agency Executive. He was also a member of the BD and some of its important committees and secretary of the Council for Jewish Refugees. Thus Bakstansky was one of the most influential figures in British Jewish life and he used his prestige to further Zionism. His sights were now set on the conquest of British Jewry's official representative organization, the BD. He supported the candidacy of Selig Brodetsky, who was a widely accepted community figure and Zionist leader.

In the debate over Britain's Palestine policy which led to the 1939 White Paper, Neville Lasky published *Jewish Rights and Jewish Wrongs*,[13] where he advocated ideas very different from those presented by the Zionists at the St. James Palace "Round Table" conference in February–March 1939. At this crucial juncture the British, meeting separately with Jewish and Arab leaders, formulated the policy later expressed in the 1939 White Paper. Lasky, who had participated in the conference as BD president, did not express reservations about the policy of the Jewish Agency. In *Jewish Rights and Jewish Wrongs*, published after the White Paper was issued, he did – much to the chagrin of Jewish Agency officials.[14] There can be little doubt that Lasky's move led Zionists, especially Bakstansky, to lobby for a Zionist candidate to succeed him. A widely-held view at the time was that a "neutral" BD president was preferable to a Zionist whose presence might spark anti-Zionist opposition. The argument was not without foundation. Under "neutral" leadership, the BD had in fact supported the *Yishuv* in Palestine and the Zionist movement at crucial times.[15]

A confidential letter sent by the Zionist Federation to Zionist delegates in the BD, noting with derision the unfortunate appearance of two competing British Jewish delegations at the Versailles Peace Conference after World War I, stressed the danger of a divided British Jewry at the next peace conference. Only the election of Brodetsky, the letter claimed, could prevent a repetition of that shameful situation. Thus the Zionist Federation demanded that Zionist delegates act as a single block, especially since their opponents were planning to propose the candidacy of the prestigious Colonel Harry L. Nathan MP, or Anthony de Rothschild.[16] Bakstansky carefully planned Brodetsky's strategy and prepared him for potential criticism.[17] Bakstansky was so intent on conquering the BD presidency that he even raised the hypothetical possibility of Weizmann himself running for the post. Therefore, as he wrote Brodetsky, "Please remember you promised me. No withdrawal except if Weizmann will stand."[18]

In the end Brodetsky was the only candidate. The other potential candidates apparently realized that the chances of defeating a united Zionist block were slim.[19]

The Board had enjoyed great prestige in British Jewry and British society from time of Sir Moses Montefiore. Its presidential nature granted its head wide authority and influence in its daily work and in policy formulation. The question is whether Brodetsky's election led to a significant change in the Board's work and achievements.

The Jewish Chronicle, for example, wondered whether Brodetsky would be able to devote the time and effort necessary to fulfill his BD duties, especially in these demanding times. The new incumbent now held three time-consuming posts: a professorship at Leeds University; the chair of the Political Committee of the Jewish Agency in London; and now the post of BD president. The last, in effect, making him the head of the British Jewish community. Would Weizmann be prepared to free him from his Zionist duties, the paper asked, adding that a Zionist at the head of the Board might endanger the unity of the community.[20] In an attempt to calm these fears, Brodetsky declared early in his BD candidacy that he would work with all sides and represent the community consensus. He also compromised his Zionist conscience when he stated that the task of the BD was to formulate a position for the peace conference that would unite all groups on Jewish issues in cooperation with American, Palestinian and French Jewry.[21] To ally the fears of non-Zionists, Brodetsky often stated that the office of president required representing the spectrum of British Jewry. His position was by no means an easy one and he was forced to emphasize different issues at different times. He adopted one stance when speaking at Zionist rallies and another at the BD. Indeed, before long New Court circles told Brodetsky that they feared that his Zionist speeches were giving the impression that all of British Jewry felt as he did.[22] Responding to Rothschild's criticism, Brodetsky admitted that he spoke in two tongues: at Zionist rallies according to his well-known views; as BD president according to the views of that body.[23] He did not, however, define those views. As we shall see, both in tone and action Brodetsky never succeeded in reconciling the conflicting pressures and finding his own way. It became even more difficult for him to do so after the British Section of the World Jewish Congress (BSWJC), with national views akin to Zionism, was established in London. In foreign affairs, the BD participated in the Joint Foreign Committee (JFC) in cooperation with the Anglo-Jewish Association, and their presidents served as co-chairman.

The Anglo-Jewish Association, established in 1871, engaged in activities similar to those of the Alliance Israelite Universelle in Paris. Initially, its brief was philanthropic assistance to Jews abroad, but later extended its activities to the political sphere by defending Jews suffering persecution. By 1878, however, when the organization established the JFC in cooperation with the BD, it ceased engaging in independent foreign operations. The agreement, renewed whenever a new Board was elected, lasted until 1943. We shall be discussing the reasons for the break between the two organizations.[24] The strength of the Anglo-Jewish Association lay in the considerable funds at its disposal, while the BD's influence derived from its broad community representation. The Anglo-Jewish Association was dominated by circles close to the Rothschilds and other established wealthy Jewish families, and its influence was enhanced by their social and political ties with the elite of British society. The Board, on the other hand, was gradually dominated by Zionists and second-generation British Jews.

In the early 1940s, Leonard Stein, a moderate Zionist, was president of the Anglo-Jewish Association. Stein, whom Nahum Goldmann considered an incorrigible minimalist, was active in British Jewish political life and during World War I, in his capacity as Chaim Weizmann's secretary, he was involved in the events leading to the Balfour Declaration, as he vividly described in his book, *The Balfour Declaration*.[25] Thus the community's foreign affairs were in the hands of Stein and Brodetsky. There were more BD than Association representatives on the JFC, but the Association's financial contribution was more significant.[26]

After the December 1939 Board elections, some Zionists called for a dissolution of the partnership. They argued that the crisis of European Jewry put political issues in the forefront of the Board's work and that it should assume full responsibility for them. Brodetsky disagreed and sought a renewal of the partnership,[27] which lasted until 1943. In 1940, Brodetsky wanted the support of Anglo-Jewry and he was afraid that dissolving the partnership would widen the rift with the circles that had just been ousted from the Board leadership. There is little doubt that had such a split taken place a rival influential political group would have evolved. By 1943, however, significant enough changes had taken place in British Jewry to preclude such a development.

The British Section of the World Jewish Congress

In the 1930s, when the condition of Europe's Jews had deteriorated drastically, Zionists proposed the establishment of an organization to guarantee the continued existence of the Jewish people and foster its unity. The plan was endorsed by the 19th Zionist Congress in 1935, which issued a plea to Zionist organizations to participate in the establishment of such an organization. The following year the World Jewish Congress was established under two veteran Zionist leaders, Nahum Goldmann in Europe and Rabbi Stephen S. Wise in the United States. Among the broad list of goals set by its founders were those guaranteeing the rights, status and interests of Jews and Jewish communities whenever threatened, representing Jewish organizations, and intervening on their behalf with governments and international bodies.[28] The BSWJC was established in London under Rabbi Maurice L. Perlzweig, an active figure in the Zionist Executive and the BD.[29] At the beginning of the war Perlzweig had called for establishing a unified Jewish front to formulate demands to be presented at a postwar peace conference. In fact, the BSWJC was involved in the same type of activities, such as combating anti-Semitism and aiding alien Jews, as was the BD. Dr Noah Barou, BSWJC secretary-general, proposed establishing a WJC faction in the BD in order to encourage that body to join the organization.[30] After the Nazi conquest of Western Europe the BSWJC assumed much greater importance than before and London became one of the three WJC centers, the others being New York and Geneva.[31]

The programs of the BSWJC "invaded" areas already "covered" by the established institutions and they were not received kindly. Criticism about competition and duplication appeared as soon as it began functioning. *The Jewish Chronicle* criticized Brodetsky for agreeing to accept one of the British Section vice-presidential posts in addition to the BD presidency, rather than objecting to their competitive roles. Brodetsky's explanation, that cooperation with the WJC was similar to that of the BD and the Anglo-Jewish Association, appears strained. It failed to convince *The Jewish Chronicle*. The paper argued that the WJC was an international Jewish organization whose authority came from abroad. As such it undermined the authority of the legal representative body of British Jewry.[32] Brodetsky was not able to reconcile the conflict and he eventually resigned his honorary WJC post.

There had been differences of opinion between the BD and the WJC even before the war broke out, and despite frequent informal meetings afterward they could not reach agreement on issues to be raised at a postwar peace conference. Perlzweig agreed that an international Jewish organization might use its local chapters as "marionettes," and that national organizations, such as the BD, Anglo-Jewish Association and the Alliance

Israelite Universelle, would act independently. On the other hand, Perlzweig argued that an international organization had the advantage of making contacts in enemy-controlled countries. An informal meeting was held on December 28, 1939, with the participation of Brodetsky, Perlzweig, Stein, Lasky and Abraham G. Brotman, BD secretary, where it was proposed that the WJC change its name to blur its international character. It was also proposed that the national organizations not be included in the WJC; that areas of cooperation not be clearly defined but remain informal; and that their work be divided in an efficient manner. Of great importance to all participants was the avoidance at all costs of a repeat of the post-World War I spectacle at the 1919–20 Peace Conference and the Evian Conference on Refugees, of July 1938. Tens of uncoordinated Jewish organizations had created confusion among the national delegations by submitting separate petitions.[33] In all events, no concrete decisions came out of the 1939 meetings because most of the proposals went against the principles of the WJC.[34]

Not only Jewish organizations had reservations concerning an international Jewish body. Undersecretary of State Richard Law said as much in a meeting with Brodetsky, Stein and Brotman. He expressed an opposition virtually unanimous in government circles to an international Jewish body to represent Jewish interests after the war: "it is advisable to resist any attempt on the part of Jewry to secure a kind of super-national status . . ."[35] Jewish nationalism was considered legitimate only in the context of Palestine and the Jewish Agency.[36] World Jewish interests in Palestine were based in law and international agreements, but the government was unwilling to extend recognition of this sort on any other Jewish issue. The Foreign Office struggled with the issue of the WJC, but even as late as 1944 had not determined its stand on the organization. Government officials were apprehensive about the growing influence of this international body, which had been expressing its views in international forums and presenting demands in the name of the entire Jewish people.

These demands were often discussed by successive governments. Eventually the opinion of a Jewish affairs expert, H. Beeley, of the Royal Institute of International Affairs, was solicited. In his report, Beeley wrote that the WJC had based it presumption to represent the Jewish people on two grounds: that Jews all over the world considered themselves one nation; and that the WJC represented that "super-national" entity. Beeley stressed the differences of opinion among Jews on the former, and the anger and the derision of many British Jews on the latter. According to Beeley, the heads of the WJC had succeeded in giving the impression that the governments of Britain and the United States took the WJC seriously. Beeley concluded that the Foreign Office considered the danger to the Jewish people in the belief that there was an "international Jewry" with political power, an idea that concurred with anti-Semitic propaganda. One should consider the WJC's opinions, he wrote, but reject its presumption of representing citizens of the allied nations. Support for the WJC, he believed, would make it difficult to solve the Jewish problem in the future European framework and encourage immigration to Palestine. The Foreign Office accepted Beeley's conclusions. It had never been favorable toward the WJC and preferred to deal with the BD and the Anglo-Jewish Association. In principle, the British government accepted the idea of a Jewish race and religion, but it did not view the Jews as members of an international body. Jews were citizens of different countries, and only their respective governments had the right to speak for them as well as for all its other citizens. Indeed, Jews had special problems as subjects of the enemy power and as the majority of displaced persons. Thus there was no choice but to conclude that there was a certain necessity to cooperate with Jewish organizations, but only on a practical, not an official level.[37]

As we shall see, the attitude of the Foreign Office toward the activists of the WJC changed according to circumstance, but as a general rule was unsympathetic and "correct." On the other hand, however, because of its American connections and prominent leaders who rubbed shoulders with British high society,[38] neither could it be dismissed.

Rabbi Perlzweig, chairman of the BSWJC, and a forceful personality, was one of the leaders with the ear of government officials. At the beginning of the war the WJC sent him on a mission to the United States. Before his departure he persuaded government officials that he could also act on Britain's behalf, especially in the area of American support for a moral boycott of Germany.[39] Perlzweig returned to London in the spring of 1940 and further strengthened his Foreign Office ties. Before a subsequent departure to New York, this time "on a special mission," he sought diplomatic status. The request was turned down, but the Foreign Office cooperated with him through the embassy in Washington. London and the British ambassador valued the Perlzweig prestige in the American Jewish community and looked forward to his reports. Perlzweig did not disappoint them. The British consul in Chicago wrote: "I am glad the Rabbi lived up to expectations." R. Butler, the deputy foreign secretary, "thought him to be o.k. I know him well."[40]

Perlzweig carried out a number of activities in the United States. He campaigned in the Jewish community for Roosevelt's re-election; gathered information about German propaganda; distributed pro-British information material; and mediated between Jewish manufacturers and the British purchase commission.[41]

Relations between Britain and the United States were at a delicate stage and Britain valued any help it could get, even from Zionists members of the WJC.[42] Perlzweig also raised funds for a children's day-care center, which he named for Chaim Weizmann, and collected binoculars and other equipment for the British army. For his efforts on Britain's behalf Lord Halifax, the British ambassador, sent Perlzweig a warm letter of appreciation. He did not, however, keep his pledge to personally submit to Churchill a letter and memorandum regarding a favorable declaration about the oppressed Jews.[43]

It is reasonable to assume that Perlzweig, before he was transferred to the New York office, was behind a number of appointments that considerably enhanced the prestige of the WJC.[44] Sydney Silverman MP, an active member of the House of Commons, succeeded him as BSWJC chairman; Eva, Marchioness of Reading, was appointed president; and Lord Melchett, her brother, one of her deputies. Through these figures the opinions of the WJC reached the upper echelons of British government and society. The Marchioness of Reading and Lord Melchett, whose father was Jewish and mother Christian, had been converted to Judaism by Perlzweig, who also served as rabbi of London's liberal synagogue.[45]

The BSWJC secretary was the energetic journalist E. L. Easterman, and Dr Noah Barou, was general-secretary. As an international and Zionist body, most local Zionist and exiled Jewish leaders such as Dr Ignacy Szwarcbart of the Polish National Council, Ernst Frischer of the Czechoslovakian State Council, and Albert Cohen, who had close ties with the Free French leadership, participated in the WJC council and committees.

In his Foreign Office contacts Perlzweig played down his WJC role and emphasized the benefit Britain could derive from his American Jewish contacts. Later, when the persecution of Jews became more severe and after the WJC improved its global information apparatus, its role changed. As documented in the BSWJC archives, the WJC began dealing almost exclusively with foreign affairs and concentrated primarily on aid and rescue plans. Other factors were at play as well. After the United States entered the war Britain no longer needed intermediaries to lobby the American public on its behalf. This was a different BSWJC than when Perlzweig headed the London office. Now with its major function, indeed that of the WJC in general, seeking help for the Jews in Nazi territory, its rescue operations proposals were usually directly opposed to Britain's policy toward the Jews. The government attitude toward the WJC remained ambivalent rather than totally negative, mainly because of the people Perlzweig had succeeded in maneuvering into the top positions of the BSWJC. But despite their high standing they did not succeed in moving the government away from its policy.

Though the international character of the WJC was problematic as far as the government was concerned, and criticized by local bodies, it had an advantage over other Jewish organizations. With branches in different countries it received intelligence that served as the basis of activities and policy formation. Agudat Israel's London office benefitted in a similar manner. At the same time the ties that had existed from the nineteenth century between the BD, the Anglo-Jewish Association and the European Jewish communities and organizations ceased to exist and the local organizations became totally dependent on information they received from the London branches of global Jewish organizations. Since the information released by these organizations was selective and often based on competitive interests, the JFC was at a severe disadvantage. Now the weakness of the local organizations, which sought to maintain their traditional policies, was evident – and they did not deny it.[46] The Riegner cable and subsequent activities provide an excellent illustration of the new state of affairs: The monopoly of the official Anglo-Jewish institutions had come to an end.

The Orthodox and Ultraorthodox: Chief Rabbi Joseph Herman Hertz, Rabbi Solomon Schonfeld and Harry Goodman

Harry Goodman, the third of the above religiously-identified personages, was an active participant in British Jewry's political affairs. He was the political secretary of the ultraorthodox World Agudat Israel which insisted on maintaining an independent stance in all areas, including the political. Despite this declared principle, however, theory and practice often diverged and when required, Agudat Israel cooperated with secular Jewish organizations. Thus, as a member of the BD, Goodman actively participated on the committees dealing with the community as a whole. On the other hand, as Agudat Israel secretary he acted independently of the Board and felt under no obligation to abide by its resolutions or participate in all of its activities.[47] The fact that Goodman was a well-to-do industrialist added to his sense of independence.

Goodman represented an anti-Zionist or at least a non-Zionist position in his contacts with government officials. They favored this stance because they were more prepared to tolerate an international religious organization than the secular international WJC. This attitude is evinced by Goodman's appointment, in the early stages of the war, as Information Ministry spokesman to world Jewry.[48] The chief rabbi and the BD were disturbed by the surprise move which they believed was meant to counter Zionist influence.[49] In accordance with Agudat Israel's separatism, Goodman acted independently of the BD and the Anglo-Jewish Association and there was nothing they could do to change it.

This was not the case with the dealings of ultraorthodoxy's other major representative, Rabbi Solomon Schonfeld. Though he was a member of

Agudat Israel and a rabbi of Adas Yisroel, the Union of Orthodox Hebrew Congregations (of the Agudat Israel system), his political activity was carried out as director of the Chief Rabbi's Religious Emergency Council (REC). Schonfeld was Chief Rabbi Dr Joseph Herman Hertz's son-in-law and this family connection was probably the reason for his appointment despite the fact that Adas Yisroel did not accept Hertz's religious authority.[50] The REC, active between 1938 and 1948, arranged for the immigration to Britain of hundreds of rabbis and scholars, an influx which helped strengthen British ultraorthodoxy and alter Anglo-Jewish life.[51] Schonfeld had an independent mind and acted as he saw fit.[52] Thus even though he was ideologically close to Agudat Israel he did not feel bound by its policies. Most of the ultraorthodox were recent arrivals from Germany, Austria and Czechoslovakia who had not integrated sufficiently into British life to provide competition for the independent-minded English-born Goodman and Schonfeld. The latter's position was unusual in that, though he was clearly an ultraorthodox leader, he was actively involved in the official British Jewish life and represented the chief rabbi on the REC. But as we shall see, his primary aim was to further ultra-orthodox interests in Britain and abroad.

Rabbi Hertz, like his son-in-law, was a forceful personality who had no qualms about acting independently or challenging the policies of the lay leaders.[53] Just as Schonfeld did not always bow to Agudat Israel discipline, Hertz, though an ardent Zionist, did not feel bound to official Zionist policy. He held moderate views in the religious sphere, but nevertheless zealously defended the status of orthodox Judaism.[54]

The BD was a scrupulously secular institution. In accordance with its constitution, it cooperated with the chief rabbi as a religious authority only when it deemed necessary, but kept him out of day-to-day affairs.[55] Brodetsky and his Zionist colleagues were especially careful in this regard.[56] This approach was apparently a reason for Hertz's support for Schonfeld's separate political activities and, as we shall see, his conflicts with Brodetsky and his circle. Hertz was not an "insider," and he was brought into political activity only when necessary as an important repre-sentative of British Jewry. This situation had a negative influence on Brodetsky's status.

Though the ultraorthodox Adas Yisroel did not recognize the religious adjudicative authority of the chief rabbi, after Schonfeld's marriage to Hertz's daughter hopes were raised of a reconciliation between the two groups.[57] Indeed, Schonfeld used his influence to arrive at a formula whereby the ultraorthodox would recognize the chief rabbi as the Jewish community's central religious authority.[58] The emergency situation also made it important for Hertz to be placed above sectarian conflicts, so Hertz and Schonfeld developed a common front.

The chief rabbi was elected by the United Congregations of the British Empire whose central body, the United Synagogue, comprised eighty large London congregations. According to its constitution, the Chief Rabbi of the British Empire was also the supreme religious authority of the United Synagogue in London. Thus the chief rabbi was not dependent on any single organization, such as the United Synagogue, but had a relationship with many other community bodies.[59] This was the source of the authority, prestige and political status he enjoyed in both the Jewish and non-Jewish worlds.

The British system accepted as legitimate the independent stance of the chief rabbi as head of a "church," and of his spokesmen on public and political issues. The heads of the Anglican Church sit in the House of Lords, play an active role in political and constitutional matters and, germane to this study, they were involved in the political issues concerning the extension of aid to European Jewry.

This was the context in which the chief rabbi was able to sanction actions taken by his religiously extreme and anti-Zionist son-in-law. In some cases he even approved them in his capacity of Chief Rabbi of the British Empire.[60]

Jewish Leaders in the British Exile

Despite the peculiar formal structure governing Anglo-Jewish life, the political leaders of British Jewry during the Holocaust worked in an atmosphere of competition, overlapping functions and mutual interference. The president of the BD served for a period of time as deputy president of the British Section of the World Jewish Congress in addition to being an active member of the London-based World Zionist Executive. Members of the WJC Executive were also members of the BD and its committees; Bakstansky was active on all these bodies and in the Zionist Federation; Harry Goodman belonged to a number of institutions, including the BD and the Anglo-Jewish Association; and because of his family tie to the chief rabbi and membership in Agudat Israel, Schonfeld was able to influence the activities of various institutions and organizations. We shall study the influence of these affiliations on the political work of British Jewry at the time. This overlapping jumble influenced the political activities of the Jews in London.

Previously, we discussed the Jewish alignment that handled negotiations with the British government when it was formulating policy toward the Jews suffering under their common enemy. However, before appraising the government's position on European Jewry, we must first describe the continental Jewish leaders who served with the governments-in-exile and who participated in Jewish political activities in London. An examination of the BD archives shows that the new leadership under Brodetsky paid great attention to foreign issues. At the end of 1939, the BD established ties with Morris Tropper, Paris representative of the Joint. The outgoing Board president, Neville Lasky, had already sought information from him on money distributed to Jews in occupied Poland. Tropper had tried to arrange for the Joint to receive £6,500 of BD funds obtained for distribution among the Jews of Vilna. Abraham Brotman, BD secretary, informed Tropper, in the name of the incoming president Brodetsky, that the money, most of it raised by the Torah Fund, would be distributed directly by British Jews in Kovno. Both the British authorities and the Board wanted the money distributed on an official British basis.[61]

The new leadership viewed its visit to wartime France in April 1940 as an important phase in their political work. Brodetsky, Stein and Brotman hoped to strengthen their ties with the Alliance Israelite Universelle and the Paris offices of the Joint and the WJC. They also met with officials of the Polish government-in-exile, then located in Angier in western France, to discuss the Polish Jewish refugees who had escaped to the Balkans and the attitude toward the Jews in the future new Poland. The Poles attempted to allay the anxiety of the Jewish representatives by noting the official state aid extended to Polish refugees in Rumania and Hungary. Moreover, they presented a plan for large-scale American help to Poland via the American Red Cross. As to the future, Professor Kot, the Polish Deputy Prime Minister, did not have much to say in the way of encouragement. He told the British Jews that he did not believe that the new Poland would have room for millions of Jews. Many of them would be forced to emigrate and he revealed a plan for a concentration of East European Jews near Odessa. The Jewish leaders were aghast. They warned the Poles against pursuing the plan and demanded an immediate declaration of equality for all Polish citizens regardless of ethnic origin and religion.[62] The British Jewish representatives were especially disheartened by the suspicion that the French supported the Poles' anti-Jewish policies.[63] The Polish delegation in London, for its part, had an exaggerated estimation of the influence of British Jews. The Polish ambassador, Count Radzinsky, sought their cooperation and suggested holding regular meetings with the JFC through a liaison officer.[64]

The actual extension of aid for Polish Jews was initiated by other institutions. A fund to assist Polish Jewish refugees was established under the presidency of Lord Moyne and an unsuccessful financing attempt was initiated by the London based Aliya Bank. Some religious groups established the Polish Jewish Refugee Fund under the presidency of Rabbi Yehezkel Abramsky, the supervision of Harry Goodman and Rabbis Eli Munk and Solomon Schonfeld, and Hertz as honorary president. Christian members of Parliament, such as Commander Locker-Lampson and George Lansbury, were appointed honorary trustees. The fund extended aid to the Polish Jewish refugees in Kovno and Vilna.[65]

Preoccupation with the Polish issue led Brodetsky to an attempt to concentrate all matters pertaining to Polish Jewry in the hands of the BD. He proposed the establishment of the Council for Polish Jewry along the lines of the Council for German Jewry that was established in 1933 as an independent body and officially authorized to undertake public fund-raising campaigns.[66] According to information that reached *The Jewish Chronicle* in April 1940, the Council for Polish Jewry was to begin work in May, jointly managed by the BD, the Organization for Rehabilitation and Training (ORT) and the Ouvre Secours aux Enfants (OSE).[67] Because of these independent BD activities, Brodetsky turned down a WJC request to participate in a meeting with Polish Prime Minister General Władysław Sikorski on his visit to London.[68] We have no knowledge of any results of the plans to establish the Council for Polish Jewry. However, since April and May were fateful months in the war, we may assume that events over-took them, especially the transfer to London of the Polish government-in-exile, including Dr Ignacy Szwarcbart, the Jewish repre-sentative on the Polish National Council.

In London, Szwarcbart established the Representation of Polish Jewry, claiming that he and his colleagues were its only official representatives. The JFC recognized this body and extended financial assistance.[69] The BD thus remained basically a representative body. It had little chance of expanding its activities because its regular budget was based on dues paid by member organizations and it required outside funding for any out of the ordinary activity.[70]

There was great anxiety over the fate of Polish Jewry, and Jews in the free world believed that the attitude shown toward them would be crucial for the fate of Jews elsewhere in Eastern Europe. Few then imagined the total annihilation planned for them.

Suddenly, British Jews were forced to come to grips with the problem of Polish Jewry. After the Dunkirk evacuation, the Polish government-in-exile was transferred to London. Polish soldiers encamped in the Scottish Highlands, and Polish statesmen and refugees launched political, social and cultural activities. Polish infighting was played out before the eyes of the British public and British Jews could not sit idly on the sidelines. Polish soldiers, officers and chaplains were openly anti-Semitic and deliberately fostered anti-Semitism as a ploy to gain support for their discriminatory policies and plans for a *Judenrein* Poland. Coming on top of homespun British anti-Semitism, local Jews experienced a sense of real danger and reacted accordingly.[71]

A rightist Polish group published a brazenly anti-Semitic newspaper,

Jestem Polakiem, which enjoyed financial support from anti-Semitic British Catholic subscribers of *The Catholic Herald*.[72] Jews lodged official complaints against the Polish paper and questions were raised in Parliament,[73] but because of *Jestem Polakiem*'s support for the war effort and its popularity among Poles, the Foreign Office, arguing the right of freedom of the press, objected to its closure. The Ministry of Information, on the other hand, which fought all displays of anti-Semitism, succeeded in halting the paper's publication on technical administrative grounds.

Actually, *Jestem Polakiem* ceased publication in June 1941. The authorities also closed down the Polish socialist newspaper, *Robotnik*, ostensibly out of "fairness." For further "balance" the Home Office reacted strongly against the Polish Jewish newspaper *Wiadomości Żydowskie*, which published generally moderate articles in English, but fiercely attacked anti-Semitism among the Poles in England. The Home Office sought Anthony de Rothschild's assistance in persuading the paper to modify its tone. After de Rothschild's appeal, Brodetsky agreed to talk to the editors of the paper. When it appeared that Brodetsky's efforts were of no avail, policemen, arguing that *Wiadomości Żydowskie* was wasting paper needed for the war effort, appeared at the paper's office in an attempt to intimidate its editors.[74]

The rampant anti-Semitism in the Polish army led many Jewish soldiers to desert and seek to enlist in the British Army. There were a number of such waves of "desertion," the last of them on the eve of the 1944 invasion.[75] The Jewish soldiers sought support in the British Jewish community and even held demonstrations outside the prime minister's residence on Downing Street, outside the BD offices and in the streets of the East End.[76] All this was reported in the British press and discussed in Parliament.[77] In a Commons speech, Sidney Silverman warned the Poles about their anti-Semitism and *The Jewish Chronicle* attacked them vehemently.[78] Brotman, through an appeal to its director, Leonard Stein, who also served as co-chairman of the JFC, tried unsuccessfully to persuade *The Jewish Chronicle* to modify its tone on the Polish issue.[79]

The Polish government was composed of a wide political spectrum which also included anti-Semites. It was subjected to pressures by Jews and liberals in Britain and the United States, as well as by rightist Polish refugee groups and the rightist underground. The latter was not content to let the inexorable solution to Poland's "Jewish problem" take its course.[80] The Polish government maneuvered gingerly among these different interests. Polish Labor and Welfare Minister Stanczyk, a socialist, who along with the moderate Prime Minister Sikorski was usually delegated to meet with Jewish spokesmen, issued statements designed to allay Jewish fears.[81] This was apparently nothing but obfuscation because the Poles, through diplomatic channels, continuously tried to turn high British officials against the unfortunate Jews still left in Poland.[82]

This was the atmosphere in which Szwarcbart and his colleagues were forced to work. Alongside the moderate Zionist Szwarcbart were two other Jewish activists in the Polish Delegation, both identified with Revisionist Zionism: Dr J. Dogolevsky, the government secretary, and Dr Manfred Lachs, who was in charge of personnel and the press.[83] These Jewish appointments might have been the result of the wish of the Polish government to preserve the good relations established with the Revisionist Movement in pre-war Poland. No wonder that Jewish Agency officials opposed the nominations because they feared a Polish–Jewish agreement that might include a plan for the "evacuation" of the Jews to Palestine,[84] as called for by the Revisionist platform. This fear still dominated at a time when the sword was being pressed against the throat of Polish Jewry.

Since Szwarcbart was a member of the Polish National Council, he was expected to protect Polish interests, especially in the area of preventing a deterioration of relations between British Jews and Polish exile leaders. Szwarcbart succeeded in convincing Brodetsky and Brotman of the need to reassure local Jewish communities, especially in Scotland, on the Polish issue.[85] It may be assumed that the Poles were pleased about Szwarcbart's relations with Jewish bodies. At various times he relayed reports to the Jewish institutions about the current situation in Poland and his activities in Britain, but it was his superiors who determined the nature of the information released to him. Szwarcbart balked when a source of information was closed to him and he appealed to the BD to be helpful in supplying him with information.[86] He was not authorized to deal personally with British officials, but would guide local Jews in their foreign contacts concerning Polish Jews.[87] Moreover, he demanded prior consultation and coordination of positions. He was not always successful. The Anglo-Jewish leaders were not prepared to bow to his dictates and preferred to operate independently, according to their interests and views, in their dealings with the Poles. On the contrary, at various times they demanded coordination before taking a certain action, and had no qualms reminding Szwarcbart that his financial support came from them. Szwarcbart was also limited by his official position, a dependence expressed by his requests to local Jews that they act in his stead.[88]

The relations between Szwarcbart and his colleagues and the BSWJC were even more complex. He had assumed that he would be appointed to the Executive of the WJC as the recognized representative of the large Polish Jewish community, but he was mistaken. The BSWJC had good reason to seek to remain essentially British and did not coopt foreign nationals on principle. However, Szwarcbart and other exiled Jewish leaders were allowed to join the Congress Council. In response to Szwarcbart's demand to be accepted as a member of the Executive Committee, he was told that the BSWJC was not ready to coopt a member of the Polish establishment in the Executive because it might involve seeking Polish approval of their moves. The BSWJC, for its part, did not obligate Szwarcbart to accept responsibility for its decisions.[89]

The attitude toward Szwarcbart was based on experience: as a Polish delegate he was obliged to defend Polish interests. A question tabled by Sidney Silverman in the House of Commons in March 1941 about anti-Semitism in the Polish army upset the Poles. Szwarcbart argued that such a question from the chairman of the BSWJC could strain relations between the Poles and the Jews, and he demanded that Silverman consult with him before acting. Silverman rejected the demand out of hand. He argued that as a matter of principle he would not brook any interference in his activities as a member of Parliament and that moreover, Szwarcbart was nothing more than a servant of Polish interests.[90] Conflicts of this sort with Szwarcbart continued throughout the war and the BSWJC met with Polish ministers without briefing the Polish Jewish delegates.[91]

Szwarcbart reacted in kind. In October 1943, he broadcast a speech on the BBC without prior consultation with the heads of the WJC. Silverman, arguing that the absence of coordination caused damage to the Jewish cause, was incensed. Szwarcbart responded by turning Silverman's argument around: He would agree to limit his privileges as a member of the Polish National Council on condition that Silverman consult with him before discussing Polish Jewry in Parliament.[92]

The nature of the BSWJC was the subject of endless discussions with the World Executive of the WJC in New York. The exiled Zionist leaders considered themselves the spokesmen of their silenced communities. They objected to their inferior status in the very organization meant to represent world Jewry at the very hour critical decisions were being made in London, the headquarters of the governments-in-exile. The arrangement eventually reached provided for the preservation of the "British" character of the BSWJC while granting the exiled Jewish leaders a certain status and framework of operation in a European Division established to work in cooperation with the BSWJC. In actuality, however, local Executive activists ran the affairs of the European Division. A study of the BSWJC archives shows that the terms "British Section" and "European Division" were used interchangeably. In all events, the same officials acted in the name of both departments. The aristocrats among the local leadership, however, mindful of the animosity displayed by the government toward the international nature of the Jewish organization, continuously endeavored to preserve its "British" singularity.[93]

In 1940, Bund leader Szmuel Zygielbojm escaped to London from the Warsaw Ghetto and was appointed to the Polish National Council. Established in 1897, as the labor movement of Russian and Polish Jews, the Bund advocated a socialist revolution and secular cultural and linguistic autonomy as the solution to the Jewish national problem. The Bund was vehemently opposed to Zionism which they condemned as a nationalist bourgeois utopia.[94] On the eve of World War II, it was the second most powerful Jewish organization in Poland.

After arriving in London, the Bundist Zygielbojm declined to establish contact with the WJC or the Jewish Agency. According to the archives he established only loose ties with the BD and the JFC. On the other hand, Zygielbojm actively cultivated relations with exiled Polish and local British leftists and sought their influence for the sake of the Jews in Poland. He also cultivated ties with the leaders of the British Labour Party.[95]

While the Zionists based their activities on the realities of the *Yishuv* in Palestine and the imminent attainment of Jewish independence, the human matrix of Zygielbojm's ideology was going up in flames. Moreover, his ideological counterparts in Britain stood by and turned a deaf ear to his pleas to launch an operation to save the Jews from total annihilation. The Warsaw Ghetto was destroyed and the Jewish revolt was snuffed out. After the failure of the Warsaw Ghetto Uprising, in absolute despair and as a protest against the apathy, Zygielbojm committed suicide on May 12, 1943. The Labour Party newspaper, *The Daily Herald*, reported that Zygielbojm had implored Jewish leaders to demonstrate against the world's indifference and commit group suicide on the steps of 10 Downing Street: "Then and only then," he said, "will the world see what the slaughter of a people means."[96] Zygielbojm's dramatic step did nothing to influence the course of events.

In the war's early stages, Dr Eduard Benes, the president of Czechoslovakia, put an end to the illusion of a continued liberal attitude toward the Jews of his country. He made great efforts to convince Jewish leaders of the necessity to evacuate the Jews from the postwar Czechoslovak republic. Those who opted to remain, he said, would have no minority rights. Benes argued that his stand was consistent with his support for Zionism.[97] He tried to gain Zionist support by stressing Czechoslovakia's bitter experience with the German and Hungarian minorities who had tried to undermine his country's political foundations. A Czech–Slovak republic would be established, he said, but without a surplus of minorities. The recognition of a Jewish minority would violate this principle. With Czechoslovak–Zionist cooperation, Benes suggested, the Jews could be evacuated. Negotiations were handled without publicity and Zionist leaders, including Weizmann, did not protest as they did in the case of Poland.[98] It is possible that both the changing times and Benes' liberal record were behind the Zionist attitude. Neither did they protest against Benes' remarks in 1944 to an audience of Czech army officers in England, that it should be made difficult for Jews to seek a return to Czechoslovakia.[99] Benes remained consistent. The political manifesto issued by him on the eve of his return to Czechoslovakia stated that the Germans and Hungarians were abusing their minority rights. Thus neither should the Jews enjoy that status. It should be noted, however, that the manifesto declared the Czechoslovak government's readiness to encourage the emigration of Jews to "their own National State in Palestine."[100] By that time Benes knew that only a few pale embers were left of a once flourishing Jewish community. His adherence to this policy toward the Jews undoubtedly connected to the plan to remove the German and Hungarian minorities, and raises serious misgivings about the motives behind Benes' attempts, as mentioned above, to pacify the Jewish public during the Holocaust.[101]

Czechoslovak government leaders in London were opposed to the appointment of a Jewish representative on the National Council.[102] This attitude had not always prevailed, but was, as noted, the result of bitter experience with minority nationalities. After World War I, the Czechoslovakian Republic had scrupulously accepted the principle of unlimited national minority rights, and representatives of the Jewish community sat in its parliament. East and Central European Zionists, unlike the assimilated Jews who accepted Benes' stand, still insisted upon the representation of a Jewish nationality in exile and refused to acquiesce. Eventually, Benes bowed to pressure and agreed to the appointment of a Jewish representative to the National Council, Ernst Frischer, a Zionist who left Palestine to take up the post. It is almost certain that Benes' capitulation was the result of American sensitivity to the ethnic minority rights issue.[103]

At the beginning of the war Czechoslovak ultraorthodox Jews established the Federation of Czechoslovak Jews in London. Raphael Springer, an Agudat Israel activist who had arrived in London before the war, was secretary. Hertz was asked to serve as president and Harry Goodman as director. Arguing that most Czechoslovak Jews were ultraorthodox, the Federation demanded that for the sake of balance an ultraorthodox representative be appointed to the Czechoslovak National Council. Despite Springer's close ties to Foreign Minister Jan Masaryk, his demand was turned down,[104] probably because unlike the Zionists he had no American backing.

Despite his defeat, Springer continued to press until he was given an official interior ministry appointment as representative of Czechoslovak orthodox Jewry. Now, and this might have been his motive all along, he demanded to be present at all JFC discussions of Czechoslovak Jewry. Frischer fought the move. He even threatened to appeal against Springer's appointment on legal grounds. However, he reneged because he did not want to involve Czechoslovak officials in Jewish infighting. The JFC resolved the dispute in a sophisticated manner: It promised to invite

Springer to JFC meetings when Czechoslovakian Jewish religious issues were on the agenda.[105]

Frischer established close working ties with Benes and his government and his position was secure. He was loyal to Benes and conveyed the Czechoslovak government's optimistic reports about the Jews in Europe.[106] In August 1944, he resigned from the WJC as a protest to the WJC demand that a Jewish official be appointed to oversee Jewish affairs in liberated Czechoslovakia. Constantly loyal to Benes, he refrained from emphasizing Jewish interests because of the German minority problem.[107]

Jewish–Christian Cooperation

The Christian Council for Refugees from Germany and Central Europe, an organization which extended aid to Christian refugees of Jewish descent and the children of intermarriages, was established in the 1930s. The secretary of the council, which had close working ties with the Jewish Refugee Council, was the Anglican minister, W. W. Simpson. In 1940, Simpson, a tireless fighter against anti-Semitism, also established the Youth Council for Jewish–Christian Relations. The BD, which considered the Youth Council an instrument to fight anti-Semitism, extended financial support.[108] Among the council's directors were Dr Israel Feldman, chairman of the Jewish Defence Committee of the BD, and Sidney Solomon who was the Jewish Defence Committee's press officer. Jewish–Christian cooperation increased during the Blitz in London in directions many Jews would have preferred to avoid. The distress shared by Jews and Christians alike in the public bomb shelters brought them closer: In the face of death both turned to the common Father in Heaven. In March 1941, at a Jewish–Christian Council meeting, a proposal for common prayer in the bomb shelters and weekend outings was raised, and a resolution passed to compose a prayer book with Psalms to be recited in the shelters by both Jews and Christians.[109] Another example of such activities was a lecture by Simpson on "Jesus in Christian Doctrine," and another by Rabbi I. L. Swift, the Jewish co-chairman of the Youth Council, on "The Torah and its Importance for the Jews."[110] Sidney Solomon grew enthusiastic and proposed the publication of a common booklet on Jesus' crucifixion.[111] For their part, the Christian partners in the council pledged to fight both manifest and latent anti-Semitism.

The Emergency Regulations and the struggle against black marketeering grew more severe as the war progressed. The Home Office was responsible for both and manipulated its press reports for the benefit of its own policy. The trials of forty black marketeers, about half with ostensibly Jewish names, were extensively reported. The BD Defence Committee considered the coverage malicious because it entailed a minuscule number of the thousands of violations of the Emergency Regulations dealt with every month. Solomon also contended that compared to the punishments meted out to convicted Christians, those given to the Jews were disproportionately severe. Hence he sought Simpson's aid with government officials and Scotland Yard in an attempt to redress the publicity and legal imbalance. Simpson, however, was not able to help.[112]

Because of incidents such as these, the support of religious leaders and Jewish–Christian cooperation had to be set on a solid institutional basis. Two possible frameworks were the Ministry of Information and the Royal Institute for International Affairs. At a conference held at the initiative of Simpson and Brotman in November 1941, Rabbi Hertz angered the Jewish participants by openly expressing his fears that the proposed body would devote itself to spiritual matters when its main function should be the fight against anti-Semitism.[113] What Hertz really meant to say was that he was opposed to missionary activity of any kind in exchange for Christian support. Indeed, some Christians had hoped to combine the fight against anti-Semitism with missionary activity. When they understood that it could not be done in the proposed framework they withdrew their support.[114]

The Archbishop of Canterbury, Dr Cosmo Lang, who was not particularly warm toward the Jews, retired in early 1941 and was replaced by Dr William Temple, a philosemite and zealous advocate of extending aid to the Jews of Europe. Simpson reported that the new archbishop considered anti-Semitism spiritually harmful to Christianity and advocated close relations and mutual understanding between the two religious communities.[115] Hertz, for his part, stuck to his guns. He insisted that the proposed organization focus its struggle on manifest anti-Semitism. Temple acquiesced to Hertz's wishes and also expedited the establishment of the Council of Christians and Jews.[116]

Anti-Semitism in Britain, apparently with a nod from high places, grew worse in 1942. There was a link between this development and the rescue plans proposed after information had arrived indicating that a systematic annihilation of the Jews in Europe was is progress. Thus the establishment of the Council of Christians and Jews came at an appropriate time.

The Home Office was asked to respond to the pleas to help rescue Jews. However, instead of doing so its officials contended that as the authority responsible for immigrant absorption, the Home Office would find it difficult to help because of Jewish involvement in the black market. In fact, an official "in highest position" bluntly told Brotman: "You will not get British support for Jews unless you manage to get over anti-Jewish feeling in this country and get rid of the causes of such feeling."[117] The quoted Home Office official was almost certainly Lord Vansittart who had already offered "friendly advice" that a high Jewish authority condemn black marketeering. Lord Vansittart went so far as to link such a move with the extension of the British help that was crucial for the future of European Jewry.[118] It is virtually certain that these Home Office arguments deterred the BD from organizing protest demonstrations for European Jewry. As we shall see, it was also behind their desperate pleas for the cooperation of the governments-in-exile and the Council of Christians and Jews.

The Home Office had hoped that by snaring the Jews into an impossible situation they would get the sought-after condemnation: the East End immigrants were responsible for the delay in attempts to rescue their endangered brethren; if they changed their ways and abandoned black marketeering, the government would be "able" to comply with Jewish requests for help. Meanwhile, if Jewish leaders publicly condemned their wayward brethren, as demanded, the government would also have "confirmation" of their suspicions that Jewish merchants were exploiting the war for profit. The problem was that a public condemnation by the Jewish leaders would be tantamount to admitting culpability and lead to increased anti-Semitism. In the end the Board gave in and decided to cooperate with the authorities in fighting Jewish black marketeers. Even the chief rabbi was recruited.[119]

The truth was very different. By April 1942, 47,000 cases of black marketeering had been brought to court. Of these about 400, less than their proportion of the British population, involved Jews. The figure is all the more remarkable considering that a relatively high proportion of Jews were engaged in commerce.[120] Hence the arguments were baseless and apparently the result a Home Office attempt to link Jewish external and internal affairs for the benefit of the government's political agenda.

The presidency of the Council of Christians and Jews consisted of the Archbishop of Canterbury, the spiritual leader of the Anglican Church, the leaders of the non-conformist churches, the Archbishop of Westminster, head of the Catholic Church in Britain,[121] and the chief rabbi. The executive was composed of members of different faiths, with Brodetsky, Israel Feldman, Anthony de Rothschild, Sir Robert Walley Cohen and Rabbi I. L. Mattuck, of the liberal synagogue, representing the Jews.[122] At Hertz's request, Rabbi Isser Unterman, who in the 1950s became Ashkenazi Chief Rabbi of Israel, was also appointed.[123] According to the protocols of the council meetings there was much discussion of the publicity given to Jewish involvement in the black market and a subcommittee was established to deal with the issue.[124]

Politically, however, the council could do very little. It was apparently hampered by the composition of its membership, which included Sir Arthur Wauchope, who had served as High Commissioner in Palestine (1931–8). Wauchope had cultivated reasonable relations with the *Yishuv* in

Palestine which flourished during his incumbency. After his retirement he continued to display an interest in the fate of the Jewish people.[125] The membership of Sir Herbert Emerson was even more problematic. Sir Herbert served in a dual capacity. He had been nominated High Commissioner for Refugees by the League of Nations and appointed director of the Inter-Governmental Committee on Refugees (IGCR), which was set up in London after the Evian Conference of July 1938. Thus Emerson was *ex officio* deeply involved in refugee politics, as we shall soon learn. Now he tried to gain a foothold in this council, whose goal would soon be to fight the prevalent refugee policy.

Only at the end of 1942, in the wake of the impact made by knowledge of the Final Solution, did the council take steps to arrange a meeting of some of its Christian members with Sir Herbert Morrison, the home secretary, and Richard Law, undersecretary in the Foreign Office. A Jewish delegation met with Anthony Eden at the same time. The council members stood firmly against the minister.[126] Soon afterward, the council's political activity declined because the framework was not suited for the intense political activity demanded by the Holocaust events. On the other hand, a nucleus of European Jewry activists established the informal Parliamentary Committee for Refugees. Public figures outside of Parliament soon joined its sessions, and the non-partisan, non-sectarian, National Committee for Rescue from Nazi Terror (NCRNT) was established in March 1943. Emerson's attempt to limit the committee's activities was quashed by the timely intervention of Lord Samuel, and he was forced to resign.[127]

Lord Crewe was elected president. Its executive included church leaders, the chief rabbi, Professor Hill MP, Sir William Beveridge, Lord Cecil, The Lord of Huntingdon, The Lord of Perth, Lord Davies, Victor Cazalet MP, Lord Rochester, Dr Grenfell MP, Mrs. Blanche Dugdale, Lady Reading, Lord Samuel, Brodetsky, Berl Locker and Harry Goodman. The committee's leading spirits were Eleanor Rathbone MP, and Victor Gollancz, the well-known leftist Jewish publisher. By any measure this was an impressive list of public figures, representing a wide range of British society. Gollancz covered the committee's expenses and for a period of time was its main propagandist.[128]

3

The British Blockade of European Jewry

> Mr Jabotinsky and his associates will surely devise with all the cunning and skill of their race means of using money for illegal immigration.

The war situation "released" the British Government from the effort it had launched toward the end of 1938 to evacuate Jews from Greater Germany to the British Isles. To make matters worse, after war broke out in September 1939, the British began interning German nationals, including Jews, behind bars. There was even a government directive that German Jews would no longer be allowed into Britain even if they held visas issued before the war, even if they had in the meanwhile succeeded in escaping to neutral countries.[1] The home secretary, Sir John Anderson, was willing to make certain concessions if their entry would be of benefit to the war effort.[2] As we shall see, the British stuck to this policy toward Jews under enemy rule throughout the war and the efforts of Jews and sympathetic Christians on the rescue issue led to no more than minor theoretical changes. Thus to all intents and purposes, the government prevented the entry of Jewish victims of Nazism into the British Isles.

The pre-war evacuation policy was closely linked to the government's stand on Palestine. As long as large waves of immigration reached that country in the 1930s, Britain did not show the Jewish refugees the same generosity offered by some of Germany's neighbors.[3] The high unemployment rate and anti-Semitic propaganda in Britain were two of the factors which deterred the government from opening the gates. As to immigration to Britain, the government's stand underwent a radical change after the Munich agreement of August 1938, and *Kristallnacht* in November of that year. Then, in the context of its preparations for imminent war, the British, as a political move, began appeasing the Arabs. The White Paper of May 1939, which restricted Jewish immigration into Palestine, was the real expression of this appeasement. Thus when the Jews needed refuge more than ever, the possibilities of entering the main haven were drastically curtailed and an alternative was needed.

The White Paper contained three provisions:

1   The establishment within ten years of an independent state in Palestine with an Arab majority.
2   Severe restrictions on land purchase by Jews.
3   In order to ensure an Arab majority, Jewish immigration would be limited to 75,000 over a period of five years, to be renewed only with Arab approval.

The third clause, especially in the present circumstances, exacerbated political tensions between the Jews and the British, who had adopted measures to limit Jewish immigration to Palestine even before the White Paper. However, criticism and protests of Jews and non-Jews over the Palestine immigration policy had the positive effect of moving the government to display greater liberalism toward the entry of Jewish refugees into the British Isles.[4]

The government was in a difficult situation. The Colonial Office sought to set severe limits on *aliya*, but unemployment in Britain was high and the trade unions opposed the entry into the country of more job-seekers. On the other hand, Jews all over the world, especially in the United States, launched angry protests against British policy. In reaction, the Foreign Office prodded the Colonial Office to permit Jewish refugees to enter British colonies, such as Northern Rhodesia and British Guyana, because "if we have to limit dramatically, or stop all together, Jewish immigration into Palestine, we shall be on stronger grounds if we can find refuge elsewhere."[5] The pace of events in Europe was swift, and directing Jewish refugees to primitive regions was not considered practical because of the lengthy preparations and great investment required to prepare those territories for the absorption of a large European population. Indeed, only two of the states controlled by London were capable of answering the needs of urgent immigration – the British Isles themselves and Palestine. In the wake of the restrictions on *aliya*, the government decided that Britain would have to be the "Island Refuge," a decision that angered the Zionists.

Immediately after *Kristallnacht*, the *Yishuv* in Palestine offered to adopt 10,000 German Jewish children. By the end of the month, however, the Jewish Agency increased the demand to include all of the 100,000 Jewish youngsters still remaining there. On December 14, Malcolm MacDonald, the colonial secretary, informed the House of Commons that he would not agree to the evacuation of the German Jewish children to Palestine. Considerable pressure was placed on the government. MacDonald suggested that the British Isles provide shelter for the 10,000 children until the Palestine policy was finally clarified, on condition that welfare organizations, not the government, assume the burden of their care. The government kept its promise. From November 1938 until August 1939, Britain saved 9,354 Jewish children.[6] A. I. Sherman, who carried out a study of British refugee policy, concludes that the demand to allow the entry of 10,000 children to Palestine was closely linked to the policy of British local refuge. The Zionists were upset because they felt that the government had taken an extreme move in order to bypass them and that this step was an indication of future British *aliya* policy. An eyewitness testified to the dramatic clash on the issue between MacDonald and a furious Chaim Weizmann: "Malcolm offered to take the children *here*, but without guarantee that they should go on. Chaim refused. He said to Malcolm: 'We shall fight you – and when I say fight I mean fight'."[7]

Even before MacDonald's announcement, British Jewry had been lobbying the government to extend refuge in Britain to different categories of refugees. On November 7, 1938, two days before *Kristallnacht*, Lord Winterton of the Home Office received a high-level Jewish delegation. Lord Samuel, the delegation's spokesman, argued that every Jew who remained in Germany would be killed. He demanded a speedy evacuation of all Jews. Lord Samuel also insisted that camps for refugees be established in Britain, or elsewhere, until suitable locations were found for their final settlement. The delegation, composed mainly of members of old established families, sought to base its request on purely humanitarian grounds. They sidestepped two traps. They did not raise the issue of the Palestine refuge, and since London did not relish the prospect of more Jewish refugees, Lord Samuel emphasized the transient nature of their stay in Britain, saying that they would be housed in camps until permanent locations were found elsewhere. Herbert Samuel had been chairman of the Council for Jewish Refugees from Germany since 1936, and was about to turn the position over to Lord Reading.[8] He had intimate knowledge of the financial difficulties involved in refugee care and now, with the need greater than ever, he demanded government help in maintaining the refugee camps.

There is no doubt that the members the Jewish delegation who met with Winterton were acutely aware of the results of the Evian Conference.

At the initiative of President Roosevelt, representatives of thirty-two states convened in the French resort city of Evian on July 5, 1938 to determine policy on the deteriorating refugee situation in Europe. The conference resolutions were a disgrace as far as the victims of Nazi persecution were concerned, and the gala opening, including a festive concert, was in sharp contrast to the tragic agenda. After Evian, the Inter-Governmental Committee on Refugees (IGCR) was established under the chairmanship of a Briton, Sir Herbert Emerson, who recently had been appointed the League of Nations High Commissioner for Refugees. As we shall see, the IGCR was little more than a tool serving British interests. The relevant Evian paragraph for our purpose was that private funds and organizations would assume sole responsibility for the refugee maintenance. This paragraph, in effect, limited the refugees' geographical options.

At the Home Office meeting, Lord Samuel had tried to reach a compromise: The government would maintain the camps with supplementary aid from the private organizations that would also finance emigration from Britain. The response was unequivocal: Agreement to establish the camps, yes. Government funding of any sort, no. Lord Winterton did not base his position on the outrageous Evian Conference. He proffered a reason, which, however offensive, was well-understood by the Jewish delegation: The Poles and Rumanians, for example, would consider any British budgetary generosity as an opportunity to get rid of their Jews by forcing them to emigrate. Winterton's position was not pulled out of thin air. Delegation member Sir Robert Waley Cohen, director of the Shell Oil Company and a relative of the Rothschilds, immediately grasped the implications of Winterton's stand and shouted out: "If something was not done rapidly, all potential refugees would be dead."[9]

A week after the Home Office meeting, the colonial secretary made a statement in the House of Commons which endorsed the principles raised by the home secretary. On the face of it, the government appeared generous: The gates of Britain were opened to the refugees; there was an alternative to Palestine and balm for conscience. The refugee advocates had the opportunity to utilize the British haven. If they could not raise the necessary funds they could even be censured.[10]

Refugee funds were established, the most important of which was headed by Lord Baldwin, a former prime minister, which succeeded in quickly raising £552,000 from the general public. The money was used for the maintenance of 8,000 refugee children.[11] The Jews also canvassed for funds. From 1933 to 1939, £3 million was collected, a considerable sum at the time. The requirements, however, grew immensely with the continued distress of German Jewry.[12] From 1933 to 1939, 56,000 refugees arrived in Britain, 40,000 of them Jews.[13] With the rapid deterioration in Germany in 1938, the pressure of Jews seeking to leave increased, but the Jewish organizations in Britain could not supply the number of guarantees demanded by the Home Office. Eleanor Rathbone MP, a stalwart refugee advocate and member of a well-known Quaker family, repeatedly demanded in the Commons that the government reject the Evian policy and establish, at its own expense, camps for 50,000 refugees. Her calls fell on deaf ears. The government did not alter its policy.[14] As to the Jewish organizations, they succeeded in establishing at their own expense a camp in Richborough, but only for 3,500 men.[15]

Until the BD's change of guard at the end of 1939, community affairs, including responsibility for foreign issues, were in the hands of the old established families. Most of them could not be defined as Zionists, but many were sympathetic to Zionist concerns and supported the *Yishuv* in Palestine. We have seen that they did not involve Palestine in the problem of Jewish distress in negotiations with the government. They based their arguments on humanitarian grounds and urged the adoption of rescue measures within the limited geographical framework of the British Isles. This approach was compatible, as we have seen, with British policy. With the election of Selig Brodetsky as president of the BD, and the entry of the World Jewish Congress into the London arena, the influence of non-Zionist circles decreased and the Zionist view became more pronounced in negotiations with Whitehall. There was a distinct tendency to align with Weizmann and his colleagues and to link the emergency needs with Palestine, a bone of contention between the Zionist Movement and the British Government. There is no doubt that the line dominating Zionist policy until the closing stages of the war caused British attitudes to harden. We shall see that within the Jewish community there were fierce struggles over the manner in which political figures should be pressured on the rescue issue outside of the context of Palestine.

Be that as it may, the government had the temerity to argue that its contribution to Jewish emigration to Palestine had helped alleviate the refugee problem.

In the framework of the White Paper the government allocated 50,000 entry certificates for Jews over a five-year period. It added an additional 25,000 special certificates as its contribution to the solution of the refugee problem, thus bringing the total to 75,000.[16]

The announcement of the quota of certificates for refugees was little more than "window dressing." In actuality, the policy dictated by the White Paper cast a long shadow over the rescue issue, and impeded any sympathetic consideration of it throughout the war. The Colonial Office and the Home Office played important roles in the overall framework determining policy toward European Jews. The influence of the Home Office, however, insofar as setting policy on entry into the British Isles, was radically changed after the war broke out. Now it was entrusted with preventing the renewal of the flow of refugees into the country. The influence of the Foreign Office, which handled all issues concerning the Jews in the Holocaust, was paramount in all decisions. It arrived at policy decisions in constant consultation with other relevant administration bodies. The concentration of such power helped the Foreign Office, under Anthony Eden, to fashion a monolithic policy from which it never wavered. It was the Jews' bad luck that Eden, a powerful and prestigious cabinet member, was the overseer of their problem. According to his personal secretary, Oliver Harvey, Eden loved Arabs and hated Jews.[17]

Along general lines, what was this policy? From the beginning of the war, the British were guided by a general view, which in effect meant a blockade of the Jews caught in the Nazi net. Moreover, the British were not content with a "sit still and do nothing" policy. The main reason why they adopted a hard line toward the Jews was the pro-Arab Palestine policy exhibited in the White Paper, and of which Eden was a staunch supporter. To the minds of British policymakers, extending a hand to the Jews of Europe might "flood" the Middle East with Jews and would make short shrift of declared British policy in a sensitive region. On the other hand, preventing the entry of Jews into the British Isles, a logistical problem in itself throughout most of the war, and other territories under British control, derived from the fear of having to assume any new obligations toward the Jews: The British were still smarting from the experience of the Balfour Declaration and the Palestine Mandate, viewed by the bureaucracy and most politicians as a dismal failure. As for the territories, they believed that there was little chance of absorbing refugees in underdeveloped colonies. To make matters worse for Britain, the Jews sent there might very well seek to join their brethren in Palestine. Internal and external pressures led to certain changes and maneuvers, but in reality made no difference at all. Only in *aliya* to Palestine could there be a display of flexibility over Jewish needs, and only to the extent of a "leeway" allowed for by the White Paper in the allocation of certificates toward the end of the five-year period.

The first test of the refugee provision of the White Paper came after the German invasion of Poland. In September 1939, the Polish consul-general in Tel Aviv met with the secretary-general of the Palestine Government to seek approval for the immediate immigration of 25,000 Polish Jewish children. This would have eased pressure on the Poles, would not have required a departure from the quota framework of the White Paper, and actually be in accordance with the spirit of the document: "as a contribution toward the solution of the Jewish refugee problem, 25,000 refugees will be admitted as soon as the High Commissioner is satisfied that the adequate provision for their maintenance is ensured, special consideration being given to refugee children and dependents."[18] The Mandate secretary-general, however, rejected the request out of hand.[19] In coordination with the Polish request, Weizmann wrote to the colonial secretary on September 15, requesting that 20,000 children from Poland be directed to Palestine. In accordance with the stipulations of the White Paper, Weizmann guaranteed their maintenance.

The Colonial Office discussions reveal aspects of the foundations of the policy toward the Jews that evolved during the war. Participating in the consultations were representatives of the Colonial Office, the Foreign Office and the War Ministry. The colonial secretary listed various negative points that government officials would later repeat. Firstly, the certificates meant for the refugees should be dispensed over the five-year period of the

White Paper and to refugees from different countries. Secondly, a mass *aliya* would have serious consequences for the Middle East, and might divert British military energies away from the primary consideration, the enemies' defeat. The colonial secretary raised two more reasons, ludicrous in themselves, and meant perhaps for public consumption, but of the kind usually formulated according to circumstances. It would not be wise, he said, to alleviate the strains on the German economy by evacuating 20,000 people that they would otherwise be forced to feed. Moreover, Christians, too, were entrapped in the tragic situation and they were far more numerous than the Jews. The Foreign Office representative in the discussions confirmed that adherence to this line was necessary, even though the Jews were suffering terribly and that Lord Halifax, then foreign secretary, would undoubtedly have wished to help the Polish Jews. Weizmann's appeal met with a vague reply: In light of the war situation there was no alternative but to turn down the request.[20] Jewish leaders would continue to hear government representatives give this and that reason for their opposition or abstention from taking rescue measures.

Jewish identification with the goals of the war against the Germans left no room for doubt. Unlike World War I, they had no choice but to be allied with the British. This total lack of room to maneuver made it relatively easy for the British to formulate policy unilaterally and the Jews were at an obvious disadvantage in any negotiations. The British soon realized that there was no need for *quid pro quo*, either for the loyalty or help of World Jewry. Moreover, a price could even be exacted from the Jews because of their desire for a British victory over the most dreadful enemy the Jews had ever encountered in their long history. On the eve of the war Chaim Weizmann proclaimed in the name of the Zionist Movement that the Jews stood on the side of the British.[21] Even Vladimir Jabotinsky, leader of the opposition Zionist Revisionists who were vociferously opposed to British policy in Palestine, declared absolute loyalty to Britain in a letter he wrote to Prime Minster Neville Chamberlain. However, in a meeting with the colonial secretary Jabotinsky raised the possibility of disturbances in Palestine, and this was seen as a warning and a reservation about total loyalty.[22] Jabotinsky's stand was closer to that of David Ben-Gurion, chairman of the Jewish Agency, who declared his support for Britain in its war against the Nazis as if the White Paper did not exist, and war against the White Paper as if there was no war raging. Weizmann, unlike them, emphasized time and again the Jews' unconditional loyalty. He went even further. He entreated British leaders to accept the help of World Jewry without the fear of being asked for concessions. Lord Halifax was left with the impression after a meeting with Weizmann in October 1939, that the Jews "felt it to be more truly indeed their war than ours . . . " Nonetheless, he feared that in the end the Jews would demand concessions for their help.[23] Halifax exploited Weizmann's commitment in the name of the Jewish people. In a letter to Weizmann, Halifax actually declared that all the stipulations of the White Paper would remain in force despite the promise of unconditional support for Britain. He continued: We are in a life and death struggle against Nazi Germany which is persecuting the Jews of Central Europe, and destroying that regime would be "a supreme service" to the Jews. Because of Weizmann's sentiments, Ben-Gurion criticized his upcoming visit to the United States as unconditional and that he was acting as an "unofficial" envoy for Britain.[24]

Halifax's comments raise the possibility that he was thinking about the history of the Balfour Declaration, when the Zionist leader had exploited political circumstances, personal connections, and his own role in the war effort (Weizmann, a chemist and professor at Manchester University, had devised a method of producing explosives). As noted, the Balfour Declaration raised highly unpleasant memories for British politicians. Weizmann, for his part, went to the extreme in his identification with the British conception. He even agreed that nothing should be done as far as European Jewry was concerned that might delay Hitler's defeat or even cause the British embarrassment.[25]

The conception of the British government was that only the final defeat of Germany would redeem the Jews of Europe and satisfy the Jewish and non-Jewish advocates of rescue. If the person standing at the head of the movement that called for an intense struggle against British policy in Palestine repeatedly expressed unconditional loyalty to Britain when the Jews of Europe faced life and death, a crisis largely linked to British Palestine policy, could any less be expected of local Jewish leaders whose loyalty to their besieged country had to be above reproach? And it was these leaders who would have to take a stand in the demanding struggle for rescue and welfare operations.

In light of all this, Foreign Office officials set about evaluating the strength and influence of Jews in the world. In a secret memorandum submitted by Winston Churchill, then First Lord of the Admiralty, to the British cabinet on December 25, 1939, he argued that the Balfour Declaration was not issued for sentimental reasons, but out of consideration for the great influence of American Jewry. Now, too, that influence should not be taken lightly. Churchill argued that Britain needed the help of the Jews in fighting against American anti-British isolationist sentiment. It was crucial for Britain that Roosevelt be re-elected, and the Jewish effort on his behalf was important. Weizmann had promised, Churchill wrote, that in his forthcoming visit to the United States he would do whatever he could to balance the scales in Britain's favor. Thus his task should not be made more burdensome by an inflexible British stand on the White Paper.[26]

Foreign Office officials, who constantly monitored the situation in the

Near East and the Jewish world, thought otherwise. After considering Churchill's memorandum, L. Baggallay, the head of the Near East Department, submitted an analysis which was fully endorsed by Halifax. Baggally rejected the inference based on the 1917 situation. To his mind the Jews now had much less influence. Rejecting Churchill's argument, Baggally wrote that implementing the White Paper policy would not turn the Jews against Britain because Britain was the Jews' only hope of saving millions of their brethren. The Arabs, on the other hand, did have an alternative and because the White Paper had acquiesced to their basic demands the region was quiet. To Baggally's mind, Britain should adhere to the White Paper and its positive influence on the Arabs rather than seek the sympathy of American Jewry, whose support was in any case secure. Furthermore, American Jewry had its own insecurities because of anti-Semitic outbursts.[27]

Baggally's memorandum was certainly more reflective of the 1939 situation than that of Churchill, which was grounded in the atmosphere of the critical days at the end of 1917. Russia was then set to leave the war, the United States had not yet entered, and it was in the context and pressures of that time that the Balfour Declaration had been issued. In 1917, the British were convinced that at that critical hour it needed the support of American Jews who, they believed, had great influence over United States policy.

In his memorandum to the cabinet, Lord Halifax went to the other extreme in relation to the Zionists. He argued that Zionist support of Britain was no advantage.[28] We shall see that the reason for an argument such as that of Halifax's was the fear of the Nazi propaganda campaign which was spreading the notion that Britain was fighting the Jews' war. Thus the attempt to prevent any British identification with the fate of the Jews. The Nazi line was also fostered by pro-German British fascists. As can be imagined, all this was highly disturbing to the Jewish public.[29] The Nazi propaganda met with some success, especially in the early days of the war,[30] and it strengthened the Home Office's resolve not to allow more refugees into the country.[31]

As mentioned above, Britain stopped the inflow of enemy nationals, including Jews, after the outbreak of war. So much for the mother country. But what rule should govern Jews from enemy countries who sought entry into Palestine? The British had a special obligation toward the Jews as far as Palestine was concerned. Moreover that country was still far from the front. Nonetheless, the stand adopted from the outset of the war precluded any displays of compassion. No entry was permitted to Jews from enemy territory even if, as noted, they had succeeded in escaping to neutral countries or to Britain's allies.[32]

Among the other justifications for this hard line was the fear that

German secret agents might infiltrate the Middle East in the guise of Jews. After the swift Nazi conquest of West Europe in May 1940, bizarre stories about a "Fifth Column" in the overrun countries made the rounds as the reason for the ignominious defeat. The Colonial Office admitted to the Foreign Office that there was no certainty that German agents had arrived along with the "illegal" immigrants to Palestine. The Foreign Office was asked not to publicize the fact that in the entire period only fifteen suspected agents had been detained and that these, too, had been released. The Colonial Office's advice was to present the issue in general terms.

Lord Lloyd, the colonial secretary, succeeded in entrapping Weizmann when he raised the suspicion, in the Zionist leader's presence, of the penetration of enemy agents. Weizmann agreed that the "Gestapo plan" to infiltrate agents among the illegals had to be stopped. This implied a stoppage in the illegal immigration, and he promised to allay American and Palestinian Jewish anger over the issue. This took place at the end of 1940, before the Nazis had decided on the destruction of the Jews, and when they were still pressuring the Jews to emigrate. Groups of Jews were setting sail down the Danube for Palestine in hazardous conditions and rotting ships.[33] The true reason for this episode was the panic that had gripped the government over the illegal immigration, which together with legal immigration had by February used up a third of the White Paper certificates quota. The British now stepped up their campaign against the illegals' ships out of fear that the entire quota of 75,000 certificates would soon be used up. Thus the categories of Jews not permitted to enter Palestine because of the war situation was devised only to serve the policy of the White Paper. On the other hand, the pressure of the illegal immigration served the activists of the Zionist leadership who worked toward nullifying the White Paper immigration quota. The refugees running for their lives were caught in the middle. Many tragedies, discussed below and documented in the historical and general literature, resulted from these desperate flights.[34]

After the September 1939 request for the *aliya* of 20,000–25,000 Polish Jewish children was rejected, British leaders concluded that it was crucial to ascertain, from the British standpoint, how the White Paper refugee quota could be optimally exploited.

Who was to be considered a refugee? IGCR director, Sir Herbert Emerson, who was entrusted by the international community with the refugee issue, defined "refugee" as someone who fled his country for another because his life was in jeopardy. The oppressed, so long as they remained in the country where they were being pursued, did not qualify as refugees and were responsible for their own fate. When was Sir Herbert obliged to act? From the moment the person in question had arrived in a country willing to grant refuge and was no longer in danger. The assistance of the IGCR included, among others, transference from the country of refuge to the country of final settlement. While granting "protection" to "authentic" refugees, Emerson also served his country's interests. A case in point is the assurance he gave to the Colonial Office that he would seek to dissuade the Joint's London representative from funding passage for the unfortunate Jews heading down the Danube for the Black Sea after the ice began to thaw in late February 1940. According to the refugee official's reasoning, after these potential illegals arrived in Palestine they would eat away at the quota for "authentic" refugees, i.e., those who had already reached a safe haven. This was sufficient reason, Emerson apparently thought, for cautioning the Joint against damaging the interests of his committee's clientele.

Lord Strabolgi, the Jews' advocate in the House of Lords, assailed this insult to the thousands of desperate Jews on boats in the Danube. He demanded that the IGCR extend them assistance, and since they had fled from Germany classify them as refugees. In his response to Lord Strabolgi, IGCR chairman Lord Winterton concocted explanations to justify the abandonment of these refugees: The committee did not deal with refugees in enemy-controlled territory, or those who had fled from there; and certainly no assistance should be extended to these special refugees because they were intending to immigrate illegally.

Emerson's conclusion from this principle, as can be seen from his meeting with the colonial secretary, was that he should be entrusted with the distribution of the 25,000 refugee certificates. The colonial secretary displayed caution. Apparently, he was apprehensive of the growing tension between his office and the Jewish Agency, which in practice had the privilege to determine the candidates for *aliya*, and informed Emerson that certificate distribution was not under his control.[35]

The Foreign Office also deemed the refugee certificates to be in a special category. In a discussion held at the ministry, it endorsed Sir Herbert's definition of "refugee," and decided that "generosity" in the allocation of special immigrant permits should serve British, or at least Western interests. Eastern Europe was already steeped in intense anti-Semitism, the officials reasoned, and removing a number of Jews from there would change nothing. Western Europe, on the other hand, was only now experiencing intense Nazi anti-Semitic propaganda. Thus the evacuation of part of the refugees there might make a serious dent in its influence.[36]

Another cabinet decision concerning the transfer of the temporary residents from Britain was appended to this universally accepted, but simplistic approach: that preference in the distribution of certificates be granted to Britain's Jewish guests. Furthermore, the Foreign Office had foreseen that the British Jewish welfare organizations would be overwhelmed by the fast pace of events, and believed that in the final analysis the government would have to assume the financial burden for the refugees.

If part of them were to be transferred to Palestine it would lessen the government's burden. Therefore, an order of priorities for entry into Palestine should be set giving preference to the Jews who had reached Britain and Western Europe. At the bottom of the scale were the Polish Jews who had fled to Rumania and Hungary, even though, the Foreign Office admitted, it was they who were in imminent danger. The minutes of this discussion indicate the attitude of the Foreign Office which was often called upon to deal with the issue of Jewish victims of the war.[37]

In May 1940, the war was bleak for the Allies. Western Europe had been swiftly overrun by the Wehrmacht, Britain was cut off and stood alone in the breach. The idea of transferring refugees to Palestine was dropped and replaced by another stance.

"Fifth Column" hysteria spread like wildfire and increased suspicion of refugees. The government took harsh measures against enemy nationals in Britain, and initially refused to distinguish between Jews and others of German origin. Even women were jailed. Young Jews were categorized as "dangerous," bunched together with Nazis and shipped to Canada and Australia. It was a disgraceful affair. Brutal fights broke out between Jews and Nazis and the sailors robbed them. On July 2, 1940, the *Arandora Star* was sunk by a U-Boat and 600 passengers and crew lost their lives. The tragedy raised a storm of protest and the British public demanded that a distinction be made between Jewish and Nazi German nationals.

Influenced by the "Fifth Column" stories, Jewish leaders hardly raised their voices in protest against the sweeping measures taken against the Jewish refugees. After the conquest of Western Europe and the "blitz," *The Jewish Chronicle* was also gripped by the hysteria. It condoned the detentions because it believed that "the very life of the nation is at issue." Eventually, but only after the protests of the general press, the *Chronicle* came to its senses and lent its voice to the criticism of the Home Office, the ministry responsible for the detention of aliens. The paper published shocking accounts about the conditions of the Jewish detainees. Jewish leaders also fell in line and joined the call for a reappraisal of the detentions policy.[38]

By now, however, hundreds of thousands of Jews in Western Europe were caught in the Nazi net. German influence had also spread to the Balkans. Masses of Jews were poised to flee southward and the British were afraid they would "flood the Middle East" and make a shambles of the White Paper policy. In a telegram of September 21, 1940, the High Commissioner for Palestine petitioned the government to classify the expected invasion of illegal immigrants as "enemy nationals" rather than immigrants,[39] for it would be easier to declare war on enemy nationals than on refugees. As mentioned above, British officials believed that the intention of the Zionists was to infiltrate as many Jews as possible into Palestine, fill the White Paper quota and force the government, under the pressure of circumstances, to alter its policy.[40] These contradictory trends determined the resistance of the British government toward the help and rescue efforts.

At an earlier stage, a cabinet decision had set a policy principle, not concealed from the Zionist leadership, of not helping Jews leave German or German-held territory and turning them into refugees.[41]

As to immigration to Palestine, the British decided that no Jew who had fled Poland after October 1, 1939 would be permitted to enter Palestine.[42] Neither did the pleas of the Jewish Agency to permit the entry of Zionist leaders, who could hardly be suspected of being enemy agents, prove effective. In the end the British agreed to permit the *aliya* of Jews with certificates in their passports issued before the outbreak of war, but only if they had been issued in Germany. A fierce argument ensued between Selig Brodetsky and Malcolm MacDonald, the colonial secretary, with Brodetsky reiterating Weizmann's accusation that MacDonald was sending Jews to their death.[43]

In the same month, January 1940, the Foreign Office, on behalf of Lord Halifax, reminded the Colonial Office of the decision not to allow "this kind of people," i.e., Jews, to leave Germany.[44] In order to block a potential loophole, the Foreign Office denied the Americans staffing the British consulates in Germany access to the safes where certificates were stored.[45] It should be noted that Whitehall had earlier agreed to the *aliya* of Jews holding certificates issued before the war.

The Polish ambassador in London requested permission for the *aliya* of Polish Jews who had escaped to a neutral country. He was turned down because these Jews had fled after the set date of October 1, 1939. In a marginal note meant for internal ministry consumption, a Foreign Office bureaucrat wrote that the Poles were apparently willing to transfer all their Jews to Palestine.[46]

The total nature of the blockade against the Jews was hardly limited to Palestine. In July 1940, the British minister in Bucharest was asked to prepare a plan for the evacuation of Polish refugees in Rumania. No mention at all was made of the date of their escape from Poland. London, however, aware that many Jews were among them, suddenly abandoned the hallowed principle against "discriminating" between Jews and others. The application of this principle, however, was contingent on upholding the even higher principle of locking the Jews into the continent. Now Jews received special treatment. The refugees were to be evacuated to Cyprus with a *numerus clausus* of five percent set for Jews. If the *numerus clausus* could not be met then at least let there be "as few Jews as possible." Eventually the British decided to evacuate only "decent and intelligent" Poles, a flexible yardstick, indeed. Thus without fear of being accused of racism, any Jew could be disqualified and the *numerus nillus* was reached.[47]

In the same period, before the second front was opened in Eastern Europe, many refugees, including heads of Polish *yeshivot* and many of their students, fled to Kovno, Lithuania. Seeking any possible means of leaving Europe, they witnessed a "miracle" at the hands of Sempo Sugihara, the Japanese consul. Totally disregarding instructions from Tokyo this low-level diplomat issued, wholesale, Japanese transit visas to any Jew who could wave a permit to enter the Dutch Caribbean possession of Curacao. As to the Curacao visas, they were obtained from the Dutch consul by the orthodox rabbi of Stockholm.

Sugihara issued 3,400 visas for Jews to enter Japan via the Soviet Union. Many arrived in Kobe. A book and documentary film recount the remarkable story of Sugihara, who has been declared a "Righteous Gentile" by the Yad Vashem Martyrs and Heroes Memorial Authority, in Jerusalem, and has had a tree planted in his memory in Yad Vashem's Avenue of the Righteous Among the Nations.

In London, officials became suspicious that this traffic to the far reaches of the eastern hemisphere might open yet another illegal route toward Palestine. In the wake of Sugihara's activities, Foreign Office officials continuously monitored Jewish activities in the Baltic countries, now Soviet republics, and in May 1941, about a month before the German invasion of the Soviet Union, discussed methods of preventing the continued exit of Jews from these countries.[48]

Even earlier, in October 1940, when there was a brisk flow of refugees to Japan via the Soviet Union, the British extended the geographical area of its blockade. It barred the entry into its territories, especially Palestine, from any part of the Soviet Union. Since the Soviet Union was still neutral, the move was neither legally nor formally valid. Therefore, the Foreign Office instructed its Moscow ambassador, Sir Stafford Cripps, not to make the decision public.

This British move coincided with Brodetsky's meeting with MacDonald about the *aliya* of Jews from the Polish territories grabbed by the Soviet Union in accordance with the Molotov–Ribbentrop Pact. The colonial secretary, however, objected and advised caution, for close Russo-German cooperation might facilitate the infiltration of German agents into British territories. Howard F. Downie, the head of the Colonial Office's Palestine Desk, openly told the Jewish delegation that any positive steps taken by the British would encourage Jews to flee to neutral countries with Palestine as their ultimate goal. Therefore, the Jews should not be encouraged to leave the lands of their residence.[49]

On June 22, 1941 the German invasion of the Soviet Union solved the problem as far as the British were concerned. Now an area extending from the Baltic to the Balkans, where conditions were "favorable," as it were, for an "invasion" of Jews into Palestine, was enemy-held territory and subject to blockade regulations. Millions of Jews in that vast area were now under the Nazi heel. But the waters leading to Palestine were quiet. The Danube River flowed to the Black Sea through areas with large concentrations of Jews, and cheap passage and sailors with itchy palms were readily available. Lax maritime supervision and widespread bribery facilitated the organization of illegal immigration. In the war's early stages the routes were free of belligerent action. Consequently the British launched diplomatic, political and military efforts to block this serious breach toward Palestine.

Many Jews were employed by the Rumanian petroleum industry, an important supplier of oil to the European market, and about fifty of them steadily furnished the British Legation in Bucharest with information about this strategic industry. In 1940, when they were fired and replaced by German experts, they turned to the British to grant them refuge in Palestine or another British territory. The Foreign Office turned the request over to the Colonial and Dominion Offices. Even though their lives were in imminent danger, they were turned down.[50] The oil employees' request came at a difficult time. The British were fuming over the swelling tide of illegal immigration to Palestine from Rumanian ports, and were engaging in very unpleasant "battles" with the illegals off the coast of Palestine.

As long as the British were represented in the Balkans they pressed the countries of embarkation to take steps against the illegal immigration. However, to their chagrin they soon learned that the Balkan states were as interested in the Jews leaving as the British were in keeping them away from Palestine. The British even acknowledged that the Balkan authorities were pressing the Jews to climb onto ships and leave. The Turks, for their part, made polite gestures toward the British, but imposed only minor restrictions on passage through their territorial waters.[51]

Since no one else would carry out the dirty work for them, the Colonial and Foreign Offices prodded the British armed forces to act. First they lobbied the Navy, successfully, to wage war on the Jewish ships. The result was an historic tragedy: the very first shots fired by His Majesty's forces in World War II were directed at the bodies of Jews off the coast of Palestine on the freighter *Tiger Hill*. In their escape from the common enemy of both the British and the Jewish People two unarmed "illegal" immigrants were killed.[52]

Actually, the Navy was far from happy about using its might against persecuted civilians and tried to avoid the mission. The Colonial Office, on its part, was furious at the Navy commanders for refusing to deviate from regular patrol routes in order to hunt down refugee ships, as if searching for contraband. The relations between the Colonial Office and the Navy were delicate and the attitude of Winston Churchill, the First Lord of the Admiralty, was, according to the Colonial Office, "lukewarm." As early

as January 1940, Churchill issued general orders concerning the intercep-
tion of refugee ships, adding that the search for contraband was not a
suitable explanation in wartime. When the Colonial Office demanded that
the refugee ships intercepted on the high seas be apprehended, Admiralty
officials objected and responded that Churchill should be consulted about
its legality. Churchill's stand was well known. In February 1940, a senior
Admiralty official expressed distaste for the entire issue and refused to
order the permanent stationing of a pursuit vessel in Haifa harbor to
operate against the refugee boats. In response, the colonial secretary and
the High Commissioner for Palestine argued that it was the Navy's duty
to prevent the entry into Palestine of undercover German agents in refugee
guise. Admiralty officials, for their part, expressed sympathy for the
"persecuted refugees." The Colonial Office attributed the sentiment to
Churchill. They noted in the minutes that such sentiments were "out of
place in an official expression of opinion from a Service Department." The
colonial secretary, however, succeeded in bypassing the Admiralty.
Churchill was furious. He protested strongly against the minister who gave
the order to send warships against "those wretched people" and demanded
a report on the Jews apprehended.

In the autumn of 1940 British suspicions grew about the illegal immigration from the Danube basin. From October to December, five
overcrowded vessels made their way to the shores of Palestine. British
influence in the region was on the wane, and the activity of British warships
declined. The decision to confiscate the ships had little effect because their
value in any case was low and the owners had already received a fat fee for
them. Thus the argument that the shipowners would be better off hauling
a "cargo of timber in substitute for Jews" had little to offer them.[53]

The British authorities were in a bind. The refugees, being without
documents, could not be sent back to their countries of origin, and even
the subtraction of their number from the certificates' quota actually served
the interests of the Jewish leadership in Palestine. Moreover, the prospect
of a year's imprisonment in Palestine could hardly deter the refugees from
Nazism.

To a great extent the Colonial Office correctly understood that the
illegal immigration served the interests of the Germans, who at that early
stage wanted to expel the Jews, while for Jews flight from Europe was a
matter of life or death. Against this background there was "collaboration"
between the Gestapo and Jewish organizations and individuals who were
organizing the sailings to Palestine.[54]

According to the Colonial Office, the Germans had further objectives
in encouraging Jewish immigration: to incite tension between the British
and the Arabs and facilitate the infiltration of Nazi agents into the Middle
East.

In their anxiety over the increasing illegal immigrant traffic, senior Colonial Office officials in the autumn of 1940 sought means of deterring Jews from leaving Europe. Thus they decided that apprehended illegals be exiled to faraway places and kept in camps under conditions similar to those the Jews experienced in Europe. They found that the island of Mauritius, in the Indian Ocean, was suitable for their plans. This tropical island, infested with malaria which "killed women and children," was deemed unsuitable for British refugees from Gibraltar, but just the place for detaining "illegal Jews." According to witnesses, 40–50 percent of the Jews transported there contracted malaria.[55] This was in October 1940, before the German decision to totally destroy the Jews in occupied Europe. Thus the comparison with conditions in Europe was not far-fetched.

The Colonial Office was aware of the severity of their decision, but believed it could prevent illegal entry into Palestine. They were apprehensive about the Jewish reaction. To forestall Jewish protests, the ministry turned to Churchill, now prime minister, with the alternative of either sending the Navy to chase the ships back to Europe or expulsion to Mauritius. Churchill approved the Mauritius option, adding: "provided these refugees are not sent back to the torments from which they have escaped and are decently treated in Mauritius. I agree. W.S.C."[56]

Decent treatment, however, was far from what the Colonial Office intended. The Mauritius detainees were treated like criminals. They were put behind barbed wire and separate camps were established for men and women.[57] Moreover, a decree was issued geared to taking the wind out of the sails of potential illegals: Anyone attempting to enter Palestine illegally would never be issued an immigration permit.[58]

Howard F. Downie of the Colonial Office was a zealous fighter against the Jews seeking to reach Palestine. He rejected American sensitivities about the Rumanian pogroms and did what he could "to keep the Jews out of Palestine." Rumania was a relatively convenient place for the illegals to embark. A friend said of Downie: "He was in this sense happy that the German occupation of Rumania had give an opportunity in Palestine to make a profit on the immigration account."[59]

From the outbreak of the war until March 1941, about 11,000 illegal immigrants succeeded in reaching and settling in Palestine; 1,700 refugees were shipped to Mauritius; about 400 drowned on their way to Palestine; and about 500 survived the war in detention camps in Italy. On the other hand, 1,200 Jews fleeing for Palestine were shot by the Nazis in Yugoslavia. Despite the efforts of the IGCR's Sir Herbert Emerson, the Joint in this period invested $550,000 in helping the illegals make their way to Palestine.[60]

The traffic ended when the war spread to additional fronts. After the sinking of the illegal immigrant ship *Struma* in February 1942, new procedures, to be described below, were introduced in the issuing of certificates. The illegal immigration was renewed only in 1944 and continued until the establishment of the State of Israel in May 1948. The British did not succeed in sealing Palestine off from the refugees from Europe. Here there was an active struggle.

The British blockade of the Jews of Europe was zealously effected. Hardly any were helped to leave Europe. On December 12, 1940, a modest request was submitted to Foreign Secretary Lord Halifax by the Luxembourg government-in-exile. The 700 Jews of that country were under threat of expulsion to Poland, and the Foreign Office was asked to grant them refuge in Britain or Tanganyika. Since so few Jews were involved, the Luxembourg officials expected a generous British response.[61] Their optimism was misplaced: Only military experts would be allowed into Britain. (How could the British expect Luxembourg, of all countries, to have military experts?) Moreover, Tanganyika was closed to refugees. R. T. Latham, of the Foreign Office, agreed that the situation of the Jews was pitiable. However, since the Luxembourgers were not fighting the Germans, and thus not war refugees, their Jews were only refugees of racist persecutions. "It is decent of the Luxembourgers to look after these Jews of theirs," the minutes read, "because it won't win them any popularity." Anyway, who are these Luxembourgers whose contribution to the war effort was nil.[62]

The Foreign Office obsessively followed every movement of Jews out of Europe, even when their interest in that movement was marginal. In July 1941, a Jewish refugee ship sailed from Spain to the Americas. The passengers were duly equipped with the consent of the British naval attaché in Madrid, as was required because of the war against contraband. The Foreign Office was dissatisfied with this sailing and warned against the infiltration of German agents in refugee guise into the United States. The bureaucrats recommended putting an end to these sailings with the weird argument that the Jews were succeeding where the English had failed: They had managed to procure Spanish vessels for their refugees while the British could not find ships for their own refugees.[63]

The following incident also reeks of Whitehall's zealous vigilance against all attempts, even those with hardly a chance of success, that might bring a Jew to Palestine. In the war's early stages the Aliyah Bank in London asked the government for permission to transfer funds to Jews in Polish ghettos in a manner that would avoid harming the economic war against the enemy. The Treasury's supervisor of the Department of Trade with the Enemy, E.F.Q. Henriques, a Jew of Portuguese ancestry, recommended that the bank's plan to transfer money to Poland be approved on the basis of Sterling deposits being kept in the bank's London branch until the end of the war. In exchange, the bank would empty its accounts in

Poland. The money would be given to the Polish Jews whose relatives in Britain would deposit equivalent sums in the bank's London branch. All transactions would take place under strict Treasury supervision. The Foreign Office thought that the plan was acceptable. However, when it learned that Vladimir Jabotinsky, the Zionist Revisionist leader, served as a director of the bank its doubts started bubbling and it turned to the Colonial Office for advice. The latter was immediately suspicious. According to one of its bureaucrats, J. E. M. Carvell, "Mr Jabotinsky and his associates will surely devise with all the cunning and skill of their race means of using money for illegal immigration."[64] Thus crucial funds that could have saved the lives of starving people was denied to the Polish ghettos.

By September 1942, it was clear that the Jews of Europe were being destroyed. In that same month the Foreign Office came up with a new reason for rejecting a proposal to exchange European Jews for Germans expatriates in Ecuador and Colombia: there might be reserve officers among the Germans whose knowledge of South American geography could be of strategic importance to the enemy.[65]

Britain's policy of blockading the Jews of Europe was based on a totality of strategic war considerations. So was its Palestine policy part of the overall conception. Thus the decision to appease the Arabs so that the sensitive Middle East be free of disturbances that might divert military energies to the region. The appeasement of the Arabs, as well as the desire to counter the effect in Britain of the intensive Nazi propaganda, deterred the government from showing favor to the Jews because it could be interpreted as an identification with them. Britain was afraid of opening the gates of Europe lest it encourage a Jewish exodus to Palestine or the British Isles.

Intervention in immigration to countries beyond the seas was apparently the result of a general cabinet decision to do whatever it could to prevent Jews from leaving Europe. According to Whitehall's way of thinking, the Jews were part of Europe, should be left to "stew" there, and it was in Europe that a solution to their problem would be found after the war.[66]

Despite expressions of anti-Semitism, some of which we have presented, it is difficult to gauge the extent and the influence of anti-Semitic sentiment on the measures adopted against the Jews, and the persistence usually zealous in fulfilling them. How is one to fathom the strict bureaucratic rulings involved in the blockade of the Jews, even in marginal instances which could not possibly have posed any real danger to British policy? Whitehall's uncompromising stance was an obsession on all decision-making levels. It prevented the adoption of even the slightest of humanitarian gestures. On the other hand, many MPs, church leaders and broad segments of the British people were sympathetic to the Jewish plight and were prepared to extend assistance.

According to the unequivocal testimony of a Briton, Col. R. Meinertzhagen, a Christian sensitive to Jewish issues who was well-acquainted with British officialdom, the Colonial and Foreign Offices were "one hundred per cent anti-Semitic."[67] Indeed, the Jewish leadership in London sensed the anti-Semitic atmosphere in government offices, especially after the Dunkirk evacuation and during the Blitz. Some examples of this sentiment were: the exclusion of Jews from certain military units, about which Rothschild was asked to make discreet inquiries;[68] rumors spread about East End Jews exploiting bomb shelters;[69] and the prominence given by the Home Office to verdicts delivered against Jews for black marketeering.[70]

For external consumption, the authorities employed various rationalizations to justify their blockade of Europe's Jews: the infiltration of enemy agents along with genuine refugees, and the benefit to the German economy if it had fewer Jewish mouths to feed. These arguments had no basis in reality, but were convenient public relations ploys because they seemed to have a direct bearing on the course of the war. If the Gestapo was pressing the Jews to leave, wasn't it to make life easier for the Germans and more difficult for their English enemies? Even Chaim Weizmann swallowed this line.[71]

The Foreign Office presented two more aspects of the problem, one formal and the other pseudo-ideological. Officials doubted whether Jewish organizations had the right to plea for their brethren. After all, Jews, like Christians, were citizens of sovereign states. From the formal standpoint, at least, Jewish organizations should petition the different governments to help their Jewish citizens. And, as we shall see below, if an issue required the assistance of the British government it should be sought by a diplomatic or government representative of those countries. We have already discussed the lack of willingness of the British to recognize an international Jewish organization. Nonetheless, even though they occasionally referred them to other governments, the British never refused to negotiate international issues with Jewish organizations or leaders. However, the Jewish leaders considered it their duty to represent and defend oppressed Jews who were enemy nationals, for who else would take up their case. Here, too, as we shall soon learn, a solution was sought.

The pseudo-ideological approach posited absolute equality: Jew and Christian were in the same boat. Even though Jewish suffering was greater, both were suffering under the Nazis. The demand made by Jewish organizations that extraordinary measures be instituted on behalf of the Jews of Europe gave credence, according to the British, to the Nazi ideology of racial discrimination when, after all, weren't we engaged in a war to destroy racism?[72] This was the long and the short of the blather used to assuage the collective conscience of British officialdom.

The Riegner cable sent shock waves, for a while, at least, that threatened this approach. After it arrived, the three great powers, in the name of all the Allies, published a sharp protest against the annihilation of the Jews and threatened, when the time came, to exact punishment from the Nazi criminals. The declaration was published of December 17, 1942, without a hint, however, of any commitment to take practical measures to save the oppressed from their oppressors.

The war spread. Most of the Balkan states joined the battle against the Soviet Union. Europe was sealed. As the war dragged on the Nazi fist came down even harder on the Jews. The Nazis decided on the Final Solution. The Jews of the free world, for their part, explored avenues to help their fellow Jews.

From this point we shall be describing the activities of the Jewish leaders and organizations in London on behalf of the entrapped Jews of Europe, and their struggles with the British government, whose stand we have discussed above.

4

Years of Vacillation: The Jewish Leadership, 1939–1942

We got nowhere, we wasted hours protesting and composing and criticising memoranda which had no hope of serious attention by the government . . . yet all these measures did not save bodies and souls.

The war caused radical changes in the life of British Jewry and the leadership faced new challenges. Men were conscripted into the armed forces and many women, children and the elderly were evacuated to provincial areas. Familiar frameworks broke down and new temporary patterns evolved with great difficulty. Much effort was invested in establishing educational and religious frameworks in the towns and villages where part of the Jewish urban population relocated.[1] The new Jewish neighbors were not always cordially received and at times it was necessary to help both Jews and Christians to learn how to live together in harmony.[2] Anti-Semitic feelings also took their toll because many believed that it was in the interests of the Jews to pursue the war. Thus, faced with the challenge, the Jews were forced to take a stand in the peace or war debates that were still taking place in British public life.[3]

The fascist agitators who opposed British participation in the war were not the Jews' only problem. As mentioned briefly in the previous chapter, the Home Office suddenly announced that Jewish refugees, victims of Nazi Germany, were suspect like all other enemy nationals. Severe restrictions were placed on their movement, and many were arrested and thrown into detention camps alongside Nazis. After the Dunkirk evacuation surveillance of the refugees intensified and the detentions were extended. The BD's protest was muted, but a *Jewish Chronicle* headline accused the Home Office of "Gestapo Methods in Britain – Cruelty and Sabotage." The *Chronicle* followed the lead of the general British press which had compared the Home Office measures to those of Goebbels and his henchmen.[4] Consequently, the BD, which did not wish to appear to be less critical than the British press, took vigorous measures for the Jewish detainees.[5] The emergency situation raised the need for change in the organization of the community's institutions, greater awareness of events and the need to draw up contingency plans in order to prevent organizational paralysis in cases of extreme emergency. Lively discussions were held in the community and in February 1940, an Executive Committee was established within the framework of the BD with the participation of the heads of the Foreign Affairs and Constitutional committees, and five other members chosen by the plenary.[6]

After the establishment of the Executive Committee, its relation to the political work of the Joint Foreign Committee (JFC) of the BD and the Anglo-Jewish Association had to be dealt with. Leonard Stein, the Association co-chairman, argued that the agreement between the two organizations guaranteed the independence of the JFC and that its agenda was not subject to the approval of the new Executive Committee.[7] This stand was accepted and the JFC's independence was maintained until its dissolution in the summer of 1943.[8] This independence may very well be the reason why the BD terminated the agreement with the Anglo-Jewish Association.

The JFC cultivated ties with the Jewish affairs experts of the Royal Institute for International Affairs, "Chatham House," which served the Foreign Office and other government bodies. These experts were: Professor Arnold Toynbee, the well-known anti-Jewish and anti-Zionist historian, H. Beeley[9] and Hope-Simpson.[10] The JFC needed access to the library of Dr Alfred Wiener at the Central Jewish Information Office (later renamed as the Wiener Library), whose wartime use was restricted to the Foreign Office, the BD and a number of other organizations approved by the authorities.[11]

The JFC drew up a grandiose scheme of harmonious cooperation between different bodies. Unfortunately, its program was based on the illusion that all these bodies, Jewish and non-Jewish alike, shared the same interests in the struggle against Hitler. Accordingly, the JFC collected information about the Jewish diasporas and presented its conclusions to the relevant officials and institutions in the belief that British Jewry could influence the future of postwar Jewry. The heads of the committee knew that the World Jewish Congress and the American Jewish Committee were preparing similar materials, but they had hoped that cooperation between them would prevent overlapping. Furthermore, the cooperation of the Jewish Agency for Palestine, Agudat Israel, the American Jewish Congress and the Alliance Israelite Universelle was also required. The hoped-for cooperation also included non-Jewish organizations, such as representatives of German anti-Nazis, Czechs, Poles and Austrians, virtually all the exiled groups in Britain. It was also suggested that permanent contact be maintained with diplomatic representations and international organizations such as the Inter-Governmental Refugee Committee (IGRC). The detailed work plan was to be submitted to the Foreign Office along with a request to advise and be advised on all issues concerning Jews. The plan's authors were certain that the Foreign Office would willingly agree to a continuous association. In order to carry out these goals a special budget of £2,000 was allocated. The JFC hoped that it would develop into a kind of government agency for Jewish affairs, drawing from available and less accessible sources and justifying its existence on the benefit to be derived both by itself and the government.[12] We shall see that the JFC's plans were based on extreme naivete and a total lack of understanding of political realities.

The utter discrepancy, as we have seen, between the approaches of government officials and Jewish leaders was most unfortunate. Moreover, the misreading of the political map was remarkable in light of the fact that the plan's main author was the lawyer and experienced community activist and historian Leonard Stein, who no doubt was well acquainted with the notions of Toynbee, a dominant Chatham House figure. Stein had served as Chaim Weizmann's secretary in World War I, was present at the birth of the Balfour Declaration, and his comprehensive and fascinating book about that document displays political savvy.[13] Stein's program was approved by BD president Brodetsky, despite the latter's intimate knowledge of the government and the anti-Jewish animus of the White Paper. The optimistic expectations seem strange. Perhaps they can be explained by the feeling that the declaration of war had created a natural alliance between those fighting the Nazis and their victims. Even Jews racked by Nazi torture had that sense of a pact.[14]

Therefore, when the action or lack of action of the government showed what its true intentions were Jewish leaders felt keen disappointment and frustration. Years later Brodetsky wrote, without blaming the government: "There was little we could do, except protest, send food parcels with Government permission, and get the BBC to speak to them about the freedom for which we were fighting." Norman Bentwich, who in utter despair left the JFC, grasped the situation precisely. The Jews' activities, he wrote, were "a monotony of unreality. We got nowhere, we wasted hours protesting and composing and criticising memoranda which had no hope of serious attention by the government . . . yet all these measures did not save bodies and souls." Nahum Goldmann pointed the finger of blame at the Jewish organizations as well: "They lacked the courage, vision, and resolution to risk radical and drastic moves. In all my years in Jewish politics I have never felt so impotent, so grimly bitter, as I did over this. All of us who spoke for the Jewish people in those days, and I emphatically include myself, bear a share of the guilt, some of us a heavy share, some of us a lighter one."[15]

The bitter taste lingers on in Holocaust research. Students of the period still gauge the attitudes, actions and failings of governments on the issue of the destruction of Jewry by moral standards. In the judgment of history we find against those nations which sat on their hands: They turned their backs, if not on brothers, then at the very least on close allies in troubled waters.

The Jews of the free countries were emotionally unprepared, and from the practical standpoint perhaps unable, to force their governments into responsible action. Jewish leaders were loyal citizens and found it difficult to devise situations where their governments would be forced to adopt the aid and rescue measures appropriate to the exigencies of events. Thus the pressure they applied on the captains of states was mainly in the moral realm. Very seldom did they succeed in creating political situations where governments were pressured into taking steps that could be of benefit to the Jews.

The interests of the Jews and of the Allied countries not only did not coincide, they were usually opposed to each other. We have encountered this theme before and will continue to encounter it. Therefore, the prior conditions necessary for any independent Jewish rescue operation was a rejection of loyalty obligations toward one's government and absolute devotion to the Jews in enemy-occupied territories. The Jewish leaders were not hewn from rock which makes for independent thought and action. They were incapable of adopting the radical measures demanded by the enormous plight of their brethren. There were a few exceptions which we will describe below. But even then, the steps taken were of a limited nature and scope. For the sake of historical perspective, however, we must consider the circumstances of a total war. Many aspects of life were under strict government supervision and it was difficult for an unofficial body to take vigorous action. During wartime, patriotism is the ultimate value and maximum loyalty to the homeland is expected from all individuals, organizations and their publications. In such a situation the Jews desperately tried to avoid any action which could lead to the suspicion of harboring an additional and perhaps contradictory loyalty in their relations to their coreligionists. It is in this light that we should view the hesitancy of the central British Jewish institution, the BD. In order to remove any suspicion of disloyalty the heads of the BD sought the backing of non-Jewish individuals and organizations and the general press, whose initiatives they might join, in the pursuit of a policy meant to benefit the Jews of Europe.

Let us to return to the "sins" of Nahum Goldmann. In March 1943, he received a cable originating in the Warsaw Ghetto, "desperately appealing to the leaders of American Jewry to take drastic and dramatic steps, such as a dozen of them staging a sit-down strike outside the State Department, until the United States Government launched a vigorous campaign to save

Polish Jewry. Today, it seems to have been a rather naive demand. Nonetheless, I believed then as I do now that desperate extraordinary measures might very well have caused something to move. Perhaps in such incomparably outrageous times, so extraordinarily removed from the routine and acceptable, leaders are indeed morally required to abandon the routine and conventional for the daring and extraordinary. However, in light of the nature of the Jewish organizations in the United States, it was unlikely that the leaders of this Jewry would display such courage and decisiveness, even in such an ominous hour."[16]

Goldmann's description is eminently suitable to the Anglo-Jewish leadership as well.

At the beginning of the war German Jewish refugees appeared to have found a safe harbor in the neutral countries of West Europe and those fighting against Germany. Neutral Italy was an exception because it was allied to Nazi Germany. The Italian government enacted discriminatory legislation against the Jews even before Italy joined the Axis war, and the British press published reports of refugees being turned over to the Germans. In October 1939, an Italian Jew submitted a plan to Neville Lasky, then president of the BD, to save the refugees by bringing them to Britain. Only a few months earlier, until the end of August, such German Jewish refugees had been allowed to enter *en masse*. The Italian Jew also suggested that they be held under guard so that there be no fear of them operating against British interests.

After consulting with the heads of the refugee relief bodies Lasky rejected the plan. Moreover, these organizations declined to petition the British government to intervene with the Italians because they assumed that Britain would take no measures against Italy or ask a neutral country to accept the refugees. Neither would Britain accept more immigrants because of the state of war. Thus an approach to the government was not even made and the issue was passed on to the Paris branch of the Joint.[17] This policy was maintained even after the BD change of guard when Brodetsky, an active Zionist, was elected president.

A case in point is that of a German Jewish mother of three who succeeded in fleeing to England. She received no help from official Jewry in her attempts to bring her husband to England. Her husband had succeeded in reaching Budapest in neutral Hungary after the war broke out and had applied to the British legation for an extension of the visa he already held, but was turned down. Upon considering this request for family reunion, the BD ruled that no Jewish institution could intervene to seek entry for a refugee national of an enemy country, even through the narrow opening provided by Home Office regulations. The Jewish leadership maintained the same severe stand in other heart-rending cases, which, according to the woman's lawyer, had caused "a great degree of hardship."[18] And this was during the "Phony War," after the cessation of the large German Jewish emigration, and when Britain was not yet considered to be in any real danger.

Today we wonder how those Jewish leaders, who but a few months earlier had pressed the government to accept refugees in their thousands, suddenly hardened their hearts. After all, as we have already seen, Britain's open-door policy derived from its deplorable European and Palestinian policy, and the outbreak of war merely served as a convenient excuse for the government to radically change its policy of hospitality. It would seem that the Jewish leaders, most probably influenced by the sudden transition to a state of war, followed an exceedingly loyal line. We shall see that only in the wake of the shock of the bloodbath in Europe, and after pressure from different quarters, did official British Jewry demand far-reaching changes in the government's approach to the Jews of Europe.

At the same time that practical measures to save Jews by petitioning for their entry into Britain were rejected, the JFC, faithful to its tradition, studied the problems of the Jewish communities in Europe. It was involved, for instance, with the problems of the Jews of Rumania where anti-Jewish agitation was rampant. Early in 1940, laws were enacted depriving Jews of civil rights. Many Jews lost their source of livelihood, and the fascist Iron Guard harassed them.[19] Rumania was a signatory to the post-World War I Versailles treaty, which guaranteed minority rights. The JFC believed that the Western governments still had some influence and could demand that Rumania honor its treaty obligations.

The heads of the JFC sought the advice of Professor Mitrany, a Rumanian scholar at Chatham House. Mitrany, along with Beeley, advised them not to press the Foreign Office to submit a protest to the Rumanian government because of the delicate nature of the relations between the two countries. They suggested instead that the American press might condemn the measures taken against the Jews in violation of a treaty to which Rumania was a party. At the same time the two scholars invited the Jewish officials to make use of the services of the Royal Institute.[20] The Jewish leadership dropped the idea of trying to influence the Foreign Office to seek to ensure the rights of the Jews in Rumania. BD secretary Abraham Brotman, however, tried to involve the heads of the Ministry of Economic Warfare. He turned to a senior Jewish official in the MEW, Lionel Cohen, arguing that the Jews constituted the only pro-British element in that country and that any deterioration of their economic status could be detrimental to British interests. Cohen, however, refused to raise the issue with his superiors. He referred Brotman to the Foreign Office, but advised him that it was doubtful that they would pursue the issue.[21]

The Rumanian issue did not drop from the agenda. In early 1941, information about the persecution and killings reached London. The BD plenary protested strongly against the "bestial" persecution in Rumania, which was about to join the German alignment.[22] The situation deteriorated further in the fall of 1941, when thousands of Jews were mercilessly slaughtered by the army and tens of thousands expelled to Transnistria. The leader of the Jewish community in Bucharest, Dr Wilhelm Filderman, succeeded in smuggling a letter crying for help to Rabbi Isaac Herzog, the Chief Rabbi of Palestine, arguing that only emigration could save the Rumanian Jews.[23] Rabbi Herzog and the Rumanian immigrants association in Palestine turned to the BD pleading that it petition the government let them emigrate to British territorie.[24] The BD appealed, but government's response was not encouraging. It stuck to the line that Jews should not seek entry into British territories, and that efforts should be made to help those who remained in the countries of their residence, a concept that simply no longer held water. Since the minorities treaty was still in effect, at least from the formal standpoint, Brodetsky turned to the Earl of Lytton, chairman of the League of Nations Union. Lord Lytton, however, could offer no solution in the given circumstances.[25] A request to Anthony de Rothschild that he seek a meeting with Eden was met with the response: "My first impression is that there is little that can be done."[26]

In the period between the evacuation of the British forces from France and the time information about the systematic destruction of the Jews became known, Whitehall occasionally discussed requests for the rescue of individual Jews and groups.[27] These petitions were turned over to the aid societies, or in certain instances to the Polish Jewish representation. When political action was required, the general trend was one of evasion and acceptance of the reality. A case in point was that of a Polish Jewish activist who had extended assistance to refugees who succeeded in fleeing the country. He reached Kobe in Japan, from where he requested asylum in Canada. Another case was that of a Polish Jewish family stranded in the Soviet Union that begged to be removed from there. The JFC turned both requests over to Szwarcbart, the representative of Polish Jewry in London.[28] Szwarcbart felt powerless. He sought the intervention of Brodetsky and his associates, but to no avail. The same helplessness was displayed in helping relatives of British Jews who had reached Vichy France.[29]

In 1941, Jewish international organizations sought refuge for Jews who had arrived in Japan and Portugal, countries which inclined toward Germany. The Polish government obtained the agreement of the authorities in Australia and Canada for the immigration of Polish citizens, but the Dominions did not relish the idea of Jewish immigrants.[30] Szwarcbart asked the JFC to attempt to influence the Dominion governments not to discriminate against the Jewish refugees.[31] The Foreign Office, for its part, contended that it had no influence over the issuance of visas to the

Dominions or to India and Burma. Brodetsky and Brotman approached the Minister for India and Burma, L. S. Amery, of the "Zionist wing" of the cabinet,[32] but it did not solve the problem of the refugees, most of whom were students of Polish *yeshivot* who had landed in Japan.[33]

During a visit to London of MacKenzie King, the Canadian prime minister, Szwarcbart pressed Brodetsky to arrange a meeting so that the two of them could lobby King. They did not succeed in arranging the meeting, but the immigration officer of the Canadian High Commission demanded guarantees from both the Jews and the Polish government for 300 Jewish candidates for immigration. He also demanded that he be supplied with detailed information about each one of them.[34]

Because of the opposition of the High Commissioner of Palestine, Rabbi Herzog had no success in arranging for their entry into Palestine. Two thousand rabbis were already in the country, the high commissioner said, and that was more than enough. He also said that the rabbinical students would have to seek other employment. Furthermore, since it would be difficult to identify them they might pose a threat to security.[35] Thus as long as Japan remained neutral, Canada was the only hope of the refugees. Rabbi Hertz took up the cudgels. He initiated the consideration of their applications by the colonial secretary and succeeded in obtaining 80 Canadian visas. The colonial secretary's agreement to lobby the Canadians, an extraordinary measure, was apparently the result of an attempt to release the pressure on Britain to grant the youths entry into Palestine. The Canadians set a *numerus clausus* for the Jews in the framework of the Polish immigration quota. According to Szwarcbart, the approval of the 80 visas went beyond the number allowed. In a further attempt to arrange for the entry into Canada of the 370 students remaining in Japan, Henry Pelz, secretary of the Chief Rabbi's Emergency Council, asked the BD to have Brodetsky lobby the Canadian prime minister. Brotman immediately wrote a note in the letter's margins that the issue should be handled by Szwarcbart. Szwarcbart was not eager to do so. He replied that Brodetsky should press the issue despite the poor odds. Brodetsky then told Pelz that since Hertz had already achieved success he should continue to deal with the issue.[36]

The surprise attack on Pearl Harbor put a swift end to the prospect of leaving Japan. Nonetheless, Canada continued to be considered a harbor for refugees in distress. The Czechoslovak government signed an agreement with Canada about accepting immigrants, but the Canadians were strict about the Jews among them. Ernst Frischer said the Canadian position was influenced by racial prejudice; they had even restricted the entry of Christians of Jewish origin. He requested that this fact be held in confidence. Frischer believed that Brodetsky and Brotman should seek an annulment of that shameful restriction, either by direct appeal to the

Canadians or via the British government. London circles close to the Canadians suggested that the issue should not be raised, and it was not. Brotman sufficed with a letter to the official in the Rothschild bank who handled its Canadian affairs.[37]

Another case displaying the hesitancy of the Jewish political institutions on refugee issues was the cable Brotman received in November 1941, from the Jewish immigrant association, HICEM in New York, about the ship *Cavohorno* that was wandering in the open seas with 85 Jewish refugees. All had valid Paraguayan visas. After the refugees were denied permission to disembark in Argentina, they sought temporary asylum in Trinidad, but the British governor disliked the idea of hosting Jews. The BD was asked to intervene, but Brotman passed the issue to another secretary, M. Stephany, secretary of the Central Jewish Refugee Council. Stephany, as representative of a philanthropic organization, turned to Sir Herbert Emerson, the High Commissioner for Refugees. Emerson then asked the Dutch government to grant temporary asylum in its Curacao colony with the Joint supplying the necessary monetary guarantees.

Lord Melchett approached the issue differently. He sent a personal letter on the stationery of his company, Imperial Chemical Industries, a corporation with global interests, to Anthony Eden describing the travail of the Jews being shunted from one South American port to another. Melchett wrote that he had received the information from the "Jewish Committee for Great Britain," in Buenos Aires. Britain had an obligation toward its Jewish friends in Argentina, Melchett admonished Eden. Denying these Jews entry at the port of Trinidad would raise doubts about the seriousness of British sympathy. Eden replied that he had been informed that the refugees had temporarily debarked in Argentina and promised to examine the possibility of their entry into Canada. In all events, according to Eden Trinidad was not a suitable venue. As we have seen, the truth was that the Foreign Office had encountered the vigorous opposition of the Trinidad governor. Melchett replied that the Jews had not, in fact, been allowed into Argentina and were sailing to Curacao. As a result of strong Foreign Office pressure, the Dutch approved the admission into their colony of the 15 Czech Jews on the ship. From the memorandum we see that the Foreign Office was apprehensive about the reaction of Lord Melchett, who continued to prod Eden, and American criticism, especially on the part of Congressman Sol Bloom. They also feared that the ship would head toward a port in Britain itself.[38] Even though a confluence of circumstances in this instance favored the Jewish refugees, one should note the positive reaction to Lord Melchett's strong letter where he succeeded in pointing to a clear British interest. The Jewish leaders did not manage to create a similar situation again.

Toward the end of 1941, more and more information about the

increasing severity of the Nazi war against the Jews was reaching London. The public was deeply disturbed.[39] In the inner chambers of the Foreign Office there was talk of the destruction of between a half and one million Jews in Eastern Europe. Half of Dutch Jewry had already been incarcerated in camps and destroyed,[40] and a report arrived from Switzerland about the use of gas to kill the Jews.[41] The Jewish public became increasingly agitated, but its leaders were still afraid to issue a suitable response.

In October 1941, Dr Hans Blum, a religious Jewish lawyer and refugee from Germany, wrote an anguished letter to John Harris of Cambridge, an Anglican priest, arguing that it was high time that large-scale rescue measures be instituted to save the threatened Jewish masses. He suggested that for the duration of the war, camps for Jews who escaped the jaws of death be set up in neutral European countries and overseas. The camps would be funded by an obligatory levy on all Jews. "Quickest help has to be tried if it shouldn't be too late!" Blum wrote. Harris sent the letter to Brotman who gave it to the philanthropist Otto Schiff, the head of the Central Jewish Refugee Council. Schiff thought that the neutral countries would not be willing to cooperate because of the large numbers of refugees and funding required. Brotman replied that he was not willing to reject the idea. No matter "how farfetched his [Blum's] idea of a neutral refugee country for refugees is, it ought not to be altogether put out of court."[42] No steps, however, were taken. A year later the extension of guarantees to the neutral countries would be a major Jewish demand to induce them to accept the Jews who had escaped with their lives.

Eventually the war came to a turning point. The Russian front stabilized, the German Blitz of the British Isles was broken and the United States had entered the war. When the Germans saw that their luck was running out they became even more bestial in their treatment of the occupied peoples. The heads of the governments-in-exile in London then convened the Inter-Allied St. James Conference, so called because of its St. James Palace venue, to discuss the German terror. On January 13, 1942, the conference issued a declaration about the suffering of the peoples under the Nazi yoke, threatened dire retribution against "those guilty or responsible" for criminal acts, and established a permanent investigative apparatus. There was no mention whatsoever of the Jews.[43]

For some reason the preparations for the conference were made in the innermost chambers. Only at the beginning of January 1942 was an article published by *The Times* about a conference called to deal with German atrocities. The Jewish organizations went into action. On the basis of *The Times*' information the secretary of the BD approached the Foreign Office. Its representative still did not officially know about the arrangement of such a conference. He explained that if indeed such a conference was held it would encompass only the occupied states. Brotman understood the implication and immediately asked that material on the persecution of the Jews be prepared for the conference by Dr Alfred Wiener. Leonard Stein had second thoughts. He argued against specifically emphasizing Jewish travail because the Jews were included in the suffering of all the trampled European peoples. The only Jewish issue Stein agreed to submit was the expulsion of the Jews of the "Reich" into Poland because they were not included in the bailiwick of any conference participant. In the end no material was submitted because, as Brotman explained, there was insufficient time for its preparation.[44]

The British Section of the World Jewish Congress reacted more vigorously and objected to the absence of any specific mention of the Jews. In a letter of February 18, 1942, to Polish Prime Minister Władysław Sikorski, the chairman of the St. James Conference, the head of the BSWJC demanded that a declaration be issued specifically about the Jews. The BSWJC reasoned that the Germans should not gain the impression that the world was apathetic to the fate of the Jews against whom they were committing crimes essentially different from those against other peoples. On May 1, after two and a half months went by without a response, the BSWJC sent a reminder. Eight days later a reply finally arrived. Sikorski wrote that the signatories of the St. James Declaration had condemned the crimes against the Jews just like those against all others. In what on the surface seemed an adroit but which was also a hypocritical response, Sikorski reasoned that the Jews had not been noted in the declaration because specific mention of them would constitute a tacit recognition of the race theory that had to be rejected out of hand.[45] Here, too, the JFC lagged behind the British Section. After it received Sikorski's letter, it also wrote a letter of protest and received the same exact response.[46]

The heads of the Foreign Office and the Ministry of Information were pleased with Sikorski's stand because it was identical to theirs. Moreover, they believed they could even learn something: it "seems to point the way for us." They especially appreciated Sikorski's logic that specific mention of the Jews could be seen as a recognition of the race theory. The writer of the relevant minutes wrote in the margins of Sikorski's letter: "This is H. G. Wells's favourite dig of the Jews."[47] With this comment the official adopted Wells's anti-Jewish stand. In that same year, Wells published *The Outlook of Homo Sapiens*, in which he dedicated a chapter critical of Jewish influence in the world, somehow comparing it to Christianity and aggressive Nazism.[48] Sikorski's position constituted much of the cornerstone of the Allies' policy toward the Jewish Holocaust. There were only temporary exceptions from this principle and invariably the result of great pressure, such as when the Final Solution was confirmed. The rule not to "discriminate" against the Jews was very convenient when the government was evading practical measures to help them. At times there was a readiness to admit that the Jews were experiencing greater suffering, but in principle no distinction should be made between suffering and suffering. A shocking and reprehensible example of this attitude can be seen in a letter sent by Oliver Stanley, the colonial secretary, to Harry Goodman of Agudat Israel, on October 22, 1942! This is how the colonial secretary explained the refusal of His Majesty's Government to help rescue Jewish children: "I find, moreover, that it would be contrary to His Majesty's Government's policy to treat Jewish children in occupied territories differently from other children. Undoubtedly, the Jews are bearing a great part of the suffering and persecution which exist in German occupied Europe but the non-Jews also are suffering greatly."[49]

In spirit, the St. James Conference absolved the free world governments from adopting any extraordinary measures and finding immediate solutions to alleviate Jewish suffering. There was but one solution for both the Jews and their neighbors – victory. The sooner it arrived the sooner many lives would be spared and it was incumbent upon the Jews of the free world to contribute to their brethren's rescue by stepping up their war effort.

That was the spirit of Churchill's address to the Jewish rally in New York's Madison Square Garden on July 21, 1942. The British prime minister, however, stressed the Jewish contribution to the war effort, especially that of the *Yishuv* in Palestine, which had mobilized 10,000 soldiers and 20,000 policemen and women – words undoubtedly meant to warm the cockles of the hearts of the thousands of Jews who had crowded into the huge hall. But Churchill did not relate to the very purpose of the rally – raising public awareness of the need to save European Jewry. One should not suspect happenstance or any lapse on Churchill's part to the rally's objective.[50] Certain Jewish circles were also willing to link a speedy end to the war to Jewish survival because it combined British patriotism with responsibility toward brethren in distress. This approach prevailed even in the most critical of times when the entire world knew about the murder of the Jewish people. As *The Jewish Chronicle* put it, on December 18, 1942, in response to the Allies' declaration, "An Answer to the Mass Murder" is a vigorous Jewish war effort.[51]

The parity of suffering of Jews and Christians could not stand up to the information which reached London in the summer of 1942. In carrying out the Final Solution the Nazis demonstrated murderous consistency in their "discriminatory" treatment of Jews in relation to others. Furthermore, the destruction of the Jews was meant to be carried out according to a certain schedule and within a set period of time. According to the intelligence in the offices of the WJC in Geneva, and relayed to London in August 1942 by Gerhart Riegner, the destruction of European Jewry was scheduled to be completed by the following winter. The death sentence, in other words, would be carried out much earlier than any victory over Germany! In this moment of truth the Allies made an exception to their rule of parity, and on December 17, 1942 issued a declaration dedicated to the suffering of the Jews of Europe.[52]

In light of the BD's lukewarm stance, other groups began pressing the official Jewish leadership to adopt a vigorous stand, which it belatedly and not entirely willingly did. Early in 1942, reliable information was steadily arriving about the bitter fate of Polish Jewry. As a result, the Polish Jewish organizations, with the exception of the Bund, banded together in the Council of Polish Jews in Great Britain. The organizations involved were the Federation of Polish Jews in Great Britain and Ireland; the Polish Sector of Mizrahi, Polish Agudat Israel, the New Zionists (Revisionists); and the Nahum Sokolow Polish Zionist Association. The council, however, believed that their appeal to the public would be at a disadvantage without the cooperation of the Anglo-Jewish establishment. Thus at the beginning of March 1942, it dispatched a letter to Brodetsky signed by Szwarcbart, in his capacity as a member of the Polish National Council, and by B. Margulies, chairman of the Council of Polish Jews. They noted in sorrow that they were incapable of alleviating the suffering of their brethren caught behind the ghetto walls, "But it is at least our duty to express our deepest sympathy with their fate. Furthermore it is our task to arouse public opinion to the existing state of affairs and to make it known to all these to whom human suffering is still of any momentum." They intended to embark upon a series of public rallies and asked Brodetsky to be the patron of the committee established for that purpose. The BD displayed caution and Brotman asked for details before determining its stand. The council planned a "Polish Jewry Day" to draw attention to the suffering of the Jews in Poland, with mass rallies in London and elsewhere and the participation of Allied representatives. They also had a political goal: "The policy behind these publicity arrangements is to force upon the authorities the idea that 'something must be done' to help Polish Jewry survive."

Brodetsky declined the offer of patronage. He and Brotman met with the Polish Jewish activists and succeeded in convincing them that the time was not ripe for mass rallies and public campaigns. Their arguments are not recorded in the sources. In all events, the activists lowered their tone and sufficed with the promise of occasional meetings with members of the JFC to discuss the Polish Jewish situation and the measures required. They also asked for a monthly allotment of £25 to fund their activities. Brodetsky evaded a positive response to their request for regular consultations and their request for the money was turned down. The only allotment the JFC was willing to make was for a certain sum for the maintenance of Szwarcbart's office. The Czech refugees also requested a budget for their activities. Brotman feared that similar requests would be made by other organizations and that there would be no end to the applications. All the initial enthusiasm ended with one small demonstration, which Brodetsky declined to attend, where Szwarcbart and Zygielbojm discussed current affairs. That was how the political activity of the Council of Polish Jews in Great Britain faded, at least for the time being.[53]

At the time of the Polish Jews' agitation, information was received about a pending mass expulsion of Slovakian Jews.[54] Different streams of Czechoslovakian refugees in England reacted in different ways. They had two organizations, Ernst Frischer's, which was affiliated with the World Jewish Congress, and the Federation of Czechoslovakian Jews affiliated with Agudat Israel. Frischer's organization did not publicly express the anxiety of the Slovakian Jews. The Federation, however, led by Raphael Springer, published a protest against the expulsion and asked for the BD's cooperation.[55] Like in the case of the Polish Jews the BD declined to cooperate. In a letter, classified as secret, the JFC informed Springer of its plea, in cooperation with Chief Rabbi Hertz, to the Vatican to intervene in the expulsion, but without success. In this way the JFC was telling Springer of its cooperation with a factor close to the World Federation of Czechoslovakian Jews, of which Rabbi Hertz, a native of Slovakia, was president. The JFC was at most, it wrote, willing to discuss Springer's proposals.[56] It would seem that Brodetsky and his colleagues wished to maintain a distance between themselves and the organizations of recent arrivals, whose demands went against the grain of the BD policy which was to work "decently" and refrain from making noise. The emotional threshold of the religious Czechoslovak organization, however, was somewhat lower. It organized a public demonstration without the cooperation of the BD, thus avoiding the pitfalls encountered by the Polish Jews. The rally was held early in June 1942 in a hall near the offices of the BD. Invitations were sent to Brodetsky and Brotman, but they declined to attend. Brodetsky was also asked to send a declaration, but sufficed with a letter to the chief rabbi, who as noted served as the Federation's president and chaired the rally. In his letter, Brodetsky wrote that the public condemnation of the atrocities would leave a deep impression in every human heart.[57] Springer had succeeded in bringing together an impressive array of speakers: the Bishop of London, the Czechoslovak interior and rehabilitation ministers, two Christian MPs, one of them Commander Locker-Lampson, and Harry Goodman.[58] After the rally, the Federation published a pamphlet with a dedication by President Benes and a foreword by Goodman about the Slovakian persecutions.[59] This was the first(!) protest demonstration held in London. When Rabbi Hertz informed Brotman about the preparations for the rally, his response was: "I did not think it would do any harm, but I did not think it would do any good."[60] If this was the reaction to a *fait accompli*, it may be assumed that the heads of the BD believed that the pain should be concealed, and that such issues should not be brought to the attention of the public.

It would appear that the shrewd action of the World Federation of Czechoslovakian Jews made a strong public impression and led to a conflict between the advocates of the quiet and the public approaches. The purpose of the rally was not only to express anger, but as is the nature of such demonstrations – to create an atmosphere of pressure on the authorities to attain certain goals. Indeed, the hour of a turn was near; the public was incited and outside pressures increased. Brodetsky, Stein and Brotman were pushed into action as if possessed. At the demonstration, Rabbi Hertz, as chairman, expressed disappointment at Brodetsky's absence. Even Eden and Cardinal Hinsley, the Catholic Primate, had sent statements to be read in public, but all the president of British Jewry did was to send an indirect letter. Brotman tried to alleviate matters by saying that Brodetsky had been at his home in Leeds. Brodetsky was in London three days of each week and the rest of the time was in Leeds, where he taught mathematics and aeronautics at the university.[61]

The way the Slovakian issue was handled was characteristic of the hesitant approach of the heads of the JFC in the period before the Final Solution became public knowledge. On the other hand, Rabbi Hertz and his circle had already called for political activism at an early stage. On June 11, 1942, Hertz had told Brotman over the telephone that Lord Strabolgi (who was close to the Revisionist circles) had suggested that Britain issue a public warning to the Quislings of Slovakia that responsibility for the expulsion of the Jews would be placed upon their heads. The rabbi was prepared to arrange a meeting with Eden through Lord Strabolgi in order to discuss the proposal. Brotman asked that the meeting with Eden be made cooperatively by the chief rabbi and the co-chairmen of the JFC. Brotman apparently had attempted to arrange a meeting with Eden through Lord Rothschild, but not in a very convincing manner. For some reason he had told Rothschild that the proposed meeting was to discuss the outcome of the request to send medicine to the ghettos. Rothschild refused to mediate because the issue did not appear important enough to involve the foreign secretary himself. Stein also thought that the Slovakian issue was not enough of a reason to seek a meeting with Eden. Thus if Hertz so desired he should arrange the meeting himself and incidentally raise the issue of the help for the ghettos.[62] There is no evidence in the sources of a meeting having taken place between the chief rabbi and the foreign secretary.

In May 1944, Rabbi Hertz, addressing a memorial day sermon for the Warsaw Ghetto, lashed into the secular leadership for its dithering in those critical times: "What has Anglo-Jewry done to arouse world opinion in regard to a moral cataclysm that threatens to engulf half the Jewish race? ... Although the Nazi killing of thousands daily began early in 1941 it was the 29th October 1942 before the lay leaders of Anglo-Jewry arranged a public protest meeting. Some of these leaders were distressed even over the Day of Mourning and Prayer I proclaimed in the December following. I need not now comment on such Olympic calm, reticence and indifference. Suffice it to say that they were not calculated to stir the men at the helm of the political universe to speedy action in human salvage, so that dismay seized many a one at the procrastination and inertia of those who alone had the power to save."[63]

Both Jews and concerned Christians wondered why so little was being done when hair-raising details about events in Europe was being published openly.[64] From the beginning of the year the British press was reporting the murder of a million Jews throughout Europe.[65] According to *The Daily Telegraph*, 700,000 Jews had been killed in Poland alone. The report angered Brotman who thought that the number was exaggerated and he regretted its publication. He conferred with Brodetsky about ways of verifying the information with neutral sources, and thus proposed to seek the help of the Foreign Office.[66]

In Christian circles various ideas were raised. In June 1942 Mrs. Henry Martin, who engaged in welfare activities for Soviet women and children, was shocked by the newspaper reports, quoting Bund leader Szmul Zygielbojm, about the persecution of the Jews in Poland. She proposed that public leaders, especially Christians, issue a declaration to the conscience of the world and to the Germans to stop the murder. She promptly prepared an invitation for a gathering of public figures and sought the assistance of A. M. Kaizer, of the Fund for Jewish Refugees from Poland. Kaizer suggested that among the Jews Brodetsky, Stein, Frischer, Zygielbojm, Szwarcbart, the chief rabbi, Silverman, Easterman and other figures be invited. Brotman wanted to stall the meeting. He said that the Jewish leadership needed time to think about it, especially when invitations would be issued to such figures as Churchill, Roosevelt and the archbishop. Neither did he believe that a relatively anonymous woman could direct such an important movement. As a matter of fact, all Martin wanted was to spur the process on, not be prominent in the committee itself. At Brodetsky's instigation Kaizer dampened Martin's activities. And if it was too late to prevent the publicity, Brotman argued, then at least let the demonstration coopt Christians and be at the initiative of the Council of Christians and Jews.[67]

Thereafter in October 1942 there was another private attempt by a Christian to awaken the public. Mrs. Peter Haslup, Lord Samuel's neighbor, sought to mobilize MPs to set up a committee to press for relaxing the restrictions against the entry of refugees into Switzerland. Lord Samuel gave Haslup his blessing. Brotman, on the other hand, was furious.[68]

Similar ideas were later raised by the Jewish organizations. The Polish

Jewish refugees and the rank and file of London Jewry were upset that no public expression had being given to their pain and protest. The Czechoslovak Jews, part of them at least, had only recently lifted their voice in public protest. The Polish Jews decided to renew their efforts to prod English Jewry into action. Early in July, the Polish Jewish Council called a meeting to which they invited representatives of various organizations and institutions. This time Szmul Zygielbojm of the Bund participated. We have Brotman's report of the meeting where he expressed disdain for the bitter cries of the speakers. The truth is that Brotman had arrived late and left early. The BD president did not attend because he was busy at Leeds University. Brotman sent him, by express mail, a sarcastic summary of the meeting: "We arrived at about 6 o'clock and found Szwarcbart in full swing. We learnt later that he had been speaking for an hour. Zygelbaum [sic] had apparently opened the ball. Barou, Schnur, Cang, Michael Levy and a gentleman called Barnett (who gave himself out as the representative of the masses in Whitechapel) all made vehement speeches."[69]

Dr Barou, the general-secretary of the British Section of the World Jewish Congress, demanded action. If the JFC was not forthcoming he threatened a mass protest demonstration organized by his organization. Others cast blame on the BD for being too slow in its handling of urgent problems. Doubts were also expressed about whether a protest demonstration would take place at all if the BD was in charge. Despite the heavy pressure Brotman delivered only a lukewarm message. He gave assurances that the Board was prepared to consider any proposal "which could be of any use," and expressed his belief that no steps would be taken without it. His estimation turned out to be correct. The Polish Jews did not act independently. Brotman still maintained that a reaction against events in Europe should be under the aegis of the Council of Christians and Jews. The British Section had a different view. A few days before the meeting with Brotman it called a press conference where Silverman quoted German newspaper articles openly reporting the physical destruction of the Jews. The BSWJC believed that with this press conference an end had finally been made to the conspiracy of silence.[70]

It would appear that Brodetsky agreed with his secretary and co-chairman Stein. He was still opposed to any Jewish protest that portrayed the Holocaust as a uniquely Jewish problem. The BD leaders viewed the reaction to the Holocaust in connection with the problems besetting the community, specifically anti-Semitism and black marketeering on the part of some Jews. Elsewhere, we have discussed how the Home Office maliciously linked these issues with the desire of the Jews to help their co-religionists in Europe. These pressures on the part of a government body apparently hit their mark. Brodetsky and his colleagues were apprehensive about depicting the Holocaust as a uniquely Jewish phenomenon and they preferred coopting non-Jews in any protest against the atrocities in general.

Consequently Brodetsky attempted to set up an unofficial committee of Yugoslavs, Poles, Greeks, Czechs and Jews to deal with the publications, radio broadcasts and meetings connected with Nazi atrocities against Jews and others. Interestingly enough, he found support in Zygielbojm, who had adopted the Polish government's fears about the fate of its people. At a JFC meeting on July 15, 1942, Zygielbojm reported the direct murder of two hundred thousand Jews in Poland and the death by starvation of another million and a half. According to Zygielbojm, the Germans were planning to destroy both the Jews and the Polish intelligentsia and proposed protesting against the two together.[71] Brodetsky apparently sought to prevent both an exclusively Jewish protest and have the Jews coopted into the work of the St. James Conference on an unofficial basis. In order to further these goals he entered into negotiations with the ministers of different governments. Czechoslovak Foreign Minister Jan Masaryk took it upon himself to summarize the discussions.[72] The Yugoslav government inclined to agree with Brodetsky, but the Czechoslovak and Polish governments demurred. Masaryk explained the move by saying that both in his country and in Poland there was a large Jewish population and an agreement to establish a common committee might open the door to other Jewish demands, such as the appointment of an observer to the War Crimes Commission.[73] In short, they perceived certain dangers in a diversion from the principles of the St. James Conference.

The negotiations carried out by Brodetsky and Brotman with the heads of states drew the attention of the Information and Foreign Offices. Once again the problem of a broad "Jewish nationality" arose. They understood that Jewish elements, the WJC in particular, were lobbying to be represented at international conferences. The British officials' fears were allayed after they learned that the stance of their allies was identical to theirs – namely that there was no "distinct Jewish nationality." They were, however, concerned about Sikorski's contact with the Zionists and Revisionist Zionists and proposed sending him a private note about this. They emphasized that in principle the Jews should be viewed as citizens of the different states. Consequently, the British did not acknowledge Chaim Weizmann's cable announcing the Jewish Agency's endorsement of the United Nations declaration, and considered the Jewish lobbying to be part of a propaganda campaign for a Jewish state in Palestine. As to the concrete issue at hand, the British believed that Masaryk had damaged the accepted approach because of his personal belief that the Jews should be invited to the war crimes discussions. As an official put it, Masaryk's "humanity is better than his judgment."[74] Benes was undoubtedly closer to the British view. In light of Brodetsky's failure there was no choice but to hold a Jewish rally despite his preference to depict Jewish suffering as part of the general travail of all nations under the Nazi heel.[75]

Early in August, Masaryk, speaking for the Allies, rejected Brodetsky's proposal to cooperate with the St. James Conference. Toward the end of the month Rabbi Hertz pleaded with the BD to arrange a mass demonstration.[76] On September 9, Brodetsky finally yielded and presented a plan to the BD Executive Committee for a public demonstration to be held on October 29 at the vast Royal Albert Hall, even though Brotman believed that it was not a good idea to gather 10,000 people "at one blow" over the issue. Brodetsky found justification for holding a Jewish rally in the prime minister's speech of the previous day, when Churchill roundly condemned German cruelty against the Jews.[77] Churchill's statement was not meant as a conciliatory measure toward the Jews, but to allay the St. James signatories of any qualms they might have had after a speech by Roosevelt condemning the persecutions.[78]

During those days, Jewish officials were receiving the reports that had reached the World Jewish Congress and the Jewish Agency in London about the dimensions of the systematic slaughter of the Jews. Those who were against holding public rallies felt there was all the more reason to withhold the information. Brotman, for his part, was concerned that "adding despair to what they are already suffering mentally" would affect the emotional well-being of the hundreds of thousands of British Jews with relatives in Poland. Moreover, he believed that the information from the Jewish Agency in Switzerland required verification in case it was the result of a Nazi ruse.[79]

In all events, the BD made preparations for a large protest demonstration. It sought, unsuccessfully, to persuade senior government officials to attend. The two cabinet members invited to address the rally declined. The prime minister was asked to send a cabinet minister to the conference to represent him. This move was also turned down with the reasoning that the precedent could lead to pressure in the future on the government to be represented at demonstrations of the governments-in-exile.[80] Eden, arguing that the prime minister had already greeted the mass rally in New York in July and *The Jewish Chronicle* on its jubilee, attempted to prevent Churchill from sending a greeting.[81] Nonetheless, Churchill did respond and his message, read by the Archbishop of Canterbury, expressed warm support for the Jews suffering from German cruelty and promised that after the war there would no longer be oppression on racial grounds.[82] The Foreign Office's efforts to prevent the participation of high officials of other governments were not successful. General Sikorski and Jan Masaryk spoke at the rally as did Lord Cecil, Jacques Soustelle of the Free French, the Catholic Primate's representative, the heads of the free churches,

Walter Elliot MP, and Brodetsky. Rabbi Hertz, an incorrigible non-conformist, caused a stir by chastising the British people for not responding vigorously to the slaughter in Europe. He also sharply criticized the press for its apathy and reservations, which to his mind served to encourage the Nazis to continue the slaughter. The rally was widely reported in the press and radio. It concluded with a resolution formulated with the agreement of the Archbishop of Canterbury, vilifying "the deliberate policy of extermination which the Nazis have declared against the Jews." The resolution did not call for rescue efforts, but unreservedly condemned and emphasized the fate of the Jews.[83]

The rally put an end to the inhibitions of the Jewish leaders. They now embarked upon an open and protracted struggle to save the Jews of Europe. The results, however, were tragically inadequate.

During the time that the British Jewish leadership felt too constrained to adopt vigorous measures, the British Section of the World Jewish Congress was also irresolute and gave no clear public expression to the information it had received. This, however, was not the result of local policy, but of the hesitant stance of World Jewish Congress headquarters in New York. British Section secretaries Noah Barou and Alex Easterman had complained that New York was not responding to its letters and cables. There was no lack of indecision on the European side of the Atlantic Ocean. On June 23, Barou and Easterman cabled Stephen Wise that the British Jewish public was deeply disturbed about the killings and prodded him to call for mass public protests. But the officials in New York had no clear plan because they were awaiting the results of its appeal to the United States Government. Headquarters thus advised London to make do, for the time being, with pressuring the British Government to at the least allow medicines to be sent to the Jews of Poland through the Red Cross or the Polish minister of welfare.[84] Since this was an inadequate response to their urgent appeal, the British Section decided to take an independent and public Jewish stand.[85]

The Polish government called a press conference for July 9, 1942. The British Section, however, called one on June 29 where Silverman declared that the conspiracy of silence surrounding the destruction of the Jews of Europe was over. Moreover, he stressed that the Germans had made no secret of their diabolical intentions. Szwarcbart gave statistics about the extent of the murder and Ernst Frischer demanded that the Germans be warned of dire retribution. Only such a threat, he argued, could stop the terror. The BSWJC believed that the press conference had been "highly successful."[86]

Szwarcbart also spoke at the press conference called by the Poles. Brendan Bracken, British minister of information and a Churchill confidant, introduced the Polish spokesman, Deputy Prime Minister Stanisław

Mikołajczyk. Mikołajczyk told the forty reporters present that the Germans had instituted a reign of terror in Poland. The destruction of the Jews, he said, was but a prologue to their ultimate goal: "The extermination of the whole Polish population so as to make it possible to include the whole territory ... into their *Lebensraum*." According to Mikołajczyk, the entire population of Poland could be destroyed in a short period of time.

Szwarcbart was less extreme about the Poles. He spoke of the mass murder of Jews and the enslavement of Poles, and mentioned the Nazis' use of poison gas. He also cautioned that the purpose of the expulsions to Eastern Europe was to concentrate the expellees in a proscribed area in order to facilitate their destruction.[87]

Two weeks later Szwarcbart informed the BSWJC that the Nazis had initiated the mass murder of the inhabitants of the Warsaw Ghetto. He asked that the intelligence information, which he had received from the Polish Interior Ministry, be held in confidence.[88] Three weeks later, on August 17, Gerhart Riegner's cable, confirming the horrendous German plan to murder all the Jews, was handed to Sidney Silverman.

The conspiracy of silence had been laid to rest. The Jewish leadership realized that the only recourse was a public declaration about the systematic murder in Europe – *the Jewish Holocaust*.

5

Attempts to Break the Blockade and the Meager Results

The Foreign Office, the sentinel of the blockade of European Jewry, did not view the Belgian plan favorably. Harold Lasky argued in its favor, but some members of the International Labour Committee abandoned it. Thus another plan to save Jews was snuffed out.

Toward the end of the period when British Jewish organizations underwent internal reshuffling, measures were also adopted in the area of foreign policy. The decree ordering the expulsion of the Jews of Slovakia to Poland, the first of the mass expulsions, came without warning. The information arrived quickly in the West along with a plea to agitate for its annulment. Since Catholic clergymen stood at the head of the Slovakian state, it seemed appropriate to appeal to the Vatican.

On March 16, 1942, the Swiss office of the Jewish Agency cabled the London branch that the March 7 decree, ordering the expulsion of ninety thousand Slovakian Jews to Poland, was meant to be executed within two weeks. They appealed for British Catholic leaders to intervene with the Pope. The following day a cable from Gerhart Riegner in Geneva arrived at the BSWJC asking Cardinal Arthur Hinsley, the Catholic Primate in Britain, and the Czech government-in-exile, for intervention. The BSWJC sought a meeting with the cardinal and Chief Rabbi Hertz, and through Archbishop Godfrey, the Apostolic Delegate in London, implored the Pope to intervene with Father Tisso, the Slovakian president.[1] On April 14 the Apostolic Delegate informed Rabbi Hertz that the Pope had approached Tisso, but it was uncertain that it would lead to anything.[2] The archbishop's uncertainty was well-grounded in reality.[3]

Alarming information about the fate of the Jews in Europe kept arriving. Moreover, the sinking of the refugee ship *Struma* on February 29, 1942 off the Turkish coast, caused public alarm.[4] The tragedy was the result of both

British and Turkish policies. The British refused to grant entry permits to refugees attempting to reach Palestine illegally, and the Turks did not allow travellers without visas to pass through the country. The Jewish Agency had asked the British to issue Palestine entry permits to the *Struma* refugees in the framework of the White Paper quota, but was turned down. After waiting off the Turkish coast for two months, its passengers suffering terribly, the ship was forced to sail on February 24, 1942 and sank that very day.

In the wake of the *Struma* tragedy, a Labour Party delegation headed by Professor Harold Lasky (Neville Lasky's brother), the Labour Party ideologist, met with Colonial Secretary Lord Cranborne to press the government to allow Jews fleeing Europe to enter Palestine. The fate of the *Struma* laid heavily on the consciences of the heads of the Colonial Office, and according to reports received by the Zionist Executive in Jerusalem they accepted the resolve of the Labour Party delegation that the *Struma* affair never be repeated.[5]

Just a few weeks later, with the memory of the *Struma* still fresh, two fishing boats with illegal refugees were chased away from the coast of Turkey. One boat capsized. Its passengers made their way to shore but were threatened with expulsion by the Turks.[6] The other sailed to Palestine. Pressure from different quarters was brought to bear on the British government to alter its stance, again making prominent the connection between the Holocaust and Britain's Palestine policy. Brotman and Dr Israel Feldman, the non-Zionist chairman of the BD Palestine Committee, called on the Foreign Office Refugee Department on March 31, 1942, and complained that Jewish refugees, unlike the French and Norwegian refugees who were granted entry into Britain, were subject to discrimination. The official contended that since their flight was organized and Palestine, a delicate issue, was involved, the Jewish refugees were in a different category.

In their attempt to appease the officials the Jewish leaders mentioned that the criticism of the government over the *Struma* affair had been exaggerated and they offered their help in correcting the resulting impression. In the meeting's minutes, A. Walker, the refugee department head, suggested that since neither of the two men had a Zionist bias they might be useful in helping to promote the anti-Zionist propaganda planned by non-Zionist American Jewish organization.[7] This official, who was charged with dealing with Jewish issues, disclosed that he was not well-versed on the balance of power in the Anglo-Jewish community. As a matter of fact no anti-Zionist moves could be observed in any secular Jewish circle. In all events the government decided to sympathetically consider the fate of the boat refugees, an attitude that Brodetsky thought was an achievement of his organization's intervention.[8]

The connection made between the fate of European Jewry and the war against the illegals was irksome to the government. At the meeting with Cranborne, Harold Lasky stressed that he was not a Zionist and that his plea was based solely on humanitarian grounds. He also noted the discrimination between the Jewish and non-Jewish refugees, which drew criticism from Cranborne for fighting on the Zionist opponents' side. Lasky responded by saying that he was carrying out his duty as a Jew, especially since the colonial secretary had not displayed generosity toward them. He added that if his grandfather had not emigrated to Britain he, too, might have been one of the *Struma* refugees.[9] Under the circumstance the government felt constrained to make a gesture, however small, toward the Jews. The result was a decision that illegal refugees reaching Palestine through their own efforts would no longer be expelled, but that they would be counted in the White Paper quota. There were, however, reservations: Under no circumstances would Palestine entry certificates be issued to refugees who had reached a neutral country from enemy territory, including those now in Turkey. It should be noted that Turkey had just threatened to expel them. At the most Cranborne was willing to ask the Turkish authorities to remove the expulsion threat. Behind the British attitude was the prospect of many Jews fleeing the Balkans for Turkey on the way to Palestine. Since, according to the Jewish Agency Istanbul representative Haim Barlas, the Turkish threat still hung in the air, the Jewish Agency's political committee in London was preparing to pressure the government by issuing a public declaration even if it meant a break with the Colonial Office. Brodetsky supported the drastic move, but Mrs. Dugdale ("Baffy"), acting for Chaim Weizmann who was about to leave for the United States and who strongly rejected any idea of a break with the government, begged the committee to reconsider.[10] In the end no declaration was issued.

The Cabinet, worried about public opinion, adopted measures based on Cranborne's "concessions": (1) refugees reaching neutral countries would not receive Palestine entry permits. This put the option of Turkey as a transit station for Jews fleeing from the nearby Balkans in jeopardy; (2) on the other hand, refugees who succeed in reaching Palestine directly would eventually be released from detention at the expense of the *aliya* quota; and (3) nineteen Jewish refugees then in Turkey would be issued Cypriot visas as a one-time "act of charity."

The Jewish Agency's Political Committee was aware that alongside the relaxation of restrictions for Jewish refugees arriving from enemy countries, there was now an obstacle facing those who reached a neutral state. Moreover, Turkey would cease to serve as a staging point for Palestine, a cynical implication of the slogan, "*Struma*, Never Again," and the refugees would have to make their way in open seas to the Promised Land.

Cranborne, in an attempt to avoid a public confrontation with the Jews, tagged a condition onto the deal: If the Cabinet decision was made public, if there was any public confrontation or if a query was raised in Parliament, it could fall through. Thus the members of the Jewish Agency's Political Committee were held hostage for the sake of refugees threatened with expulsion back into the inferno.[11] Judging by the minutes, the members of the Jewish Agency Political Committee apparently did not grasp that the attempt to silence them derived from government weakness and for the time being, at least, did not press for the use of Turkey, a natural land bridge, to Palestine. Moreover, it is virtually certain that the British offer of Cypriot visas for the refugees whose ship had floundered stemmed from the British desire not to press the Turks. On the contrary. They approved of Turkish hostility toward the Jewish refugees and considered it a building block in the blockade wall. Because of widespread sympathy in Britain in the summer and fall of 1942 for the Jews of Europe the authorities did not want to increase the tension with the Jewish leadership, but neither did they wish to press Turkey to relax its entry policy, because it would encourage *aliya*.[12]

The British persevered in the blockade of European Jewry, but because of pressure they were sometimes forced to make minor concessions. A case in point is the agreement to allow the entry of children from Bulgaria, Hungary and Rumania into Palestine within the quota framework. In the months of May and June 1942, such a plan was devised and the consuls of Switzerland were asked to identify the children and prepare them for the journey to Palestine. The Foreign Office was angry at the impatience of the Jewish Agency which constantly pressed Whitehall to speed up the evacuation of children from the Balkans. The Foreign Office, for its part, blamed the Swiss for the delay.[13]

In the fall of 1942, when organizations were agitating for rescuing children without any connection to *aliya*,[14] the High Commissioner for Palestine agreed in principle to allow the entry of children from all areas of German occupation.[15] These concessions in the Palestine blockade were made during Cranborne's tenure as colonial secretary.

Cranborne, a member of Churchill's inner circle, had always opposed the White Paper, and despite everything related above he was the colonial secretary most sympathetic to Jewish concerns throughout the war. He described his cabinet struggles to cancel the ban on the entry of illegals into Palestine to Dugdale.[16] Much to the Jews' sorrow, he served only a short tenure as colonial secretary. Cranborne had publicly rejected the notion that Nazi agents might infiltrate Palestine along with bona fide refugees. Eden, however, had no compunctions about resuscitating that canard. In the context of the demand to evacuate the seventy thousand Jews of Bulgaria he said to United States American Secretary of State Cordell Hull:

"Furthermore any such mass movement . . . would be very dangerous to security, because the Germans would be sure to put a number of their agents in the group." He repeated these notions to President Roosevelt.[17]

In the fall of 1942, the Belgian government-in-exile initiated a plan to evacuate the Belgian Jews living in Vichy France. In a display of generosity it also expressed a willingness to include French Jews. Szmul Zygielbojm was privy to this plan and in cooperation with the Belgians tried to win the support of the Labour Party's International Labour Committee. He submitted a list of countries that might receive the Jews, but Palestine, "curiously enough," in the words of Berl Locker of the Zionist Executive in London, was not among them. Locker suggested issuing *aliya* permits, but British friends advised against raising the Palestine question in this context. The Foreign Office, the sentinel of the blockade of European Jewry, did not view the Belgian plan favorably. Harold Lasky argued in its favor, but some members of the International Labour Committee abandoned it. Thus another plan to save Jews was snuffed out.[18]

In August 1942, Dr Manfred Lachs, an expert in international law and an aide of Dr Szwarcbart's, argued in a research paper on the legal status of unoccupied France that as a neutral country it was prohibited by international law from turning its citizens or foreign residents over to the Germans. A synopsis of Lachs's research was published in *The Times* in the hope that it would serve as a warning to the Vichy government. Moreover, the Americans, who maintained a diplomatic representation in Vichy, protested strongly against that regime's handing of Jews over to the Germans[19] and Churchill, on September 8, 1942 severely censured Vichy in a Commons address.[20]

After the rejection of the Belgian plan the governments of Belgium and Poland had to suffice with a limited plan to save Jewish children by sending them from France to England. It was difficult to reject the new proposal, for horrifying reports were reaching the West about children being torn away from parents expelled from France to the East. France was not cut off from the outside world and much reliable information flowed from there. Nonetheless, Home Secretary Morrison tenaciously defended the blockade and argued in the cabinet against transferring the children to the British Isles. His arguments, by now common coin, were: (a) in principle, only refugees needed for the war effort should be accepted; (b) why, indeed, Jewish children. After all, tomorrow other Allies could demand refuge for their children; (c) large numbers of American soldiers were entering Britain and there was a lack of housing. This was meant for American consumption; and (d) the "humanitarian" argument that the evacuation of orphans would encourage the collaborationist Vichy to "create" them by expelling the parents.

Since Whitehall felt constrained to offer a compromise, Morrison agreed to the entry of "approved" orphans, those with close relatives in Britain, twenty of which were located. Even Morrison understood that this was a ludicrous concession and, indeed, two additional proposals were submitted to the cabinet. Sir Herbert Emerson was then seeking entry permits for a thousand children. The president of the Council for Jewish Refugees, Otto Schiff, apparently not informed of Emerson's petition, proposed granting visas to children with parents in Britain and orphans with first degree relatives in the country, a grand total of three hundred to three hundred and fifty children. Naturally, the Jewish proposal was the one accepted[21] and it got the home secretary off the hook.

The pressure applied on the government did not let up. At the end of October a parliamentary delegation approached the Home Office and various organizations made appeals to the government. Ironically, succor for the home secretary, which helped to extricate him, came from Palestine. At the beginning of October the High Commissioner for Palestine approved the entry from France of one thousand children and two hundred accompanying adults. Then the home secretary, arguing that every single British colony had already accepted as many refugees as it could, advised Eleanor Rathbone, head of the delegation, to drop her demands since they could not be fulfilled. As for Palestine, its quota was set biannually by the High Commissioner on the basis of its absorptive capacity.[22]

After the Allied invasion of Morocco in November 1942, the Germans occupied southern France and the possibility of evacuating even those few candidates slated for rescue was quashed.[23] Again Whitehall was "saved" by the Germans.

In summary we may conclude that in the autumn of 1942, when it was public knowledge that Jews were being systematically exterminated on orders from the highest echelons of the German government, the British blockade of Europe's Jews, both in principle and on the ground, remained in force. After much hesitation the British government made stingy concessions, such as allowing the transfer of a few hundred children from France to England; others from Europe to Palestine within the quota framework; and the acceptance of illegals arriving unaided on the shores of Palestine. The blockade remained in force in the case of Jews who had fled the inferno and succeeded in reaching a neutral country. They would not qualify for entry certificates, even as the sword of expulsion back to Nazidom dangled ominously over their heads.

As we shall see, with Lord Cranborne's help another chink in the blockade wall might have been chipped away by Rabbis Hertz and Schonfeld.[24] But bureaucratic sloth and meanness sealed the concessions into the hypothetical realm and the champions of blockade could celebrate with another "triumphant" blast of their relentless horn.

6

The Declaration of December 17, 1942

Knowledge of the Final Solution had already been made public and various organizations, uncoordinated with the others, had already taken steps to make connections and take action. The processes and conceptions described here illustrate the discord among them even when they were apparently intent on cooperation.

Paradoxically, it was the "separatists" who raised the idea of cooperation and coordination among the major Jewish organizations in London. As early as February 1941, Harry Goodman, political secretary of Agudat Israel, proposed that the JFC appoint a sub-committee to coordinate the activities demanded by the extreme emergency situation. Brodetsky demurred because he believed that the organizations adopted operative decisions independently. However, he agreed that a coordinative framework to liaise with bodies beyond Britain's borders, especially in the United States, was warranted.[1]

On September 7, 1942, when the Jewish community was grappling with its response to events in Europe, Raphael Springer of Agudat Israel suggested to Brotman that Agudat Israel and the JFC establish such a framework and that the WJC and the Revisionists be included as well. The "group" would cooperate on issues such as assistance to the Jews of Europe and their later rehabilitation. Brotman did not believe that the Revisionists should be included because they advocated evacuation, not rehabilitation in Europe. He did, however, believe that the Jewish Agency should be part of the framework and suggested that the JFC serve as the umbrella organization. Each body would submit its proposals independently and the JFC would be obliged to present its ideas to the others only if it believed they were useful. Actually Brotman was seeking power of attorney for the JFC to approach the different authorities in the name of all the others.[2]

At the time of that meeting the London office of Agudat Israel had knowledge of the mass murder of Jews in Poland. Harry Goodman also knew of the cable sent by Riegner to the BSWJC and WJC headquarters in New York. It is possible that the censor had asked his opinion about the contents of the cable.[3] Goodman did not reveal its contents to Brotman in their telephone conversation on September 23, 1942. Goodman was highly distraught and as early as July he called for a meeting between representatives of the WJC, the Jewish Agency, Agudat Israel and the JFC.[4]

Also in July, after many details of the mass murder in Europe had been made public, the BSWJC suggested guidelines for cooperation with the JFC but was turned down. On October 2, the British Section again asked for a meeting and this time Brodetsky could not refuse.[5] Brodetsky, himself, had complained about the community's lack of discipline in a published article. He criticized the circles that refused to accept clear guidance; their lack of understanding, absence of discipline and irresponsibility had made it difficult for him, as president of the BD, to fulfill his task.[6] No doubt Brodetsky was referring to the heads of the BSWJC, about whom he had already complained that their decisions were "sometimes taken in a hasty manner."[7] Thus when the BSWJC asked for a meeting to discuss events in Europe, it could not be dismissed. Brodetsky, however, preferred Goodman's formula: a meeting with the representatives of the four organizations.[8] Meanwhile, Brodetsky learned about Hitler's plan to kill the Jews from Lord Melchett. Melchett alerted the Jewish Agency's Political Committee and argued that it could not refrain from taking action. He advised that the facts be set before the House of Lords either by Lord Cecil or the Archbishop of Canterbury. Moreover, he asked Brodetsky to first convene a meeting of all the Jewish members of the House of Lords and hold a separate meeting with Viscount Samuel.[9] Thus the BD was being prodded from different quarters to initiate action.

The Board wanted to preserve its senior status and at the same time improve its relations with the BSWJC. The prevailing assumption was that the BSWJC was the representative of a world organization with headquarters in New York, but that it was the BD, the elected and representative body of British Jewry, that was empowered to speak in its name. The BD's view was that the BSWJC was a mediator of information from the Jewish world, while the BD was the body that made the decisions.[10] Its perspective was indicative of a lack of understanding of the new balance of power in the present situation. The BSWJC's influence stemmed from its global connections and it was well aware of it. Accordingly, Easterman approached Berl Locker, head of the Jewish Agency in London, for a meeting to coordinate their activities.[11]

The JFC was afraid that it would be pushed into a less significant role, and it called for a meeting with all the major bodies the Jewish Agency, the British Section of the World Jewish Congress and Agudat Israel, as well as with Szwarcbart, Zygielbojm and Frischer to discuss the state of European

Jewry. At that meeting, held early in December, the four organizations established the Consultative Emergency Committee (CEC).[12] Knowledge of the Final Solution had already been made public and various organizations, uncoordinated with the others, had already taken steps to make connections and take action. The processes and conceptions described here illustrate the discord among them even when they were apparently intent on cooperation. The question was: Which would play the leading role, the WJC or the JFC? Rivalries, some stemming from matters of principle, others from personal and practical issues stood in the way of cooperation. Thus the CEC, whose very function was to plan the political steps demanded by a public agitated over the desperate situation of European Jewry, was at times paralyzed by competition and jealousy.

December 17, 1942, the Tenth of Tevet on the Hebrew calendar, the Jewish fast day of mourning for the destruction of Jerusalem by the Romans, was an unusual day in the docket of the House of Commons. The MPs rose in silence for the murdered Jews of Europe. Just moments before this demonstration of solidarity with the victims, Foreign Secretary Anthony Eden read a declaration sharply condemning the persecution and mass murder of the Jews in Europe and warned the murderers that they would be held personally responsible for their actions. The declaration, whose wording had been agreed upon by Britain, the United States and the Soviet Union, was proclaimed in the name of the United Nations and published simultaneously in the capitals of the three major powers.[13]

Details of the mass slaughter of the Jews of Eastern Europe had been appearing in the British press since early 1942,[14] but only at the end of 1942 did the Allies fighting Germany reach an accord about the need for a united declaration on the Jews of Europe. Thus for a fleeting moment the principle of the St. James Conference opposing any "affirmative action" in favor of the Jews as distinct from all the suffering citizens of occupied Europe was suspended.

As discussed earlier, the WJC and the Polish government called news conferences in June and July, which made a strong impact. The British people and government were shocked and taking a stand could not be avoided. Hints from Germany and information from the United States[15] set the end of December as zero hour for European Jewry. Meanwhile, despite the authenticated information about the Final Solution that reached Whitehall from different sources, the Foreign Office still maintained that the basis for saying that a final date had been set was tenuous. Nonetheless, it refrained from making this anxiety "allaying" information public. What was publicized was the version given to a gathering of MPs, including Silverman, and with the guest participation of Brodetsky and Szwarcbart: The Nazis had prepared plans for the systematic mass destruction of all the Jews in occupied Europe by the end of the year.[16] The MPs accepted the information literally because details, such as the progress of the destruction of the Warsaw Ghetto, were also arriving at the time.[17] It is virtually certain that the Foreign Office wanted the timing to be emphasized in order to justify the "discrimination" in favor of the Jews expressed by the December 17 declaration. The foreign secretary's Commons announcement had been delivered in response to a Private Notice question of Sydney Silverman's, which stressed that the Jews would be "put to death by the end of the year,"[18] and that there were only two weeks left! The question was composed after intensive discussions between Silverman and the Foreign Office. Richard Law, Under-secretary of State for Foreign Affairs, argued that the declaration should not be postponed because the new year was about to begin.[19] Later, when it became know in public that the Final Solution was not dependent on a specific date it would be easier to slide back onto the principles of the St. James Conference and there would be no need for further specific mention of the Jews.[20]

The December 17 Declaration was issued after the Nazis had declared their intention "to exterminate the Jewish people in Europe." It describes how the Jews from all over Europe were being shipped to Poland: "which has been made the principle Nazi slaughterhouse, the Ghettos established by the German invaders are being systematically emptied of all Jews except a few . . . required for war industries. None of those taken away are ever heard of again. The able-bodied are slowly worked to death in labor camps. The infirm are left to die of exposure and starvation or are deliberately massacred in mass executions. The number of victims of these bloody cruelties is reckoned in many hundreds of thousands of entirely innocent men, women and children."

In the declaration were other strong condemnations of the policy of destruction, but only one operative paragraph at the end: "They (the Governments) re-affirm their solid resolution to ensure that those responsible for these crimes shall not escape retribution, and to press on the necessary practical measures to this end."[21]

As pertains to the Jews of Europe, the declaration clearly stresses that there would be no operative change ("re-affirm") in the Allies' policy regarding war criminals. This was exactly in line with the St. James Conference whose influence is evident in the words, "those responsible." Indeed, the Poles participated in the wording of the declaration.[22] The British Section was apprehensive about this wording because the reference to "those responsible" could be interpreted as applying only to the heads of the Nazi regime. If that was indeed the case the declaration would have no effect on the tens of thousands of lower rank and file who were carrying out the orders of destruction on a daily basis. The Foreign Office eventually bowed to pressure and agreed that Silverman raise the question in Commons and that Eden's response specifically mention that the threat of retribution was also aimed at those carrying out the atrocities with their own hands.[23]

Since the declaration did not refer to any practical measures, Silverman asked the foreign secretary about the possibility of immediate assistance. Eden replied that Silverman himself was aware of the difficulties involved in rescue attempts. Nonetheless, the government would do what it could, but it was not very much. Eden purposely hinted that Silverman held a similar view. As chairman of the British branch of the WJC, which had assumed the representation of distressed Jewry, Silverman had only recently told a press conference that only a speedy Allied victory would redeem the Jews from their suffering. Until that longed-for day, Silverman said fatalistically, four million Jews would be killed. He had also cast doubt upon the worth of declarations and demonstrations. However, the conscience of the free world was aroused and demanded that a voice be heard.[24] On the other hand, the BSWJC and Silverman himself insisted upon bombing German cities in reprisal for Nazi atrocities, as had been demanded by the Polish government, but rejected. Silverman had also pressed for such actions in his talks with the American ambassador.[25]

To return to the debate in the House of Commons: After Eden's reply, James de Rothschild MP, speaking for British Jewry, delivered a moving speech. The declaration, he said, would serve as encouragement for Jews struggling to maintain their human dignity.[26]

A different tone was heard in the House of Lords. Viscount Samuel opened the discussion. He praised the declaration but wondered what practical measures had been adopted to save as many Jews as possible, especially the children. "Will His Majesty's Government," he asked, "will the listening to the cries of people in agony bring them succor?" Had the government sought the assistance of the neutral countries? The Bishop of London demanded that the gates of all Allied countries be opened to the Jews. He insisted that guarantees be issued for refugees who found a safe harbor in neutral countries until their final placement after the war. Other members of the Lords spoke for the Free Churches and the Catholic Church. All stressed that the evidence cried out for rescue and Samuel and others listed the efforts of different groups to prod the government into action.[27]

The criticism of the House of Lords echoed beyond Westminster. A *Jewish Chronicle* editorial asked, "What Now?" It criticized Eden's hesitancy, arguing that he was hiding behind a wall of formalistic, security and geographical excuses in order to avoid action. He had missed an historic hour, the paper claimed. Britain could have been held up to the entire world as a haven for the persecuted. There wasn't a moment to lose, the *Chronicle* pleaded, because the killing was proceeding at full blast. Neither did the home secretary escape criticism. The paper argued that he was not doing enough to deal with anti-Semitism in the factories and elsewhere in the country, as indicated by the anti-Semitic graffiti scribbled on many walls.[28] *The Jewish Chronicle* had yet to grasp the connection between foreign and domestic policy.

Indeed, rescue proposals had been raised in Jewish and non-Jewish circles and in Parliament by the Archbishops of Canterbury and York.[29] The "historic" declaration and demonstration in the House of Commons had created a suitable atmosphere in the public for bringing to pressure to bear on the government, but it could peter out.[30]

Let us now examine the readiness of the Jewish leadership to act. What preoccupied them after the CEC was established.

The major contenders were the BSWJC and the BD. Each argued that the December 17 Declaration was the fruit of its initiative. On the surface, at least, the declaration was a respectable achievement which received widespread media coverage at home and abroad. The BSWJC, for its part, announced that it alone was responsible for the achievement. Brodetsky, on the other hand, said that it was the result of his appeal to the Foreign Office on October 1, 1942. After the Jewish Telegraphic Agency gave publicity to Brodetsky's claim, Alex Easterman, the BSWJC secretary, was furious. He claimed that Undersecretary of State Richard Law told him that neither Brodetsky or his colleagues raised the issue at their meeting in Whitehall. Easterman accused Brodetsky of seeking undeserved accolades and expressed disdain for the JFC's political activities. However, an examination of the documents demonstrates that the first item on the agenda of the October 1 meeting of Law, Brodetsky, Stein and Brotman was the proposal that the government issue a public statement condemning the persecution of the Jews. However, at this early stage the Foreign Office was unprepared to do so. Law argued that Churchill's occasional denunciations of the persecution of the Jews would have to suffice.[31]

This was the kind of inane dispute that a *Jewish Chronicle* editorial labeled, "A Miserable Position Alone: Koved [honor] Hunting We did it." The British Section was apparently correct. As they cabled WJC headquarters in New York: "can now tell you allies declaration entirely congress work." Officials of the Foreign Office did indeed prepare the declaration in coordination with Silverman who took part in the House of Commons performance. And as we have already seen, the Polish leadership in London also had a part in the formulation.[32]

Had their political antennae been more finely calibrated, the heads of the WJC in London might not have fought so hard for the credit. In fact, they had actually given Eden a tool to save his policies on the issue of European Jewry. Why did the Foreign Office bring such heavy pressure to bear on the American State Department, which had expressed its reservations about participating in the December declaration?[33] Eden even succeeded in coopting the United Nations, including the Soviet Union, which was consistently against separating the Jewish issue from the suffering of all anti-fascists. But Eden was one step ahead. With the increasing information and glaring certainty about the Nazi plans of total destruction, strong feelings were aroused among the British people to come to the aid of the unfortunate. It must be said in favor of the British that even in their darkest hour many sympathetic and concerned people turned the distress of the Jews into a national issue, and prodded the government to do something when every "something" was against the path the government had set out for itself.

Therefore, the declaration achieved two goals. The sharp public condemnation of the atrocities would satisfy the Jews and the respected figures and bodies that supported them. But it went further. The declaration supported by all the nations fighting against the Germans turned the issue around. The obligation assumed for the Jews' suffering would no longer be Britain's responsibility alone. Now any national or local British initiative could be rejected in favor of international initiatives. There were certain distinct advantages for Whitehall in international "initiatives": Time could be gained and failures could be papered over. After all, public control over such initiatives in wartime was virtually nil. The wool could be pulled over the public's eyes in the name of wartime security and confidentiality. The new policy led to the perfidious Bermuda Conference of April 1943, at the very time the Warsaw Ghetto was going up in flames and its remnants engaged in a desperate and hopeless armed struggle against the Nazis. The following correspondence contains most of the elements we have been discussing.

On January 8, 1943, Dr W. Temple, the Archbishop of Canterbury, wrote to Winston Churchill proposing that international guarantees be issued to neutral countries willing to accept refugees, and that asylum be granted in all of the United Nations countries. However, he also addressed a request on the British national level: "It has been in my mind to issue an appeal for offers of hospitality in order that I might be in a position to tell the Government what measures of welcome, with readiness to support Jewish children, might be forthcoming. But I have not liked to do this unless I knew that the way would be open for them afterwards to come. If you have any counsel for me about this matter, I should be most happy to receive it. Our chief anxiety is the time factor; our process of consideration takes so long, and the Jews are massacred daily. I repeat this, because it is the whole cause of our urgency in the matter."

Since the Jewish issue was Eden's bailiwick, Churchill passed on the archbishop's letter with the note: "Foreign Secretary. Will you kindly deal with this?" George W. Randall added in the margins: "There are more visas for children available than there are children."

If this was indeed the case, in practical terms the archbishop could have been granted leeway to act according to the dictates of his conscience. Eden, however, would not allow Britain to take unilateral action. He rejected Dr Temple's proposal with the ungrounded reasoning that allowing the entry of refugees into Britain was undesirable because of an international development on the refugee issue: "[To] *His Grace the Most Reverend The Lord Archbishop of Canterbury.* In spite of the many complexities of the situation, we are making an attempt to deal with it as far as possible on an international basis. We are getting on with this and in the circumstances I really do not think that an appeal on the lines suggested in the last paragraph of your letter would be very opportune. I expect shortly to receive a Three-Party deputation in private, when I hope to be able to give some account of the progress which we are making. It is up-hill work . . . ."[34]

This new line now confronted the Jewish and non-Jewish organizations. And while the cabinet was designing its policy the Jewish organizations were vying with each other for a place in the sun. BSWJC circles expressed disappointment with Brodetsky. How could he, whose status in the Zionist leadership was so high, lend a hand in fortifying the "Anglo complex" of the Jewish leadership. How could he shove aside the British Section of the WJC which was basically a Zionist institution. But as to the British Section, Brodetsky believed that now, under his presidency, the BD was "Zionized" and there was no longer a need for WJC operations in London. Neither side spared the rod of derision and scorn. As for the British Section, it claimed that Brodetsky's self-concept was that of a new Sir Moses Montefiore. (In the nineteenth century, Montefiore intervened politically in Jewish causes all over the world.) Neither did the British Section refrain from involving the WJC Executive in New York, which in turn sent a sharply-worded cable to Brodetsky. They also attempted to draw Chaim Weizmann, then in the United States, into the dispute. However, Weizmann, as the chief Zionist leader, refrained from getting involved in local problems. Weizmann suggested that Brodetsky be invited to New York and coaxed into reaching an agreement.[35]

Harsh words about the leaders of the BD also came from "Anglo complex" opponents of the WJC at *The Jewish Chronicle.* The paper was relentless. It opposed the activities of the British Section, the representative of an international Jewish organization, and argued that British Jewry had a traditional elected representation, the BD. However, it sharply criticized the Board because as Zionists they were under the influence of international Jewish organizations and their London branches. Be that as it may, the *Chronicle*'s editorial board was openly pro-Zionist. They directly and obliquely criticized Brodetsky who was a member of the Zionist Executive and had even been vice president of the British Section.

The paper saw a blurring of authority in the fact that the same figures were active at one and the same time in competing organizations. There was rivalry, competition and duplication. *The Jewish Chronicle*, read in virtually every Jewish home in the country, went so far as to issue a warning in a glaring headline: "A Community or Mob?" and "Too Many Cooks; End the Chaos." The editor complained that the Board was impotent and incapable of attracting people of serious intellect.[36]

The attacks met their mark. Brodetsky was nudged toward the "Anglo-Jewish" position, but as a result left open to attacks from Zionist circles, and BSWJC officials and supporters.

The BD plenary convened the day after the December 17 Declaration. Brodetsky was subjected to severe criticism. It was argued that Silverman and his BSWJC colleagues had taken the initiative and credit while the president of the BD trailed along like a junior partner. It was blow to its status as Anglo-Jewry's central institution.[37]

At the same time Brodetsky was preparing for a post-declaration meeting of a Jewish delegation to discuss European Jewry with Churchill or Eden. The British Section was against a meeting at this stage. If it took place anyway then only the four organizations of the CEC should be represented. In other words, no non-Zionist organization aside from Agudat Israel. Brodetsky, as president of the community, could not accede to this demand. Without consulting the CEC he invited a broad Anglo-Jewish delegation. At the last minute he also invited Lady Reading, BSWJC president, but she declined to attend. Among others at the meeting were the chief rabbi, Viscount Samuel, James de Rothschild, Neville Lasky and Sir Robert Valley Cohen. The BSWJC thought the meeting was a serious blow, threatened to leave the CEC and immediately warned WJC headquarters in New York about this "private" design of Brodetsky's.[38]

The delegation had sought to hold the meeting with Churchill, but he referred them to Eden.[39] Churchill would continue to direct to the foreign secretary all issues pertaining to the Holocaust and consistently declined to intervene in favor of the Jews. When Eden had doubts about certain measures and asked for his advice Churchill, as we shall see, despite his consistently warm words of consolation and sharp condemnations of the persecutors, tended to be strict with the Jews.

The only Jew who discussed the Holocaust with Churchill was Harold Lasky. He refused to tell Locker about the contents of the discussion, only that the prime minister was moved. Moshe Shertok, however, who did succeed in bringing Lasky to share his thought, found him devastated about Britain's attitude toward the Jews. Lasky divulged that though Churchill seemed to identify deeply with the Jews, at that stage he was not prepared to do anything for them. Lasky was angry that on the Palestine question Churchill referred him to the colonial secretary. Lasky said that there was hope for the Jews only if the United States undertook rescue operations. Thus he suggested transferring the activities of British Jewry to the United States and seeking a meeting with President Roosevelt. The BD cabled the suggestion to various contacts in the United States, but received no reply. The Political Committee of the Jewish Agency in London believed that the Foreign Office would not grant approval for the plan, but thought that a Jewish–British–American meeting could spur action. Weizmann believed otherwise. He cabled from the United States that nothing would come of the plan and it was stricken from the agenda.[40]

Interestingly enough, Lasky had received an invitation to the White House as a guest of the Roosevelt family. Lasky asked Churchill to invest him with some kind of official capacity, but was turned down. Lasky was one the few figures during the war to criticize the prime minister, and Churchill wanted to prevent him from presenting his views to Roosevelt.[41] Thus Lasky lost the opportunity to transfer his efforts for his Jewish brethren to the highest echelon of the American government.

As to Churchill, Colonel Morton, a close associate, told Lord Melchett that the prime minister, "deeply moved" by the deep distress of the Jews of Europe, had tried to do something for them, but had encountered resistance. In light of this report it is difficult to accept at face value what Churchill told the House of Commons after the war: "I had no idea, when the war came to an end, of the horrible massacres which had occurred to millions of millions that have been slaughtered . . . "[42]

In the discussions of the Jewish Agency Political Committee in preparation for the meeting with Eden there were differences of opinion over raising the issue of a refuge in Palestine. Brodetsky, Locker and Professor Louis Namier thought it should be mentioned as a possible haven, but without touching upon the White Paper, Shertok agreed. Opposing him were Lord Melchett and Simon Marks, a member of the delegation, who demanded that Palestine be the main point. Locker argued that many Christians were opposed to exploiting the catastrophe to advance the Zionist program. According to him the public was only interested in the aspect of saving Jews.[43]

The members of the Political Committee need not have worried. The Christmas Eve meeting with Eden was exceptionally "Zionist" because Eden had nothing else to offer but Palestine. It was, after all, the only territory prepared to grant refuge, and that within the existing framework of British law. When the Jews spoke of the need to evacuate refugees from Spain, Eden said that they could be sent to Palestine. As to the rescue of Balkan Jews, Eden said that Britain had approved the *aliya* of 4,000 children. When Brodetsky said that there might be a possibility of saving 70,000 Bulgarian Jews, Eden said, first start with the children. Even Rothschild turned temporarily Zionist. Following the foreign secretary's lead he "left" England and wondered whether the Iraqi authorities might change their policy and permit the *aliya* of the "Teheran children," children who had escaped the Nazis in Poland, traveled in a roundabout route for Palestine through the Soviet Union, and were stuck in Teheran. The most sweeping suggestions, both within Britain's bailiwick, were raised by Viscount Samuel, the first High Commissioner for Palestine. Samuel, who had recently returned from there, believed that the country was capable of absorbing two million Jews! He didn't stop at that either, but demanded that immigration restrictions to Britain be relaxed. Eden promised nothing. On the other hand, he expressed a willingness to try and influence the Pope to raise the persecutions issue in his Christmas message. None of these demands appeared in the official resume received by the cabinet, and there is only a faint allusion to the possibility that restrictions on the entry of refugees into Britain might be relaxed.[44]

According to Brodetsky, the minister was congenial and understanding and the atmosphere was optimistic.[45] Even the heads of the BSWJC, apparently still affected by the spirit of the December 17 Declaration, felt the same way. After a meeting with the Soviet ambassador they even cabled New York with satisfaction that "the Soviet anxious associate helpful attitude toward catastrophe."[46]

It is possible that as a maximalist, Viscount Samuel was disappointed, but so was Rothschild a few days later. According to Rothschild, Eden's contention that he was "anxious to do whatever possible to help . . . " was tested and found wanting.

This was the result of a request he had appended to a letter to Eden expressing appreciation for the cordial reception. Rothschild asked that asylum be granted to the wife and child, stranded in Italy and threatened with expulsion to Poland, of a Polish Jewish refugee in Britain. Eden's reply: This was but one tragedy among many, and until general guidelines were established individual cases could not be dealt with.[47]

A delegation of the heads of all the Christian churches led by the Archbishop of Canterbury met with Undersecretary of State Richard Law the day before the declaration. Though they represented the Council of Christians and Jews they purposely did not include Jews in the delegation. They were expecting the declaration to cast responsibility for the atrocities upon the perpetrators, to call on Christians in Europe to protect the Jews, and for refuge to be granted in British and other United Nations territories. The delegation was disappointed at the wording Law read to them. The undersecretary cautioned against submitting a plan to save only Jews and relayed the home secretary's opposition to entry into Britain because of the food and housing shortage. The Christian delegation also suggested that Britain provide guarantees to neutral countries that Jewish refugees would be relocated elsewhere after the war. Law countered by pointing to the danger that Britain might never rid itself of such a "Super-Balfour Declaration." Nonetheless, he promised to ask Switzerland and Sweden to help those who succeeded in reaching their borders. Law felt that the delegation could not just be dismissed, and he believed that it was difficult to bridge the contradiction between a strict line and a declaration of good will toward the unfortunate.[48]

Earlier, at the end of October 1942, another distinguished delegation met with Herbert Morrison, the home secretary, to discuss rescuing Jews from Vichy France. The Archbishop of Canterbury, the Bishop of the Catholic Church in Britain and the Quaker, Eleanor Rathbone MP, wanted more than just lip-service. Their main demands were for two thousand visas to be issued for children; unrestricted entry into England for the elderly; and that the British government provide Switzerland with monetary guarantees so that it open its gates. Morrison, who was accompanied by officials of different ministries, did not relate to the practical points. He claimed that since 1933, Britain had done much for refugees and was still extending aid, and that Palestine had absorbed many Jews during the war. Moreover, Britain was engaged in war, had suffered a harsh Blitz and therefore should not be asked to save others. To Britain's credit, the author did not find an argument of this kind elsewhere. Morrison warned his distinguished guests that raising their demands in Parliament and in the press could be detrimental to the Jews, for just as they enjoyed support among some, among others there was animosity. Thus the home secretary did not accept any of the suggestions.

The delegation had also raised two proposals that did not involve any obligations on the part of the government: that British families host refugee children at their own expense and that the delegation, via private organizations, ask South American countries to accept refugees. But Morrison, the Labour representative in the War Cabinet, was apparently zealous to lock the Jews up in Europe. He opposed any individual arrangements because, he said, they had no grounding in the general policy. Moreover, the United States was sensitive to the South American question and should not be embarrassed by direct approaches to South American countries through private organizations.[49]

There were different opinions among the Jewish delegation about Whitehall's attitudes on the Jewish issue. At a Jewish Agency meeting in London Simon Marks said that he had been positively impressed by Eden's sympathetic attitude and willingness to help. He rejected Dugdale's view that Eden was the Jews' enemy in the Cabinet. Brodetsky was more sober. He said that Eden was only prepared to help in minor issues. As to Morrison, Brodetsky thought that he had been influenced by the anti-Semitism prevalent in his ministry. The BD was familiar with that anti-Semitism. In all events, Eden was more elegant than Morrison, for whom the Church heads felt disdain.[50] They did not know that Eden and his War Cabinet colleagues were at that very time formulating a policy that to all intents and purposes was a withdrawal from the spirit of the December 17, 1942 Declaration, a policy whose objective was for the United Nations, especially the United States, to fall into line with Britain.

Eden's memorandum to the newly established War Cabinet Committee on the Reception and the Accommodation of Jewish Refugees, pleads: ". . . no differentiation should be made as between Jewish and non-Jewish refugees and that the refugee problem should be dealt with as a whole . . . the problem should be regarded as a United Nations responsibility in respect of which each nation should agree to make a definite contribution."

The following paragraph seems to be the most important: "The next step should be to try and persuade the United States Government to agree that the problem should be dealt with on those lines . . . "[51]

The composition of the Jewish delegation that met with Eden might have placated the "English" circles but, as we have seen, it led to a rift with the Zionist circles of the BSWJC. Consequently, Brodetsky and Brotman spent much time and effort mending rifts, conciliating the opposition and patching up the unity within the Consultative Emergency Committee framework. It was imperative that positions be coordinated in relation to the government and Parliament, and the non-Jewish organizations active in the rescue issue. They feared that each body would again act independently and that their efforts would lead nowhere. These frantic activities paralyzed all sides.[52] A peripheral body exploited the situation and for a while succeeded in raising new ideas and a new direction in Jewish foreign policy. Rabbi Solomon Schonfeld, the director of the Chief Rabbi's Religious Emergency Council, suddenly jumped into the central political arena. By so doing he angered the leadership of the both the BD and the BSWJC, and in order to neutralize him they quickly began cooperating with each other.

Schonfeld raised the idea of mobilizing many members of Parliament from both houses to support a resolution that would force the government into adopting rescue measures. In order that such a resolution succeed it would be necessary to advance a proposition without controversial points. For political reasons it would be difficult to force the government into rescue operations. So Schonfeld played down the political and stressed the humanitarian in his attempt to rally a broad spectrum of parliamentarians. To his mind there were two sensitive political points. One was the demand of Zionists and allied Christians to throw open the gates of Palestine, especially for the Balkan refugees. The extreme position went beyond the White Paper quota, the moderate one was willing to suffice with the permits still available within its framework. The other obstacle, according to Schonfeld, was the option advocated especially by non-Jews that Britain itself have an "open door" policy.[53] The Home Office was strongly against liberalizing immigration. It argued that such an act could spark anti-Semitic sentiments and as such undermine the fighting morale of the people.[54]

Swiftly and adeptly Rabbi Schonfeld built up his connections with both houses of Parliament to press for a resolution obligating the government into rescue action. The Parliamentary Committee for Refugees, established with the assistance of Sir George Jones MP, was set up for this expressed purpose.[55]

Brodetsky, who by chance learned of Schonfeld's activities, asked him to explain why he had undertaken separatist action. Schonfeld's response was that every British citizen had the right to approach Parliament, and as the head of an important community (the ultraorthodox) he was acting according to the dictates of his conscience. On January 11, Brodetsky sent a letter to Rabbi Hertz complaining that Schonfeld's actions were detrimental to the unity achieved by the CEC, of which Hertz himself was a member, and asked him reign Schonfeld in. A few days later Hertz sent a letter to Brodetsky, but without relating to Brodetsky's letter. The chief rabbi did not mince words. A month had gone by since the declaration in Parliament, he wrote, yet *"nothing has yet been done"* and both Jews and non-Jews were asking why. According to Hertz, Brodetsky might be fighting for unity and dealing with formalities and organization, but feasible rescue opportunities have not been exploited. In order to correct the situation Hertz suggested that an official be appointed to liaise between Jews and the United Nations. He suggested Viscount Samuel, who had entry into high places and who would not allow a retreat from the promises given. Admonishing Brodetsky that there was a chance of saving tens of thousands of Jews from death, Hertz charged him with the sacred task of persuading Samuel to accept the mission. If you succeed, Hertz wrote, the entire community will praise you. The rabbi was well aware of personality weaknesses and pleaded that the BD sacrifice its status for the sake of higher objectives.[56] Thus Hertz's response to the "Schonfeld problem." Because of the pressure Hertz applied in his letter, the JFC sent its co-chairmen to meet with Samuel. Stein saw him separately, and was turned down. Brodetsky did not report the reasons Samuel gave for his refusal. He did, however, mention the unquiet in the community because no rescue efforts were evident.[57] Hertz was not reconciled to Samuel's refusal and asked Professor A. V. Hill MP to organize a number of colleagues and speak to Samuel,[58] but neither did that bring him about. At the same time Hertz and Schonfeld carried out a limited and secret rescue operation, more about which below.[59]

Meanwhile, Schonfeld distributed to members of the Lords and Commons a draft resolution calling on the government to save Jews and others by allowing them into Allied and neutral countries. They were asked to sign the draft and call a preparatory meeting in the House of Commons. After Brodetsky persuaded Jones to pull out of the initiative, Schonfeld enlisted the aid of Lord Josiah Wedgewood and the Bishop of Chichester.[60] Certain points considered by Schonfeld and others as "too risky" were not mentioned in the draft: i.e., neither Palestine or entry into the British Isles. Since, according to Schonfeld, the issue of the Holocaust was presented in purely humanitarian terms, he was certain that broad support would be achieved and that the government would feel pressed to do something.[61] Schonfeld claimed that his formula influenced the declaration issued shortly thereafter by three Anglican archbishops in the name of all the bishops, calling for immediate refuge for Jews reaching the territory of the British Empire and elsewhere. They demanded that British Government serve as an example to other governments. In their announcement they actually mentioned the prospect of six million Jewish victims.[62]

The draft proposal suggested by Schonfeld had three more operative paragraphs: a plea to countries contiguous with the Nazi-occupied areas to grant temporary refuge or transit to Jews; an offer to help those governments; and a call to the Allies to adopt similar measures.

Schonfeld sought a "de-Zionization" and "de-politization" of the Holocaust issue. He even sought a "de-Judaization" by seeking only the signatures of Christian representatives. This displeased the Jewish parliamentarians because of the parliamentary tradition that they always participated actively in issues concerning Jews.[63] Eventually, Schonfeld's opponents accepted the principle and hundreds of Christian figures, including members of Parliament, heads of the churches, leaders of the political parties, trades unions and universities signed a petition. It was cabled to the foreign secretary, who was then in the United States prior to the Bermuda Conference. The signatories declared that Britain was prepared for any sacrifice and stalwart rescue measures required.[64]

There were differences of opinion among both Jews and Christians about Schonfeld's draft. Eleanor Rathbone pressed for the inclusion of the word, Palestine, in order to placate the Zionists. Professor Hill, on the other hand, agreed with Schonfeld that it would be a "dangerous" move. Lord Melchett, who had demanded that Palestine be at the center of the discussions with Eden, now believed that a mention of Palestine would alienate the support of certain important figures. On the other hand, Berl Locker and Sidney Silverman pressured Schonfeld that the final draft be drawn up by representatives of the BD, MPs, as well as Schonfeld in order to find a way to refer to Palestine. Schonfeld rejected the proposal, saying that a change of wording would be tantamount to a deception of, among others, the Archbishop of Canterbury and Lord Crewe who had helped draft the resolution. Schonfeld thought that the Zionists would be satisfied with the words "territories under British Supervision." Saving lives was the primary goal and the conflict with Britain over Palestine was secondary. Schonfeld was not prepared to endanger an agreed upon enterprise which had been signed by 280 members of Parliament.[65] However, when pressed, Schonfeld recommended leaving the decision to Viscount Samuel, Lord Wedgewood or Rabbi Hertz. In the end this proposal was turned down.[66]

More than a hundred members of both houses attended the advisory meeting. Silverman, however, announced that the parliamentarians were about to enter into negotiations with the government over the issue and suggested that a decision be put off to a later date. It was agreed to meet again on February 3. Schonfeld was very upset over the loss of spontaneity. He wrote to his father-in-law Hertz that a heavy responsibility would rest forever upon the Jews who had agreed to the postponement.[67]

The atmosphere turned increasingly acrimonious after *The Jewish Chronicle* published a letter of Schonfeld's accusing Brodetsky and his associates of sabotaging his effort and lack of action. He wrote that the attempt to delay a decision had left an unfavorable impression on Parliament. Brodetsky's reply appeared in the following issue of the paper. He defended himself more than he attacked Schonfeld, whom he accused of having exceeded his authority and disregarding important issues, i.e., Palestine.[68] Brodetsky turned again to Hertz, this time complaining that Schonfeld had threatened retaliatory action against him. Since Schonfeld had not succeeded in achieving another formula it was necessary to postpone the issue. It was arranged by Silverman.[69]

In the end, Schonfeld was isolated. His colleagues in Agudat Israel, who had initiated the idea of an advisory committee of the central Jewish organizations, were asked to intervene. Goodman wrote to Schonfeld that he might have acted in a manner similar to this fifteen years earlier, but not in an hour such as this. Agudat Israel informed the secretary of the BD that Schonfeld was prepared to accept Agudat Israel's position against individual initiatives taken without consultation. Conciliatory letters were exchanged by Schonfeld and Brodetsky,[70] but the former was not yet ready to capitulate.

It was clear to Schonfeld that he could not persevere in his struggles without public backing, and he no longer took the chance of a struggle in the name of the Chief Rabbi's Emergency Council. Consequently, he established the Committee for Rescuing Victims of Nazi Massacres, and operated in its name. However, it was a committee of one man and he failed to win the support of public figures.[71] Schonfeld could not prevail against the two public organizations established for fighting anti-Semitism and struggling to save Jews: the Council of Christians and Jews and the National Committee for Rescuing from Nazi Terror. Jews and Christians cooperated closely on both committees, each of which enjoyed a prestigious public base. Only in mid-March was the resolution initiated by Schonfeld, now revised, tabled in the House of Lords. The operative paragraphs were worded in much milder terms than the original draft. It said in general terms that the House would support considerable and generous measures to extend assistance and temporary refuge to Jews and others in danger of their lives and capable of flight. The government succeeded in postponing the debate until Eden's return from Washington, when he would announce the convening of the Bermuda Conference. Now all looked forward to Anglo-American cooperation. In the meanwhile, there was no place for unilateral steps on the part of Britain. Hopes were pinned on this new development and it might possibly have been the reason why the House of Lord's resolution was watered down to general terms. In all events, a disappointed Schonfeld accused Silverman of an intervention which had resulted in "a much weaker non-committal motion."[72]

Schonfeld also tried to lobby the upper echelons of government. On February 7 he sent Eden a letter requesting a meeting, and to introduce his position he attached a copy of the resolution that he had launched. Eden had recently received many delegations on the Holocaust issue and would meet with Schonfeld only if he could present new ideas. Schonfeld again came up with a surprise. He requested permission to go to Turkey to manage rescue operations. He argued that he had the means to carry them out, the support of important bodies such as the Chief Rabbi's Emergency Council, the Federation of Organizations Assisting Refugees, and the Fund for Aiding Jews, chaired by Lord Cecil. The Foreign Office did not turn him down at once; they did so only after conferring and seeking the advice of the British Ambassador in Ankara. Schonfeld had hoped, among other objectives, to find a haven for Jewish refugees in Ethiopia and Egypt, and by promising funds for their upkeep until their evacuation, to soften the Turk's attitude toward the refugees.[73] It may be surmised that because it was against British policy, this point led to Schonfeld's failure.

In contrast to the Foreign Office's caution and reservations, the Colonial Office expressed interest in Schonfeld. There is no doubt that he was more amenable to British policy and the view of the Colonial Office that Palestine could not solve the Jewish refugee problem. In mid-March, while the Foreign Office was discussing and eventually rejecting Schonfeld's request to go to Turkey, Schonfeld received a letter from Colonial Secretary Oliver Stanley informing him that visas for a certain British territory had been issued to two families numbering twenty persons. Furthermore, Stanley promised Schonfeld visas for another one hundred people on the basis of a list to be submitted by him. These candidates for rescue were currently residing in enemy territory.[74]

Elsewhere, we have dedicated a chapter to the granting of visas for

Mauritius initiated by Rabbis Hertz and Schonfeld. They achieved some theoretical success in breaking the blockade. Schonfeld's wish to travel to Turkey was also connected to this operation.

Before and After the Bermuda Conference

To the end of her life Eleanor was haunted by the thought of the Jews who might have been saved . . . And to the end of her life her heart was hardened against Herbert Morrison. Neither then nor later was she disposed to credit him with a substratum of warm humanity beneath the efficient exterior of a busy Secretary of State. She did not believe it was there.

Rabbi Schonfeld's parliamentary initiative had repercussions in several directions. As he had intended all along his move prevented the rescue issue from being dropped from the agenda. Furthermore, it may reasonably be argued that the dispute over his initiative prodded influential circles into taking a stand. Schonfeld's main aim was to encourage as many parliamentarians as possible to prod the government into acting upon its declaration. However, the apparatus to coordinate among all concerned groups, Jewish and Christian alike, was lacking. It was in this context, as discussed in the previous chapter, that a core of parliamentarians, the Parliamentary Committee for Refugees (PCR), and Jewish activist, formed a coalition and in March 1943 established the National Committee for Rescue from Nazi Terror (NCRNT). Its leading figure and spokeswoman was the energetic and dedicated Eleanor Rathbone MP.

As early as January 1943 the PCR distributed a memorandum listing ways of saving the Jews in Nazi Europe: (1) After assuring that state security would not be harmed, Britain would declare its willingness to grant asylum to each refugee; (2) the Dominions would be encouraged to do the same; (3) the United States would be asked to grant refuge in its own territory and in the South American countries where it had influence; (4) Britain would release the remaining 37,000 White Paper framework Palestine entry permits; (5) it would encourage neutral countries to open their gates to refugees, and together with its Allies guarantee their upkeep and evacuation after the war; and (6), it would encourage Germany's allies to allow the Jews to leave, especially since it suited their own policies. Another proposal was that the Germans themselves be asked to let Jews leave. In order to achieve these goals it would be necessary to involve the neutral countries, possibly with the cooperation of the Pope. Britain, according to the memorandum, would be immediately required to establish a suitable apparatus, involve the United States at the initial stage and later the United Nations.[1]

This program contains almost all the points that would be raised with the government until the end of the war. If the proposals to exchange German and Italian citizens or prisoners of war and the issuance of open visas be added, the list of all rescue proposals is virtually complete. Needless to say, except for one principle, that of cooperation with the United States, most of the proposals went against government policy. The framers wanted to include the United States in the net of refugee responsibility in order to spare the British government embarrassment. The government saw what was brewing. Thus in order to stem the pro-refugee tide it set up a high echelon committee, the War Cabinet Committee on the Reception and Accommodation of Jewish Refugees, whose purpose was both to withstand public pressure and free the government from having to carry out any real rescue measures.

With its establishment in March 1943, the NCRNT published an outline with practical proposals: readying the Isle of Man for the absorption of refugees and providing the British consuls in the neutral countries with visas *en bloc*. These decisions should be seen in the context of the Anglo-American conference on refugees, whose planned venue was Ottawa, but transferred to Bermuda. In light of the possible joint British-American action, the NCRNT executive called upon the government to present an example to the Americans.

Activists in London had the impression that the British Government was ready to act but that the Americans were hesitant. Thus the decision to cable Eden, who was then in Washington.[2] The leftist publisher and pro-refugee Jewish activist Victor Gollancz succeeded in gathering the signatures of 206 public figures, the elite of British society. Jews were not asked to sign. The cable expressed the public's full support for refugee assistance "as one of extreme urgency." Eden was asked to use his visit to Washington to accelerate the adoption of real rescue measures.[3]

The BSWJC also appealed to Eden after it received a cable from Riegner reporting the expulsion of Jews from western Europe and the escalated killing. Riegner appealed for immediate action even before the Anglo-American conference was convened. The BSWJC reported the cable's contents to Eden and requested that the planned conference adopt concrete rescue measures rather than sufficing with an examination of the situation.[4] However, Eden's Washington negotiations took a different turn. American Secretary of State Cordell Hull pressed Eden on March 27, 1943, to arrange for the evacuation of 60,000 to 70,000 Bulgarian Jews. Eden rejected Hull's request out of hand: "If we do this then the Jews of the world will be wanting us to make similar offers in Poland and Germany. Hitler might well take us up on any such offer and there simply are not enough ships and means of transportation in the world to handle them." Neither did Eden forget to wave the threat of the infiltration of enemy agents disguised as refugees. Furthermore, he implored the Americans not to make broad promises to save Jews before the issue was discussed at Bermuda.[5]

Since the problems of the Holocaust were discussed at the War Cabinet Committee Eden came well prepared for his Washington meetings. After all, the committee had been established by the government to protect it from the strong pro-refugee winds blowing from the public. In fact, the issue was considered so important that three senior cabinet officials, the foreign secretary, and the home and colonial secretaries, were appointed to the committee. When the pressure grew even greater it coopted Deputy Prime Minister Clement Attlee, the leader of the Labour Party.[6] Attlee expressed the view that he was weary of lobbying for the Jews. The government was being inundated with pleas from all sides the Labour and Conservative Parties, various other circles, and from public rallies. Surprisingly, even the Trades Unions, which understandably were always strongly against immigration, joined the demand to open the gates to persecuted Jews. This is an indication of the feelings among the British public even when their country was embroiled in a life and death war against the Germans. The motto, "Britain shall give the lead," was the refugee lobby's response to government attempts to make assistance conditional upon international action.[7] The name of the cabinet committee is itself evidence of the government's concerns about public opinion and it could serve as a cover for its decisions to do whatever possible not to receive and accommodate Jewish refugees.

At the War Cabinet Committee the ministers raised the old worn arguments and rationalizations for sitting on their hands: Britain had done more than its share – after all had it not already accepted 100,000 aliens, most of them Jews? The number apparently included immigrants to Palestine and the colonies. The colonies, the government argued, were already flooded with refugees and prisoners of war. If the Americans applied strong pressure the home secretary could agree to accepting 1,000 or 2,000 refugees into the British Isles, but no more.[8] In the end the committee reaffirmed the principle raised by the colonial secretary not to discriminate between Jewish and non-Jewish refugees. Indeed, the word "Jewish" was eventually stricken from the committee's name. Ironically, the committee actually rejected its Cabinet brief "to consider what arrangements could be made for the reception and accommodation of such Jewish refugees as might be able to find their way out of enemy territory through Bulgaria or Portugal." This rejection appears in the committee memorandum submitted by Eden to the War Cabinet.[9] In the previous chapter we discussed the policies laid down by the committee. As early as January 9, 1943, Eden submitted a memorandum to the government about the committee's policy. There were two strategic objectives: a blurring of the distinctions between the fate of Jews and non-Jews in occupied Europe categorizing the refugee problem as a common United Nations concern. Only within such a framework would Britain be prepared to do its share and, as had already been resolved, even that would be as modest as possible. Persuading Washington to be a dedicated partner to this policy was so crucial that the foreign secretary himself undertook to do the work in his March 1943 visit.

Each War Cabinet Committee minister was accompanied by a bevy of senior ministry officials whose brief was to help the minister fortify the policy line that refugee responsibility was a common Allied concern and that the United States had to help in their absorption. The cabinet itself, at the behest of the home secretary, decided not to allow the entry of 1,000 or 2,000 refugees without it being part of a common United Nations effort.[10] During his visit to Washington, Eden succeeded in convincing his American colleagues of the need to convene a refugee conference. Thus the Bermuda Conference came into being. Initially it raised hopes among pro-refugee circles. However, the very nature of its conception soon dampened their expectations. The objective was to formulate inter-governmental or international responsibility for the deficiencies in order to make it easier for the British government to stave off parliamentary and public pressure.[11]

The rescue proposals raised by different Jewish and Christian groups were therefore totally out of line with what the government intended. Refugee Commissioner Sir Herbert Emerson's deputy, Dr Gustaw Kuhlmann, a Swiss, defined the problem in a discussion with Norman Bentwich and Abraham Brotman in January 1943: There was no chance of agreement on any grandiose plans such as an appeal to Hitler to let the Jews leave Europe. If Hitler indeed agreed to such a step it would be to burden the Allies with hundreds of thousands of refugees as a ploy to hamper their war effort. Thus Kuhlmann suggested plans of limited scope such as the channeling of 50 refugees a day to Spain as a way station; 4,000 refugees to the Isle of Man; temporary residence in South Africa for potential Palestinian immigrants; and an appeal to Turkey to permit the passage of Bulgarian Jews *en route* to Palestine. Kuhlmann believed that such plans might win British approval because of the favorable public opinion. He did not believe that similar pro-Jewish feelings were as prevalent in the United States. Even from the tactical standpoint his proposals were worth considering because grand proposals could serve as an excuse to reject even those on a small scale.[12]

The purpose of the meeting with Kuhlmann was to examine the operative possibilities of the rescue proposals. The large-scale examples raised with him, in contrast to those of a more limited scope, were apparently the subject of differences of opinion between the WJC and the JFC. As we have seen, cooperation in the framework of the Consultative Emergency Committee had not succeeded, either in the hopeful days of late December 1942 and early January 1943. Therefore, each organization submitted separate memoranda to the government and its representatives met separately with Undersecretary of State Richard Law to discuss operative measures, at it were.

The BSWJC's program was maximalist and that of Brodetsky's associates minimalist. A week after the major meeting with the foreign secretary, Brodetsky presented a limited rescue plan to Law. The following is a list of the plan's points and a summary of the undersecretary's response to each one:

1 Warning the Laval government in France and Italy, Rumania, Hungary, Bulgaria and Slovakia through radio broadcasts and air-dropped leaflets that it desist from persecuting the Jews.
   Law: There was no need. The French people opposed the anti-Jewish measures and Laval's men knew what was in store for them. Moreover, as learned from a similar experience dropping leaflets over the German town Essen, it would be difficult to relay the proposed warning.

2 An approach to the Vatican that it issue a warning to the Catholic peoples of Europe.
   Law: The British representative had already done so, and the Pope's secretary of state had responded that they were doing whatever they could.

3 Supplying food and international guarantees of speedy evacuation of Jews after the war to encourage neutral countries to accept refugees and by declaring its readiness to receive refugees Britain would serve as an example to the others.
   Law: An approach to the neutral countries would only succeed in angering them. In all events they were not impeding the arrival of refugees.[13] The acceptance of refugees by the Allies was predicated on inter-government negotiations and Britain was waiting for the American stand before drawing up a final plan.

4 The evacuation of refugees from the neutral countries via Spain and Portugal to North Africa.
   Law: The decision was in the hands of the American military authorities in the region.

5 The transit of Jews to Palestine via South Africa.
   Law: Discussions were being held with the South African authorities.

6 Asking Argentina to appeal to Germany to allow the Jews to leave.

Law: That "is probably a wild goose chase."

7 Increasing the flow of refugees from Bulgaria and Rumania to Palestine.

Law: The government of Palestine had agreed to accept 5,000 Jewish children from Bulgaria and Youth *Aliya* children already in Rumania.

In the end Law stressed that only victory would be of benefit to the Jews.[14]

The BSWJC's Easterman was called to Law's office in the first week of 1943. A day earlier Easterman had sent Law two memoranda, one concerning rescue measures, the other a report of a meeting between Monsieur Haccius, the London representative of the International Red Cross, and Ben Rubenstein, the BSWJC's treasurer. These memoranda were in the realm of large-scale proposals. According to the Easterman plan it would be necessary to find a way to absorb two million refugees. In order to carry out such a huge evacuation plan an international body under United Nations' aegis with budgets and operative authority would have to be established. This body would also settle refugees in Palestine, coopt the neutral countries and issue guarantees. Understandably, the Red Cross would take part in the rescue operations and would have governmental authority over the refugees. Finally, "The World Jewish Congress will wholeheartedly offer the fullest possible cooperation in securing the effective execution of the measures envisaged in the foregoing plan." After reading the memorandum, Law gave vent to his feelings in a marginal note: "What in the world am I to say to all this, which strikes me as completely unreal?"

The following is Law's account of his meeting with Easterman: "I said that I was afraid that they (my comments) would have to be discouraging. The memorandum spoke of the possibility of removing 2 million Jews from Europe. I said that . . . it seemed to me that a programme of this kind will be quite impossible unless we were prepared to abandon for example the campaign in North Africa or in the desert . . . ; it would be impossible in war. Mr. Easterman then argued that in fact the figures would be nothing like that, and that the Germans would not let them go. At the most there would be 100,000, mainly children. He asked me whether I did not agree with him. I said that my personal opinion was that this Jewish campaign was one of the things the Nazis really believed in and that the worse things went with them in the military sphere, the more determined they would become to get a victory in this one. Not everyone, however, would agree with me and we could not take the risk of the Germans calling our bluff." He countered Easterman by saying that such a grand rescue plan went against the war effort and that an appeal to the Germans should only be chanced if no more that 100,000 refugees were involved.

The sides also discussed Rubenstein's report of his meeting with

Haccius, which was meant to provide the basis for the first memorandum. Haccius had contended that the Red Cross was capable of assisting in large-scale rescue only if different countries were willing to accept them, and that food and clothing could be supplied if trains and ships were available. Haccius believed that Switzerland alone could grant asylum to 100,000 children. He was prepared to send an emissary to Berlin. What is astonishing about Rubenstein's memorandum is that it is anchored neither in reality or an understanding of international relations, including Red Cross policy: Haccius "declined to believe that the International Red Cross, with its vast resources and the Allied Governments with their good intentions, should not be able to save a very large number of lives." It is possible that this second-hand report of Rubenstein's was intended as a means of applying pressure on the Foreign Office. In order to initiate an operation on behalf of Europe's Jews the Red Cross representative sought a formal appeal by the WJC to be dispatched to Switzerland, preferably with the endorsement of the British and American envoys in Berne. It is difficult to fully fathom Haccius's intentions. In all events, Law rejected the endorsement request because, as he said, licenses without concrete plans were useless.

However, Easterman was full of expectations. Thus in order to assuage him Law said that negotiations were being carried out with the Americans on a "less ambitious but more practical" plan of transferring refugees from Spain to North Africa. No special international body, only discussions between the two powers were required. Easterman, who was loathe to leave empty-handed, inquired into the possibility of stationing a Jewish observer in the soon to be established United Nations aid organization (UNRRWA). That would be superfluous, Law said, because New York Governor Herbert Lehman, a Jew, was involved,[15] thus intimating that the organization was in faithful Jewish hands.

The maximalists and the minimalists had identical achievements: nothing. The government refused to budge from its adamant stand.

Its do-nothing policy was stamped with official approval by Deputy Prime Minister Attlee. In an address to the House of Commons on January 1, 1943 the Labourite said that the ceremonial December 1942 declaration had been issued to *help* put an end to the destruction of the Jews. As to real salvation, that would come only after victory. Meanwhile since secret negotiations were in progress with various countries it would be prudent of the Jews to keep silent. In principle, Attlee pronounced, one must get away from the idea that only Jews were suffering. Perhaps it was true of the 1930s, but now millions of others had joined the ranks of the suffering.[16] Attlee's stand was a retreat from the December 1942 declaration.

After the deputy prime minister's disheartening statement the BD plenary met to consider a response. Brodetsky tried to haze over the harsh impression left by Attlee. The government, according to the Anglo-Jewry's official leader, had already undertaken significant action. Brodetsky did not elaborate. Goodman was more forceful. He proposed issuing a clear expression of the community's disappointment. The British government had directly approached the Germans over the issue of the evacuation of wounded soldiers and the treatment of POWs, Goodman said, and must now be approached on behalf of the Jewish refugees. Bakstansky argued that the government would only act under the pressure of public opinion. Therefore the churches must be asked to organize demonstrations. Others raised the oft-heard complaint that Brodetsky's manifold activities prevented him from fulfilling his BD brief properly.[17]

The disappointment was keenly felt in London BSWJC circles as well. Its president, Lady Reading, sent a letter to Prime Minister Churchill imploring him to take action on behalf of Europe's Jews. Five weeks passed before she received a personal reply attached to a memorandum sent to Churchill by the Foreign Office. It stated that if the Germans allowed the Jews to leave all the means of transportation in the entire world would not be enough. The lines of escape cut through war zones and the war effort took priority. The real difficulties "cannot unfortunately be dismissed as 'fetters of red tape'; but we shall do what we can." In the meanwhile *aliya* permits were being issued within the framework of the White Paper, the government was intervening with the Turkish authorities on behalf of the refugees and some had been transferred to British territory. Greater rescue efforts would be only possible after the intervention of all the Allies, an objective the foreign secretary was working toward.[18] Clearly, balm for the Jews would not issue from the prime minister's office. The Foreign Office had his full backing; Churchill's letter even strengthened its stand.

Meanwhile, the WJC, in a letter to Eden, retreated from its maximalist stand and the demand for an "open-door" policy and was prepared to make do with less.[19]

The British Government conferred with the United States Government on three issues: (1) Apprehensions about criticism from the other Allies if preference was given to the Jews (i.e., a retreat from the St. James Conference); (2) an examination of the capacity of the means of transportation before granting assurances about receiving refugees (the "practicality" excuse); and (3) the fear that the Germans and their satellites would begin mass expulsions and flood the world with refugees.[20] On the other hand, the Foreign Office recognized the refugee problem as an international issue weighing on the public's conscience. But it also believed that Britain's balance on the issue was favorable since Britain and its territories, including Palestine, had contributed in the absorption of refugees. Furthermore, it was still willing to accept them. This was apparently a reference to Morrison's offer of 2,000 permits. But since the United States was capable of a more serious contribution a conference should be convened to deal with the problem.[21]

The third issue, the fear of an endless stream of refugees, worried the British government since there were signs that Rumania, in the hope of receiving a princely ransom, preferred expulsion to murdering the Jews. The Cabinet Refugee Committee dealt at length with this problem. Concerned over American pressure Attlee, as early as January 1943, demanded adherence to the policy of limiting entry to Palestine to a specified number of children accompanied by women. Home Secretary Morrison, who was entrusted with protecting the British Isles from an "invasion" of refugees, advocated seeking alternative havens.[22] In all events the War Cabinet Committee instituted a great principle as a bulwark against the pressure applied on the government by members of Parliament: "It was essential to kill the idea that mass immigration to the United Kingdom and the Colonies was possible . . ." In other words, maintain the blockade against Europe's Jews. None other than Eden cultivated the ideological motto that the solution did not lay in transferring them, but in "making Europe fit for Jews to live in." This was one of the aims of the war.

The immediate practical conclusions were: a rejection of the idea of exchanging Germans and others for Jews and preventing the transfer of refugees to Britain from Spain, which was liable to be drawn into the war or agree to a German request for them to be returned. It would appear that the exchange principle was advanced because of Rathbone's appeal to exchange Jews for the Belgian, Dutch and Danish citizens stranded in Britain who had appealed to her to help them return home.[23] In the spirit of this hard line all the proposals to negotiate with the Germans to seek permission for Jews, even in strictly defined categories, to pass into neutral countries, were turned down. Neither did the pleas of the Norwegian government-in-exile to rescue Norway's 500 Jews on the verge of expulsion to the country where they would be destroyed fall on ready ears: "This proposal could not be entertained."[24] A description of the fate of these Jews would be superfluous. Such and other decisions were made by the War Cabinet Committee on Refugees that was composed of senior government officials bearing ministerial responsibility.

At that time the Foreign Office received a Jewish Agency report of the Rumanian proposal to ransom the 70,000 Jews subsisting in Transylvania and transferring them to Palestine upon Rumanian vessels. The home secretary's response: The proposal was impractical because such rescue operations might cause Britain to "lose the war."[25]

Weizmann, then in Washington, beseeched Lord Halifax to give his backing to the Rumanian proposal. Halifax, who was also a member of the cabinet, passed the request to Eden. The rejection of a proposal that stood a good chance of success was considered so important that Eden's letter to Halifax on the issue was distributed to all members of the government.[26]

The Parliamentary Committee on Refugees headed by Eleanor Rathbone was also disappointed by the government's stand and opposed the tendency to cast responsibility for refugees onto the United Nations in general. In a memorandum sent to four government ministers, Rathbone severely attacked the government bureaucracy and raised a number of proposals that she believed could be carried out if the government and its officials displayed good will. The officials were insulted by the insinuation and angrily rejected the Quaker MP's assault. In a "counter"-memorandum, A. G. Randall, head of the Foreign Office Refugee Department, let loose a broadside against the "impatient idealistic" Rathbone. In principle, Randall wrote, the Jewish tragedy was integral to the general problems in Europe such as the starving children, the destruction of the Polish and Czech intelligentsia, the forced labor and the spiritual poisoning of the youth. Using the oft-used excuses Randall rejected all of Rathbone's practical suggestions. The officials, on their part, were offended because according to the rules of the democratic game an MP could attack the government, but not its civil servants. Rathbone, who was well-aware of the problem, countered by saying that if the machinations behind the scenes were made public the officials would have no excuse for being upset. "But as long as 'official channels' discharge nothing but an icy flow of discouraging answers to parliamentary questions, what can we do but go on prodding?"[27]

Meanwhile, as described above, the organizational framework of the forces striving to spur the government into action was coalescing. The NCRNT was established and it immediately struggled against the government's foot-dragging and the excuses layered over by the verbiage about the need for an international committee to deal with the refugee issue.[28]

Upon its founding in March 1943, the NCRNT published a twelve-point rescue plan:

1   expediting the granting of entry visas for the United Kingdom;
2   encouraging neutral countries to accept refugees;
3   establishing camps for refugees;
4   increased use of transport facilities to carry refugees;
5   increasing the rate of entry into Palestine within the White Paper framework by removing the adult restrictions;
6   pressuring the German satellite states to stop the atrocities and allow the Jews to leave;
7   applying the arrangements reached with the Bulgarians to additional states – Hungary and Rumania – to free refugees for *aliya*;
8   examining the possibility of exchange with enemy nationals;

9   radio broadcasts and air-dropped warning leaflets;

10 setting up a new government apparatus to deal with the array of problems involved in rescue;

11 the appointment of a high commissioner under United Nations auspices to handle these plans;

12 and finally, the "Adoption of the principle that whatever other nations may do or leave undone, the British contribution to the work of rescue should be the speediest and most generous possible without delaying victory."

Practical suggestions accompanied most of the proposals.[29]

This plan contained certain points that differentiated it from the maximalist proposals. It did not demand that the Germans be approached, only their collaborator states. Neither did it speak outright of an open-door policy, but that the granting of United Kingdom entry visas be liberalized.

The next step was seeking public support. According to a Gallup Poll survey, 78 percent of those canvassed favored the entry of refugees into Britain the greatest majority in Gallup's history. Fifty percent favored unlimited entry of refugees and only 13 percent were opposed.[30] The Jews' champions exploited the public's support to the hilt against the government. Rathbone was so merciless with the home secretary that she was accused of defaming the homeland. According to her biographer, writing a few years after the war: "to the end of her life Eleanor was haunted by the thought of the Jews who might have been saved . . . And to the end of her life her heart was hardened against Herbert Morrison. Neither then nor later was she disposed to credit him with a substratum of warm humanity beneath the efficient exterior of a busy Secretary of State. She did not believe it was there."[31] Rathbone's booklet, *Rescue the Perishing*, demolished the government's excuses, especially the claim that means of transportation were lacking. She argued that troop-transport vessels returning to Britain and the United States could carry refugees; that ships of neutral countries and the space taken up by non-vital imports could be used. Britain had managed to find ships to transport tens of thousands of pilgrims to Mecca, Rathbone wrote. Nonetheless, the government argues that it has no means of transportation for refugees. In every edition of her booklet Rathbone listed more and more examples of lives lost because of Home Office strictness and regulations.

Mobilizing public support was generally entrusted to the parliamentary committee's non-Jews. The exception was the wealthy leftist publisher Victor Gollancz, who dedicated the income from his pamphlet, *Let My People Go*, to covering the expenses of the committee, whose office premises he supplied. The first edition, an unprecedented publishing success selling a quarter of a million copies within a few months, was released in January 1943. Gollancz broke the Jewish silence, but did not demand that Jewish activists follow his lead: "Leave any attack or agitation to others, as a Jew be silent. Nor do I keep silent for even if I did not believe as I do believe, that I must speak as a Jew, the duty to speak as a man would still be absolute."[32] He labeled the government's policy one of "revenge" that would not even save a single life. The emphasis on "revenge" was a cover-up for not carrying out rescue. His stand influenced some serious newspapers.[33] Gollancz was also sharply critical of the assumption that rescue was solely dependent upon victory. To the contrary. When the suppressed nations of Europe saw that Britain was defending them and fighting against the atrocities, they would be encouraged in their struggle against the enemy.

Gollancz's pamphlet raises practical rescue proposals of the kind we have already seen. He is a maximalist and emphasizes the need to demand that Germany and the other enemy states let at least some of the Jews leave. He demands that the gates of Palestine be opened and refers to their closing as complicity to murder! He appeals directly to the public to apply pressure on the government by beseeching government ministers, MPs, newspapers, and organizing public demonstrations of solidarity with the victims. He rejects as a shameful libel the argument that the entry of refugees would lead to a wave of anti-Semitism. Gollancz identified with the victims with all his being: "For a few brief moments, *be* just one of these human beings whose body, with its nerves that can suffer so, and whose mind and soul, with all their resources of terror and despair, are concealed by cold abstraction of 'one hundred and fifty' and 'ten thousand' and 'six million.' And then *be* another, and another. *Be* the mother flinging her baby from a sixth-floor window; *be* a girl of nine, torn from her parents and standing in the dark of a moving truck with two corpses pressed close against her; *be* an old Jew at the door of the electrocution chamber. And only then, when you have been each of these for a few short moments, do the multiplication . . . "[34]

In 1943 Gollancz lectured throughout the country. Before each appearance he shut himself alone in a room for twenty minutes and performed identification exercises with the Nazi victims. His lectures flowed with deep feeling.[35]

In each edition of his pamphlet Gollancz updated his attacks with quotations showing how government ministers were sneaking away from rescue operations, and quotations from Christian figures who accused the government of apathy and complicity to murder. Naturally, government ministers could not defend themselves *directly* against such attacks. Instead, in response to the argument that the British populace favored daring rescue operations,[36] the Home Office was busy with encouraging anti-Semitism.

Sir Oswald Mosely and his coterie were released from detention early in 1943 and British fascists began to operate openly.[37] The anti-Semitic graffiti which began to appear in the months before their release included slogans such as "it's a Jewish war" and "Mosely was right." Fascist rallies were openly held in London and anti-Semitic publications were distributed.[38]

The conservative weekly, *The People*, printed an article in March 1943 that linked anti-Semitism, black marketeering and Jewish behavior in the East End shelters with the rejection of plans to rescue Jewish refugees. The supervision and suppression of such activities was the bailiwick of the home secretary. As we have described earlier, the Jewish establishment had already experienced the attempt to link rescue activities and anti-Semitic accusations. Even in the critical Spring of 1943 the anti-Jewish agitation reached such worrying proportions that the BD circles discussed a proposal to appeal to the home secretary to activate the emergency regulations against the agitators. They dropped the idea because they were certain that in Morrison's current mood he would do nothing to protect the Jews of his country. Brodetsky was frustrated because at the very time rescue negotiations were in progress the black market issue and the part played by Jews suddenly emerged. Neither did an attempt to lobby the Minister of Information, Brendan Bracken, a man friendly to the Jews and an intimate of Churchill's, bear any fruit.[39]

As to the Foreign Office, it will be recalled that its officials and members of the War Cabinet Refugee Committee sought cooperation with the United States. When Washington tried to shrug off the attempt, the British threatened to announce its stand, or the lack of it, as the case may be, in Parliament.[40] The pressure worked. In March, during his Washington visit, Eden succeeded in gaining US agreement for the refugee conference. That same month, after undergoing the transmogrifications described above, Schonfeld's initiative of January was finally tabled in the House of Lords by the Archbishop of Canterbury, along with a ceremonial declaration that the British were standing "at the bar of history, of humanity, and of God." The timing was convenient for the government. Lord Cranbourne, its spokesman, used the opportunity to announce to the Lords that Eden himself had used his Washington visit to press the Americans into an acknowledgment of the urgency of the refugee problem.[41]

The conference was scheduled to convene in Bermuda on April 19. It was Passover eve on the Hebrew calendar, and on that Festival of Freedom the remnants of the Warsaw Ghetto rose up against the Germans. Sidney Silverman, chairman of the BSWJC, appealed to Richard Law to make transportation to Bermuda available to its representatives. Law, arguing that for the sake of stemming anti-Semitism it was undesirable at a refugee conference for the Jews to be mentioned exclusively, turned him down.[42]

What Law really intended to say was that it was not possible to include representatives of all the bodies dealing with refugees. This reasoning was explicitly mentioned when the BD asked that a representative be sent to Bermuda as an observer. Anglo-Jewry was afraid that it would be at a disadvantage *vis à vis* American Jewry, which had succeeded in convincing the State Department to include US Congressman Sol Bloom in the American delegation. (The British Ambassador in Washington was immediately instructed to coordinate positions with the State Department in relation to Bloom.) Brodetsky did not give in easily, but he was given the run around and in the meantime the conference was convened.[43]

In the end the Foreign Office agreed to submit to the conference a BD memorandum listing all the current proposals ranging from an appeal to Germany to immigration arrangements with the Turks. Since the Jews wanted the conference to decide on operative measures and not be limited merely to an examination of the situation, the BD memorandum dealt only with practical measures.[44]

The Anglo-American conference on the refugees raised great hopes. Brodetsky expressed certainty at the BD plenary that now many Jews would be saved. He even used Schonfeld (!) to support his view, for at that very time draft resolutions signed by two hundred and eighty members of both Houses of Parliament were being submitted to press the government into action.[45]

In the somewhat optimistic atmosphere before the opening of the Bermuda Conference, the Zionist circles associated with the Jewish Agency began negotiating with the Rothschild circles and the Archbishop of Canterbury and his colleagues about raising funds to assist the masses of refugees about to leave the European inferno. Most of the money would be dedicated to absorbing the Jews in Palestine.[46] When the hopes were scotched so were the plans.

However, there was not only hope but also suspicion. Silverman wondered why isolated Bermuda, rather than the original venue of Ottawa, was chosen.[47] The struggle to include observers was also accompanied by suspicions about the possibility that the representatives of the Allied Powers were seeking to escape the public eye and criticism.[48] Memoranda were submitted but not acknowledged; the line seemed to have been set beforehand. The British Government set the policies of its delegation which was headed by Undersecretary of State Richard Law. Its task was to persuade the Americans "that it was out of the question to enter into any undertaking whatever with the Axis powers to accept refugees from Central Europe." Nevertheless, the British did try to achieve some kind of result. Thus they demanded that the Americans allow its immigration quota to be filled, just as the British were doing in Palestine. Moreover, they wanted the Americans to establish refugee camps in North Africa to house refugees and evacuees from Spain. Under strong American pressure the British undertook to accept a grand total of 5,000 refugees in all the territories of its Empire. And if the pressure to evacuate all the Jews from Bulgaria was maintained, they would try to settle them in Turkey but never in Palestine. One may legitimately surmise that the Turks would not have agreed to such an exodus.[49] Because the Americans adopted the British policy of doing as little as possible to save the victims, the British delegation to the conference obtained "better" results than originally expected.[50]

Under the pretext that news of its achievements might find its way into the hands of the enemy, the conference "results" were kept confidential. Rathbone had doubts about just how *bona fide* that confidentiality was.[51] In all events, on May 19 some of those results were made public in the House of Commons: reserved assurances to evacuate refugees from the neutral countries of Europe and maintaining the policy of granting children entry into Palestine. The conference had another "achievement." By courtesy of Britain three additional categories of refugees would be permitted an Albion haven: (1) parents of children serving in the armed forces; (2) refugees the authorities were willing to conscript; (3) parents of children below the age of sixteen who were residing in Britain and who had arrived without them. Two hundred souls all told.

Eden, in the Commons, made no effort to hide the truth. "I do not believe that great things can be achieved," he said. "I do not believe it is possible to rescue more than a few until final victory is won."[52] The conference had entrusted responsibility for carrying out its decisions to the Intergovernmental Committee for Refugees under Sir Herbert Emerson, who also served as High Commissioner for Refugees. The IGCR had been established after the Evian Conference. Its function, as described above in chapter 3, was to deal with refugees who had fled Greater Germany and Bohemia. Now its authority was expanded to include the *persecuted* from all of Europe. This novelty countered the Jews' contention that no organization aside from theirs was concerned with oppressed stateless Jews or Jewish nationals of enemy states. In order to handle its new function the IGCR would undergo reorganization.[53] The British representatives had won a "great" victory. Until then the IGCR had done very little for the refugees. Now it had a mandate to continue doing just as much for more people in greater danger than ever before.

As Mark Wischnitzer concludes, in a study of the World War II refugee problem: "The proceedings of the Bermuda Conference were shrouded in mystery. Its decisions were kept secret . . . the immediate practical results were nil . . . "[54] Henry L. Feingold, in *America and the Holocaust*, entitled the chapter dealing with the refugee conference, "The Bermuda Conference Mock Rescue for Surplus People."[55]

The May 19 discussion in the House of Commons revealed much of the truth about the Bermuda Conference. Eden and Home Office Undersecretary Osbest Peake, who had attended the conference, defended the government. Peake, basing himself on the Bermuda resolutions, flatly rejected the notion of an appeal to Hitler.[56]

If we raise the possibility that by the longed-for victory no Jews would still be around to save, Peake sought to apply the term "persecuted" to the one hundred twenty million Europeans under the German yoke, all of whom wanted to flee! He mentioned the eight million Poles suffering directly. In other words, the Jews should not be the focus. Peake managed to stir up the MPs' ire and they shot questions and demands at him, such as the entry of 10,000 refugees into Britain which would only mean an annual loss of fifty-six grams of food for each British resident, transporting refugees beyond the seas and other demands. Peake of the Home Office was unmoved: Britain had already done its share. Even now it had allotted Palestinian entry permits for 4,000 Bulgarian Jewish children, but no ships were available to transport them. Moreover, 40,000 non-Jewish Poles had been evacuated from Russia to Persia and the burden of their care was on Britain. The undersecretary also yanked at the anti-Semitism scarecrow. If the Jews were allowed into the Kingdom they would crowd into the East End and intensify anti-Jewish feeling. Finally, the undersecretary said that he could not talk about all the issues because they were confidential. Peake attacked Rathbone and the Bishop of Chichester for their publications. The MPs became even more angry and raised many more demands. Especially active was the indefatigable refugee champion *par excellence* Eleanor Rathbone. Eden jumped into the fray to rescue his colleague. He attempted to allay the agitation by expressing an identification with the MPs and by stalwartly revealing a secret: that the efforts on behalf of the persecuted were in the faithful hands of an extraordinary committee headed by three members of the War Cabinet.[57] If anything, the discussion sharpened the Common's sense of outrage and intensified the disappointment of the Jews.

Colonel Victor Cazalet MP, for the NCRNT, sent an angry letter to *The Times* about the Bermuda Conference's purpose of being an "explanatory consultation." Cazalet warned that if no real results emerged, there would be "a mounting wave of indignation in Britain which may surprise those who have failed to appreciate how deeply the public conscience is stirred . . . "[58]

The Jewish Chronicle ran a sharp editorial, "Never Again," after that Commons meeting saying outright that the Jews had been abandoned by their friends.[59]

The keen disappointment over the Bermuda Conference led to confusion in the Jewish leadership. The main Jewish organizations met in the framework of the Consultative Emergency Committee, but they did not succeed in agreeing on a statement over Bermuda. The BD feared piquing the government and agreed only to a tepid announcement of disappointment released for the Jewish press.[60] The BSWJC, on the other hand, influenced by New York headquarters, issued a critical public statement.[61]

After Bermuda the Jewish organizations were not prepared to take public protest action. The British Section's censure damaged its relations, once again, with the BD. Brodetsky was vehemently accused of leading the Jews of Britain and other countries toward chaos and oblivion.[62]

Now even Lord Melchett was ready to come out against the dictatorial tendencies of the BD, but was soon deterred from doing so.[63] We have already seen that its members were unable to present a clear and open Zionist stand against the government, even though their president was a Zionist.

The crisis within the Jewish community was so deep that it was necessary to mobilize the aid of the Anglo-Jewish aristocracy to reconcile the parties. On May 1, 1943, a meeting was arranged between Brodetsky, Stein, Sir Robert Waley Cohen and Brotman from the BD, John D. Mack, Daniel Frankel, Daniel Lipson and Major Gluckstein, and the Jewish members of Parliament, Sidney Silverman and Lords Swaythling, Jessel, Samuel and Nathan, to discuss the chaos gripping the Jewish community. Silverman sought to bring about a compromise between the BSWJC and the JFC. He was afraid that there would be a request to cut contact with the WJC.[64] In the conciliation negotiations the deep differences of opinion appeared. BSWJC–BD relations deteriorated further when it became clear that various BSWJC activists had begun organizing community branches throughout the country. This development greatly alarmed BD leaders who feared that the community might fall apart.[65] The BD demanded that BSWJC activities be limited and proposed an understanding between the two organizations based on the following: Externally, the BSWJC, as the representative of World Jewish Congress headquarters in New York, could approach the London-based governments-in-exile, but not the British government. Otherwise, the impression would be gained that Anglo-Jewish policies were dictated from the United States. Likewise, the BSWJC would not appeal to the British public because that was the function of the local organization. Internally, the WJC would refrain from organizing local chapters and from speaking in the name of Anglo-Jewry.[66]

The BSWJC submitted its counter proposals in June: The BD would be recognized as the over-all representative of Anglo-Jewry, including external affairs in the framework of the JFC. The British Section, however, as the representative of the global World Jewish Congress, would be empowered to act in the political sphere without limitation. In order to prevent duplication the BSWJC proposed that a joint committee coordinate the activities of the two organizations. On the other hand, the BSWJC had no reason to refrain from recruiting support within the community.[67]

Bridging the gap appeared to be an impossible task. It was a struggle akin to a jostling tournament between Jewish knights. Lord Nathan of Churt, an active BD member, wrote a warning letter and called the Jewish MPs to another meeting over the issue. Lord Melchett, of the BSWJC, suggested a simple division of labor: the Board would act on British Jewish issues, the WJC in global Jewish matters, and the Jewish Agency on Palestine. And if they could not reach an agreement each organization would go its own way, but with mutual respect.[68]

In the same month of June 1943, BD elections were held and the numbers of Zionist and WJC supporters in the plenary increased. It is therefore surprising that at the new Board's opening meeting, on July 4, resolutions were passed in favor of the government and an identification with the view that victory alone would put an end to Jewish anguish. Among other matters, the Board was cognizant of the "desire" of His Majesty's Government to rescue the Jews from their bitter fate and that it "appreciate[d] the measures of rescue, though so far of limited character, which have been announced as a result of the Bermuda Conference . . . " Moreover, the elected deputies "believe that the government would use all opportunities to increase its [rescue] efforts and in the end a speedy victory would bring redemption to the Jews and all the nations of the world!"[69] The purpose of all this was, apparently, both to mollify the Jewish public and to let the new Board express abject loyalty to the government. In light of the widespread information about the destruction of their brothers and sisters in Europe, this was nothing more than irresponsible gliding away from the glaring truth.

The official Anglo-Jewish leadership was composed of conformists. The non-conformists were to be found elsewhere among the non-Jewish members of the NCRNT which issued a sharp reaction and resolved to embark upon a campaign of publicity and protest rallies.[70] At a press conference, Rathbone and her colleagues expressed bitter disappointment at the Bermuda Conference and the secrecy which served as a cover for the absence of any positive steps. The Archbishop of Canterbury announced that every day after the famous December declaration tens of thousands of Jews were murdered and that not one single child had been freed. The government had even put hurdles in the way of the implementation of the White Paper when it announced that children alone would be allowed into Palestine. The government was also blamed for the failure of the plan to rescue Jewish children in France.[71] In order to show some kind of achievement, the Foreign Office attempted to find places for refugees on troop carriers, or procure Rumanian or Swedish ships to transport 4,000 children from Bulgaria to Palestine and evacuate refugees from Spain. The Foreign Office saw the step as politically urgent, "a case for high priority."[72] However, its Refugee Department did not even manage this meager achievement. In all events, the government stood firm in the midst of the stormy debates in Parliament, and the public's interest in Jewish suffering grew dimmer. Rathbone complained about the scant participation of journalists at the NCRNT press conference, which was attended only by representatives of the press agencies. In order to arouse public opinion a new edition of *Rescue the Perishing* was published with remarks about the Bermuda Conference.[73] However, here too the government had the upper hand.

After the true intent of the Bermuda Conference became clear, there was widespread despair. Leonard Stein, the JFC co-chairman, who had great hopes when the war broke out of a fruitful cooperation between the Anglo-Jewish leadership and the British government, accepted realities. He admitted that there were practical difficulties that delayed rescue and warned against having any illusions.[74] Shortly thereafter his high public prestige declined. The Joint Foreign Affairs Committee of the BD and the Anglo-Jewish Association fell apart and the Jewish community faced more division.[75]

Other circles still clung to a straw of hope. The WJC in New York eventually hoped that the secrecy that clouded some of the Bermuda Conference decisions might actually be a cover for real measures. As to the disclosed decisions, perhaps the refugees would be evacuated from Spain and Portugal and rescue from the Balkans would be carried out. One path still remained: the retribution committee that was to be established in the framework of the St. James Conference. The heads of the WJC in the United States discussed this with Czech President Eduard Benes. They also accepted the hopes of the BSWJC that the Red Cross would be an anchor of rescue for the Jews.[76] It soon transpired that the vision of Jews protected from the storm under a Red Cross umbrella was but another illusion.

8

The Bermuda Policy and
its Opponents

According to some historians British Jewry was more concerned with this battle than with any other during war years. Richard Bolchover states that the efforts invested in the European tragedy "were dwarfed by the conflict between [the] Zionists and non-Zionists."

More Splits in the Jewish Community

The BD elections in the summer of 1943 strengthened its Zionist component, especially as described above, which aligned with the World Jewish Congress. Easterman was chosen by the new plenary as chairman of the Palestine Committee instead of the non-Zionist Dr Israel Feldman. Another step taken to remove the non-Zionist influence from external affairs was the dissolution of its partnership with the Anglo-Jewish Association in the Joint Foreign Affairs Committee. The decision was reached in July 1943 by a narrow majority of only 154–148.[1] Instead of the JFC, which had existed since 1878, the BD established a Foreign Affairs Committee (FAC).[2] Zionist groups approved of the move, but the Rothschild circles and Agudat Israel did not. Harry Goodman, who had been an AJA representative on the JFC now refused to take part in any BD committee. Non-Zionist groups accused the Zionist Federation of distorting the elections by buying the votes of synagogues that were in financial difficulty, and the demand was raised to invalidate the elections.[3] The claims were without foundation: The BD electoral system was based more on historical political interests (like the "Rotten Boroughs") than on the democratic process. The Zionists, who were more politically savvy and determined than their opponents, took advantage of the system.

In the 1943 BD elections the Zionist struggle for hegemony was over. According to some historians British Jewry was more concerned with this battle than with any other during war years. Richard Bolchover states that the efforts invested in the European tragedy "were dwarfed by the conflict between [the] Zionists and non-Zionists." In May 1942, the Zionist leaders under Chaim Weizmann and David Ben-Gurion convened at New York's Biltmore Hotel and declared that the new goal of the Zionist Movement was that "Palestine be established as a Jewish Commonwealth" (the Biltmore Program). An identical resolution was adopted at a large convention in the United States with the participation of organization delegates representing two million Jews. The Biltmore Program was a declaration of war against the Britain's White Paper, a struggle that led to the establishment of the State of Israel in 1948.[4] Thus for the Zionists it was crucial that the official representatives of Anglo-Jewry were their allies when critical issues were on London's agenda.

The AJA did not end its involvement with external affairs. After the split it established the General Purpose and Foreign Committee under Leonard Stein, the AJA president, and so informed the Foreign Office. Furthermore, the AJA joined the NCRNT as an independent body.[5] AJA leaders now embarked on a round of making contacts and establishing their own ground. Stein and Otto Schiff, for the AJA, met with Sir Herbert Emerson who promised to consult with the association on refugee issues.[6] The financial strength of the AJA was based on its close relations with the financially strong Jewish Colonisation Association (JCA)[7] and its foothold in distinguished and influential circles in British society. Rabbi Hertz served as vice president, a position he emphasized when he was a member of delegations that met with the heads of the government.[8] In order to prevent the rabbi from representing the AJA exclusively he was coopted for the first time to the BD Executive.[9]

Six British Jewish organizations now raised external issues with the government and legations and embassies in London: the BD, AJA, BSWJC, Agudat Israel, the Chief Rabbi's Religious Emergency Committee and the Political Department of the Jewish Agency.

There was no defined division of labor among them. Some had established interests in certain areas. Otherwise there was considerable overlapping, even on Palestine, presumably the exclusive bailiwick of the Jewish Agency, and Agudat Israel and the AJA; and even the BD intervened each from its own perspective. The Consultative Emergency Committee, set up at the end of 1942, did not function properly because it was ignored by the BSWJC and the AJA was not even invited to participate after the break-up of the JFC.[10]

An examination of the sources shows that the AJA's political activity was extremely limited and soon waned.[11] It began developing international connections and strengthened its ties to the anti-Zionist American Jewish Committee led by Judge Jacob Proskauer and with French Jewry's Alliance Israelite Universelle, but they were useless in these critical times. The heads of the AJA admitted their weakness. Thus they limited their goals to stemming the increasing WJC influence in the BD. According to the AJA, the moderate Brodetsky was a captive of his extreme Zionist colleagues. The AJA struggled for its independence and against the influence and dictates of the international Jewish organizations aimed more at the BSWJC than against the local branch of Agudat Israel.[12]

The BD leaders were concerned about the prospect of the AJA's independent and overlapping political activities. Thus after the dissolution of the JFC they sought a new framework of cooperation. However, the WJC and the AJA had an aversion to each other and the AJA resolved not to join in any activity "involving or implying cooperation with the World Jewish Congress."[13]

Thus it was necessary to enter into a tripartite agreement, with the BD in the middle, which held separate discussions with each body. The negotiations lasted three months and the AJA refused to accept any restricting conditions.[14] The point of contention with the BSWJC was the BD demand that its representatives alone be empowered to approach the British Government, a demand that was rejected.[15] Brodetsky tried to limit the AJA by proposing consultative cooperation within the framework of a BD subcommittee. This was also rejected and the AJA now displayed its independence by approaching external bodies.[16]

In April 1944, separate agreements were signed between the BD and the two other organizations. Mediated by Nachum Goldmann, an agreement with the WJC was signed by its European Division, which had been established to involve refugees in congress activities.[17] From the formal standpoint it was apparently more convenient for the BD to sign an agreement with the European Division than with an organization that bore the name *British* Section. The arrangement called for an obligatory exchange of information and occasional consultations. The information, unless decided otherwise, would remain confidential. In actuality each organization acted independently.[18] Thus the BD waived its demand for exclusive representation in external affairs. According to the BSWJC the agreement was neither sound nor sufficient, but it was hoped that a period of quiet work would ensue.[19]

The BD agreement with the AJA also involved an exchange of information, meetings and consultations. There were also limiting clauses, apparently as a result of BD pressure. One clause freed each organization from the obligation to consult with the others if there was an urgent need to take action. Thus this agreement, too, allowed for independent action. The other clause made it obligatory to hold prior consultations before any political decision on problems concerning the postwar period. In this way the BD Zionists believed it would be possible to forestall the adoption of positions inimical to Zionism.[20] Consequently a formal balance was reached between the different bodies, but the lack of detailed clauses impeded the anticipated cooperation. The organizations submitted complaints, mainly against the BD, about violations of the agreement.

By May 1944, shortly after the agreements were signed, the BSWJC complained that the BD had submitted a memorandum to the Foreign Office and the prime ministers of the Dominions about issues such as defining the crimes committed against the Jews and the enactment of laws against anti-Semitic propaganda, without prior consultations. Moreover, Brodetsky and his colleagues approached the Soviet ambassador and the United Nations War Crimes Commission over matters concerning Jews outside Britain when according to the BSWJC's Easterman, his organization, because it represented all Jewish communities, should deal with such issues. Easterman threatened to annul the agreement if it was not grounded in practical activities and he proposed holding regular weekly advisory meetings. In reply, Brotman argued that the BSWJC had violated the agreement when it contacted the Soviet ambassador. A contentious correspondence ensued between the secretaries of the two organizations. Furthermore, Easterman suspected Brodetsky of undermining the BSWJC. He was certain that Brodetsky had instigated the NCRNT's inimical attitude toward the WJC and believed that the "Committee appears to be merely another vehicle for Brodetsky's antics."[21] This was a clear confrontation between different principles: that for which the WJC was established, to represent World Jewry; and the view of a proud Anglo-Jewry as guardians of suffering Jews, wherever they may be, as was exemplified by Sir Moses Montefiore.

The agreement with the AJA was certainly an achievement in that its status was recognized by the central British Jewish organization. Be that as it may, their relations were shaky. The AJA, too, complained about the violation of the agreement by the submission of the memorandum to the Dominions without prior consultation. They were also upset over the FAC's handling of the problem of the Jewish soldiers who had deserted the Polish army in the spring of 1944. In response, Stein, Rothschild and Lord Bearsted, for the AJA, met with Polish Foreign Minister Tadeusz Romer to press for the retraction of the verdict against the Jewish soldiers.[22]

The attitude of the authorities to the proliferation of Jewish representations was not uniform. The Foreign Office expressed annoyance over the proliferation of entreaties from different Jewish sources.[23] Refugee Commissioner Emerson, on the other hand, appreciated the elaboration of the many facets of the refugee problem presented by "a hundred Jewish organizations,"[24] but requested that a uniform Jewish delegation attend the regular monthly meetings with him under the auspices of the IGCR. The Jewish organizations, however, did not succeed in reaching agreement. Because it opposed mixing welfare with political activities, the Central Council for Jewish Refugees under Otto Schiff insisted that it be represented separately. The WJC argued that because of its international status it should be granted the same right. Lady Reading even thought that the Americans might frown upon the prospect of a Jewish representation under the British flag on an international body. Her words were aimed against the BD and the AJA. The Jewish Agency, for its part, demanded the right of separate representation by virtue of its political status as recognized by the Mandate.[25]

For whatever the reason, at its first meeting early in July, the new BD plenary resolved to issue an appreciation of the government for the rescue measures, however limited, adopted in the wake of the Bermuda Conference. This position, however, could not be maintained very long. By October Brodetsky expressed despair over political activities because of Whitehall's meager response. After this admission of failure a BD member raised a lack of confidence motion against the Executive. After the BD Constitutional Committee ruled that there were no legal grounds for the move, the same member proposed obligating the president to establish a rescue and rehabilitation council along with prominent Jewish figures outside the BD. Brodetsky rejected the proposal. He argued that it was not the handling of the problem that was defective, but that the Germans and their allies had rejected all the rescue proposals submitted by Britain and the United States. On the other hand, the Zionist representative, Dr S. Levenberg, said that it was clear from the announcements of the Foreign Office and the IGCR that the refugee problem was not being dealt with properly. According to Levenberg, the time had come for the Jews of Britain to openly state their stand on the issue. Brodetsky cautioned against saying anything unfair about government officials despite the insignificant achievements.[26]

Brodetsky consistently maintained that the best way of achieving anything was to induce the government to consider the stand of the British Jewish community. He attempted to persuade the plenary that "whatever was possible in the present situation to do was done."[27]

Brodetsky believed that the BD was a great asset because it was the major independent representative of the Jewish community. Moreover, it had a long venerable tradition and was in contact with one of the most powerful governments. It was in order to preserve and strengthen this crucial asset that he entered into a confrontation with the competing Jewish organizations, the BSWJC and the AJA, which were vying with the BD for supremacy. As to the BD's lackluster political results, Brodetsky explained: "When you are dealing with governments you must not put any government in a position in which it finds itself unable to pull out its feet without creating a position of great difficulty for itself. You are dealing with dynamite in this matter."

This was when the Holocaust was gripping Hungarian Jewry. But Brodetsky, the conformist and loyalist, considered it necessary to defend the government. He contended that the complex relations between the Allies toward the end of the war, and the critical hour before the opening of the second front, was difficult for the government, hence the scanty results of the BD's efforts.[28]

The Political Struggles of the National Committee for Rescue from Nazi Terror

Despite Brodetsky's display, at this time the BD cut down its independent political activity and its FAC mainly dealt with the preparation of material for the postwar period. The BD was well-represented in the NCRNT. The NCRNT included members of both Houses of Parliament and as a non-sectarian organization it could handle two objectives: pressuring the authorities and mobilizing public opinion so that it, too, apply pressure on the decision-makers.

After the bitter truth of the Bermuda Conference was exposed the NCRNT felt helpless. Toward the summer of 1943, when the situation in the Balkans deteriorated, its executive felt that it would be more beneficial to personally approach the relevant ministers rather than appeal to the public at rallies. However, at the end of July 1943 Rathbone expressed her deep disappointment at the government and the NCRNT because nothing had been accomplished. The ministers were elusive and the meetings with them were occasional and brief. The government apparatus worked slowly, refused to refer to experts on the issues it dealt with and considered the NCRNT a nuisance led by amateurs. Eden refused to receive parliamentarians representing the organization. He referred them to his deputy, Law, who made assurances only about secondary issues. Rathbone thought it was high time the NCRNT changed its tactics.[29]

The committee, however, feared that it would not be able to arouse the masses. It is remarkable that at the same time it published a lukewarm brochure, *Fourth Front*. No reference was made to the government and it heaped praise onto Emerson.[30] It may be that the committee was influenced by the attitude of the BD as expressed by the plenum resolution.

Rathbone refused to accept the committee's lassitude. On October 1, 1943, she distributed a memorandum among her colleagues listing the government's failures: It had not protected the Jews in northern Italy; had not provided ships for the transport of refugees from Spain to Palestine; and had done nothing to prevent the expulsion of the Jews from the Balkans. It had not issued guarantees to the Swiss to accept refugees on a temporary basis, neither had it done anything to further the Adler–Rudel Scheme to rescue children by sending them to neutral Sweden, and it had not even relaxed the restrictions on the entry of refugees into Britain.[31] Not even minor promises were kept. Rathbone demanded that a public campaign for rescue funds be carried out so that the committee have an added dimension such as that enjoyed by the Joint Distribution Committee and the JCA. These funds would support organizational activities throughout the country, distribute literature, and fund actual rescue activities such as the evacuation of Danish Jewry in that same month of October 1943.[32] This proposal was never accepted. The sum of the committee's accomplishments were the sending of a letter to Churchill and meetings with Foreign Office officials and Emerson. This development spurred Victor Gollancz to demand "an extremely militant attitude both inside and outside the House of Commons." Consequently, Rathbone drafted a militant brochure to be distributed among the public.[33]

The government tried to prevent a renewed storming of Parliament by "refugee enthusiasts." Now they raised the demand that the promise to issue guarantees to neutral states to facilitate the absorption of refugees be instituted immediately. The Foreign Office made sure to warn Rathbone that a parliamentary query on the issue might be harmful. By way of compromise Rathbone suggested that the government announce that the issuance of guarantees was being actively discussed.[34]

Brodetsky accompanied Rathbone and her associates in the different delegations. They met with Emerson, who disclosed the nature of the guarantees that Britain and the United States were supposed to issue to the neutral countries. It was in line with Eden's views: After the war the powers would provide suitable conditions for the repatriation of the refugees. Rathbone argued that the enemy would conclude from this declaration that it could continue its acts of cruelty without concern. The assurance would not be acceptable to the neutral states; neither would the European governments intent on getting rid of their Jews let them leave (i.e., rather let them die where they were) because of the dread of their return after the war. Why don't Britain and the United States undertake to accept the refugees who could not return to their native lands after the war, they argued.[35]

A parliamentary delegation led by Rathbone was finally received by Eden who also asked the heads of Foreign, Colonial, and Home Office departments to attend. The only Jew at the meeting was Lord Melchett. Rathbone again raised the issue of guarantees. She demanded that the conclusions of the Danish example be drawn; that Jews be ferreted into Britain, and the route taken by downed British flyers from France to Spain be used. The delegation also requested that more Jews be permitted to enter Palestine. According to the report of the meeting, Eden, using his diplomatic talents, again succeeded in creating an atmosphere of tranquility. Appealing to patriotic sentiments he maintained that of primary importance was the safety of soldiers escaping from the enemy and the lives of POWs in Germans camps. One must, of course, also consider what may be of benefit to the Jews themselves. If too many broadcasts were made or British visas issued their lives might be endangered. Furthermore, the government had no power over matters such as the Adler–Rudel Scheme. That was a matter to be dealt with by Emerson's commission and the Swedish Government. As to increased immigration to Palestine, weren't the Turks to blame for limiting the numbers of Jews making there way eastward?[36]

In January 1944, Rathbone's organization distributed a brochure describing a plan to save Jews, but it had few innovations. There were only ten clauses (the "Ten Points Programme"), the last of which demanded "that the British contribution to the work of rescue should be the speediest and most generous possible without delaying victory."[37]

The position of Rathbone and her colleagues underwent some ups and downs. Because of government influence at times they moderated their stand, at others it was more forceful. Rathbone was unflagging and refused to let the committee fade. After she "recovered" from the meeting with Eden a new strongly-worded brochure, *Continuing Terror – How to Rescue Hitler's Victims*, was issued. The Foreign Office was not at all pleased with this brochure. Its officials suggested coming openly out against Rathbone and her organization, which seemed to be casting Hitler's crimes onto a British Government fighting for its life.[38] It would seem that the Jewish members of Rathbone's organization, with the exception of Victor Gollancz, were not particular active at this time in the organization.

The Struggle for a New Declaration and Warning Broadcasts

During the period under discussion the BSWJC, sensitive to all issues involving the European Jewry, stepped up its activities considerably. In the first months after the Bermuda Conference disappointment sank deeply in wide circles.[39] Even Eduard Benes, who had not been a partner to Chaim Weizmann's pessimism over the situation of the Jews of Europe, agreed that the conference was a disappointment. The Foreign Office's Richard Law and Dr Benes contended that the US State Department had delayed implementing the conference's decisions for political reasons. Hence it was suggested that Easterman and Barou address a dramatic appeal to President Roosevelt in the name of the King of Norway, the Queen of Holland, and the presidents of Poland and Czechoslovakia. Benes was opposed. He was afraid that the move might be leaked to the American press and that a negative American reply would be an insult to the heads of state. Benes suggested sufficing with making allusions to the US ambassador that such an appeal was being considered.[40]

After the aborted proposal the heads of the BSWJC tried another tactic, one which was not dependent on any muddling Anglo-American cooperation: radio broadcasts warning of retribution. The BBC occasionally issued such warnings to the enemy about its atrocities. Ernst Frischer, a Jewish member of the Czechoslovakian State Council, believed that the alleviations in the Theresienstadt Ghetto in the summer of 1943 were the outcome of such warnings or perhaps even of the United Nations December 1942 declaration. Consequently, he called for the WJC to strive for another public declaration. Easterman had but recently pressed in that direction. But according to Frischer, not hard enough, because the situation in Europe was deteriorating rapidly. Frischer had obtained a report that Riegner had written about the atrocities in the camps at Birkenau (Auschwitz) where synthetic rubber plants were operating. Easterman rushed the information to Law because he believed that it could help the war effort.

In the accompanying letter the BSWJC asked for approval to transfer money and provisions to the Jews in Europe through the International Red Cross. In his reply, Law did not even relate to the strategic information supplied by Easterman. Easterman had not mentioned the atrocities being committed in Birkenau. His main objective was to get a new declaration and he kept on singlemindedly pressing the Foreign Office.[41] After Law's secretary, Paul Grey, resisted issuing a "Jewish" declaration Easterman was prepared to accept a general declaration on condition that the December 17, 1942 declaration be mentioned.[42]

When he received no reply, Easterman rushed a further letter to Law. He accepted the argument that rescue efforts were being delayed by the exigencies of war, but that was not an excuse for delaying a warning declaration. Fully a month and a half later, on October 25, the Foreign Office, steadfast in its position, replied that a declaration was an issue between a number of governments.[43]

Easterman persevered. He met with the Soviet ambassador, Ivan Maisky, who had recently been appointed deputy foreign minister and was about to return to Moscow. He explained that it was imperative to renew the declaration of eight months before and requested that even now the Soviets participate.[44]

Easterman also approached a number of the foreign ministers of the governments-in-exile, but they, too, turned down his request. Even the Czechoslovak Jan Masaryk, a philo-semite, repeated the same refrain: "In the first place it was pointed out that in no case could any distinction be drawn between the persecuted Jews and other inhabitants . . . "[45] In his despair Easterman was prepared to accept a general declaration on condition that there be some mention of the Jews, because their destruction was based on doctrinaire and not political reasons. According to Easterman the many declarations and warnings issued, but without mention of the Jews, had left the impression that the world had abandoned them.[46]

Meanwhile, the Foreign Office was dealing with Easterman's appeal because of information that Hitler was planning to destroy all the Jews by the end of the war. They found difficulty, however, retrieving the spirit of December 17, 1942 and agreeing to an explicit mention of Jewish travail. Now the Dutch Government was raising obstacles against "discrimination" in favor of the Jews.

At the Foreign Office a declaration of censure was being drafted to be issued at the planned Moscow summit by Stalin, Churchill and Roosevelt. It declared that all those responsible for the atrocities would be brought to justice. The Foreign Office regarded this as meeting the WJC halfway. Churchill, however, rejected the Anglo-Dutch formula and demanded a "Jewish" declaration such as that of December 17, 1942. However, as the summit date drew near the prime minister was nudged back into *realpolitik*. His officials proposed to Stalin and Roosevelt that a sharp declaration of condemnation be issued warning the Germans and their lackeys of dire punishment over their cruelty. The officials argued that the Jews were included even without their explicit mention.[47]

On the anniversary of the December 17 declaration Easterman warned the Foreign Office about an abandonment of the Jews, since no mention of them was contained in the condemnation of war crimes at the Moscow summit on November 2, 1943.[48] Easterman pressured the new Soviet ambassador, Fyodor Gusev, but was told that according to the Moscow warning all acts against civilian populations, including those against the Jews, would be punished.[49] The critical point in the Moscow War Crimes Declaration was the explicit pledge of vengeance for the war crimes committed against Cretan peasants, but no mention was made of the Final Solution. From this the Nazi leaders could conclude that the Allies were apathetic to the fate of the Jews.[50]

Thus the BSWJC was concerned about the Moscow declaration, and it struggled its amendment. Although Dr Nachum Goldmann and Dr Arieh Tartakower, two WJC leaders then in London, were aware of the danger, they advised against a further appeal to Churchill. The Marchioness of Reading did not follow their advice. On February 22, 1944 she issued a moving appeal to the prime minister, again through his close associate Information Minister Brendan Bracken. Lady Reading wrote that it was necessary "to leave no stone unturned" in the effort to save the remnant of European Jewry. She suggested that a ceremonial joint warning of the three major Allied leaders might deter the murderers, and that those carrying out the slaughter of the Jews would know that the Allies stood at the side of the victims. She also appealed to Churchill to permit the transfer of funds to the Polish underground to help conceal and smuggle Jews away from the Nazis. Her letter hinted at US approval of such a move. "I appeal to bring this to the personal knowledge of the Prime Minister; our hope lies in him; please do not fail us." "Friend" Bracken, however, once again took the short-cut and gave the letter directly to the Foreign Office.[51]

That same day, Lady Reading's brother and BSWJC deputy president, Lord Melchett, sent a similar letter to Eden, who had a reply: The government was awaiting the opinion of the Polish Government about the transfer of funds to the underground; as to a renewed declaration, serious negotiations were in progress with the United States. Eden mentioned his doubts about the wisdom of such a declaration, because it might harden the enemy's heart.[52]

The British Government could no longer withhold issuing a declaration, not necessarily because of the lobbying of Rathbone's group. There was a new factor to contend with: the War Refugee Board (WRB) established by the US Government in January 1944. Its executive director, the energetic John Pehle, formulated a declaration for the president and Britain was asked to participate. When the Foreign Office advised the Americans that the rhetoric about Jewish suffering was likely to work to their disadvantage, Pehle wrote a furious note such, that the State Department modified it into a "more friendly and courteous tone." Pehle claimed the Foreign Office's reasoning intimated to Berlin that the Allies had no objection to the destruction of the Jews.[53] Consequently Eden relented and agreed to an "amended," though moderate declaration. The Foreign Office, however, made strong efforts to moderate its language. It demanded that the words "*war* crimes" be cited in connection with the Jews in order to exclude the Jewish citizens of Germany. After all, crimes committed against a country's own citizens were not war crimes as such. Those crimes should be considered internal affairs. Otherwise it would harm the principle of the Jews remaining attached to their original citizenship in each and every country and related to accordingly. In this way a distinction could be made between the Jewish citizens of Germany and those of the ally Poland. Foreign Office officials still contended that warning the Germans would do harm and recommended that it should be aimed only at the Germans' satellite states. The cat was out of the bag. Eden disclosed to his War Cabinet Refugee Committee colleagues that the consequence of such a declaration "is likely to be redoubled pressure on us for measures of rescue." However, for lack of an alternative Eden finally recommended joining the United States in a declaration.[54]

On March 24, Roosevelt issued a stirring declaration mentioning the atrocities which had commenced in Hungary. On March 30, Eden issued one more reserved to the House of Commons warning the Quislings not to cooperate with the Nazis. Like the previous declaration it, too, was in response to a private question tabled by Sidney Silverman. The warning was directed to the policy of destruction in general. As to the oppression of the Jews, it "has in particular been of unexampled horror and intensity." According to Randall's minutes this sentence was entered only at the last minute for fear of "the Jew enthusiasts."[55]

The Russians, the third partner to the Moscow War Crimes declaration, tried in vain to convince the others to change their stand and refused to issue a comparable statement. According to its London embassy clerks, the Russians had suggested issuing a joint declaration and had been insulted by the discussions held by Britain and the United States without them.[56] The suddenness of the president's declaration put pressure on London and Moscow. We have seen London's reaction. Moscow, being offended, did not react at all. Its position was far better because it had, in the words of a Foreign Office official, no Jewish "pressure groups."[57]

In all events, an expression of self-satisfaction from Easterman was not long in coming. He sent his BSWJC Executive colleagues and Council copies of a congratulatory letter that Lord Melchett had sent him on "a very successful piece of work."[58] There is room to surmise that Easterman had not been made privy to the negotiations with Washington that had led to the declaration.

From time to time the idea came up of broadcasting warnings or airdropping leaflets to deter the murderers and encourage the partisans and civilian populations to undertake rescue efforts, or at least not cooperate with the Jews' killers. A year earlier, in March 1943, when the information about the transports of Jews eastward increased, D. Robertson MP demanded that Eden order daily radio warnings for a month. The Foreign Office turned it down.[59]

Frischer tried to reach an agreement directly with the BBC, but he, too, was turned down. Easterman now set his sights on the same objective.[60] From March 1943 nothing was heard about the endeavors to issue radio warnings. Then, in October of that year, intelligence about the expulsion of Greek Jews to the land of slaughter reached London. Now there was a positive response to Easterman's request: The Germans were warned that the day of judgment was nigh. However, an appeal to broadcast a call to the Greeks to come to the Jews' aid was turned down. The repeated broadcasts made a great impression on the BSWJC and Easterman sent flattering letters to the relevant Foreign Office official.[61]

The good will displayed by the readiness to use the BBC did not last long. In December 1943, Silverman was informed about the hunt in France by the Germans and their French collaborators for concealed Jewish children. Both Easterman and Joseph Linton of the Jewish Agency asked the Foreign Office to broadcast an appeal to the French people, but were refused with the reasoning that broadcasts could intensify the tragedy. The Foreign Office official wrote in the minutes that this was a real possibility, and for the same reason Britain stopped broadcasting warnings concerning the Jews of Greece.[62] In countering the arguments of the BBC's experts, Easterman wrote to the Archbishop of Canterbury, whose help he was soliciting for broadcasts to the Germans, that the terror against the Jews was so intense it could get no worse, and that broadcast warnings could only help.[63]

Be that as it may, Easterman expressed a different view in a letter to the Foreign Office. He admitted that broadcasts to the Germans would not be of much help, but that an appeal to the French would hearten those who were hiding children. In the wake of Easterman's incessant intense pressure the Foreign Office acceded and indicated that its propaganda experts would determine the content of the broadcast at the appropriate time. The Foreign Office's intention was to combine the issue of rescuing Jewish children with an appeal to the French to assist evacuees in the framework of the military preparations for the invasion.[64]

The broadcast dispute came up again during the German invasion of Hungary in 1944. The BSWJC pressed for broadcasts to the Hungarian people. In response to its request the Archbishop of Canterbury sent a speech to the BBC to be broadcast to the Christians in Hungary. Easterman submitted Riegner's opinion to Undersecretary Law, that Eden's and other warnings should be repeatedly beamed at Hungary. According to Easterman, Riegner had intimate knowledge of the Hungarian situation and knew what could be of benefit. The Foreign Office, however, had its reservations.[65]

Activities on Behalf of the Jews of France, Italy and Transnistria in the Wake of Changes at the Front

The Foreign Office adhered to the principle of not giving the Jews any leeway even in the more modest BSWJC requests.

In September 1943, Easterman asked the Foreign Office to recommend that the censor approve the maintenance of an information service through the WJC office in Geneva for relatives of Jews in Britain living on the continent. Some officials argued that a letter service might jeopardize the recipients. The main objection, however, was voiced by Randall of the Foreign Office Refugee Department. He suspected that Easterman was preparing the ground for the Zionist demand for the Jews to have a recognized national status. The request was refused. The Foreign Office suggested to Easterman that the Jews suffice with the services of the Red Cross and the Thomas Cook travel agency.[66]

At another time "the persistent Mr. Easterman" drew attention to the danger hovering over the heads of the Jews of France and the need to save the ten thousand Jews of Turkish origin living there. Indeed, the Turks decreed that their citizenship was not to be renewed, but happily the French still recognized them as Turkish nationals. Easterman appealed to George Hall, parliamentary undersecretary at the Foreign Office, to ask Ankara to renew their citizenship in order to save them from expulsion to the death camps. Randall again interfered and recommended not approaching the Turks. His recommendation was accepted.[67]

Between 1943 and 1944, thousands of Jewish children went into hiding in France. Different organizations saw to their concealment and with Berne's consent hundreds began making their way to Switzerland. Dr Gustaw Kuhlmann, Emerson's Swiss deputy, returned from Switzerland in February 1944. He advised Emerson, who in a detailed memorandum analyzed the situation in France and Switzerland and concluded that the IGCR could assist in the financial upkeep of the children if the blockade authorities approved the transfer of funds. In the meanwhile, the BSWJC thought that it would be able to smuggle some of the children to Spain. The leaders of the Free French in London agreed that the WJC spirit two emissaries into France to assist in the evacuation on condition that the British approve. The Foreign Office refused to do so. It argued that a Jewish organization could not be allowed to engage in rescue operations or examine possible escape routes. There was a note of annoyance in Randall's minutes: "We can't have the World Jewish Congress butting in here."

The Foreign Office and the intelligence services believed that a refugee flow along the France–Spain escape routes could endanger the exit of people vital for the war effort, presumably for the invasion preparations. The Foreign Office referred Easterman to Emerson and Dr Gustaw Kuhlmann, who had been entrusted by the Bermuda Conference with wide authority. Actually, the issue was on the agenda of discussions between the governments of Britain and the United States.[68]

The advance of the Allies into enemy territory in 1943 created a new situation and raised Jewish hopes, and the Jewish organizations in London began working on the diplomatic level.

In the summer of 1943, the Allies invaded Italy. The BD and BSWJC appealed to the British legate at the Vatican to ask the Pope to be concerned with the fate of the Jews during the battles. At the end of June 1943, the Foreign Office told the Jewish organizations that the Pope had prevented the expulsion of the Jews from Italy, even those originally from Poland. Szwarcbart thought that the pressure applied by the BD had led to greater results than the attempts of the Polish Foreign Ministry to obtain the Pope's help.[69]

After Mussolini's downfall there was fear that the Germans would take over the northern Italy and Croatia. Fifty thousand Jews would then be in danger of their lives. Brodetsky asked Richard Law to warn the Italians against turning refugees over to the Germans, but Law immediately refused. The Allied commander warned the Italians about the treatment of prisoners of war, but the warning was not extended to include all civilians. Moreover, the endangered civilians were not British or Allied citizens. The same rule applied to the warnings issued to the Balkan governments via Switzerland. The policy not to relate to endangered non-British civilians had an advantage, Law added, because the requested warning might draw the attention of the Germans to the Jews.[70]

As early as 1943, there was contact with Rumania over the possibility of the exit of seventy thousand Jewish refugees from Transnistria to Palestine in return for a large ransom. Weizmann discussed this possibility with the State Department. The Foreign Office was deeply concerned both because of its Palestine policy and fear for the breakdown of the economic blockade. In general they concluded that at this stage "any large-scale solution of the Jewish Problem" should not be considered. Such an operation, according to the Foreign Office, would jeopardize the war effort and it was certain that Lord Halifax would succeed in convincing Weizmann to accept the British stand.[71]

With the Russian advance in the winter of 1943, the Rumanian stand changed and they put out feelers to the Western powers about the price of peace. Easterman thought that the hour was ripe and he again raised the issue of the ransom of the Jews in Transnistria. He was turned down because the Americans believed that ransom was blackmail. They were, however, willing to send a warning to the Jon Antonescu regime via the diplomatic route that had been opened with Rumania.[72] The danger hanging over the Jews of Transnistria deepened in the first months of 1944. The Foreign Office was asked to issue a warning to the Rumanians because the Jews were caught in a death trap. The Foreign Office replied that the warnings had been inflated and suggested that the WJC itself approach the governments of the United States and the Soviet Union. The Foreign Office had ruled that out since the WJC was not a British institution it could approach governments at its will.[73]

It would appear that the lack of willingness to apply concentrated pressure on Rumania, which had been soundly pounded and was on the verge of surrender, derived from a warning of Randall's to the Colonial Office. Randall argued that if the British assumed any obligations toward Turkey concerning refugees liable to reach its territory, they would be confronted by a flow of refugees eastward from Rumania and Bulgaria. This would pose problems for Britain: Ships would be needed to transport the refugees; the White Paper entry quota for Palestine would be filled up; and the Hagana, the illegal Jewish military force, would gain in strength. The flooding of Palestine with Jews would cause unrest throughout the Middle East and would require the deployment of troops who would otherwise be sent to invade Europe. Nonetheless, for humanitarian reasons the Turks should be informed that all refugees reaching its territory would be issued Palestine entry certificates, at the Jewish Agency's request, so that they might issue transit visas.[74] But in order to be correct with all sides the British ambassador in Ankara was instructed to inform the Turkish foreign minister, but only orally, about the humanitarian decision. He was to add that if the flow of refugees to Turkey increased the British Government would reconsider its policy. The Jewish Agency for Palestine was also informed about the change in policy and was requested to keep it secret.[75]

Silverman and Easterman approached Eduard Benes in their quest to help the Jews of Transnistria because of his close ties to Stalin. They appealed to him to ask the Russians to make the exit of Jews from Transnistria a precondition of their negotiations with Rumania. Secondly, they asked Benes to try to persuade Stalin to agree to emigration to Palestine; and thirdly, that he order the Red Army to rescue Jews during its advance. Benes did not believe that the Russians would agree to this Jewish precondition for the negotiations with Rumania. Neither did he believe that the Nazi satellites would seriously oppose the Germans on the Jewish question, or that the partisans and paratroopers could assist. Nonetheless, he promised to approach Stalin.[76] Easterman also appealed to the Soviet ambassador, but was only given vague assurances.[77]

The BD also dealt with these issues. Brodetsky met with the Soviet ambassador and discussed the public warning to Rumania and Hungary and the appeal to the populace to grant refuge to Jews. The ambassador replied that his country would not issue a warning to the nations under the Nazi regime.[78]   Externally, the BSWJC pointed to its political "gains." The following astonishing remarks appeared in a report presented to the BSWJC council on December 13, 1943: "No details can be given of these deliberations and activities. It can, however, be stated that the Executive has been successful in finding a way to send relief on a large scale and with little delay to the Jews in Southeastern Europe."[79]

A different tone appears in a letter of Easterman's to Lady Reading: Success should not be expected. He lists a series of failures from Greece and Bulgaria to Sweden. He does not, however, throw up his hands, but suggests keeping up the pressure on the United Nations and especially on the Foreign Office. He also referred to the proposal of appealing to the Rumanians to let the Jews go.[80]

The Council for Rescue of the Jewish Population in Poland

It was clear that the chances of any significant help from abroad for the remnant of Polish Jewry were virtually nil. The only escape route led to

Hungary. Its regime treated the refugees who arrived from Slovakia and Poland tolerably, a situation that changed only after the German occupation in March 1944. Dr Szwarcbart succeeded in obtaining the concession of the Polish government-in-exile for the underground to assist Jews fleeing to Hungary. Swiss currency was needed to bribe both Germans and Hungarians. Szwarcbart appealed passionately to the British Government to help but a few thousand of the remnant of Polish Jewry to escape. He did not ask for monetary assistance, for that could be obtained from Jewish organizations. What was required was a permit to transfer funds through the blockade. Randall expressed deep sympathy, but mulled over measures to torpedo the request. He understood from the meeting with Szwarcbart that the Polish Government preferred averting the submission of an official request. He advised his colleagues not to turn Szwarcbart down because then he might appeal to the Americans. And due to the upcoming elections the Americans were purporting to be "the champions of humanitarian schemes, held back only by British red tape." Thus British officials understood that for political reasons it would be difficult to refuse Szwarcbart's request.[81]

Now the ball was passed to other ministries for their opinion. The Treasury was sympathetic, believing that avenues to extend aid to potential escapees must be found. The Ministry of Economic Warfare (MEW), on the other hand, opposed acceding to Szwarcbart. The MEW was prepared to look again into the request if the Polish Government agreed to allocate only Hungarian currency for this purpose. The proposal was rejected immediately by Szwarcbart because those taking bribes were voracious for currency. The two economic ministries were particularly concerned about the black market in German exit visas that Jews used at the end of the 1942. At the time the MEW intervened vigorously and boasted of being "unexpectedly successful in suppressing" that black market. Now they couldn't very well lend a hand in canceling such a fine achievement.[82]

The tactics used by H.M. Ministry for Economic Warfare to win such an illustrious victory over such "a dangerous enemy" are not listed in the sources. One needn't stress that smearing a palm was hardly an economically strategic hazard.

In order to strengthen Szwarcbart's hand and do something to save the remnant of Polish Jewry, Lady Reading appealed to Bracken and Lord Melchett to Eden. Eden avoided a clear response. He said that negotiations were still in progress with the Polish Government and Dr Szwarcbart. As to Bracken, he as usual sent Lady Reading's letter on to the Foreign Office and not, as she had asked, to Churchill.[83] We have previously referred to these letters in connection to the request for a new declaration. Both requests were regarded as extremely important. No other sources cite this activity of Szwarcbart's and it may be assumed that the issue was dropped.

Later, on June 17, 1944, the Polish Government established the Council for Rescue of the Jewish Population in Poland, and assigned the task of preparing a budget proposal to Dr E. Scherer, a Bund representative on the Polish National Council. Scherer believed that two to four million dollars would be enough to ransom the Jews from all over Europe who were still concentrated in Poland. He thought it would be possible to get 60 percent of the sum from the Polish Government and 40 percent from Jewish contributions. For the latter amount he approached the Joint in New York. The American Embassy in London asked the opinion of the Foreign Office, whose officials doubted the intentions of the Polish Government.[84] No further historical material exists for this subject. The Foreign Office then had information that there was a real possibility for Jews to escape the concentration camps and find places to hide. A source they considered reliable, Sir Herbert Emerson, had informed them that the price for a forged document was $400 and for liberation from the camps $500. Sir Herbert continued, "The work is necessarily on a limited scale, but it could be increased if more resources were availabl."[85] The month was March 1944.

The last knell of the Council for Rescue of the Jewish Population in Poland is found in a letter to Eden. Written on official Republic of Poland stationery, it cried out for the rescue of the remaining Jews: The remnant that had fought in the Warsaw Ghetto was now fighting for the liberation of Warsaw. Since the letter did not raise proposals for action the officials in the Foreign Office declined to respond.[86]

This was at the end of September 1944. In August, the Polish underground revolt against the Germans was brutally quelled. The battles were fought on the streets of Warsaw, which was razed to its foundations. By the end of September it was clear that the revolt was petering out. Hundreds of thousands of Warsaw residents fled or were expelled and tens of thousands were killed. How many Jews were there to be saved? Very few were still hiding in the city after the Warsaw Ghetto Uprising of fifteen months before. London followed the events of the Polish underground revolt in Warsaw, day by day and hour by hour. The British air force even airdropped aid to the rebels.

British Adherence and American Withdrawal from the Bermuda Conference Policy

As a rule, in the period under discussion the British Government did not deviate fundamentally from its stand on the Jews of Europe, either in principle or in practical terms. The exception was Palestine immigration policy. Previously we described the "relaxation" of restrictions in relation to refugees making their way to Palestine after the *Struma* ship disaster and some more concession for *aliya* via Turkey in March 1944. The British Government adhered to the White Paper immigration quota and regulated *aliya* accordingly. Great generosity was not displayed. It presented the *aliya*, a policy set before the war and meant to limit Jewish entry in Palestine, as its significant contribution to the rescue effort. Thus in order to curb the utilization of the White Paper framework immigration quota the British opposed emigration from countries where Jews were not in immediate danger.[87]

In September 1943, Sir Jonah Walker Smith MP demanded in the name of Christian conscience that the Germans be asked to let the Jews go. Again the government's response was evasive. At the Bermuda Conference it had been categorically resolved not to enter into negotiations with the Germans on behalf of the oppressed. And indeed "from our point of view, fortunately, the German Government appear to be intending to persist in their refusal to allow Jews to leave Germany."[88] However, on February 4, 1944 the Swiss Government conveyed a letter to the British legation in Berne with a proposal to transfer 5,000 Jew to Britain in an exchange framework. The Germans, who had initiated the proposal, made one condition: that these Jews not continue on to Palestine in order not to impinge on the sensibilities and interests of the Arabs.[89] The British minister did not rush the proposal off to London and it reached the Foreign Office only at the beginning of March. The ministry's clerks advised against revealing the proposal to the pro-Jewish lobbies as they considered it an invitation to blackmail.[90] Moreover, they stated in their minutes that legal exchanges were in progress to exchange Germans for Palestinian Jews. If the Germans announced the British refusal it would lead to a deterioration in the relations between Rathbone's group and the government. In such a case the British would publicize the fact that 20,000 British citizens were still in Germany waiting to be exchanged and all would agree that they had priority over Jews. Therefore the Foreign and Home Offices decided on the bureaucratic level "to leave this feeler unanswered." It instructed the legation in Berne that the exchange "cannot be contemplated" and that the Swiss Government be informed "that at the present juncture at all events we should not wish any reply to be returned to the German exchange proposal."[91]

On the other hand, in January 1944 President Roosevelt announced the establishment of the War Refugee Board (WRB) under the Secretaries of the Treasury, State and War. Treasury Secretary Henry Morgenthau Jr., who had initiated its establishment, and recruited its staff from among his foremost officials. The Americans had broken the rules. The WRB's declared objective was "to take all measures within its power to rescue the victims of enemy oppression who are in imminent danger of death." This left no room for doubt about the purpose of WRB and it was invested with broad authority. Now that the president had emphasized the Jewish cause, the WRB had to struggle against the "Nazi plans to exterminate all the Jews."[92] The Foreign Office was surprised by the speed with which the WRB had been established. It made them nervous. The Americans had not only not bothered to consult with the British; they had not even informed the Foreign Office or the IGCR about the dramatic step. At first the Foreign Office thought that the move was inspired by the Zionist Revisionists led by Peter Bergson (the Palestinian Jew, Hillel Kook, who assumed the name Peter Bergson for his American activities) to the chagrin of the State Department and middle-of-the-road Zionists.[93] In a further evaluation Foreign Office experts concluded that "the affair is of limited US electoral interest." Thus in the election year the president had undertaken a "Zionist drive" which was liable to cause trouble in Palestine and conflict between the two Allies.[94] Whitehall was not yet aware of the serious shake-up in the US administration brought about by Morgenthau and his staff and which led, albeit tragically late in the day, to the establishment of the authoritative WRB.

Pro-Jewish groups stormed the Foreign Office demanding the establishment of a similar British authority.[95] The press called for cooperation with the WRB and criticized Emerson's IGCR.[96] Members of the NCRNT demanded in the House of Commons that the government follow the American example. Eden, unruffled, announced that his government had preceded the Americans when it established the War Cabinet Committee of Refugees as early as December 1942. Brazenly, he declared that this committee worked for the refugees' benefit and that its objectives were identical to those of the American president's new board. Moreover, there was no doubt in his mind that the British way was preferable.[97]

The American embassy sent an assuaging message to the Foreign Office explaining that combat units would not be used in rescue actions, but that rescue would ensue in the wake of battle. The embassy made assurances that the assistance rendered to the Nazis' victims would be "consistent with [the] successful prosecution of the war." The British were not reassured, especially since one of the heads of the WRB was the American war secretary.[98] At first, the Foreign Office decided to cooperate with the Americans and not be overly fastidious about approving rescue funds or other activities so long as there was no departure from the Bermuda obligations, such as compromising the IGCR and the war effort.[99] However, a number of approvals to transfer minor sums to feed Jews in Europe lit a warning light in the offices of the Ministry for Economic Warfare and raised suspicions that in its enthusiasm the WRB would eventually approve greater sums.[100] When the British ambassador in Washington reported that the WRB had approved the transfer of $700,000 from the Joint to the oppressed Jews of

Europe, Whitehall considered the step a gross departure from agreed policies, "even though they might not be of vital importance."[101] The
ambassador was told to make a cautious protest to the Secretary of State.
The British were careful not to damage the president's electoral efforts and
were afraid that the WRB would make the hard-line British stand public.
Its ambassador was instructed to propose exchanging the payment in
dollars for rescue and assistance with an IGCR credit system in order to
prevent hard currency from falling into the hands of the enemy. The British
Government proposed an investment of £500,000 for Emerson's
committee if the United States would invest a similar sum. Emerson was
so trusted by his country's policymakers that he was invited to participate
in the meetings of the War Cabinet Refugee Committee.[102]

The British Government did not succeed in strangling the activities of
the WRB. By May 1944 the Foreign Office understood that the WRB had
a dynamic of its own[103] and that it had no choice but to "grin and bear it."
The reports of the British ambassador in Ankara, D. E. Howard, were not
very encouraging. Ankara was the center of activities of organizations
involved in rescue and *aliya*. Now two American Jews were engaged in an
issue so sensitive to the British, the ambassador Lawrence Steinhardt and
the attach, for refugee affairs recently appointed by the WRB, Ira A.
Hirschmann. They threatened British Government interests when they
pressured the Turks to declare the right of entry for every fleeing Jew. In
order to help the Turks reach a positive decision the WRB promised to
fund the refugees' upkeep until a permanent home could be found for them.
Ambassador Howard found it difficult to stomach Steinhardt's and
Hirschmann's verve and wrote: "The whole business is rather typical of a
particular bad side of American life which I could only describe suitably
by using words which are not suitable for a semi-official letter . . . It is
partly electioneering propaganda and partly the American habit of bragging."[104]

The establishment of the WRB also distressed Emerson and his associates. Lord Winterton, chairman of the IGCR, complained to Eden that the
WRB was not consulting with his veteran organization which had amassed
great experience.[105] In the wake of the British Government's policy
Emerson entered into a cautious confrontation with the trespassing
Americans. He tried to prevent food from reaching the mouths of the
oppressed with whose welfare he was entrusted. He expressed his displea-
sure to the Red Cross about the purchase of food for Jews with Joint funds
and the permission of the WRB. While visiting Washington Emerson
formulated his opinion of the WRB, that was run by Morgenthau and his
staff, "mostly Jews." He admitted that it was established out of humanitarian urgency, but also out of a desire to win New York State for the
Democrats in the upcoming elections. He warned Eden that the WRB "in

a very real sense [was] the apple of Mr. Morgenthau's eye, and that if we wished to get anything substantial from Mr. Morgenthau we should be well advised to work with him over this comparatively small issue of war refugee policy."[106]

Various figures who worked within the framework of the WRB did not stint in publicizing their organization's activities. Clearly the strategy of this US government agency was a departure from the Bermuda resolutions. Morgenthau's staff went straight to the heart of the problems involved in rescuing Jews. The information and rumors that arrived from the "bragging" Americans gave Rathbone and her associates on the NCRNT no rest. On February 29, the NCRNT appealed to the public to attend a mass rally in London. *The Times* stated that the major demand would be the establishment of a refugee board on the American model and the appointment of refugee affairs attachés in the diplomatic representations. The main speakers were to be the Chief Rabbi, the Archbishop of York, and Members of Parliament. Panic struck the Foreign Office. Eden's assistant, Richard Law, invited two non-Jewish MPs to his office, Rathbone and D. R. Grenfell. Pushing patriotism to the hilt he warned them against praising the American measure and calling for rescue via the routes used by the partisans for escaping British airmen and Allied military personnel as it might put them in danger. He also asked them not to censure Turkey. Emerson was also drafted into the the attempt to restrain the Rathbone campaign.[107]

A well-attended public meeting took place at Central Hall, Westminster. The Archbishop of York, Dr Garbett, justified the saturation bombings of the enemy's cities as a measure that would accelerate the end of the war and bring relief to the multitudes of the oppressed. The archbishop also wanted to let the government know that it would be supported in every rescue step it took. The only Jewish speaker was Rabbi Hertz, who referred to Rathbone as "a veritable Deborah of our generation."

According to the report in *The Jewish Chronicle*, it seems that Rathbone had been influenced by the treatment she received at the Foreign Office. This was a tempered Rathbone who "did not charge the Government with indifference and passivity. She realizes the great difficulties besetting the task of rescue. But while they said to them Hush! Hush! and excelled in understatement, they seemed surprised and hurt when the public drew the conclusion that little or nothing was being done." The government lacked the "passion of conviction, fury of energy which alone overcomes obstacles," apparently a hint at the spirit prevailing in the American WRB. Under the slogan "They Shall Not Perish" the meeting urged the government to establish a British equivalent. Rathbone and her colleagues were uncompromising in this regard.[108]

In the period under discussion the external political activities of the BD diminished. Its leaders apparently relied on the efficiency of the non-sectarian NCRNT. The BSWJC, as was characteristic of this body, maintained incessant pressure while displaying a sensitivity to European events. The friction and overlapping of the two organizations continued, but eventually became less sharp, possibly because of the penetration of the BD by members of the BSWJC after the 1943 elections. Eventually an implicit division of labor evolved and neither delved into the defined arena of the other. The BD assumed responsibility for the food parcels sent via Portugal; no one interfered with the diplomatic activities of Harry Goodman in Ireland; the Chief Rabbi's Religious Emergency Council dealt with the rescue of the non-Zionist orthodox scholars; and the Jewish Agency handled *aliya*.

As to the government, it never gave in to the pressures from many sides appealing for an abandonment of the Bermuda Conference policy. It was careful not to be drawn into the American rescue activities but also not to offend them. The government sought a *modus vivendi* with the objective of maintaining the blockade on Europe's Jews. Whitehall did display greater flexibility over *aliya* and viewed it as Britain's contribution to the rescue efforts, but in all its steps it carefully maintained the policy of the White Paper.

Aid and Rescue Efforts to Comfort the Seablocked

Tell them that the Jews in the Ghettos are dying at the hands of the Nazi slaughterers with the bitter feeling that they are being let down by their brethren in Great Britain and the United States.

Food Supply

By the summer of 1941, the nations under the Axis heel were sorely feeling the effects of British blockade. Greece was the first to suffer. Much of its fleet had escaped to Allied ports, it was heavily dependent on food imports, and since its industry was of little use to the Germans' war machine they did very little to alleviate the food shortage. Britain, on other hand, because of Greece's valiant resistance on its side, felt a moral obligation to help. Moreover, they were afraid of a mass movement of hungry Greeks into Turkey and the creation of a refugee problem. Thus aid to Greece developed into a large-scale effort.[1]

Norway's situation was similar. Like the Greek merchant marine fleet Norway's also contributed to the war effort by transporting food and military supplies from the United States to Britain. Both fleets lost many ships to German U-Boat torpedoes. Neither was Belgium capable of meeting its food needs, but because of its developed arms industry the Nazis arranged a fairly regular supply. Belgium's major contribution to the Allies' war effort was the Congo's natural resources.

Because of the food shortage at home, the Belgian and Norwegian governments-in-exile opposed the strict British blockade, a stand supported by groups in the then-neutral United States. The British, however, rejected the American critics as isolationist, anti-British and pro-German followers of former president Herbert Hoover. Hoover, a Quaker, had organized aid for Belgium in World War I, and led American relief efforts after both world wars. In 1941 he initiated a campaign to extend aid to Belgium.[2]

The British permitted the shipping of wheat to Greece on Swedish ships throughout the war, but refused to relax the blockade for Norway and Belgium. The Belgians were so furious with Britain that they threatened to stop shipping vital raw materials from the Congo. Norwegian crews, on their part, threatened to moor their ships if 750,000 food parcels were not dispatched to their occupied homeland by Christmas 1942. The British were hardly moved, but they agreed to allow food parcels limited to goods already available in the blockaded zones to be mailed to individuals from Portugal.[3]

The British believed the blockade would help the Allied effort against the Axis and they maintained it even after the United States declared war.[4] The Americans attitude was, "Feed Europe Now!" but Britain chalked it up to American domestic pressures and reaching for "political credit" in Europe.[5] The British were consistent. In the spring of 1943, Churchill, who had first-hand knowledge of the effectiveness of the blockade in World War I, declared: "No relief except for Greece." He told the Minister for Economic Warfare that it was "the Ministry for Economic *Warfare* and therefore, by inference, no relief organization."[6] Churchill's stand was upheld at Bermuda, and the proposal to ship food to the starving European masses was rejected.[7]

Against that background, the attitude toward the Jews was not different. A call, apparently originating in a letter sent by the American branch of Agudat Israel to Lord Halifax in October 1941, demanded recognition of the Jews as prisoners of war, which would qualify them for aid despite the blockade.[8] Stephen Wise pleaded with the British not to discriminate between Belgians and Jews and Maurice Perlzweig wrote Lord Halifax that because the Jews supported a blockade by the neutral Americans Britain should take the initiative in sending food to starving Jews. The embassy sent Perlzweig's message to London, adding that if Jewish demands were not met their support for the blockade might end.[9] The argument lost its sting when, shortly afterward, the United States entered the war.

In February 1942, after London learned that 170,000 Polish Jews had died of typhus the previous year, Szwarcbart, through the JFC, sought British approval for the shipment of vaccine.[10] Meanwhile, Agudat Israel, citing the Greek precedent, asked Brotman to arrange a meeting with the JFC to plan the campaign for food shipments to be sent to the ghetto.[11] The BD and Brodetsky supported the plan, but his Anglo-Jewish Association JFC co-chairman, Leonard Stein, was less enthusiastic. Stein, in character, argued that the government should not be asked to prefer Jews over other starving Poles, "a request which would be inadvisable to make."[12] His fear of "discrimination" in favor of the Jews was compatible with the attitude of the St. James Conference then taking place.

Other nationalities, as well, based their arguments on the Greek precedent and the MEW feared that giving in would lead to the collapse of the blockade.[13] The British were so adamant that Brodetsky had no choice but to inform the Polish Jewish organizations that medicine could not be sent because of what he termed insurmountable economic, social and political problems.[14] By the summer of 1942, after receiving reports about the critical state of Polish Jewry, Szwarcbart entered into intense negotiations with the American ambassador and the governments-in-exile about food and drug shipments. The Polish Government and the BSWJC also lobbied the British.[15]

Finally, these efforts bore fruit. The BD came to an agreement with the British and Polish Governments about sending food parcels from Portugal to the Jews of Poland.[16] The agreement was in line with a similar arrangement with other governments. A total of four tons of food valued at £3,000 could be sent monthly in small parcels. To meet blockade restrictions all goods would be of Portuguese origin. Moreover, parcels would be addressed only to private individuals so as not to free the Germans from their obligation to feed the population in general.[17] Two serious problems arose. Considerable time had elapsed since the Jews of Europe had fixed addresses. Furthermore, the BD had been asked not to publicize the project. Consequently, address-gathering could only be undertaken by word of mouth and since no public fund-raising was permitted, financial problems soon arose.[18] The British insistence on a low profile was undoubtedly aimed at preventing public pressure to extend the food program. The British contribution consisted of the transfer of Pounds Sterling to neutral Portugal.

To maintain what the British saw as an inviolate principle that Jews of one country did not represent those of another the transfer license was not given directly to the BD, but issued to Polish Government.[19] On the other hand, the sacrosanct principle was violated when the Jews of one country were expected to accept responsibility for those of another, in this case to finance the aid rendered to the Jewish citizens of another country. Incidentally, the funds for the United States' War Refugee Board, which was established to extend aid to the Jewish refugees in Europe, were supplied by the Joint.

The governments-in-exile were often reluctant to abide by British dictates. Without bothering to consult them, Polish Red Cross officials in Lisbon organized food shipments independently and the Belgians sent home monthly consignments worth £1 million, besides the personally licensed parcels.[20]

Meanwhile, after months passed without a single parcel leaving Portugal for Poland the Jewish activists were extremely upset. Unfortunately, the Portuguese government temporarily suspended the food transfer. Moreover, neither did the £6,000 sent by the BD arrive; it was stuck somewhere between the Polish treasury in London and its legation in Lisbon.

After six months passed without the dispatch of a single food parcel, the London-based English language *Polish Jewish Observer*, on January 8, 1943, published a stinging criticism of the BD, Szwarcbart and the Polish welfare authorities: "Tell them that the Jews in the Ghettos are dying at the hands of the Nazi slaughterers with the bitter feeling that they are being let down by their brethren in Great Britain and the United States."[21] Publicizing the program was a violation of the British conditions, and the paper was censured by both Brotman and the BD.[22]

Nonetheless, the arrow hit its mark and the Joint's Lisbon delegate, Joseph Schwartz, who also represented the BD, received urgent instructions to investigate the whereabouts of the £6,000.[23] He learned that the Bank of England had originally opposed the transfer to Lisbon and authorized it only at the end of December 1942; and that, scandalously, the Polish decoder had unscrambled the message only on January 20, 1943, fully three weeks later.[24] Since public fund-raising was disallowed, the BD obtained the money from financial institutions, with the Jewish Colonisation Association (JCA) funding the first two months of the program.[25]

When the parcels were finally sent it was difficult to determine if they actually arrived at their destinations. The Czechoslovakian Foreign Ministry was optimistic. It cited cables from Switzerland affirming that Red Cross parcels to Theresienstadt and the expelees in Poland had arrived. In all events, affirmation arrived in Lisbon that parcels had been received in Theresienstadt.[26]

Meanwhile, information arrived from Poland that Jews survived in only 55 towns and that Warsaw was *Judenrein*.[27] Therefore, Szwarcbart, who was responsible for drawing up the list of addresses, suggested sending parcels to *Judenrats* for specific persons. And if those persons could not be located then the parcels would be turned over to the *Judenrats*. Another of his proposals, meant to check the reliability of supposedly "authoritative sources," was to send half the parcels to the *Judenrats* and half to private addresses. In all events, Szwarcbart wanted some of the parcels sent to Warsaw. Another demand, submitted by the Polish Jewish Council, was that the first shipment be sent to addresses supplied by relatives in England, the second to community committees, and that the person signing for a parcel automatically be listed as a candidate for another. The BD accepted Szwarcbart's proposal that the parcels be sent to *Judenrats* for specific persons and instructed the Joint's Lisbon office to do so. However, the Joint replied that only dispatch to individuals was allowed.[28]

A discouraging report arrived in April 1943 that only 108 confirmations were received for 9,229 parcels consisting of 500 grams of dried dates; 66 empty packages (the Germans kept the contents) were returned for various stated reasons: four because post offices were closed down; one because the recipient supposedly refused to accept it; two due to the elimination of the

Judenrat; twelve deaths; three because of the refusal of concentration camp commandants to accept them; and four without any stated reason. The BD then instructed the Joint to send three parcels a month of sardines, almonds and fruit juice to persons who had acknowledged receipt and from time to time to new addresses.[29]

Dr Stanisław Schimitzek, the Polish representative in Lisbon, reported in June that half the parcels were unaccounted for, three-quarters of the remainder had been confiscated by the Germans and that 90 percent of the others were signed for by the *Judenrats*. Nonetheless, there was no certainty that Jews had indeed received them. Therefore, Schimitzek proposed limiting shipments only to persons who had already acknowledged receipt, and that three parcels be sent to them for a period of one month.[30] After receiving Schimitzek's report, the BD, fearing that knowledge of the German confiscations could put an end to the program, sent a more sanguine report than that of Schimitzek's to the Ministry of Economic Warfare.[31] Nonetheless, the British severely limited the scope of shipments. They warned the BD to stop negotiating with British Quakers to intermediate with Quakers in neutral countries to help the Jews in Poland.[32] According to the letter the initiative was that of the BD.

Another example of the government's strict position concerns shipments to Holland. According to Joseph Schwartz, the Joint was planning shipments to Jews there. However, when Brotman prepared a letter to the Joint in Lisbon with the addresses of two Dutch Jews, the government returned the letter with a note that his organization was only allowed to engage in correspondence within the limits of its license.[33]

After an examination of the situation the Polish welfare authorities reached the conclusion that the shipment of parcels to Poland should be discontinued.[34] The Joint's Lisbon representative came to the same conclusion. Consequently, the BD agreed to restrict the program with the proviso that shipments to the areas of Poland annexed to Germany continue.[35]

When the BD's success in obtaining approval for parcels to Poland became known, Ernst Frischer, of the Czechoslovakian State Council, asked the BD to arrange a similar program for Theresienstadt because the British had turned down his application to do so.[36] Meanwhile, the Czechoslovakian Government submitted a request for parcels to be sent from Switzerland, Sweden, Turkey and Portugal. Only shipments from Portugal, limited to a monetary total of £3,000 a month, exactly like the Polish conditions, were approved.[37] In all events, in March 1943, the government of Czechoslovakia began sending parcels to Jewish detainees and expelees. They budgeted £6,000 for the first shipments and sought subsequent funding from local Jewish sources. Czechoslovakia insisted that the parcels be sent only to its citizens. On the other hand, the BD, in its program for Polish citizens, also supplied addresses of Jews, including those from Czechoslovakia, expelled from other countries. One time the name of an Austrian citizen was listed among the potential parcel recipients. Frischer, making apologies, crossed it off.[38]

Czech Jews had difficulty funding their food program and requested that the unused Polish funds be made available for their compatriots in Theresienstadt and Cracow. However, their request to change the terms of the license and transfer money to Switzerland was twice turned down by the MEW. Frischer's lobbying was based on optimistic Czech reports confirming the arrival of parcels at Theresienstadt and Auschwitz-Birkenau.[39]

In late 1943, the parcels programs was cut back and contrary to Schwartz's request the American legation in Lisbon delayed the shipments arranged by the Joint; £5,000 of the BD's £9,000 was left, enough to ship 10,000 parcels. Thus Schwartz went to London with confirmations of parcels received by the *Juedische Unterstuetzungsstelle in Krakau*, headed by Dr Michael Weichert, a Joint nominee, and the *Zwangarbeitslager Andrychau, Kr. Bielitz*, and succeeded in getting approval to ship another one thousand parcels.[40]

The BD then submitted a request to the MEW to transfer part of the unused Lisbon money to Switzerland for the Jews in Birkenau. The request was rejected. The MEW advised Brotman to contact the IGCR which was licensed to transfer SF100,000 to detainees in German territory. (A clerk had apparently mistaken Birkenau for German territory.)[41]

Earlier, in November 1943, the IGCR applied for permission to send parcels to Jewish citizens of Allied powers, but was turned down by the MEW which wrote: "It would appear difficult to make special arrangements for Jews." At last the money had been placed at the IGRC's disposal, but the project could not be carried out because the Red Cross had no access to camps with Jewish internees.[42]

Frischer did not rest. He pleaded for the continuation of the British aid operation, however modest. Since the Czech budget was allocated by the British, and ruled out specific aid for Jews, Czech Jews in Britain raised £5,000. Frischer then demanded that the idle Lisbon money be added to this sum for parcels to Theresienstadt. The government, however, consistently refused to alter the terms of the license.

In fact, the Joint had enough money for thousands of parcels but only a few addressees.[43] But suddenly parcel receipt confirmations arrived from the Jewish Aid Center in Cracow and all the British money was spent for new shipments. The Cracow center pleaded for clothing to be added to the food supply. Again, the MEW refused to alter the license to include goods of non-Portuguese origin; the license had to remain limited to food available in the blockaded areas.[44] Frischer, too, received optimistic reports from his government about the efficiency of the Cracow center. He demanded more money. He rejected the BD's contention that it had no funds of its own and Brotman's explanation that the BD served as a facilitator between different organizations and whose funds derived from bodies such as the JCA and the Council for Refugees. Hence a meeting was held by Brodetsky, Brotman, Frischer and the Czech minister of welfare, but the Czech's were £20,000 short of their annual welfare quota and nothing could be done. The Czech Government expressed its willingness to include aid to non-Czech Jews in its relief budget,[45] but subsequently dropped the offer. Consequently, in September 1942, Frischer again found himself in the position of having to remove the names of two Austrian Jews from the parcel list for the ghetto in the Czech town of Theresienstadt.[46]

In May 1944, Frischer submitted three reports of Dr Weichert's activity in Cracow listing food and medicine he had received and distributed.[47] However, a month later the Poles informed Brotman of a secret letter sent by two Jewish underground organizations in Poland, the Bund and ZKN, the Jewish National Council, stating that the Nazis were using Weichert's center for their own benefit and demanding an end to the Cracow shipments.[48] Schwartz and Schimitzek, on the other hand, were convinced that parcels were reaching Cracow and even increased them to 2,500 a week. Meanwhile, the British funds ran out and the BD was asked for more means.[49]

Pressure was applied from different sides. Frischer threatened to make a public appeal if the BD did not acquiesce,[50] but since all private fundraising required the home secretary's approval it was an empty threat. Brodetsky, however, was sensitive to criticism. He appealed to the Chief Rabbi who convinced the Central Council for Jewish Refugees and the JCA to allocate £9,000 each. As Brotman wrote to Rabbi Schonfeld: "the Chief Rabbi has obviously a much greater pull with these bodies . . . "[51] Ironically, just when money was available Polish Minister of Welfare Stanczyk ordered an end to the shipments. However, he changed his directive after meeting with Brotman and M. Stephany, secretary of the Central Council for Jewish Refugees, in July 1944.[52]

In September 1944, after confirming that most of the parcels were indeed ending up in German hands, the Poles finally stopped the program[53] and in March 1945 the Lisbon accounts were closed. The unused portion of the money was returned to the BD which handed it over to the Central British Fund for Jewish Relief and Rehabilitation (CBF).[54]

The threat of annihilation which suddenly engulfed Hungarian Jewry in the spring of 1944, generated a new wave of convulsions in the Jewish world. But the lessons of the past had been learned and Jews in the free world reacted quickly. In a later chapter we will discuss the part played by British Jews in the global effort to save the Jews of Hungary. The following is a discussion of the attempt to send aid to the Hungarian ghettos.

On June 2, 1944, Schonfeld proposed sending food parcels from Portugal to Hungary. He gave assurances that the Chief Rabbi would raise the required funds from the Refugee Council and the United Jewish Relief Appeal, the council's financial instrument. The chief political obstacle, however, was the MEW which permitted aid to reach territories conquered or annexed by the Germans, but not to enemy countries such as Hungary.[55] Brotman was resourceful. He appealed for parcels to be sent to Hungary by the Polish Government which curiously still maintained diplomatic ties with Hungary. Faced with the universal agitation aroused by the annihilation of the last remaining large Jewish community in occupied Europe, the MEW finally relaxed its restrictions on the shipment of parcels from Portugal to Hungary. However, because of the disorder in the European rail and postal system, the ministry doubted whether the parcels would reach their destination.[56] The Poles agreed to the program. But again, time lapsed before it was implemented and Schimitzek received appropriate instructions only in August 1944. An additional delay was caused by the need to gather individual addresses.[57]

In October 1944, after Schimitzek reported that there was no food shortage in Hungary but the Jews were impoverished, the Joint obtained permission for transferring money. In November, the Polish envoy reported that sending parcels from Portugal was futile and that only Switzerland could serve this purpose. Here, however, the British refused to budge.[58]

That was the end of the BD's parcel program. It was modest in all respects and could not be expanded because of the strict stand of the British authorities who were not willing to make the same concessions to the Jews that it had made for the Greeks. We have already discussed the principle of "not discriminating in favor of the Jews" that resulted in the food blockade against them, which was part of the British strategic policy.

The parcels program was criticized after the war. The World Jewish Congress blamed the Joint for surrendering to government dictates and not doing more. The BD also came under attack for its "clandestine relief" and was forced to publish a report of its activities. Brotman justified the BD, citing the obstacles posed by the blockade policy and the transportation and postal problems. Brotman also dealt with the moral aspect: Even though it was known that many parcels ended up in German hands, they had to be sent if only for the small number of Jews who actually received them.[59]

We conclude that not enough was done. Jewish organizations did not devise an independent welfare infrastructure and were impeded by their conception of loyalty to the embattled homeland. The government quashed innovative proposals such as cooperation with the Quakers, and the Jewish leadership abjectly surrendered without protest. The same holds in regard to the maintenance of secrecy and capitulation on the issue of publicly raising funds. Letting the information leak out, however, would have led to the support of influential non-Jewish circles which could have pressured the government. One is left with the impression that the BD preferred to suffice with the little that could be done within its restricted framework. In fact, what the Jews received was actually crumbs which fell from the Czechs' and Poles' table.

The Adler-Rudel Scheme

On January 1, 1943, the Political Committee of the Jewish Agency headed by Moshe Shertok (later Sharett, foreign minister and prime minister of the State of Israel) met in London with the representative of the Joint, Joseph Schwartz, to discuss a plan for ferrying Jews from German-occupied Denmark to Sweden. Though immigration to Palestine was not on the agenda, the Jewish Agency initiated the operation to keep Jews in Denmark "cold storage," in Shertok's words, for their eventual *aliya*.[60]

Shalom Adler-Rudel, director of the Jewish Agency's European Department and a member of the Executive Council for Jewish Refugees, was sent to Sweden with the approval of the British Government to examine the plan's feasibility.[61] While there Adler-Rudel learned that he could not help the Danish Jews or the German Jews in pioneer training camps in Denmark to leave legally, and he tried to lay the groundwork for an illegal escape to Sweden.[62]

Meanwhile, Adler-Rudel started lobbying for the transfer of Jewish children from Nazi countries to Sweden. In a meeting with the Swedish welfare minister, Gustav Moeller, which was arranged by Bruno Kraisky, an Austrian Jewish refugee (who would become the foreign minister and *Kanzler* of Austria), Adler-Rudel appealed to the Swedes to shelter 20,000 Jewish children. At first the Swedish cabinet rejected the plea, but after they were pressured they agreed to negotiate with the Germans. Eric Boheman, the secretary of the Swedish Government and a Christian of Jewish background, was delegated to work out details.[63]

The Swedes set three prior conditions to negotiations with the Germans: that the children's upkeep be covered by outside sources (the cost amounted to one dollar a day per child for a grand total of £5,000 a day); that their food be imported despite the blockade; and official assurances that the governments of Britain and the United States would eventually transfer the children to Palestine or another overseas country. As to the food imports, the Swedes then negotiated with the British for safe passage of food to Goteborg harbor and they hoped to benefit from such an arrangement.

The British minister in Stockholm frowned at the immigration clause, arguing that most of the children would be returned to liberated Europe after the war. The Swedish representative, however, argued that an agreement on immigration overseas would facilitate negotiations with the Germans who wanted a Europe without Jews.[64]

The Foreign Office was surprised at Adler-Rudel's progress, especially since the rescue program was not the reason why he had been issued the exit permit for Sweden.[65] The plan, however, came at the right time. Adler-Rudel returned from Sweden when the Bermuda Conference was in progress, and according to the Foreign Office: "the success of which [Adler-Rudel] we shall need to plug as much as possible if we are to avoid over-much criticism." Therefore, the Adler-Rudel Scheme could be presented as an achievement "it will look as if it is a direct outcome of the Bermuda Conference."[66] In actuality, the plan was used by the British as another delaying tactic to uphold their blockade.

The blockade policy had been a bone of contention between the United States and Britain over the evacuation of Christian children. From experience gained in World War I, Britain wanted strict controls over the food imports to Europe while the United States wanted to feed the hungry.[67] The British proposed high publicity steps to demonstrate their sensitivity to the suffering in Europe, but without relieving the Germans of their responsibility to provide food for the occupied populations. Hence, they proposed supplying milk powder for children or their evacuation to neutral countries to be fed. Herbert Lehman, the Governor of New York, who headed the welfare projects sponsored by the US president, favored direct aid and rejected the British proposal. In all events, the State Department later thought that the British had already gained enough "political credit" from their few aid projects, and that "the US has been outsmarted" by the British plan to evacuate children.

In reality, the evacuation of Belgian or Norwegian children could not be considered crucial or a rescue operation. The question was whether to bring food to the children or bring the children to the food in neutral countries. The British preferred the second alternative because it would attract wide public attention. The evacuation of Jewish children on the other hand, was more than a matter of alleviating suffering, but of saving them from the jaws of death. Therefore, the plans for the evacuation of Christian children were entrusted to the MEW while the Adler-Rudel plan was assigned to the Foreign Office Refugee Department.[68]

In their attempts to persuade the Americans to accept British policy, the MEW emphasized that a certain percentage of the evacuated children would be Jewish and that even the Swiss government had agreed to the plan. Lehman, a Jew, was not taken in by the British arguments.

The Ministry feared that the delegates at the Bermuda Conference would decide to send food to Europe, thus weakening the blockade. Therefore, the Ministry proposed evacuating 100,000 children, 20–25 percent of them Jewish, to Switzerland and Sweden and pledging to allow passage of food and clothing only when needed. However, this plan was not raised at the Bermuda Conference because the cables sent by Anthony Eden to his deputy in Bermuda and the British ambassador in Washington arrived too late. In the end the blockade authorities need not have worried: At the conference it was decided against sending food to starving Europe.[69]

Sir Herbert Emerson was enthusiastic about the Adler-Rudel plan and urged its acceptance by the government.[70] However, when Foreign Office officials reconsidered the plan they found that it entailed far-reaching concessions to the policy of blockading the Jews. Thus the British were only willing to offer sympathetic consideration of the request to increase the Swedish food quota for the children. Since the British had no intention of relaxing the blockade restrictions they dragged their heels as much as possible. In this case they demanded that they be consulted at all stages. The Bermuda Conference did recommend that the Allies be responsible for the financial maintenance of the refugees and guarantee their return to Europe after the war. The curious British interpretation brought about the decision to let the Swedish government be informed that expenses and repatriation would be on the agenda when final arrangements were made after the war!

As to the principle involved in the evacuation of Jewish children to overseas countries, as the Swedish government requested, Britain maintained that the Jews were Europeans and expulsion beyond its borders would be a concession to Hitler. Thus they were not willing to grant even the formal assurances that would facilitate negotiations with the Germans, "Since to do so would be tantamount to acquiescence in the *judenrein* policy for Europe of the German Government."[71] The Swedes were dissatisfied with the British stand and the negotiations were deadlocked.

In July 1943, American Undersecretary of State Sumner Welles, informed Stephen Wise and Nachum Goldmann that the United States had endorsed the Adler-Rudel plan and that the Jewish Agency could start carrying it out. Nonetheless, Agency officials in London soon learned from the Foreign Office that there were snags in American-British cooperation.[72] Meanwhile, the MEW submitted a plan of its own, and the Swedes now had two evacuation programs: that of the MEW which proposed evacuating Christian children from Norway to Sweden for certain periods of time, in order to feed them and then send them back home; and the Adler-Rudel plan. Furthermore, the MEW asked the Foreign Office to instruct the British minister in Sweden not to advance the Jewish plan without suggesting its own, which is understood as being "opposed to the Adler-Rudel Scheme." "What we wish to ensure," the Foreign Office instructed its Stockholm consul, "is that the Adler-Rudel Scheme is not pressed on the Swedes to the exclusion of reference to any negotiations about the child-evacuation scheme."[73]

It is possible that competing plans, lack of enthusiasm and the vague British response caused Stockholm to become hesitant. Moreover, British Jewish leaders did not lobby the government in favor of the Adler-Rudel Scheme and, complying with a Swedish request, kept the plan secret. Moreover, there was also doubt on whether to inform members of Parliament active in the Committee Against Nazi Terror.[74] Adler-Rudel, himself, was warned by the Foreign Office not to publicize his scheme.[75]

The secret leaked and in October 1943, the restless Miss Rathbone asked the Foreign Office for its stand on the scheme. She received no reply.[76] However, developments in the United States at the end of 1943 caused the British to revive the evacuation plan. Most important was the demand by the Senate Foreign Relations Committee that the president establish a rescue committee of diplomatic, economic and military experts to save the remnant of European Jewry. That was before the establishment of the WRB. Influential American groups laid full responsibility for the blockade at Britain's door and the British Ambassador felt pressured to ask the Foreign Office for "some indication of our proposals regarding evacuation of children to Sweden and Switzerland." Lord Halifax's main concern was public clamor for a relaxation of the blockade.[77] Finally, on December 20, 1943, after eight long months, an Anglo-American letter was presented to the Swedish minister in London asking his government to approach the Germans about the evacuation of the children. The Germans, however, turned it down.[78] Then the MEW suddenly became enthusiastic about saving Jewish children. It was in accordance with its policy of children-feeding, as mentioned. The MEW instructed Halifax to ask the negotiating Swedes to include Jewish children in every evacuation program and, if the Germans turned it down, to threaten them and the Norwegian collaborator, Vidkun Quisling, with publicizing their refusal.[79] The German refusal was already known, but the ministry instructed the embassy to stress the positive British attitude toward the evacuation plan and at the same time to make clear that it had no intention of relaxing the blockade.[80]

Adler-Rudel believed that the time factor had worked against his scheme. Indeed, almost nine months went by before the Swedish Government received the requested guarantees, though they were of a limited nature, and by then developments at the front frustrated the negotiations.[81] The scheme was revived six months later, in June 1944, when the American Government, influenced by the WRB, pressured the British to relax the blockade.[82] The Foreign Office then asked the Swedes to renew negotiations with the Germans. However, because of the now strained relations between Sweden and Germany and problems at home, the Swedes refused to do so. They had granted asylum to many Finnish refugees and were disinclined to invest an additional effort in the children.[83] Nonetheless, during the Hungarian crisis, Sweden offered to shelter 500 Jewish children from that country.[84]

The Adler-Rudel Scheme was on the agenda longer than any other rescue plan because it served as a basis for the cynical political maneuvering which simultaneously caused this rescue possibility to stumble. After the war, Adler-Rudel laid the blame for failure on bumbling indifferent bureaucrats.[85] He was mistaken. Had he been given access to British archives he would have learned that Britain merely exploited his plan to help maintain its blockade policy.

10

The Search for Refugee Havens

"We have never accepted the White Paper," he wrote, "except as a modus vivendi pending a new declaration."

In late 1942, the British Government feared that the growing public concern for the refugees would force it to grant shelter to a large number of Jews. The different ministries adopted positions according to their policy lines. Home Secretary Herbert Morrison insisted that the United Kingdom was incapable of harboring the masses of Jewish refugees that he feared would flee Europe. Thus he proposed that a search be made for alternatives besides Palestine.[1] Foreign Secretary Anthony Eden, on the other hand, believed that the Jews should continue to live in a liberated Europe.[2] Eden's views, which were adopted by his postwar successor, Ernest Bevin, determined British policy toward the Jews during the Holocaust.

Meanwhile, as part of the rescue effort and solutions for Jews who would neither wish nor be able to live in Europe after the war, British officials and the Jews began searching for suitable havens. The British wanted to use their ships for transporting refugees as little as possible and thus sought suitable nearby territories. The possibility of settlement in Libya and Eritrea, recently liberated from Italian occupation, was raised as was French North Africa, where refugee camps had already been proposed. The latter was under American occupation and French sovereignty, and Eritrea and Libya were under British military administration. Thus these areas appeared suitable for Jewish resettlement.

The transfer of Jews to the former Italian colonies was raised in discussions between Alex Easterman, of the BSWJC, and the Soviet Ambassador in London, Ivan Maiski, in January and February 1943. Maiski, whom Easterman described as a friend of the Jews, immediately confirmed the truth about the Nazi Final Solution and was one of the initiators of the United Nations declaration of December 17, 1942. Maiski displayed sympathy toward Easterman's memorandum concerning the rescue and extension of aid to Jews, especially the establishment of an international body to deal with Jewish problems. The Soviet ambassador also stressed the importance of American involvement for any large-scale operation. He also suggested the establishment of a permanent Jewish settlement in Libya. When Easterman noted that the Jews had deep historical and spiritual roots in Palestine the Russian was surprisingly sympathetic. He thought, however, that since many Jews would wish to leave Europe, Palestine should not be considered the only alternative because of its large Arab population and a "certain" i.e., negative, British policy. Though he believed the Jews should press for a Jewish state in Palestine, he suggested that one might also be established in Libya in federation with Palestine. As we shall see, even though he denied it, Maiski had heard of the Libyan plan from the British. He said the USSR supported such a plan and asked Easterman to raise it with his colleagues. There is no doubt that Maiski was heralding the dramatic change in Soviet policy toward Zionism that led to the unreserved Soviet support for the establishment of a Jewish state in Palestine (the November 29, 1947 UN resolution).

The BSWJC was against the Libyan proposal, but believed that Maiski's attitude showed that the Jews could expect Soviet support for a territorial concession. Mentioning to the ambassador the cordial relations with Ethiopian Emperor Haile Selassie, the BSWJC resolved to positively pursue temporary Jewish settlement in Eritrea as a step toward permanent settlement in Palestine. Maiski expressed enthusiasm, asked for a detailed memorandum and promised Soviet support.[3] What lay behind the conundrum of the BSWJC seeking Soviet support for activities in an area so sensitive to British strategic interests? Perhaps it was a naive conception of the relations between the British and Soviet allies.

Ben Rubinstein, honorary treasurer of the BSWJC, studied the Eritrea proposal and handled the negotiations regarding Jewish colonization in Eritrea. On February 2, 1943, prior to Easterman's second meeting with Maiski, Rubinstein wrote Lord Melchett, who favored territorial schemes, that Eritrea was six times larger than Palestine, sparsely populated and, according to Rubinstein, close to Palestine and the rich Belgian Congo. (Rubinstein was entrusted with the negotiations because as an importer of wood from the Congo he was supposedly an expert on Africa. Geography was apparently not one of his stronger points.) He also expressed his belief that the British would favor the existence of a strong Jewish army in the center of the Muslim world and that Italian-Americans would not oppose taking Eritrea from Italy, but might not feel the same way about a Jewish state in Libya. Rubinstein, recounting the legends of King Solomon and the Queen of Sheba, was certain of Ethiopian friendship. Neither did he forget to mock Brodetsky's helplessness and he elaborated on his ideas with gusto. Though Lord Melchett never replied, Rubinstein obstinately continued to write him every day demanding that Eritrea, rather than Libya, be the focal point. After the United Nations declared Eritrea a Jewish refuge, Rubinstein wrote, a quarter million Jews could be transferred immediately, an act he believed would put an end to the slaughter in Europe.[4]

The WJC cabled the London stationed Dr Haccius, of the International Committee of the Red Cross in Geneva, asking whether it could transfer Jews to Eritrea on ships sailing the Red Cross flag[5] and asked an Eritrea expert about conditions in the territory.[6] Easterman and Rubinstein described resulting optimistic prognoses to Lord Melchett and Lady Reading; even the United States government raised the idea of settling Jewish refugees in the territory.[7]

Subsequently, Sidney Silverman, in March 1943, sent a memorandum to the Foreign Office detailing Easterman's and Rubinstein's investigations and making a tempered proposal for Eritrea to serve as a temporary haven for refugees. The Foreign Office immediately responded that Italian citizens had not been removed from the territory and that their homes could not be confiscated.[8] The Foreign Office's expert thought that the Eritrean climate was suitable, but that it would be difficult to provide the amenities required by Europeans. Moreover, the political future of Eritrea was unclear because of the conflicting claims of different states. Other officials thought that Eritrea provided an opportunity to divert Jewish attention, especially that of influential American Jews, away from Palestine. The negative aspect, however, was Eritrea's proximity to Palestine and the possibility that refugees might use the territory as a way station for that country.[9]

Eden opposed the plan because Jewish settlement in Eritrea might hamper negotiations with Ethiopia on border adjustments with Sudan, Kenya and Somalia. Moreover, the Ministry of War was against settling foreign populations in the area. The reasons given for the rejection of Silverman's memorandum were "practical": inferior hygienic conditions; the lack of accommodation after the dismantling of military installations; and a shortage of employment opportunities.[10]

Support for the Eritrea plan came from an unlikely source: Winston Churchill. In reaction to the Bermuda Conference the prime minister sought to explain his negative position about the White Paper and the urgent need to find a territorial solution elsewhere for the Jews: "We have never accepted the White Paper," he wrote, "except as a modus vivendi pending a new declaration." Churchill's statement was made on April 27, 1943. A day later he made clear to the Cabinet that he did not accept the view that an Arab majority in Palestine should stop Jewish immigration. Immigration was now frozen, but a new political survey had to be conducted after the war. Meanwhile, Churchill wanted to examine the possibility of Jewish settlement in Eritrea and Libya, the latter possibly to be divided into an Arab Cyrenaica and a Jewish Tripolitania, perhaps as a branch of the national home in Palestine.[11]

At this stage Churchill believed the solution to the Palestine problem lay in partition. With his imperialist outlook he saw nothing wrong with compensating the Jews for the small area apportioned them in Palestine with territory elsewhere, even if the Jews had no affinity for it.[12] Churchill's suggestions were also a reaction to the Bermuda Conference. Foreign Office officials opposed these plans. They argued that the Tripoli plan would cause more friction with the Arabs, that Haile Selassie would not agree to a Jewish colony in Eritrea, and that the local population would be hostile to the new settlers.[13] Before all this was composed, the Foreign Office rejected the Silverman memorandum.

Nonetheless, because of the prime minister's instructions, the Foreign Office and the Secretary of State for the Middle East submitted memoranda on Jewish settlement in the liberated Italian colonies. Their reports, submitted in autumn 1943, advised against the proposal on practical and political grounds.[14]

Meanwhile, representatives of Jewish bodies entered into independent negotiations with the Ethiopian legation in London. The idea of settling 30,000 Jews in Italian-occupied Ethiopia had been raised before the war by Karel Gieldemester. Gieldemester, a Dutchman and rather mysterious figure who apparently had Gestapo ties in Vienna, claimed that he had $50 million from French, British and American sources and the agreement of the Italians to settle five million Jews in their new colony.[15] In all events, Mussolini had proposed to Chamberlain settling Jews in the Harar region of Ethiopia in return for the French port of Djibouti.[16]

In early March 1943, Rubinstein entered into negotiations with the Ethiopian envoy, Dr Ayala Gabra, for a safe haven for Jewish refugees with permits to sail from Portugal to Lorenco Marques in the Portuguese colony of Mozambique. Gabra rejected this request and all others. He even rejected the proposal to grant refuge to Jewish scientists and technicians even though they could be of benefit to the Ethiopian economy. On the last point the envoy said that out of Christian charity Ethiopia had not sought vengeance and not expelled 500 Italian technicians after their country was liberated from Italian occupation. Neither did Gabra have any encouragement for the Eritrea proposal. He told Rubinstein that Eritrea, as the cradle of Ethiopian culture, should be annexed by Ethiopia. Despite the rejection Rubinstein remained optimistic. He reported that "no interview could be more cordial and sympathetic."

In his letter to the Marchioness of Reading, Rubinstein reported that he promised the Ethiopian diplomat that the Jews would make efforts to assure that his country would have an outlet to the sea; that the British army would quell any Arab rebellion; and that Russia would be favorable, America convinced and Britain reconciled.[17]

Neither did Easterman lose hope. He sent a memorandum to the Ethiopian envoy suggesting that refugee doctors, engineers and technicians currently in Switzerland, Portugal and Spain, and a few thousand French Jews, especially women and children, be sent to Ethiopia. They would live in camps, he wrote, and be supported by Jewish organizations until they could be resettled in Palestine or elsewhere.[18] Jewish representatives did not often find a ready ear among foreign representatives. Thus when the Ethiopian envoy cordially received the enthusiastic Rubinstein, the gesture was misinterpreted.

While the British Government examined the possibility of Jewish settlement in Ethiopia, its envoy in Addis Ababa reported that Professor Jacob Faitlovitz, the noted scholar of Ethiopian Jewry, had been told by Haile Selassie that he was prepared to grant temporary refuge to a limited number of Jews. Faitlovitz proposed suggested settling the refugees among Falasha Jews in the Gondar region, but the emperor refused to make assurances that he would accept them as permanent residents. Though not enthusiastic, the British examined the issue because they wanted areas outside of Palestine for Jews who had found refuge in Mauritius and Turkey.[19]

Rabbi Solomon Schonfeld did not leave the Ethiopian arena entirely to the BSWJC. In his zeal to rescue rabbis in every possible way, Schonfeld, in May 1943, met with Gabra and submitted two proposals that the envoy undoubtedly found frightening: a modest one, regarding the immediate issuance of entry visas for a number of Polish and Slovakian rabbis and their families who would be permitted to leave Europe if a neutral country would accept them; and a large-scale scheme for mass Jewish colonization of Ethiopia that would develop into a "self-governing Jewish Dominion under the authority of the Ethiopian Emperor."[20]

Schonfeld's proposal was a serious misreading of world politics. It is unlikely that the Germans would honor visas issued by an Ethiopia liberated from their ally, Italy. Neither did Schonfeld make an effort to learn about the delicate political and religious balance in Ethiopia.

The suggestion that a "self-governing Jewish Dominion" be established outside Palestine is characteristic of his ultraorthodox anti-Zionism but it also shows that Schonfeld believed that the Jews would need their own autonomous territory. Schonfeld, Rubinstein and others who suggested these unlikely plans might be faulted for political naïveté, but not for leaving any stone unturned in their quest to save Jews from the Holocaust.

Ethiopia showed no greater willingness than most other countries to grant shelter to Jewish refugees. At their final meeting, in August 1943, Gabra informed Rubinstein that Ethiopia, resentful of the recent Italian occupation, was suspicious of foreigners. Thus they would accept no more than a small number of selected immigrants, and only after international issues were resolved and plans for a post war order prepared.[21]

In summation, despite their misgivings the British were prepared to consider the settlement of refugees in Ethiopia. The Ethiopians, however, could not be pinned down to any concrete plan.[22] By the end of 1943 the issue was dropped.

The Rescue Efforts of the Chief Rabbi's Religious Emergency Council

Thus Rabbi Hertz's proposal to rescue Polish Jewish children was turned down. Colonial Office officials, harping on familiar strings, suggested that Hertz be told that their acquiescence would be tantamount to "discrimination in favour of Jewish children" and that under no circumstances should the children of the ghettos "be singled out for special treatment."

"Rabbis to Mauritius"

In a previous chapter we described the efforts of Jews and Christians in 1942 to break the blockade on Europe's Jews. Here we discuss the endeavors of Chief Rabbi Joseph Herman Hertz and his son-in-law Rabbi Solomon Schonfeld to bypass that blockade in the framework of the Chief Rabbi's Religious Emergency Council (REC).

The division of labor between the chief rabbi and his son-in-law was such that Hertz met with and signed the letters addressed to government ministers while Schonfeld handled day-to-day affairs and initiated negotiations with officials on lower levels. In government offices Schonfeld was referred to as "the "mouthpiece" or "lieutenant of the Chief Rabbi."

In September 1942, the Colonial Office opened a special file named "Rabbis to Mauritius." It contains reports of the activities of the REC on behalf of the rabbis and families suffering in the European cauldron. The file begins with the Rabbi Hertz's activities on behalf of "the Jewish Clergy" up to September 1942. It does not deal with the problems of the orthodox Jews already living in Britain. The official opens with a description of Hertz's efforts early war on behalf of rabbis and their students in the Baltic countries and the appeals made to the government to extend them assistance. Eventually, many succeeded in reaching Shanghai and Kobe, in Japan.[1] In chapter 4 we discussed Hertz's successful effort to obtain Canadian visas for some of these rabbis and students. The visas enabled them to leave Japan, Germany's ally. Thus Hertz rescue efforts preceded those of other Jewish organizations.

Early in September 1942, Lord Cranborne was appointed colonial secretary. He displayed a greater understanding toward the Jews' plight than his predecessors. It would appear that Rabbis Hertz and Schonfeld sensed the new spirit in the Colonial Office and used the opportunity to present new ideas to the minister.

On September 9, 1942, Rabbi Hertz sent a letter to Cranborne, followed by a memorandum the following week, seeking his help in the rescue of a number of important rabbis. He proposed granting them visas to British territories such as Mauritius or the West Indies, with Jewish welfare organizations assuming the burden of their care. Hertz explained that the rabbis would be granted visas by neutral countries only if they could provide proof that they would be resettling in a final destination.[2]

Hertz's suggestion of Mauritius was a sophisticated move. Jewish Agency officials had complained about the conditions of the Jewish illegals deported to the island, and now the Zionist-minded chief rabbi pleaded that great rabbis be offered refuge there. The Colonial Office set about discussing Hertz's proposal and encountered two problems: the agreement of the island's governor before visas could be granted; moreover, instructions had already been issued not to accept refugees from enemy countries into British or American territory.[3] During Cranborne's tenure, however, in an effort to improve relations with the Jewish Agency, visa requirements were relaxed. Cranborne suggested that Hertz's proposal be given sympathetic consideration, especially since only a few endangered rabbis were involved. A display of compassion, moreover, would improve the image of the Colonial Office since "it would be concrete proof that the C.O. are not generally obstructive as regards proposals for assistance to Jews, so long as they are not asked to take action which is incompatible with established public policy."[4]

The Lord and the Chief Rabbi met. The colonial secretary was businesslike. He asked for the names and addresses of the rabbis in order to transmit them to the Foreign Office and security services for immediate consideration. Hertz also used the opportunity to ask that visas be granted to Polish Jewish children so that they might be brought via a neutral country to Cyprus and from there to East Africa. The lord's readiness to consider the rabbi's request was apparently limited. He responded that there was little chance of agreement because of the food shortage in Cyprus, a glut of Polish, Greek and other refugees in East Africa, and that the proposal was too broad.[5] We should add that the Colonial Office had recently refused to grant refuge in East Africa for Polish Jews who had succeeded in fleeing to France, but that the region had been set aside for Polish refugees arriving via Russia and Iran.[6]

Thus Rabbi Hertz's proposal to rescue Polish Jewish children was turned down. Colonial Office officials, harping on familiar strings, suggested that Hertz be told that their acquiescence would be tantamount to "discrimination in favour of Jewish children" and that under no circumstances should the children of the ghettos "be singled out for special treatment." In order to assuage the Foreign Office's Refugee Department regarding the concessions the new minister would be granting to the Jews, the Colonial Office informed its counterpart that "we are not in a position to consult any colonies at present and it seems clear also that no Colony could undertake to admit any larger number of children." Nevertheless, two days later the same Colonial Office officials concluded that Greek children would be sent to East Africa. The chief rabbi, however, was directed to the Foreign Office, which reacted according to the "facts" with which it had been supplied by the Colonial Office.[7]

The Colonial Office, previously, had also referred the BSWJC to the Foreign Office over the same issue. There was little chance of sympathetic consideration in that quarter because the head of its Refugee Department, George W. Randall, had already been encouraged by the Colonial Office to oppose in principle saving Jewish children because of the danger of the "segregation of Jews as a separate nationality." Moreover, the Foreign Office believed the case to be a minefield because the governments-in-exile might then seek to evacuate all their hungry children. Such was Whitehall's worry when it had agreed to evacuate some French children from Vichy. In all events, according to the Foreign office Greek children had priority. Since the issue was a matter of principle it was necessary to consult with the Home Office, as well. Neither did Randall neglect to mention the difficulties involved in transportation and the problematic passage through Turkey. Thus was concocted the response to Hertz's quest. Cranborne raised all of Randall's points and also mentioned that the response was disappointing.[8] In a long reply to Cranborne brimming with bitterness against the Foreign Office, Hertz wrote that its refusal to recognize the unique fate of the Jews was "somewhat out of accord with the actual circumstances." Hertz also wrote that information about the 30 rabbis for whom the Mauritian visas had meanwhile been approved would soon be available.[9] Cranborne only replied on the issue of the rabbis and suggested that Hertz turn the information over to the Foreign Office.[10] Hertz had another worry to contend with when Cranborne left the Colonial Office and was replaced by Colonel Oliver Stanley. Fearing that the issue of the rabbis would reach an impasse, Hertz sent the list of rabbis to Cranborne and Schonfeld sent a copy along with an explanatory letter to Stanley. Cranborne convinced Stanley to deal favorably with the request and told the chief rabbi, "you will have lost nothing by the exchange" of colonial secretaries.[11]

Early in December 1942, when Jewish leaders and various authorities were busy formulating the December 17 announcement about the suffering of Europe's Jews, Stanley turned the list of 25 rabbis and their families over to the Foreign Office and the security services and began asking colony governors if they would be prepared to accept them for the duration of the war. Stanley advised Schonfeld that "it must not be assumed that any future request can similarly be granted." The list contained among others the names of Rabbi Dasberg of Holland, Nahum Friedman of Lvov, Baruch Rabinowicz of Munkacz, Shmuel Schreiber of Bratislava, Simon Schreiber of Lublin and rabbis Jungreiss, Moscowitz, Perlov and Israel Shapira. There were also a number of rabbis from the *yeshiva* in Nitra, Slovakia, where Schonfeld had studied, including rabbis Altman, Jonah Fuerst, the head of the *yeshiva* Samuel David Ungar and his son-in-law, Michael Dov Weissmandel, the famous leader of the Jewish underground.[12]

Early in February 1943, the security authorities approved the list. Throughout the period Rabbi Schonfeld lobbied Parliament and, as we have discussed above, his activities came into conflict with the BD and the British Section of the World Jewish Congress.

There is no doubt that Hertz and Schonfeld's achievements, though modest, led them to believe that additional rescue efforts should be attempted. Schonfeld thought that Parliament could serve as the arena of these efforts. Hertz, for his part, believed that the lack of action on the part of the elected leadership was a serious impediment to launching rescue operations. Thus he sought to enlist the support of influential figures such as Viscount Samuel. However, the negotiations for rescuing the rabbis were still confidential.

After Schonfeld learned that the response to the rabbis' issue was positive he applied for permission to go to Turkey to lead the rescue operation from there. Randall was opposed because "We can't have a rabbi running around in Turkey. The Turks would stiffen and regard him as sent by us." Schonfeld's pleas, including the argument that no one in Turkey would be helping those destined for territories other than Palestine, were of no avail. The Foreign Office told him that the activities of the Jewish Agency in Turkey would have to suffice, even though its position was shaky. Moreover, the British Embassy in Ankara warned against sending such a Jewish delegation because of anti-Semitism in the Turkish Government. To complicate matters, the Jewish Agency was finding it difficult to establish offices there. Schonfeld was still seeking permission to travel as late as April 1943.[13]

During the deliberations over the rescue of the rabbis, the Foreign Office was discussing the status of the chief rabbi and the Jewish organizations in relation to alien nationals. According to the principle that each government was responsible for its citizens, no Jewish organization had official status in matters concerning Jewish alien nationals. Therefore the chief rabbi was asked to approach the pertinent governments-in-exile. In response, Schonfeld wrote Stanley that as "The Chief Rabbi of the United Hebrew Congregations of the British Empire" Hertz had no standing with the London-based governments-in-exile and for that reason had sought to arrange matters with Whitehall. Schonfeld presented the officials with a serious dilemma: Who would deal with the rabbis who were nationals of enemy states?

The Colonial Office did not yield. Schonfeld was again asked to turn to the governments-in-exile, and by way of compromise to simultaneously petition the Colonial Office. The Foreign Office was to be approached in the case of rabbis who were enemy nationals, but the Foreign Office asked that the requests for those rabbis not be viewed favorably by the Colonial Office.[14] A study of the relevant documents shows that the Colonial Office continued to maintain close contact with Schonfeld and avoided the requests that the issue be dealt with exclusively by the Foreign Office. The chief rabbi's Mauritius proposal was supported by the Colonial Office because it could help resolve the disagreements between the British and the Jewish Agency. After all, the Zionist chief rabbi himself had initiated trans-ferring refugees without Palestinian entry certificates to Mauritius. The colony was making preparations to receive 500 rabbinical refugees and Cyprus had undertaken to accept 400 of them in transit.[15] In the meanwhile other solutions seemed to arise. As a result of Jewish Agency pressure the adult certificates quota was made available in the framework of the Balkan children. Children were to receive 85 percent of the certificates, 10 percent would be for accompanying adults and 5 percent for officials and rabbis. Now Whitehall came up with the idea of including Hertz and Schonfeld's rabbis in this framework as a way of ridding itself of the entire rabbi scheme. The Foreign Office, in particular, favored this solution. Its officials were aware of the fact that the Jewish Agency would agree only to the *aliya* of Zionist rabbis and that Schonfeld would not succeed in getting his list approved. Schonfeld, in the name of the chief rabbi, argued that because the number of adult certificates was limited, and because stiff negotiations would ensue with the Zionist parties over their allocation, the Jewish Agency would not seek to include his rabbis. Thus Schonfeld pleaded to revert to the original plan of seeking refuge in Mauritius. In all events, Schonfeld asked that the list of rabbis be sent to Turkey and Spain for delivery to their consulates in the enemy states for the issuance of visas.[16]

Meanwhile, the governments of Czechoslovakia and Poland were asked to submit official applications for the rabbis who were their nationals. These applications were also meant to serve as guarantees that the rabbis would eventually leave British territory. The Czechoslovak deputy foreign minister, Dr Ripke, duly submitted the request and noted the repatriation.

The Polish ambassador expressed his support for the rabbis' *aliya*, but without mentioning other British territories. There is no doubt that the ambassador's move meant that there was no guarantee of repatriation to Poland: Palestine was the last stop. To the credit of the Colonial Office it interpreted the Polish application as sufficiently indicating a guarantee of repatriation.[17]

Rabbi Schonfeld's patience was at an end. More than six months had elapsed since the meeting between Lord Cranborne and the chief rabbi and yet not a single visa was on its way to Europe. Schonfeld thus asked the colonial secretary to grant the rabbis "a general British Colonial visa" with the final destination to be determined upon arrival in Turkey. The request was turned down.[18] Hertz, too, pressed Stanley after he received confirmation that Turkey would issue visas to refugees holding immigration permits for other countries.[19] Only then did Stanley send cables to the governors of Cyprus, Mauritius, Kenya and the Seychelles asking them to accept a small group of rabbis, with financial upkeep guaranteed by Hertz, until the end of the war.[20] The Kenyan governor turned down the request saying that he had enough on his hands with the small number of Jews among the Polish refugees and matters did not have to be made worse "by importing Rabbis."[21] The Seychelles governor claimed a food shortage in his refusal to accept refugees.[22] The governor of Cyprus was more magnanimous. He would accept 400 Jews on a temporary basis if, when the time came for their transfer to Mauritius, another 224 refugees already on the island would be attached to them.[23] The Mauritius governor alone was willing to accept the rabbis and their families, but on the condition that they agree to live in camps among their racial and religious brethren. Stanley told Hertz that he would have to decide whether the rabbis should be sent to camps where women and men lived separately.

Hertz immediately endorsed "this life saving scheme" and unlike the Jewish Agency declared, "In fact my reports from Mauritius indicate that conditions in the camps are highly satisfactory." Hertz attached a £25 check to cover the expense of dispatching urgent cables to the British consuls on the European continent. When on Stanley's instruction's the money was returned, an official pointed out in his minutes: "I feel very doubtful that any of these rabbis will ever get away, but we have done our best, if rather a slow best for them."[24] Tragic prescience. Eight months had already gone by since the Hertz–Cranborne meeting and in the end not a single rabbi or member of his family was ever saved by operation "Rabbis to Mauritius."[25]

The Colonial Office, on its part, began putting the plan into action. It demanded that the Foreign Office urgently dispatch the list of rabbis to the relevant consuls in Turkey, Spain and Portugal so that transit visas were issued by their representatives in occupied Europe. The Cyprus governor was asked to prepare facilities on the island because the rabbis would be permitted only a short stay in Turkey.[26]

Hertz and Schonfeld pressed Whitehall to take two additional steps: to make the list known to the Germans via the Swiss, who handled British interests in Germany; and to ask the governments involved to issue unconditional visas, in other words visas not limited to transit alone.

The Colonial Office endorsed both requests. The Foreign Office, however, refused to involve the Swiss because it would mean negotiations with the Germans, a step prohibited by the Bermuda Conference. Moreover, Churchill was very sensitive to this subject and was on guard against contact with the Germans, even at the expense of human lives. He had just written a personal note warning Eden not to negotiate with the Reich about *aliya* from Germany. The Foreign Office did, however, agree to pass the list of rabbis to the German authorities, but without the visa request that was the practice with candidates for emigration to Palestine. That action appeased the prime minister. On the other hand, the Foreign Office issued instructions to the Madrid, Lisbon and Ankara legations about the request for unconditional visas, "as we should be open to criticism if we were not to comply fully with the [chief rabbi's] Council's request."[27] Meanwhile the governor of Mauritius requested a budget to prepare for the arrival of the rabbis and their families.[28]

Thus the apparently successful completion of the first stage of operation "Rabbis to Mauritius." Now Rabbis Hertz and Schonfeld sought to expand the program.

"Rabbis to Mauritius" and Palestine Immigration Policy

The Mauritius affair coincided with developments in Palestine immigration policy.

The Colonial Office promoted a limited non-Zionist "rescue" program parallel to that of the Zionists, a stance well-illustrated by the following affair. The Czechoslovakian foreign minister submitted a request to the Foreign Office to add the names of three rabbis to Hertz's list. Approval had already been granted for 32 rabbis and their families for a total 108 people, while the original agreement had been for only 30 rabbis. The attempt to expand the list met with the opposition of the colonial secretary: "in view of the desirability of treating the refugee problem as a whole and not affecting Jews only, the Secretary of State would be reluctant to extend the arrangements to other Rabbis." Therefore, he suggested that the Foreign Office submit the following evasive reply to the Czechoslovak government: If these rabbis succeeded in reaching neutral territory, the colonial secretary would consider ways of receiving them into British territory.[29] The message left the Colonial Office on July 20, 1943. The following day Schonfeld, arguing about the number that had been agreed upon with Lord Cranborne, wrote Colonel Stanley requesting the extension of British generosity to 100 and their families.[30] Surprisingly Schonfeld's request was granted.

A study of the issue shows that the approval was due to the Palestine policy. It had been decided that every Jewish child and adult who succeeded in reaching Turkey would be granted an *aliya* permit. This was a reason to cancel operation "Rabbis to Mauritius," because Hertz and Schonfeld's rabbis could be included in this framework. British generosity, however, had its limits: they decided to keep their decision secret so as not to encourage Jews to flee to Turkey.[31] Only the heads of the Jewish Agency knew of the decision and they promised to keep it under wraps because, as the Foreign Office told them, secrecy was to the Jews' benefit. And as the government did not wish to include people such as rabbis Hertz and Schonfeld in the circle of those privy to the secret, the government was inclined to grant Schonfeld's request to broaden the framework of the Mauritius operation. The Colonial Office was, however, afraid that "there will be no end to those rabbis."[32]

The Mauritius governor agreed to accept 100 rabbis and their families on condition that the total not exceed 340 people. This happy information was immediately forwarded to the chief rabbi.[33] The officials, however, were less than happy to deal with the issue, but decided to maintain "this fiction" with Hertz. They believed that he was capable of extricating many more rabbis from Europe. In contrast, the Foreign Office thought that only a few rabbis, mainly those from Slovakia and Hungary, would be removed, but nonetheless was apprehensive about broadening the operation.[34] The Colonial Office, for its part, was prepared to add any name Schonfeld submitted. On Hertz's recommendation it even sent the Foreign Office the name of the endangered Bishop of Dalmatia, though as an official wrote, "he could by no stretch of the imagination be classed as a Rabbi!" The Foreign Office was also inclined to accept Hertz's gesture, "although the Serbian Bishop is not a Rabbi," but demurred after the Belgian ambassador sought to include the head of the Brussels Jewish community in Schonfeld's list.[35] Be that as it may, Schonfeld managed to have the widowed wives of rabbis, and teachers and other Jews included.[36]

The lists were compiled and sent for endorsement, but Turkey proved to be an obstacle when, at the end of 1943 and the beginning of 1944, it became increasingly clear that the escape route passed through that country. The Foreign Office and the British Embassy, fearing a mass emigration from Europe, kept a close watch over the transfer of Turkish visas to European capitals. Schonfeld, ever alert, made great efforts to prevent the issue from being dropped from the Whitehall agenda.[37] To forestall any negative Turkish action Schonfeld, on February 4, 1944, sought approval for the transfer of £2,000 to the embassy in Ankara in order to show the Turks that the means for the upkeep of the rabbis, their families and their travel to a final destinations were available.[38]

The Colonial Office repeatedly stressed its desire to maintain the operation, but "it is necessary to keep up with him the fiction that these rabbis may go to Mauritius," because in February 1944 the decision to allow emigration to Palestine for every Jew who had fled Europe was still confidential. If the rabbis reached Turkey they would be issued transit visas for travel via Syria to Palestine, and if they so wished they would be allowed to remain there.[39]

Palestine Chief Rabbi Isaac Halevi Herzog, who had recently returned from Turkey, wrote Hertz that only 28 Turkish visas had been issued. Schonfeld then resubmitted his request to be allowed to travel to Turkey. Eden turned him down again because the British ambassador said that only Hayim Barlas, the Jewish Agency's representative in Istanbul, was acceptable to the Turkish authorities. Not even Rabbi Herzog was able to get anything out of the Turks. Thus Eden suggested that the Jewish Agency handle the refugees destined for Mauritius.[40]

Schonfeld now lobbied even harder. In April 1944, after receiving appeals from Switzerland, he asked that the holders of the Mauritius visas be included in an exchange plan. In all events, the government was asked to recognize them "as quasi British protected persons." Both appeals were rejected by the Foreign Office because it did not believe it could tell the Germans that nationals of enemy countries, just because Britain was willing to accept them, could be considered British citizens.[41]

Meanwhile, after the quota of 100 rabbis destined for Mauritius was filled, Germany occupied Hungary. Rabbi Hertz, contending that the visas sent to Europe had saved many people, asked the colonial secretary to expand the program to 1,000 rabbis and their families. Hertz's words met with astonishment at the Foreign Office because not a single one of the rabbis had managed to flee abroad. Hertz had apparently meant that the visa holders had not been expelled from their homes. It is doubtful, however, that the transit visas for neutral countries ever reached the rabbis. When the rabbis arrived at the Turkish legation in Budapest they discovered that the Turks had canceled the visas and the British ambassador was asked to demand their renewal.[42] Now, too, the Colonial Office recommended that the Foreign Office accede to Hertz's request for an expansion of the quota. There were a number of reasons for this:

1　None of the rabbis had arrived in Mauritius, it was doubtful they ever would, and if they indeed succeeded in escaping Europe they would probably settle in Palestine;

2   the rabbis would not be included in the *aliya* quota framework because, as a Colonial Office official wrote, "the root of the trouble is that the rabbis are not *personae gratae* to the Jewish Agency"; and

3   the chief rabbi's report that the visas had saved many people should not be disregarded.

The Foreign Office accepted the Colonial Office's endorsement. In mid-July Stanley was pleased to inform Hertz that visas for 1,000 people had been approved with the agreement of the Governor of Mauritius. The island's governor had, in fact, conditioned his approval on the number not exceeding 300. In return, Hertz was asked to use his influence to ask the Jews already in camps on the island to modify their demand that they be sent elsewhere. Hertz's reply was apparently phrased so diplomatically that the colonial secretary felt obliged to vindicate himself. He wrote that he understood the feelings of the detainees, but that he had no way of removing them from the island in the near future.[43]

Surprisingly, Schonfeld neglected to note the acquisition of the thousand visas in the report of the Religious Emergency Council published after the war.[44]

When the condition of Hungarian Jewry deteriorated Schonfeld again lobbied the Foreign Office for help. Initially, he asked that it inquire into the fate of the Jews in Hungary via the Swiss, who represented British interests in that country. The Foreign office bypassed this route since it would be tantamount to negotiating with an enemy power. It did, however, instruct its ambassador in Berne to submit the inquiry to the Hungarians via the International Committee of the Red Cross.[45]

Toward the end of August 1944, Schonfeld asked that the Turkish consul in Budapest mail the visas to the rabbis so as to avoid the danger of having to appear at the consulate in person. The Foreign Office promised to send the request to its ambassador in Ankara.[46]

All this was relevant to the rabbis already registered, but the British authorities were in no hurry, despite knowledge of the existence of the crematoria, to approve any additions. The completed list of a thousand rabbis was submitted on July 24, but the security authorities approved it only on September 28.[47]

The conflict between Schonfeld and the Foreign office over Swiss involvement in rescue operations was protracted and the Foreign Office refused to yield. The reason was that Britain refused to adopt measures that would seem to involve negotiations with the enemy. For some reason, however, it was explained to Schonfeld that Swiss intervention would endanger the candidates for rescue. The Foreign Office refused to allow them to receive Swiss visas. In the end, however, it did agree to submit the list of rabbis to Switzerland so as to enable the local Jewish welfare organizations to enlist their government's aid in the rescue efforts.[48]

Schonfeld was persistent. He asked the Colonial Office to seek ways of convincing the Germans that the Mauritius visas were not fictitious. Schonfeld may have worried that the Germans would invalidate the visas just as they refused to recognize the South American passports held by Jews.[49]

Toward the end of the war there was a tendency to grant protection to Jews. This was especially the case in Hungary and only then did the British authorities use the appropriate wording. The Foreign Office sent the ambassador in Berne a declaration attesting to the authenticity of the Mauritius visas, adding that they should "act as a protective measure in the same way as visas to Palestine."[50] Ergo, "Rabbis to Mauritius" trod the path of British policy toward the Jewish Agency of Palestine.

The Attempts to Rescue the Jews of Nitra and their Rabbi

On September 12, 1944, the London office of the Jewish Agency wrote the Foreign Office expressing deep concern over the fate of the Jewish remnant in Slovakia.[51] The Germans were then quelling a revolt in that country with a heavy hand and the expulsions of the Jews resumed.[52] It was at that time of distress that Schonfeld succeeded in persuading Masaryk to relay his support for Schonfeld's and Hertz's plans to the British Government. As a result the Foreign Office immediately announced that the Czechoslovak, not the Swiss Government would find a way to locate the Jewish candidates for visas.[53] Rabbi Schonfeld had close ties to Slovakian Jewry, especially the Nitra community in whose *yeshiva*, headed by Rabbi Samuel David Ungar, father-in-law of his childhood friend Michael Dov Weissmandel, he had studied. As noted above Schonfeld had submitted a special list of Nitra residents for the Mauritian visas. In the fall of 1944, Schonfeld concentrated his efforts on saving his rabbi. He told the Foreign Office that Ungar was the greatest Jewish figure on the continent and that his rescue would be of "world wide importance to the present and future of Israel." He requested that Ungar be granted "the utmost possible British protection, as near as can be to British nationality." Schonfeld based his request on the fact that Ungar had spent various periods of time in Palestine.[54] Serious deliberations then took place in the Foreign and Colonial Offices. However, the idea of granting Rabbi Ungar the status of a British protected person, or Palestinian citizenship, was rejected. In the end Ungar, since he possessed a Uruguayan passport, received both a certificate of entry for Palestine and a visa for Mauritius. The Foreign Office informed Berne that the rabbi "is exchangeable," i.e., for Germans held by the British. In the meanwhile, Schonfeld reported that Ungar had escaped from prison and was in hiding.[55] The efforts to save him continued nonetheless and his certificate was transferred to Sweden because it had an honorary consul in Bratislava, the Slovakian capital. The consul was instructed to issue a certificate to Ungar stating, "Palestinian citizenship on completion of two years' residence," with the hope that the word "citizenship" would provide salvation. This formula was a step of sorts toward meeting the Jewish Agency demand that certificate holders be recognized as citizens of Palestine.[56] In February 1945, the British legation in Stockholm announced that the certificate sent to Ungar had been returned to Sweden with a note that he had been expelled.[57]

In April 1945, Schonfeld asked the Foreign Office to make attempts to locate his rabbi in the Bergen-Belsen concentration camp which had been liberated by British forces. By June 1945, after Ungar was not located there, Schonfeld requested that the British ambassador in Prague ask the Czechoslovak Government to look into his fate. Shortly thereafter Schonfeld learned that Rabbi Ungar had died in the forest hideout were he was concealed by Slovakian partisans. The Foreign Office expressed sorrow "that all our joint efforts on his behalf were unavailing."[58] It should be noted that the British were never prepared to adopt extraordinary measures, even in the case of a single individual. Even stretching themselves they never agreed to bypass the formalities dealing with the refugee issue.[59]

The efforts on behalf of the other visa applicants continued, and since Ungar had been declared "exchangeable" Schonfeld petitioned the Colonial Office to include all the Nitra residents in the list of candidates for exchange with German nationals. However, the Colonial Office replied that the list was full and there were not enough Germans to exchange for British and Palestinian citizens. Nonetheless, the Colonial Office told the Foreign Office, "You will agree that anything we can do we must do." The Colonial Office suggested that the list of candidates for emigration to Mauritius be resubmitted to the Germans and that attempts be made in South America to locate Germans who could be exchanged for them.[60] Three terrible months, fateful for many Jews, passed before the government issued its final answer: Exchange was impossible because of the absence of any formal basis for doing so. Thus Schonfeld asked that the list of Mauritius candidates among the Nitra residents be sent to the Germans through the Swiss. On April 4, when the Red Army was already advancing into Slovakia, the list was finally sent to Switzerland by diplomatic pouch with the hope "that they [Nitra residents] may not be deported."[61]

In early January 1945, Rabbi Schonfeld received a smuggled letter from his friend, Rabbi Michael Dov Weissmandel, who was hiding in a "cave near Lvov" after having jumped off a train taking Slovakian Jews to Auschwitz. Weissmandel listed all the members of his family and others, including the Zionist leader Gizi Fleischmann, who were with him on the train.[62] Weissmandel, well-informed from his hiding place, pleaded for them to be transferred to Bergen-Belsen through the mediation of Dr Reszoe (Israel) Kasztner. Since most of those mentioned in Weissmandel's letter were candidates for Mauritius, Schonfeld, who handed the letter to the Foreign Office, asked that now the list be sent via Stockholm to the Swedish consul in Bratislava. Furthermore, Schonfeld demanded that they be granted the rights of certificate holders, because as such they would be transferred to Bergen-Belsen. Schonfeld, of course, did not know of the controversial agreement in Budapest between Kasztner and the Gestapo concerning the rescue of a limited number of Jews via Bergen-Belsen. He thought that the certificates indeed saved lives and hoped that a similar arrangement could be attained in Slovakia. The Foreign Office agreed to send the list to Stockholm for transfer to Slovakia. However, it rejected the proposal that the Swedes be asked to appoint a consul with full diplomatic status in Slovakia since the local honorary consul was restricted in his activities on behalf of the Jews.[63]

Weissmandel, bereft of family, survived. In April 1945, thanks to a ransom paid by the Joint, he escaped to Switzerland with a group of Bratislava Jews.[64] Wiessmandel was one of the great figures of the Holocaust. He established the Jewish underground movement on Slovakia to fight for the survival and rescue of Polish Jews. His risky negotiations with the Gestapo in Bratislava led to a large-scale ransom plan ("Europa Plan"). In order to promote this and local rescue schemes he established a communication network with Western countries. It was probably Weissmandel who conceived the idea of bombing Auschwitz. His documentary book, *Min Hametzar* (From the Depths of Suffering), is a heart-rending account of the travail of European Jewry and a harsh reckoning with the secular Jewish leaders of the Free World who regarded his rescue efforts with skepticism. Rabbi Weissmandel is considered a great hero of the Holocaust by the orthodox community.[65]

Financing Efforts

The Mauritius affair unfolded alongside the efforts of Hertz and Schonfeld to obtain rescue funds. They had initially sought to transfer £2,000 to the British Embassy in Ankara to convince the Turks that funds for the upkeep and travel of the rabbis were available. The Foreign Office supported the move and it was approved by the Treasury's Department of Trade with the Enemy. Neither did the MEW object to the transfer of money to a neutral country even for the purpose of bribing border guards. It preferred that the money be in British rather than Americans hands. This should be viewed in the context of the competition with the WRB. The British ambassador in Ankara, however, suggested that the transfer be made directly to the Jewish Agency's Haim Barlas.[66] It is possible that the money issue was raised to back another Schonfeld request to leave for Turkey.[67]

At about the same time an illegal transfer of £2,050 by Hertz to welfare organizations active from Sweden, through the mediation of the Joint, was uncovered. Since Britain maintained a strict blockade on the transfer of hard currency to enemy countries, Schonfeld was summoned to the Bank of England for an explanation. No legal measures were taken against the chief rabbi, and in order not to embarrass him Eden referred Hertz to Emerson for what developed into a protracted issue. After meeting with Emerson, Hertz expressed his disappointment because "the facilities are circumscribed." The negotiations lasted almost half a year without any tangible results.[68]

With the renewal of the expulsions from Slovakia, Hertz asked that £2,000 be made available to Rabbi Ungar for the Jews of Nitria. He asked Emerson's Inter-Governmental Committee on Refugees to transfer the sum to Isaac Sternbuch, an Agudat Israel leader in Switzerland active in rescue and relief work. Hertz assured the committee that Sternbuch would exchange the Sterling for Slovakian currency. When the British Embassy in Berne was consulted about the proposed transaction it replied that Slovakian currency was unavailable in Switzerland. Thus Hertz's pledge was worthless. The Foreign Office then suggested that Hertz's organization be asked how it intended to assure that hard currency would not fall into the enemy hands.[69] Weissmandel's letters were one great outcry for ransom money.[70]

Meanwhile, the expulsions were carried out and the funds never arrived. It appears that Hertz succeeded in sending various sums to Sternbuch about the time of the Swedish transfer. Rabbis Hertz and Schonfeld had hoped to receive permission through Eden for the transfer of £100,000 in rescue funds. He had also sought the cooperation of the World Jewish Congress.[71] Naturally, the project had no chance of succeeding.

The Rescue Policy in Rabbi Schonfeld's Eyes

There is no doubt that Schonfeld considered his achievements to be the result of the "de-Zionization" and "depolitization" policy he advocated in the rescue issue. We have seen, however, that British refugee policy in general, and Palestinian policy in particular, went hand-in-hand in the Mauritius operation. Just as the British had gradually agreed, under Jewish Agency pressure, to a limited rescue *aliya*, they had also acquiesced to the entreaties of Hertz and Schonfeld by opening a crack in the blockade to the non-Zionist ultraorthodox.

A sharp public debate in Britain about the failure to save more Jews followed the Eichmann trial that was held in Jerusalem in the early 1960s. Schonfeld defended the Churchill administration. In an article in *The Times* he even mentioned "some hundreds of Mauritius and other immigration permits . . . in favour of any threatened Jewish family whom we could name." He even claimed that the British were prepared to help "openly, constructively and totally." Be that as it may, Schonfeld's argument cannot be sustained, either by the facts documented in the official files or by his personal experience. Schonfeld's intention was apparently to publicly censure the Zionists, while *"Britain was at her best"* [emphasis in original].[72] Schonfeld's stand led to a lengthy debate in *The Times* and the British Jewish press.

Schonfeld was consistently anti-Zionist. After the war he even attempted to undermine the *aliya* policy in regard to displaced persons. In another anti-Zionist move, on September 2, 1945, Schonfeld sought the consent of Foreign Secretary Ernest Bevin for "an autonomous Jewish reserve" for 100,000 Jews in northern Germany, as "poetic justice" of sorts. The Foreign Office rejected the idea out of hand.[73]

12

The Ten Million Dollar
Illusion

Cable: "Emerson stated ten million dollar fund never existed."

Jewish leaders made great efforts to bring about a basic change in the attitude of the Western powers toward European Jewry, but never managed to make even an effective dent in the blockade. Preventing Jews from breaking away from Europe was a basic tenet of British policy, according to which the Jews' fate was bound to Europe and victory alone would be their salvation. One might imagine that agreement could have been reached on the extension of humanitarian aid for the Jews inside Europe, beyond the paltry sum of £3,000 a month discussed in chapter 9, without contravening British government policy.

In this chapter we discuss a supposed $10 million relief fund, a huge sum at the time. It is a story which highlights the tragedy of Jewish intercessors roaming about in a bubble of illusions, never aware that the Allies on both sides of the Atlantic Ocean were dallying with them.

On December 21, 1943, the Jewish Telegraphic Agency cabled information that sent waves of hope soaring through Jewish hearts. Breckenridge Long, Assistant Secretary for Special Problems at the American State Department, testified before the Senate Foreign Relations Committee that the British and American Governments were prepared to extend $4 million each to buy food for Jews in Polish and Czechoslovak ghettos. He added that an American Jewish organization would grant an additional $2 million, bringing the total to $10 million. According to the plan the Red Cross would be responsible for distribution.[1] Long's role in misleading his superiors is severely censured in all the books dealing with the US attitude to the Holocaust. After this confidential information was leaked by Long, whom Henry Morgenthau, the American treasury secretary accused of being an anti-Semite,[2] the British Section of the World Jewish Congress sent a confidential circular to its members informing them that the WJC was the contributing organization mentioned.[3] Moreover, the

BSWJC boasted that the plan was drawn up at its initiative. In August it had proposed that the British and American Governments grant the sum of £5 million for the immediate supply of food, clothes and medicine to occupied Europe under the supervision of the Red Cross and the management of the Inter Governmental Committee for Refugees. After complex, arduous negotiations the two powers agreed to participate. After the leak all sides agreed to maintain secrecy! Finally, success was achieved and Easterman could write in the circular with great satisfaction that "The foregoing is only a brief resume of a notable chapter in the history of the WJC. The full details will be disclosed at a later date."[4]

Shortly thereafter, Easterman announced that Britain and the United States had undertaken to budget the entire $10 million and shelved the participation of the WJC. The Jewish organization thought "this is highly satisfactory."[5] In actuality, both governments wanted to remove the Jews from the picture because, as we shall see, they had no intention of going ahead with the plan. The WJC, on the other hand, thought that the money was already available.

The Foreign Office attempted to cool the Jews' fervor and told Brotman that even if the Germans permitted the Red Cross to supervise the food distribution, the Exchequer would be opposed to the plan. In all events, a prior condition was absolute certainty that the Germans would receive no benefit.[6] The American partner displayed interest in the WJC proposal and consulted with Sir Herbert Emerson. The IGCR director then turned to the Foreign Office where he was cautioned not to veer from the set framework.[7] Long's leak changed the rules of the game, for "it seems somewhat late in the day to suggest in effect that the Inter Governmental Committee should abandon it." Emerson advised the Foreign Office to coordinate moves with the United States, lest Britain be presented as the party refusing to deliver: "that it shall not be turned down by one without reference to the other."[8]

The director of the Foreign Office Refugee Department raised two problems. First, was it possible to establish a fund only for a specific group of Europeans? i.e., the Jews. Secondly, purchase by the Red Cross of goods in the enemy countries of Rumania and Hungary contravened the Anglo-American blockade. Only the second point was mentioned in the correspondence.[9] As to the first point, the WJC spoke of a fund to aid all suffering people, even though they meant Jews especially. The Red Cross, for its part, had no hesitation about emphasizing that the fund was meant to assist Jews.[10]

The WJC's Dr Nachum Goldmann and Aryeh Tartakower arrived in London in January 1944. When Tartakower met with Haccius, WJC officials reacted as if the money was already available and Haccius rendered advice about its use. The Jews wanted to present to the heads of the Red

Cross a written expression of their faith in the organization. Tartakower sent a letter of summation to Red Cross headquarters in Geneva, adding a flattering "expression of gratitude of the World Jewish Congress for their [the Red Cross'] splendid humanitarian work which has succeeded in saving the lives of tens of thousands of victims of war." And when Haccius returned to London, Ben Rubenstein greeted him warmly and naively saying: "We are glad to have you back in London. It is one bit of sunshine in an otherwise very depressing world."[11]

Be that as it may, in their contacts with the Foreign Office, International Committee of the Red Cross representatives displayed a totally different approach. S. Zollinger, of the ICRC, told the Economic Warfare Ministry that his organization was startled to hear that $10 million was to be allocated to help Europe's Jews. He thought the information would reach Hitler who had made up his mind to destroy the Jews. On the other hand, there were circles in Germany, the director of the German Red Cross for example, who were not reconciled to Hitler's plans. Therefore it was advisable to extend more modest assistance so that it not draw public attention. The ministry was pleased with Zollinger's stand.[12]

On the other hand, the Foreign Office took notice of the fact that the United States was in a presidential election year and that Roosevelt had only recently established the high level War Refugee Board to deal with the refugee problem.[13] The Foreign Office was in a delicate situation, for the prevailing impression was that the United States had initiated a humanitarian program for the benefit of Jews which Britain opposed when in actuality no proposal to allocate $4 million had yet been presented to the government. The British ambassador in Washington received instructions to meet with State Department officials for purposes of coordination.[14]

As to the status of the $10 million, its existence was never denied, but actually not one penny on either side of the ocean had been budgeted. Goldmann raised the issue with the Foreign Office, which suggested that the Red Cross enter into negotiations with the British and American blockade authorities in other words, back to square one.[15]

Apparently the British Section thought that in special circumstances it would be possible to revive the $10 million scheme. In July 1944, when the Hungarian Jewish crisis was at its peak, Eva, Marchioness of Reading, approached Eden for the WJC. She reminded him that in a previous meeting he had said that the Red Cross was set to extend assistance to Hungarian Jewish refugees. In her judgment the agreement concerning the fund "has not been made effective through some technical difficulties, although it was agreed in principle months ago." Eden did not deny the existence of an $8 million program ("not ten million"). According to the Foreign Secretary the program was impractical and was replaced by another that was operating properly. The information was secret and publicizing it would harm the refugees, he said, adding, "we are giving considerable help."[16] Eden was referring to the IGCR's credit program, a project limited in scope that was mainly meant to prevent means of payment from flowing out of the Allied countries.[17]

Lady Reading and the other leaders of the BSWJC persisted in their belief that a $10 million fund indeed existed. In December 1944, she toured liberated Belgium and France and was shocked by the condition of the surviving Jewish remnant. When she returned to London she met with Undersecretary George Hall and suggested that the $10 million be used for the refugees in the territories liberated by the Allies. The Foreign Office was mystified because no documentation about the fund existed. Lady Reading was referred to the International Red Cross in Geneva, which also wondered what fund she was talking about.[18]

In the meanwhile Dr Leo Kubowitsky (Kubovi), a senior WJC official in New York, arrived in London. He and Lady Reading met with Emerson and his colleagues. As to the fund, Emerson emphatically denied that it had ever existed. According to him, Long's testimony before the House Foreign Relations Committee in November 1943 was based on incorrect information, thus any inquiries by Kubowitsky should be made in Washington. At any rate, His Majesty's Government had never assumed the obligation of donating $4 million to the starving Jews of Europe.

The end of this sad chapter was succinctly expressed in the cable sent to Goldmann by Kubowitsky and Lady Reading the day after the meeting: "Emerson stated ten million dollar fund never existed."[19]

Ireland and the Jews of Europe

I am not aware of any such [deliberate cruelty] towards Jews on the part of
the German Government.

Ireland, Britain, Germany, and the Jews

The Republic of Ireland was in a unique situation in World War II. Its
agreement with Britain of 1921, after a protracted armed rebellion and
political struggle, gave independent Eire all of Ireland except for Ulster,
which had a Protestant majority. Ireland had the status of a Dominion and
was represented in London by a High Commissioner. However, unlike all
the other Dominions, Ireland did not make common cause with Britain
after it declared war on Germany in September 1939. The Taoiseach (prime
minister) and minister for external affairs, Eamon de Valera, declared his
country neutral in the conflict.

More than Irish interests and animosity toward Britain were involved.
Zealous Catholicism also played an important role. De Valera instructed
his external affairs secretary, Joseph Walshe, to ascertain the Vatican's
views on the war. "On that basis Walshe prepared the ground for Ireland's
wartime policy," which "tended to pursue the same line as Pius XII."[1]

This voluntary dependency on the Vatican was veiled by the other
reasons given for Ireland's neutrality, foremost among them the stress on
Ireland's absolute independence in reaching crucial decisions. Another
declared reason was the desire to protect the country and its citizens, a
surviving remnant of conflicts, famine and mass emigration, from destruction. But neither were "the real national arguments" absent: the hope for
an eventual unification of Northern Ireland and independent Eire.[2]

May and June 1940 were fateful months in the war. The Wehrmacht ran
over Western Europe and the British Expeditionary Force was evacuated
from Dunkirk. The British feared that the German army would invade
Ireland, now of crucial strategic importance. In its hour of distress Britain
made Ireland an offer it believed the erstwhile antagonist could not refuse:
Britain would relinquish Ulster if Eire joined in, or at least agreed to the
stationing of British troops on its soil. The offer was rejected. The Germans

had also offered their support for Irish unification and warned Dublin against violating its neutrality. Irish policymakers apparently believed that Germany would win the war, thus rendering the generous British offer worthless.[3]

The Dail, the Irish Parliament, roundly supported the policy of neutrality. Not even its only Jewish deputy, de Valera's friend and erstwhile comrade-in-arms Robert Briscoe, voted against the "Chief."[4] (Briscoe was then an honored member of the presidium of the World Zionist Revisionist Organization and close to its leader, Vladimir Jabotinsky.) Even when the fortunes of war turned, de Valera adhered to his policy. Britain often expressed resentment of Ireland because its neutrality played into the hands of the Germans in the struggle for control over the shipping lanes of the Atlantic Ocean.

On occasion, de Valera even expressed sympathy for Germany. The peak, or nadir, of this expression was the personal condolence call de Valera paid at the German legation in Dublin after Hitler's death. The heads of the Department of External Affairs cautioned de Valera, but he preferred the advice of the pro-German minister of war, Frank Aiken. The incident occurred after the cancellation of the political censorship protecting Germany's "fame," and when the public had already learned of its atrocities. The gesture was censured at home and abroad and damaged Ireland's postwar standing. The opposition in the Dail raised a storm and the Taoiseach, claiming that protocol called for the condolence gestures, found it difficult to defend his actions.

However, he let Ireland's Washington envoy, Robert Brennan, know his true feelings: "So long as we retained our diplomatic relations with Germany, to have failed to call upon the German representative would have been an act of unpardonable discourtesy to the German nation and to Dr [Eduard] Hemple [the German envoy] himself. During the whole of the war Dr Hemple's conduct was irreproachable. He was always friendly and invariably correct in marked contrast with [David] Gray [the American envoy]. I certainly was not going to add to his humiliation in the hour of defeat."[5]

Churchill's reaction was not long in coming. On May 13, 1945, in a speech marking the fifth year of his premiership, he emphasized the critical importance of British sovereignty over Northern Ireland and the control of the straits between Scotland and Ulster, "through which to bring in the means of life and send out the forces of war. This was indeed a deadly moment in our lives and if it had not been for the loyalty and friendship of Northern Ireland we should have been forced to come to close quarters with Mr de Valera or perish forever from the earth. However, with a restraint and poise to which history will find few parallels, we never laid a violent hand upon them, which at times would have been quite easy and

quite natural, and left the de Valera government to frolic with the German
... representatives to their hearts content."[6] This strategic experience might
be one of the reasons for the tragic history of Northern Ireland after the
war.

The stand of the Irish leadership on the dire predicament of the Jews of
Europe at the time can be understood against this backdrop of antagonism
toward Britain; sympathy, to one extent or another for Germany; and
zealous adherence to the Vatican's political line. In March 1944, Dublin
was apprised of the accusations of anti-Semitism hurled at the Irish
Government by American Jewish groups. In response, de Valera told his
cabinet on March 25, 1944, that his government was not tainted by anti-
Semitism. He did, however, admit that German anti-Jewish propaganda
had made inroads in his administration. The country's Jewish community,
obeisantly loyal, stood behind its government. The Irish Jewish
Committee issued an absolution from anti-Semitism, graced by Briscoe's
signature.[7]

Those anti-Semitic inroads stand out in *bas-relief* in the attitude of
Charles Bewley, the senior official of the Department of External Affairs,
who served as his country's Berlin envoy until 1939. Secretary Joseph
Walshe, the head of the External Affairs Department, asked him to explain
why the countries of Central and Eastern Europe fostered "discriminatory
measures in respect of Jews." According to Bewley, the major reason was
the Jews' failure to assimilate into society. He did not stop at that, but
accused the Jews of preferring the interests of their own "race" during times
of conflict even at the expense of the interests of their homeland. His barbs
were aimed at the Balfour Declaration, which had supposedly won the
hearts of German Jews who, as it were, subsequently engineered the downfall of their German homeland. He spouted German propaganda without
a trace of incredulity: "It is a notorious fact," Bewley wrote, "that the international white slave traffic is controlled by Jews."

Bewley not only castigated the Jews for Germany's demoralization, but
as a patriotic Irishman waxed eloquent in condemning the British for their
deliberate obstruction of attempts to solve a problem that was endangering
world peace: for "English politicians to make solemn pronouncements in
complete and often willful ignorance of the circumstances would appear
neither helpful to the cause of peace nor of assistance in finding a solution
of the problem."

Bewley sent Walshe this confidential report on December 9, 1938, a
month after *Kristallnacht*. He does not even refer to the event which
shocked the enlightened world. Tens of Jews were murdered, hundreds of
synagogues were set to the torch, and 7,000 Jewish-owned businesses were
destroyed. The Irish diplomat had neither seen nor heard. And though he
thought the activities of Jews should be curtailed, he concludes: "Naturally

this would not apply in cases of deliberate cruelty on the part of the Government, but I am not aware of any such toward Jews on the part of the German Government.[!]"

The Catholic diplomat apparently believed that his attitudes would be justified in the eyes of his Catholic colleagues in Dublin if Nazi pagan anti-Semitism was subsumed under Apostolic protection. What, according to Bewley, were the contemporary Jew-haters doing? Nothing more than the "Measures introduced by the Popes in relation to the Jews in Rome. Under various Papal decrees Jews were forbidden to have Christian servants. Christians who had recourse to Jewish doctors were excommunicated. Jews lived in special parts of the city and carried a distinctive mark (a wheel or a circle) on their clothing . . . " The broad purview of Bewley's report makes it an egregious document from the diplomatic standpoint.

Disturbingly, Bewley's Dublin colleagues entered no comments in the margins of the report they had received from this follower of Josef Goebbels. The line drawn in pencil in the margins attests to the absence of a response.[8]

The senior Irish officials who determined Ireland's refugee policy shared Bewley's views. Neither was the Department of Justice, responsible for dealing with Jewish refugees, favorable to them. Ireland was hardly a major magnet for immigrants and had no refugee problem. For generations it was a land of emigration and its population decreased from year to year. Nevertheless, the trend was to reject even the few requests for refuge submitted by Jews, even when the applicant was of potential benefit to the country.[9]

It was believed that many Jews would seek to forsake the continent of their travails and seek new homelands after the war. Consequently, Irish officials dealt with the theoretical aspects of immigration policy. The discussions reflect the accepted policy toward the Jews throughout the crisis years and the war.

Colonel Dan Bryan, of the Department of Defence's military intelligence, was asked to submit his views on the security risks that Jewish refugees might pose. In his report to the Department of Justice of January 6, 1945, he fulfilled his professional duty in one sentence: Such an immigration posed no security risk. However, he penned many sentences warning his Department of Justice colleagues not to deviate from the principle "adopted since the start of the emergency that aliens should not normally be allowed to come here." After all, "it would lead to an influx of continental Jews."[10]

After the guns were silenced, hundreds of thousands of displaced persons, a considerable number of them Jews, wandered throughout Europe. The Department of Justice discussed the problem and dedicated a special chapter of a memorandum of September 24, 1945 to the Jews. It displays an attitude toward the Jews different from that toward other refugees: "It is the policy of the Department of Justice to restrict the immigration of Jews. The wealth and influence of the Jewish community in this country appears to have increased considerably in recent years, and murmurs against Jewish wealth and influence are frequently heard. As Jews do not become assimilated with the native population like other immigrants, there is a danger that any big increase in their number might create a social problem."[11]

The Irish historian Dermot Keogh is the only one of his colleagues who has dealt seriously with the topic of Ireland and the refugees. In *Ireland and Europe 1919–1948*, he argues that in light of the Department of Justice memorandum, Prime Minister de Valera expressed a willingness to accept 10,000 refugees as Ireland's contribution to the displaced persons problem. From the relevant document it is clear that de Valera was referring to refugees, in general, not necessarily to those of the Jewish faith. It is unlikely that the Taoiseach was prepared to more than double the Irish Jewish community of some 4,000 souls.

Nevertheless, Keogh concludes that "de Valera had no sympathy whatsoever for that point of view" that reflected by the Department of Justice memorandum: "there is evidence that in the case of applications from the international Jewish community, de Valera was particularly attentive to ensure that his liberal policy was applied; he was in contact with the Chief Rabbi of Palestine, Dr Herzog, on more than one occasion."[12]

Keogh presents no evidence, but it is true, as we shall see, that in his wartime attempts to save Jews, Rabbi Isaac Herzog had turned to de Valera. Herzog had cultivated close ties with de Valera when he served as the chief rabbi of Ireland's Jewish community.

Despite his efforts to defend de Valera and his policies, Keogh is a fastidious historian except when dealing with Ireland and the Jews. He faithfully presents sources which even to his mind display a moral lacking among Irish diplomats and senior officials, but insists that those anti-Jewish views did not influence the Taoiseach, who also served as minster for external affairs,[13] again without a shred of documentary or testimonial evidence. Any trace of liberalism in de Valera's policy may be found in reference to "non-Aryan" Christian refugees of Jewish origin, about 150 of whom arrived in Ireland during the war. Their entry, as we shall see, was indeed approved by de Valera, but as we have seen in the memorandum the declared policy was not to permit the entry of refugees of the Jewish faith.

Before the outbreak of the war, the Irish Co-ordinating Committee for Refugees was established. The first page of its memorandum, *Proposals for the Settlement in this Country of Refugees from Germany and Austria*, clearly states that "these proposals relate only to Christians with Jewish blood." The committee defined Ireland's task as providing refuge only to this type of immigrant. Other countries would accept those of the Mosaic faith.[14]

Despite his desperate attempts to vindicate de Valera, Keogh can neither disprove that the practice was to prevent the arrival of Jewish refugees into Ireland, nor that the policy was supported by the prime minister.

Keogh relates the story of Gerald Goldberg, a Jew, elected as Lord Mayor of Cork, who was a member of de Valera's party. In September 1939, Goldberg's father met a Jew who had arrived in Ireland from Germany as a stowaway and whom the authorities had decided to return to the ship's port of origin. Robert Briscoe, close friend, former comrade-in-arms, member of the Dail and boundless admirer, was dispatched to de Valera.[15] Briscoe implored him to pity the poor unfortunate. But to no avail. Keogh: "The Taoiseach felt that there was little he could do." In this case evidence exists. Not only that of Goldberg, but also of the victim of Irish policy who survived the war after running the hellish gauntlet of the Nazi death camps.[16]

Keogh's note on the incident is astonishing: "But it is most likely that Briscoe persisted and his personal persistence ultimately paid dividends. Given the uncertainty of the months leading up to the outbreak of war and the determination of the country to remain neutral de Valera was not prepared to take any risks. [Where is the proportion between high policy and saving the life of a single hunted man? M.S.] As the war progressed, the Taoiseach was more prepared to seek ways around the policy when cases were brought to his department's attention. The 'assimilation' argument was never enthusiastically supported in the Taoiseach's department. Briscoe may have smuggled many Jews into Ireland during the war."[17]

No source, no reference, no evidence, no document. What is most likely is that despite Briscoe's high position, close personal and political ties with the Taoiseach and Ireland's highest decision-makers, he did not succeed in spiriting even a single fellow-Jew into an Irish haven. Briscoe's autobiography, *For the Life of Mine*, published in 1958, says nothing about attempts to save Jews. Neither does he refer to the story of the stowaway, apparently out of respect for the "Chief." Briscoe, a warm Jew and an active Zionist Revisionist, would not, in 1958, of his own initiative, have concealed a rescue action, even illegal, that he had launched if any such had taken place. Such a revelation would have enhanced both his standing and that of the Ireland that he so proudly represented. We shall discuss in detail the responses of the Irish authorities to the entreaties of Jews from abroad and when they were positive.

Keogh attempts to present a balanced picture: "De Valera, while agreeing to the general policy of restricting the entry of Jews into the country was to deviate substantially from it on many occasions during the war. While de Valera stopped short of actively encouraging the entry of

Jews, it is unlikely that individual appeals for refuge were actually turned down by the Taoiseach if brought to his personal attention. Approximately 150 non-Aryan refugees from Germany were admitted for temporary refuge during the war."[18]

This is sleight of hand. As we have seen, the non-Aryan refugees refers to Christians of Jewish origin or children of mixed marriages. After all, wasn't that the policy set forth at the start by the Committee for Refugees? Nothing else was initiated by the prime minister. We are thus left with no alternative but to conclude again that what we have here is an attempt to whitewash de Valera.

The dominant secretary, Joseph Walshe, left the Department for External Affairs in 1946 to assume the position of envoy to the Vatican. It was apparently no less important a position than running Ireland's foreign affairs, because "In Walshe's eyes, the Vatican was Ireland's most important mission abroad. Great store was set by what the Vatican thought and did in the field of diplomacy." Keogh continues: "unfortunately, little remains of the files from the legation [to the Holy See]. [Ambassador] Walshe . . . destroyed many files before he retired in the 1950s in another burst of incendiarism. It is possible that [T. J.] Kiernan [pro-British envoy to the Vatican] himself may have got rid of files for security reasons during the war years. The net result is that but for a few fragments the archives of the Villa Spadia [the Embassy residence] are of poor quality." In Keogh's notes we read: "I surveyed these archives in 1986 and found what remained very disappointing."

In spite of the unhappy fate of these primary sources, Keogh dares to conclude without citations: "But among the fragments which have survived, it is possible to show that Ireland, through Kiernan, was very heavily involved in attempting to prevent the deportation to the death camps of Jews from Hungary and other Central European countries. Both Dublin and the Vatican were together involved in these efforts. The initiatives taken by de Valera in this area won him praise from his friend Dr Herzog, the Chief Rabbi of Palestine."[19]

One must express sorrow that this passage extolling these diplomatic efforts in a general and grandiose manner is not elaborated upon. Verification could help to rehabilitate Ireland and grant some comfort to Jews. Another research problem must be mentioned. At the National Archives of Ireland, in Dublin, the archivists could not locate for me the correspondence between de Valera and Rabbi Herzog. It is listed in the catalogue, but the documents file itself is missing. The archivists made efforts to locate the file, but they could not explain its absence.

This survey of Ireland's "Jewish" policy, and the analysis of the relevant part of Dermot Keogh's study, will help elucidate Harry Goodman's efforts in Ireland to save Jews. The documents found in his personal archive are of great value in complementing the above material and other documentation from Irish sources.

Ireland and Harry Goodman

In the spring of 1943, deep disappointment set in among Jews about the possibility of aid from Britain and the United States. These countries did not conceal their view that the prospects of rescue and assistance were slight. They refused to enter into negotiations with the Germans over Jewish issues and were especially opposed to a direct appeal to Hitler. The British also rejected appeals to act via Switzerland, which represented their interests in Berlin. The Bermuda Conference bolstered this policy. Political and philanthropic activity on behalf of Jews fleeing the Nazis was carried on by local and international Jewish organizations in the neutral countries on the continent. However, the attitude of those countries was influenced by the ominously close geographical proximity of Germany.

The turn in the Allies favor began in 1942. But at the same time the condition of the Jews deteriorated and the Final Solution hung over their heads. The threat of a German invasion of Ireland had passed and the political secretary of Agudat Israel, Harry Goodman, decided to seek Dublin's aid. He hoped that activities on behalf of the Jews could be carried out by Irish diplomats in Berlin, Rome, Vichy France and elsewhere.

The idea of appealing to de Valera to grant entry to Jewish children was raised in *The Times* after the December 17th, 1942 declaration.[20] The article spurred Alex Easterman of the BSWJC to apply to the Foreign Office for permission to travel to Dublin to negotiate with the Irish. His request was turned down.[21] Be that as it may, in April 1943, the energetic Secretary of Agudat Israel, Harry Goodman was deeply involved in negotiations with the Irish High Commissioner in London, J. W. Dulanty, over the role that Ireland might play in alleviating the plight of European Jewry. First of all, Goodman sought to determine whether the Irish would supply their consuls in the German-occupied lands with open visas for Jews. Recently, the British had somewhat extended the categories of refugees who would be allowed into British territory if they succeeded by their own efforts in reaching a neutral country. The issuance of Irish visas to refugees in enemy territory could facilitate their passage to a neutral country. He was, it seems, referring to the rabbis destined for Mauritius. Goodman proposed the establishment of enclosed UN-funded camps for refugees in Ireland. The last paragraph of Goodman's appeal was for Irish ships to transport Jewish refugees *en route* to Palestine from Bulgaria to Turkey. Goodman displayed caution and put forward only modest proposals. He assured the Irish that few refugees would arrive and that the burden of their upkeep

would be met by the United Nations.[22] Goodman applied to the Foreign
Office for approval to travel to Dublin. His request was granted. He met
with Joseph Walshe and outlined his proposals.[23] They appear to be less
demanding that those discussed with Dulanty. He asked for only 100
transit visas for individuals recommended by the Chief Rabbi's Religious
Emergency Council; that the Irish consuls be empowered to grant a limited
number of visas to special cases such as individuals in possession of
Palestinian entry certificates issued before the war (the Colonial Office
tended to renew those visas after their holders reached a neutral country);
and that the Irish Government charter a ship to transfer 5,000 Jewish children from Bulgaria to Turkey and then to Palestine. A final request was
that Irish Jewish families be permitted to host Jewish orphans.[24]

Goodman used the opportunity of his Dublin stay to meet with the
Papal Nuncio, Dr Paschal Robinson, and the heads of the Irish Red Cross.
Robinson assured Goodman that he would recommend the proposals to
de Valera.[25] If the Nuncio met with de Valera it made no impact, at this
stage, on the devout Catholic statesman. Neither did Goodman's efforts at
the Irish Red Cross meet with success. They turned down his request to
send food parcels to Jewish refugees in Poland and Shanghai.[26]

After his return to London, Goodman submitted a report to the head of
the Foreign Office Refugee Department, A. W. G. Randall. Randall, who
had recently returned from the Bermuda Conference, believed that
Goodman's proposals could be carried out and was prepared for Britain to
grant transit for refugees destined for Ireland. Britain was especially interested in the exit of refugees from Spain so that it would receive others,[27] a
suggestion raised frequently after the Bermuda Conference.

Meanwhile, the Irish did not respond. In order to emphasize the issue's
importance Goodman called on Rabbi Hertz and the two met with the
Irish High Commissioner in July. As a result, Dublin announced its willingness to accept a limited number of adults and children. Not, however,
with the guarantee of the Chief Rabbi of the British Empire, but with that
of the Irish Jewish community.[28]

Rabbi Hertz began corresponding with the heads of the Irish Jewish
community. Dr Abrahamson and Edwin Solomons met with de Valera and
presented him, on behalf of the community, with the required guarantees.
Nonetheless, the Irish were hesitant. Goodman then wrote an urgent letter
to the Irish High Commissioner: "It is three months since the matter was
raised in Dublin. I am convinced that the position has deteriorated on the
Continent and I feel sure that a number of cases which might have been
saved have since been lost. If, as I am sure is the case, there is a desire on all
sides to help, the delay is particularly unfortunate."[29]

Goodman's anger did nothing to nudge the Irish out of their compla-
cency. A month later, August 9, 1943, Goodman, in a pleading tone,

appealed directly to Walshe: The danger in Europe was growing even greater. He cited, as an example, the difficulty in extricating visa candidates from Italy after a German takeover. And this was a matter of only three Jews whose names were submitted to the External Affairs Department.[30]

Meanwhile, the Irish received more lists of visa candidates. Things started to move and inquiries were made by the Irish envoys in Berlin and Vichy about the possibility of exit permits for holders of Irish visas. The answer was negative: "the result of enquiries in Vichy and Berlin" were received "about the possibility of Exit Permits being granted there on production of an Irish visa. In both cases there was an unqualified refusal to make such grants." Goodman refused to throw up his hands. He sent another letter quoting the British Foreign Office that holders of visas for neutral countries would not be expelled even if they were not issued entry permits. If that was the case, the Irish could save people from death even without bringing them to Ireland.[31] No reply came from Dublin.

A month later, on October 20, 1943, Goodman appealed again to the Irish High Commissioner for the issuance of visas even if there was no possibility of the visa holders arriving on Irish soil: "The whole point is that people who hold visas for abroad are not deported to Eastern Europe and even if interned, are in separate internment camps." Goodman cited the generosity of the Swedes, who had received thousands of Danish Jews, and Turkey, Spain, Portugal and Switzerland, which had issued thousands of visas to Jews. And where was Ireland? Goodman asked for a clear ruling.[32]

Goodman waited three weeks before sending another letter to Dulanty complaining that he had not received any information about any measures Dublin might have adopted.[33]

Goodman waited another two weeks. On November 24, 1943, he wrote to Walshe expressing his disappointment: "It does seem a pity that this plan is not materializing when a visa involving no obligation, can save the life of a Jewish family . . . I am sending this letter as a last attempt to try to bring some relief."[34] Dublin did not react.

Goodman sent a copy of his letter to Walshe to the Papal Nuncio in Dublin. In his reply, the nuncio implied that the Irish Government was in no great hurry to help the Jews. He was restricted by the parameters of his office, he wrote, and all he could do was inform the minister for external affairs that he had received a copy of Goodman's appeal.[35]

Goodman withdrew from this disappointing source of potential relief. Toward the end of the year, however, events took a new turn. Palestine Chief Rabbi Isaac Herzog informed Goodman by cable that he had been given to believe by de Valera that he would extend assistance to Jews with Paraguayan passports who were being held at a detention camp for "exchangeables," Jews and others, in Vittel, France. They had been brought from Poland and were being held for exchange with Germans in South America. Herzog asked Goodman to arrange matters with the Irish authorities. Herzog had good reasons for asking Goodman. It was difficult from Jerusalem to enter into intense negotiations with Dublin because of the slow mail connection and the strict political and security censorship. Herzog had probably been informed of Goodman's involvement in the negotiations with the Irish authorities and could rely on his well-known diplomatic talents and effective ties with leading British officials. Geographic proximity was also an advantage. Consequently, Goodman wrote to the Irish High Commissioner that he was only turning to him out of respect for Rabbi Herzog, because "my past experience has not been too happy and I am not quite sure what I should do in this instance."[36]

Dublin's reply was swift. The very next day, December 30, 1943, the Irish High Commissioner informed Goodman that his government was in contact with its envoy in Vichy and promised to convey further information.[37] No other evidence of contact between Goodman and the Irish authorities is available until the time of the German occupation of Hungary in March 1944.

From the Irish sources we learn that the Irish approach to the Vittel issue raised by Rabbi Herzog was indeed different from the approach to Goodman's appeal. At Dublin's request the Irish envoy in Berlin, Cornelius Cremin, submitted an *aide-memoire* to Wilhelmstrasse: Before the Irish Government agreed to the appeals of various organizations to grant temporary residence to 200 Jewish families from Vittel, it wished to know whether the German Government would approve their departure after they received Irish visas. He combined this with another question: Would exit permits be issued to certain other Jewish families?[38] It is possible that the second question was the result of Goodman's persistent prodding.

The results of Cremin's Berlin queries were sent to Dublin on March 24, 1944: The Germans rejected the Irish application with the formal reasoning that Ireland had no standing on the issue because its citizens were not involved. In order to induce the Irish to drop the matter the Germans sent a comprehensive explanation for their rejection: If the Jews in transit via Ireland were destined for Palestine it would imply agreement for them to penetrate into Arab territory. That was intolerable. And if you say that these Jews would be returning to the European continent it would mean that Ireland assumed that Germany would be defeated. Moreover, if the Irish intended to naturalize these Jews then "the German authorities would, I was given to understand, gladly save us the inconvenience of having so many Jews." On April 19, Walshe informed Goodman that the efforts to bring the Vittel group to Ireland had failed, "but have instructed Vittel representative to make further effort."[39] On May 16, Walshe was able to inform Goodman of an Irish achievement: Von Thadden, of the German Foreign Office, "told me [Cremin] that the Jews in question had in fact been in Vittel and had been transferred to another camp in France for purpose of deportation. The measures for deportation had been suspended pending on our *demarche*."[40]

This was actually a German deception. At the time that they were supposedly "considering" the *demarche* of a friendly state, only fourteen Jews were still left in Vittel. The rest had already been shipped to the East.[41] Goodman's satisfaction with the Irish "achievement" was short-lived: a few days later he received a cable from Agudat Israel in Geneva informing him about the expulsion from Vittel. Goodman asked Walshe to inquire in Berlin and Vichy about the fate of these Jews and asked for the Irish to renew their intervention.[42]

At Walshe's request, Goodman forwarded the names of the Vittel detainees, noting that "the list was smuggled out of Vittel and reached me through official channels." Goodman was referring to a letter written by a detainee, scholar and author Hillel Zaidman, in German and Hebrew. The detainees, according to Seidman's letter, which was written on a coat lining and smuggled into England to Goodman's address, believed that they were the last surviving Polish Jews.[43] He wrote that on April 18, 1944, 225 Jews were deported to an unknown destination. This information was confirmed by repatriated persons who reached England from France. Eventually, even Walshe understood that the Germans had deceived them and that "Some of the families named in your list are certainly deported, possibly to Bergen Belsen."

Meanwhile, the British Foreign Office succeeded in inducing the Spanish Government to make representations in Berlin about allowing the return of South American passports holders to the Red Cross camp in Vittel as exchangeable persons. On December 9, 1944, Walshe reacted: "Our Minister instructed to support Spanish representations."[44] That was the end of the Vittel episode. The Taoiseach had responded to Rabbi Herzog's plea and the Irish Government had done what it could in the given circumstances.

In the hapless month of March 1944, when negotiations concerning the few Vittel detainees were still in progress, the Wehrmacht occupied Hungary. Adolph Eichmann and his henchmen immediately set about their objective of destroying the last remaining great Jewish community on the European continent. With satanic efficiency, trains were soon transporting many tens of thousands of Jews to the death camps. In July, Goodman, noting the entreaty plea of the King of Sweden to the Hungarian head of state, Admiral Miklos Horthy, appealed to Walshe for Irish intervention on behalf of the Jews. The Irish External Affairs secretary responded quickly, noting that his government had no representation in

Hungary.[45] When the Hungarian Government announced that it would permit every Jewish child up to the age of ten to emigrate (the "Horthy Offer"), Goodman sought the cooperation of the Irish Government in the rescue effort. He applied to the British Foreign Office for permission to travel to Dublin again and seek the aid of the prime minister.[46]

Meanwhile Irish High Commissioner Dulanty was in Dublin and from there considered Harry Goodman's proposal that Ireland grant entry to 500 Hungarian Jewish children. After his return to London he conferred with the Dominions Office. The Dominions deputy secretary received the impression "that Mr Dulanty put forward these ideas not so much on compassionate grounds but from a feeling that it would be useful to Eire if she could say after the war that she had not entirely stood aside from helping . . . "[47] It would seem that stones can be thrown even by people who live in glass houses.

Be that as it may, the British view was certainly similar to that of a number of other Free World countries: At this stage of the war neutral states expressed a willingness to help save the surviving remnant of Jews. Ireland joined them, but limited its generosity to the granting of temporary asylum to 500 children.

American Embassy representatives in London and officials of the Foreign Office had empowered refugee commissioner Emerson to organize the transportation and upkeep of the children, and they referred the Irish Commissioner to him.[48]

In the meanwhile, it would seem that the American legation in Dublin carried on negotiations about the absorption of children from Hungary. However, the Irish, stressing that it was the absorptive limit of the Jewish community and the Irish economy, did not yield and the number remained 500. However, according to the American Embassy in London, the plan was being endangered by Agudat Israel. Agudat Israel's Raphael Springer turned to the Irish Red Cross with a plan to save thousands of Hungarian Jewish children without regard to age or numbers. The American Embassy in London, acting for its Dublin legation, asked Agudat Israel to drop the proposal. "Otherwise the existing agreement may be jeopardized" as the "Irish Government held to the limitation of 500 as the maximum which might reasonably be supported under the circumstances." Here, too, the old worn horse of security was trotted out of the stable: The Irish Government "maintained its view that for reasons of security the quota should include only children."[49]

Agudat Israel did not bow to American pressure. However, Springer promised to inform the Irish that his proposal should not be confused with the plan involving the 500 children, and was not connected to the agreement reached with the United States Government.[50] Neither was the British Government prepared to come to the aid of the Americans (and perhaps the Irish, too) in its struggle against Agudat Israel's plans.[51]

After information again arrived about the renewed expulsions from Hungary to Auschwitz, Goodman renewed his application for permission to go to Ireland. The Irish Government eventually agreed to the visit. But to make sure that Goodman's expectations should not be aimed too high, Walshe noted that the rescue plan was being carried out by the United States Government and Agudat Israel was asked not to interfere. In order to appease the ultraorthodox Agudat Israel, Walshe gave assurances that the local Jewish community would be consulted with regard to the children's education.[52]

Goodman's achievements on this Dublin stay were modest indeed. Walshe reiterated his confirmation of the 500 children plan, but repeatedly refused to allow the issuance of visas for adults. Eventually he agreed to consider a few individual cases approved by the British. Now Goodman expressed his warm appreciation, both in correspondence and in the press, for the Irish Government.[53] Walshe would rather have not had the praise, because, as he told Goodman, publicity might cause harm.[54]

The 500 refugee children never reached Ireland, but Ireland was not to blame. The Germans and Hungarians had refused to cooperate.

(Ironically, many months after the war Ireland was able to keep its promise to the Americans. Five hundred Jewish children did indeed arrive for a period of rehabilitation in the Emerald Isle. Here, too, Goodman, using the connections he had cultivated in Dublin, was a major player, to the chagrin of the Americans who had planned it. This group of recuperating children from the displaced persons' camp in Germany had been organized by the ultraorthodox Agudat Israel, of which Goodman was the political secretary.)[55]

After Goodman's second wartime visit to Dublin, a lengthy correspondence ensued between him and the Department for External Affairs. Goodman asked that it make inquiries in Berlin about the fate of the Jews who had been shipped to Auschwitz, those who had been in Vittel, and refugees in Shanghai and elsewhere. In the last months of the war Jewish organizations submitted such requests to all the neutral governments.

Among other endeavors, in the framework of efforts to rescue the great Torah scholar, Goodman sought a visa for Rabbi Ungar of Slovakia.[56] At Walshe's request, Goodman submitted Rabbi Ungar's name for a security clearance from the Foreign Office. The clearance was granted on November 17, 1944 "provided his journey took him [to Ireland] direct."

The Irish were incredulous because all travellers to Ireland had to pass through England. At the *end of January*, after months of negotiations, the Foreign Office finally referred Goodman to the Home Office to arrange transit through the United Kingdom for Rabbi Ungar.[57] Whitehall had been in no particular hurry to save the life of a rabbi.

On November 14, 1944, Goodman asked Walshe to make inquiries in Berlin about the fate of the Jews in Auschwitz. Walshe's response, two weeks later, seems to be based on an earlier report of Cremin's. Acting on Dublin's instructions, the envoy asked Wilhelmstrasse for a statement on the situation of the Jews in the camps. On October 25, von Thadden had told him that as the camps were abandoned, the Jews would be evacuated because the Germans were not about to relinquish such a work force. Moreover, according to von Thadden, "that rumour of intention to exterminate the Jews [is] being spread by various enemy sources, but that . . . is pure invention and lacks all foundation. The German authorities have no reason to make any statement on the subject."[58]

Walshe's report to Goodman of November 29, is basically Cremin's record of his meeting with von Thadden: "We have had a reply about the Oświęcim and Birkenau camps and we have been informed that the rumours in relation thereto are absolutely devoid of foundation. Furthermore, we have been told that, if the camps were to be abandoned, the inmates would be evacuated to another place." Goodman was apparently surprised by the information, for he wrote: "I am much relieved to hear the reports about the camps of Oświęcim and Birkenau are unfounded."[59] One wonders: What did he expect to hear from Berlin?

Wilhelmstrasse again contended that Ireland had no standing on the issue of these Jews because they were neither its citizens or relatives of its citizens.[60] In order to downplay Ireland's interest in the issue, its envoy was instructed to "say that the Jewish Community of Dublin had asked us to make enquiries."[61]

When again, at Goodman's request, the Irish envoy in Berlin submitted an *aide-memoire* to the Germans to allow the Jews incarcerated in Bergen-Belsen who held South American passports, to leave Germany, the document was returned because there was "no justification for interfering. Persons concerned not being Irish, having no Irish connection."

The German official tried to placate the Irish envoy by saying that he was willing to discuss the Jewish question, in general. However, by order of the German deputy foreign minister, no official representations regarding the Jews in Bergen-Belsen would be accepted.[62] Goodman's request was part of the world-wide effort on behalf of the Vittel internees.

Cremin then cultivated ties with his Swiss counterpart, who had greater standing because he represented American interests in Berlin. Cremin derived information of various sorts from him, including, "it is a well known practice to allow Jews to leave against a payment of 1,000 dollars each." He also notified Dublin of other rescue deals operating from Switzerland.[63]

Goodman cultivated an intense relationship with Walshe, and through Goodman the Foreign Affairs Ministry's secretary was able to spread information that enhanced Eire's prestige. On February 9, 1945, Walshe initiated steps to inform Goodman about Irish efforts, in cooperation with the Vatican, on behalf of the Jews, and emphasized by Keogh. "With regard to the Slovakian and Hungarian Jews, our Representative to the Holy see has made strong representations to both Governments in support of the Vatican demarches," Walshe reported to Goodman.[64]

Unlike the attitude of other Western European countries before the outbreak of war, the Irish were not prepared to grant asylum to Jews. Ireland's hard line was due, in part, to ideological considerations which the sources do not hide.

Harry Goodman's efforts in Eire to provide a haven for persecuted Jews were based on the conception that its neutral status and good ties with Berlin and Vichy could enable it to play an important role in the rescue efforts. However, a turn in the Irish attitude came only after Chief Rabbi Isaac Herzog of Palestine intervened with Prime Minister Eamon de Valera. Even then, perhaps because of the Irish record, Rabbi Herzog limited his appeal to the exchangeables incarcerated in Vittel and in whom the Germans had a stake because of their being potential exchangeables. For that reason they transferred the holders of foreign passports from ghettos in Poland to the Red Cross camp in France. From the outset, and openly, Rabbi Herzog coopted Goodman in his efforts and he had good reasons for doing so. After Herzog broke the ice, intense contacts ensued between Goodman, Walshe and Dulanty.

Toward the end of the war, and to a great extent because of Goodman's persistence, the Irish sought clarifications from Berlin and submitted diplomatic representations and demarches. However, when it came to practical measures, such as granting asylum to refugees, Irish policymakers remained faithful to the policy of not letting Jews "inundate" the country.

It should be noted that in this case Agudat Israel, under Goodman, acted intensively with the Irish. For some unknown reasons the London Jewish organizations did not compete with Goodman's efforts to involve Ireland, although they eagerly tried even more dubious avenues. Ireland was exclusively Goodman's arena.

14

Reactions to the Crisis of
Hungarian Jewry

In my opinion a disproportionate amount of the time of the office is being wasted in dealing with these wailing Jews.

On March 19, 1944 the Germans occupied Hungary; the last of the large Jewish communities in Europe, numbering approximately one million souls, faced imminent destruction. This time the Jews of the free world reacted without delay, within a context of declarations of warning by Britain and the United States. The War Refugee Board[1] was set up by President Franklin D. Roosevelt, thereby implanting hope in Jewish hearts. The three leading organizations in London: the Board of Deputies (of British Jews), the British Section of the World Jewish Congress, and the Anglo-Jewish Association were about to conclude their tripartite negotiations in an atmosphere of increased understanding, although their activities did overlap to a certain extent.

When the occupation of Hungary was announced, two conferences were convened in England: the one officially, by the BD, and the other, unofficially, on the initiative of the BSWJC. Participating in the former were, among others, Chief Rabbi Hertz, Professor Selig Brodetsky, Dr Schmorak, a member of the Jewish Agency's Board of Directors in Jerusalem, Mrs. Blanche Dugdale of the Jewish Agency in London, Dr N. Barou of the World Jewish Congress, Miss Eleanor Rathbone MP, and representatives of the Agudat Yisrael and of the Anglo-Jewish Association. It was held on March 21, before President Roosevelt and Foreign Secretary Anthony Eden published their warnings. The assembled dignitaries, except for the representatives of the World Jewish Congress, did not look to the promised declarations for salvation; the latter expended considerable effort and labor to have them published. It was resolved to send a small delegation to Eden to ask that he establish contact with the Russians who were then advancing toward the Hungarian border and request their help for the Jews. It was likewise decided to appeal to the government to equip the

British consulates in Turkey with open visas to Palestine for refugees from the Balkan countries.[2]

Brodetsky planned to meet with the President of Czechoslovakia, Eduard Benes, but the leaders of the BSWJC forestalled him. Benes undertook to cable Stalin, but only on behalf of the Jews of Transnistria (what was meant is probably Transcarpathia – formerly Subcarpathian Ruthenia) and not those of Hungary.[3] Ernst Frischer, a member of the Czech National Council in London, who had not been asked to participate in the emergency meetings, insisted that the Czech statesmen not be approached except on prior consultation with himself. He considered himself the representative of the 160,000 Jews of Czechoslovakia under Hungarian rule and announced that he was negotiating with his government regarding this matter.[4]

Alex Easterman met with officials of the Foreign Office and learned from them about the forthcoming declaration in Parliament. The Foreign Office people urged him not to hold demonstrations and to refrain from public statements; activity should be solely in the sphere of foreign affairs. The Jewish leaders acquiesced in this matter, and, indeed, the BD rejected the Vaad Leumi's appeal to hold a mass march of Jews and non-Jews on the streets of London.[5]

The World Jewish Congress agreed that the sole representative at the meeting with Eden be the BD.[6] But since the Anglo-Jewish Association refused to forego its representation at this meeting, it was decided that the Chief Rabbi would be presented to the Foreign Secretary as the Association's vice president.

The delegation was received not by Eden but by one of his senior assistants, Maj. Arthur Henderson MP, who attempted to reassure the representatives. Roosevelt's declaration, he said, had been broadcast in all languages, and a British declaration was shortly to be published as well. There was, he assured them, no need to set up a special council for the refugees – on the model of the American WRB – since the government was giving every plan serious consideration, even though many facts could not be made public. With regard to the transfer of funds for rescue purposes, he replied that they were discussing this possibility with the Americans, and as to specific cases, applications should, for the time being, be addressed to the Foreign Office.

The delegation brought up two proposals of an innovative nature: Britain was requested to approach the Russians on the question of aid to Jews, as the members of the delegation were convinced that paratroopers from the Russian-held region could rescue numerous individuals. Henderson's response was: "No comment." He was probably aware of the impossibility to move the Russians to undertake such action. The second suggestion was that the Government approach Marshal Tito, commander of the Yugoslav partisans, with the request that he help young Jews to flee Hungary and join his forces. Henderson replied that this proposal would have to be submitted to the Russians; he promised to weigh the matter.[7] A similar request was filed that same day with the Foreign Office by a representative of the World Jewish Congress.[8]

Contrary to his custom, Chaim Weizmann joined actively in the efforts to save the Jews of Hungary, assuming a key role in the political activities surrounding Joel Brand's mission. He had agreed even earlier to undertake the appeal to Tito to rescue Jews, when this idea was broached by the Jewish Agency's Board in Jerusalem, apparently in the wake of the parachutists' drop in Yugoslavia.[9] Weizmann contacted Churchill's political secretary, John Martin (their friendship dated back to the days when Martin had served as secretary of the Peel Commission), wishing through him to impel Churchill to contact Tito directly. The letter was transmitted to the Foreign Office. On April 5, 1944 Weizmann addressed a personal letter to Churchill, thus expediting the process. The Colonial Office and the Foreign Office were in favor of the appeal to Tito and everyone expected the Americans to provide the necessary assistance from their bases in Italy. The British Military Attaché to Tito's units was instructed, as early as April 10, to approach the Marshal with regard to the rescue of Jews from Hungary.[10] Tito replied in the affirmative, but no actual contact with the refugees was effected.[11]

At that time also, Dr Gerhart Riegner, Secretary of the World Jewish Congress in Geneva, cabled Easterman via the British Legation in Berne to enlist British personalities, including heads of churches, to warn the Hungarian people not to hand Jews over to the Germans. He asked that warnings be broadcast in Hungarian every evening for a week.[12] The Foreign Office rejected this request on the pretext that the BBC broadcasts in Hungarian were overloaded and that Eden's warning had already been broadcast in that language. Easterman contented himself with this reply and sent a letter of thanks to Richard Law.[13] The AJA, in cooperation with the BD, sent its president Leonard Stein with Viscount Bearsted to one of the BBC directors to enlist the aid of the broadcasting service on behalf of the Jews of Hungary; all their proposals were rejected.[14] Upon the suggestion of the BSWJC the Archbishop of Canterbury agreed to prepare a broadcast to Hungary. The BBC had its doubts as to the effectiveness of such a broadcast, which would present the Jews as "the pampered favorites," so to speak, of Britain.[15] In the meantime it was learned that the Germans were planning to concentrate the Jews of Hungary in three districts in order to isolate and then annihilate them. Riegner and Lichtheim, Secretary of the Jewish Agency in Geneva, suggested broadcasting instructions to the Jews there to destroy all documents and lists on file in their community offices, to cease functioning, and to join the partisan forces. Alex Easterman and Abraham Brotman approached the Foreign Office regarding the proposed broadcast. The Foreign Office opposed it; it was decided to continue broadcasting the warnings of Roosevelt and Eden without addressing the Jews directly, so as not to cause panic in their midst. The veto also applied to the transmission of instructions by other means.[16] They did, however, agree to broadcast a warning to the officials and gentile citizens of Hungary against taking part in the embezzlement of Jewish property.[17]

Eleanor Rathbone's organization, the NCRNT, evinced genuine concern for the fate of Hungarian Jewry. First of all she asked Churchill to include in his speech an appeal to the satellite states.[18] After her suggestion was rejected on the grounds that a declaration by the Allied Powers was forthcoming, she suggested that leaflets be dropped from aircraft. She also demanded support for the Chief Rabbi's appeal to the Vatican representative and for pressure on the Turkish Government to grant visas in Budapest to those who held immigration certificates to Palestine. The officials of the Foreign Office reassured Eleanor Rathbone but categorically rejected her demand to appeal to Moscow since no cooperation existed in that area.[19] They moved with extreme caution because they were apprehensive about bursting the dams from Hungary and the Balkan countries and flooding the Middle East; they hoped that in the future, too, not many Jews would succeed in escaping and that thus no breach would be secured of the terms of reference of the White Paper.[20]

Every shred of information arriving from Hungary evoked reactions from the organizations concerned. All the suspicions proved to be well-grounded, and masses of Jews were carted off to the death camps in Upper Silesia. Easterman drew up a memorandum running to dozens of paragraphs about the steps that were mandatory to prevent the killing and to expedite the rescue operations. Some of these steps had already been brought to the officials' attention, while some were of no use whatsoever.[21]

Lady Reading maintained that protests and "nagging" would not produce results; in her opinion, Parliament was indifferent to the fate of the Jews. The Government of Britain entrusted the handling of this matter to Sir Herbert Emerson and she suggested that he be consulted. She declared that the entire subject required re-examination by means of a serious investigation and methodical, business-like deliberations – "don't let us drift into Continental Jewish habits."[22] She, of course, was not aware that the Hungarian issue had taken a dramatic turn in the wake of the still secret Yoel Brand Mission: Word of the trucks-in-exchange-for-Jews deal had reached the Government. The fate of the Jews of Hungary now lay in the hands of the leaders of the Great Powers.[23]

As the frightful news from Hungary proliferated Chaim Weizmann appeared for the first time in his life at a plenary session of the BD that was convened on June 18 as a protest conference. Weizmann delivered the keynote address in which he disclosed his involvement in the rescue operations (he was dealing with Brand's mission). He censured the Jews of the world for not doing enough and lauded the extensive rescue efforts being made by the Jewish community of Palestine. "They have even helped in the fight of the Warsaw ghetto" [sic].[24] If the Jewish communities of the world would only devote similar efforts to this goal, it would be possible to save many more, declared Weizmann. At that assemblage Brodetsky reassured the public, justifying the paucity of assistance and warning against over-emphasizing the sufferings of the Jews.[25]

The leaders of the BSWJC had long felt that the authorities were not cooperating with them fully; even the London representative of the War Refugee Board refused to furnish them with any information regarding his activities. Easterman was convinced that Dr Nahum Goldmann, President of the World Jewish Congress, possessed a magic wand which enabled him to change this sad reality. Not only the Americans had reservations: "All authorities appear to be adopting an uncooperative, uncommunicative attitude," he asserted.[26] It may well be that the lukewarm attitude of the Americans was prompted by conclusions reached in April by both United States officials and the Foreign Office. They felt that the World Jewish Congress on both sides of the Atlantic was pursuing an aggressive political policy which the conservative Jewish circles found distasteful. According to them the aim of the Congress was to establish itself as a body that would represent World Jewry in peace talks.[27]

The same sense of frustration stemmed from the refusal to grant the BSJWJC's delegation an exit permit to attend the Emergency Conference of the World Jewish Congress which was scheduled to convene in the United States on May 20. Sidney Silverman MP was to have headed this delegation. He appealed to Eden who replied that his office was in favor of their going but that General Eisenhower had vetoed the trip in the light of preparations for the invasion.[28] In the meantime the date for the conference was postponed to the autumn. The Ministry for India likewise objected to Silverman's leaving Britain as he also served on the Council for India's Independence. Isaiah Berlin, the attaché at the embassy in Washington, who was closely following the mood prevailing among the Jews of the United States, asserted that the World Jewish Congress "is wholly Zionist and rather bogus," and proposed that the delegation be limited to two representatives only.[29]

In July, Silverman again filed an application for an exit visa to New York in order to discuss the grave condition of Hungarian Jewry. The officials were again reserved, but this time Eden was forced to approve the request.[30] George Hall, Deputy Foreign Secretary and member of the Labour faction, tried to delay Silverman with the argument that he dare not abandon his district on the eve of elections.[31] The new date set for the conference was in the meantime approaching rapidly. Finally the delegation's going was approved – after Silverman undertook to report on the activities of all its members to the ambassador in Washington. The delegation was warned not to discuss sensitive matters, such as Palestine, Zionism and the Indian problem; otherwise the Ambassador would be authorized "to arrange for the immediate return to the United Kingdom of any or all of the members of the delegation."[32] The Section representatives behaved with propriety and no complaints were forthcoming from Lord Halifax.

At that time relations between the Foreign Office and the World Jewish Congress deteriorated for an additional reason. On June 30, *The Star* reported that the murder of Hungarian Jewry was being stepped up and would be completed within twenty days. The members of the BSWJC intensified their activities, and in this context Silverman was anxious to raise the subject in Parliament in a private question. Hall and Eden attempted to dissuade him from this but he remained adamant. In his reply to the question on July 5, Eden promised nothing: Only a rapid victory, he stated, would put an end to the tragedy.[33] At that time Silverman knew nothing about Joel Brand's mission, and when the news was leaked to the press on July 20, he was furious with Hall for having misled him just before he raised the question: He accused him of an antagonistic attitude toward the World Jewish Congress and of ignoring his obligations "as a private backbench member of Parliament." Hall claimed that Weizmann and Shertok (Sharett) were privy to the secret and that the news item was leaked to the London press via Ankara. This was a complete distortion of the facts, for the information regarding Joel Brand was passed on to the diplomatic reporters of three leading newspapers by the Foreign Office. With his back to the wall, Hall admitted that his office had done so in order to forestall the American announcement on this matter.[34]

Following *The Star*'s disclosure, the British Section cabled to the Pope, to the Archbishop of Canterbury and to Nahum Goldmann in New York. Lord Henry Melchett requested an interview with Churchill and upon being refused, sent a written plea.[35] Upon the urging of the BSWJC, the Archbishop of Canterbury addressed a similar call to the Prime Minister; he demanded forceful action against the persecutors and promised the support of the Christians for all rescue acts.[36] On July 13, Churchill answered the Archbishop as well as "My dear Henry" with a disappointing reply that was merely a repetition of Eden's response to Silverman's question.[37] Two days prior to the sending of these two letters Churchill had expressed his view of Brand's mission in a personal note to the Foreign Secretary: "There should in my opinion be no negotiations of any kind on this subject." In place of negotiations he suggested issuing public declarations to the effect that those involved in the crimes would be caught and put to death.[38] The connection between this note and the above-mentioned letters is clear. In all three documents Churchill employs identical expressions of condemnation: "The greatest and most horrible crime ever committed in the whole history of the world – by scientific machinery by nominally civilized men . . . " He thereby refuted Eden's statement of the previous week: "that the declarations have had the effect of making the anti-Jewish atrocities worse"[39] – which had been made in reply to Churchill's laconic answer to the cable regarding the annihilation of the Jews of Hungary by gassing: "What can be done? What can be said?"[40]

Heavy pressure was being applied on the top government echelon from other directions as well. On July 6, Rathbone demanded that Churchill contact Stalin in a non-routine manner and suggest voicing a severe warning to the Hungarian nation. Unless dramatic steps were taken immediately, she insisted, not one Jew would survive in Hungary. Eden promised to deal with her suggestion without delay.[41]

On that same day Weizmann and Shertok discussed Brand's mission with Eden and also the bombing of the death camps of Auschwitz and of the railroad tracks leading to them. Weizmann, too, raised the possibility of eliciting from Stalin a sharp, impressive denunciation, and Eden supported this suggestion.[42] Churchill's reply was: "I am entirely in accord with making the biggest outcry possible." But as concerned the proposal that Brand had conveyed, his unequivocal reaction was: "On no account have the slightest negotiations, direct or indirect, with the Huns!"[43] He expressed his readiness to take vengeance on those Huns, since the Gestapo had murdered fifty officers of the Royal Air Force, and suggested weighing the possibility of publishing a declaration about the Jews of Hungary and linking it to the murder of the officers. He hoped thereby to bring about a rupture between the Wehrmacht and the Gestapo. He also demanded that fifty officers among the German prisoners be condemned to hard labor. This suggestion was rejected by the Cabinet being contrary to the Geneva Convention.[44] To the end Stalin was not asked personally for a declaration and warning, and the request was transmitted to the USSR Government.[45] No positive reaction came from the Russians,[46] and from Britain "the biggest outcry possible" was not issued. The BBC broadcast a number of appeals to Hungary – by heads of churches, and by the secretary of the British Transport Workers to their comrades who drove the death-cars in Hungary.[47] The panic touched off by the news that the Jews of Hungary were to be annihilated within a few weeks' time was not shared by the British authorities. In the meantime a pause in the killing occurred in Hungary. The manifold pressures brought to bear, and above all the declarations issued by the King of Sweden and by the Pope, had their influence on the government, and Horthy issued an order on July 6 to stop sending transports. Later he announced that his government was prepared to allow every Jewish child up to the age of ten and holders of certificates to Palestine to emigrate from Hungary ("the Horthy Offer" – see below).

In the light of the horrifying news emanating from Hungary, Chief Rabbi Hertz addressed a personal letter to the Prime Minister in which he suggested that a declaration be published to the effect that "all Jews in enemy territories are under British protection and as such must be offered facilities deriving from their status, including the provision of travel documents, facilities for exchange and places of refuge."[48] Churchill transmitted the letter to Eden for his attention, but the Foreign Office objected to granting any kind of special British status to Jews. The Refugee Department recalled the German proposal for exchange in February, which had caused a panic, and in consequence the officials held to their conviction: "This is entirely contrary to our policy."[49]

They were also "concerned" lest the preferential treatment of Jews intensify anti-Semitism on the part of the population of the conquered countries. Moreover, it was essential to handle the Jews with caution lest they demand for themselves the status of British citizens after the war.[50] This time the ideological angle was not neglected: Accepting the suggestion would be interpreted as tantamount to recognition of the Nazi doctrine of discrimination against the Jews. In the light of the Brand Mission, Herz's proposal was again discussed. The alarmed officials foresaw enormous dangers arising from the Brand mission which were bound to please the Germans: "along the lines recently proposed by the Gestapo, that we should receive and maintain all the Jews they wished to select and send us."[51] Most of the arguments were brought at once to Churchill's attention, with the addendum that the Russians would not welcome any preference given to the Jews.[52] Churchill found it necessary to seek the support of the Cabinet for the negative reply proposed by the Foreign Secretary.[53] On June 28, Eden's answer was sent to the Chief Rabbi; it contained some of the above-mentioned arguments and the warning that the declaration might backfire since it might "stir the Germans to even worse measures." Eden reassured the Rabbi by adding that the Allied Powers together with the Inter-Governmental Refugee Committee, by dint of patient labor, could already chalk up a number of rescue acts to their credit.[54]

This subject was not removed from the agenda for many months and the Foreign Office was presented with a number of formulas aimed at guaranteeing protection for the Jews. Chaim Barlas of the Jewish Agency in Turkey proposed that British citizenship be extended to the Jews of Hungary alone. This suggestion was rejected out of hand.[55] The Colonial Office, however, was inclined to accept a more modest proposal made by Shertok: to grant Palestinian citizenship to 5,000 veteran Zionists in Hungary. Even though there was no legal basis for such a step, the Colonial

Office took into account the danger of death that was hanging over these people; the Foreign Office, however, objected.[56] The High Commissioner for Palestine also objected, claiming that one could not be certain that they would not repay the good deed with bad ones.[57] A compromise was reached whereby the consuls in Switzerland were to grant visas to individuals declaring that they would be Palestinian citizens after two years residence in that country.[58] Norman Bentwich proposed the publication of a declaration based on the Minority Treaty signed with Hungary, according to which killing a Jew was equivalent to killing a subject of the United Nations. Bentwich's suggestion was rejected.[59] A proposal in the same spirit was laid before Eden by a large delegation of representatives of the NCRNT. The intention was to lay the full responsibility for the fate of the Jews first on Hungary and subsequently to extend it to other countries. Eden cited the old arguments against giving the Jews a new status, but, as was his wont, nevertheless reassured them, promising to consider the suggestion.[60] Other elements demanded protection for the Jews.[61] Sir Clifford Heathcote-Smith, a representative of the IGCR, addressed to several ministries and personalities a memorandum headed "Saving Lives of Threatened Internees," which dealt mainly with Jews. He suggested that they and other persecuted people be accorded temporary British-American protection, while at the same time conducting intensive psychological warfare against the Germans, terming this "A Whirlwind Campaign." This was in his view the last chance of preventing a bloodbath.

The Chairman of the Committee, Sir Herbert Emerson and its Executive Director, Lord Winterton, berated Sir Clifford for exceeding his authority. Having no alternative, the Foreign Office together with the Department of Psychological Warfare subjected the plan to a precise scrutiny and rejected it with the claim that most of the suggestions had already been tried, although admittedly not in the measure demanded; and further, there was another order of priorities in the conduct of the war.[62] It may be that some benefit emerged indirectly from these lengthy, many-faceted deliberations for at a later stage various countries such as Sweden and Switzerland did not hesitate to grant their protection to the Jews of Budapest.

The suspension of deportation from Hungary in the month of July, and Horthy's offer to the International Red Cross that it handle the departure both of children up to ten years of age and of bearers of Palestine certificates, created a new situation. The urgency was manifest as there was no way of knowing how long the Germans would consider this suggestion valid or how long Horthy would remain in power. In London a new series of pressures was brought to bear, only to be met by renewed reservations on the part of the Government. It was not easy to object to Horthy's offer, as it was advanced with no conditions or price attached, as opposed to the

Gestapo deal. All of the problems pertaining to the absorption of Jews from enemy areas, even in small but undefined numbers, had already been discussed in connection with the Brand mission and it was these deliberations that now determined the attitude to the Horthy Offer. The Home Secretary, Herbert Morrison, studied the documents relating to Brand's mission and warned the Foreign Office that "the further reception of refugees here might be the ultimate outcom."[63] Brand's mission could be rejected on the grounds of political complications and suspicions as to its true intentions. Horthy's offer, on the other hand, struck Eden as sincere, and he emphasized this to his colleagues on the War Cabinet Committee on the Reception and Accomodation of Refugees.[64] The Government of the United States urged Britain to join it in united action "to care for all Jews who are permitted to leave Hungary and who reach neutral or Allied Nations territory," underlining the fundamental urgency to reach a decision. The Red Cross announced that it would prepare a transport of 40,000 individuals or more to Palestine.

On August 4, the Cabinet Committee for Refugees met to consider the two announcements. The Colonial Secretary feared that Palestine would be flooded with Jews at a time when there remained only 15,000 entry permits from the White Paper quota. The Home Secretary claimed that the feasibility of absorbing such immigrants in the British Isles was practically nil. There began therefore a search for other sites; a survey showed that the camps in Tripoli and Phillipville were capable of absorbing approximately 50,000 souls. Switzerland promised to accept 50,000 children and the Swedes, too, expressed their willingness to receive children. The Colonial Secretary was prepared to make some use of the remaining 15,000 entry permits to Palestine for this project, while stressing that "there were no other possible places in the British Empire or territories." Finally it was decided not to take action on mass emigration from Hungary. The Red Cross was informed that there was no objection to saving 40,000 Jews but that they would not be permitted to enter Palestine. It was also decided to draw the attention of the American Government to the fact that there were definite limits to the assistance that Britain could give the Jews of Hungary; the British were, however, careful not to forego the right to have a voice in the final decision. They pointed out, furthermore, the need to consult with the countries of South America and with the Inter-Governmental Committee on Refugees. The government in Washington objected to including Emerson's men in the work of rescuing Hungarian Jews because, as the British suspected, "it might steal the thunder of the War Refugee Board." The Americans, on the other hand, were afraid that the committee's sluggishness might compromise the operations.[65]

The Cabinet Committee did not arrive at any final decision since it faced a difficult choice: Rejecting the Horthy Offer would engender antagonistic public opinion in Britain and the United States, while accepting it might well mean civil war in Palestine. It therefore asked the War Cabinet to decide. With the Colonial Office objecting and the Home Office in favor, the Foreign Secretary recommended that the Horthy Offer be accepted in a joint Anglo-American communique.[66] The War Cabinet accepted the Foreign Secretary's recommendation but rejected the American demands for a guarantee of refuge for the deportees.[67] The War Cabinet was pleased that the Americans had agreed to delete the words "all Jews" from the announcement, adopting instead the formula included in the Horthy Offer, i.e., sixty to seventy thousand souls. What is more, the Americans realized that not too many obligations could be placed on the shoulders of the British.[68] Yet, nonetheless, the announcement alarmed the Colonial Office which proposed that only 2,000 certificates be granted to the Jews of Hungary.[69] The Foreign Office counselled: "The 10,000 odd places must be spun out as long as possible."[70] The "danger" was to all effects quite tangible, for the Red Cross had initiated preparations for bringing 8,000 families into Palestine. The Foreign Office informed them of the fact that there remained certificates for only 8,000 individuals.[71]

In September and October, when it became known that the neutral countries were to grant protection to the Jews, the Colonial Office agreed to Shertok's suggestion that the Swiss Consulate in Budapest manufacture "bogus certificates" as it saw fit, to serve solely for purposes of rescue, but tried to prevent the issuing of these certificates unless there was positive proof that they were indeed saving Jewish lives. The Foreign Office ruled that this project was not to be suspended,[72] after learning of the thousands of protection-passports that were produced by Wallenberg, the Swedish Attaché for Refugee Affairs in Budapest.[73] But when it came to actual rescue, which was likely to storm the gates of Palestine, the Foreign Office hesitated. It rejected, for instance, the suggestion made by Brotman at the end of August that Rumania, which was already outside the arena of the war, be asked to accept refugees from Hungary – because of the Foreign Office's "concern" lest "a Jewish invasion of Rumania reawaken the anti-Semitism there"[74] Rumanian ports served as transit stations for illegals en route to Palestine. On September 5, Shertok approached the Foreign Office asking them to send Chaim Barlas to Bucharest to try to save Hungarian Jews. Approval was granted in principle, on condition that he rescue only the holders of immigration certificates, for others would not be permitted to enter Palestine. Besides, his departure for Rumania was to be delayed until the British Minister's arrival there.[75]

What actually became of the British solemn acceptance of the Horthy Offer? It evolved that the German Foreign Office had initially agreed to the proposal in principle but in August it added the proviso that the first group of Jews should leave for the United States whereas Horthy was referring to immigrating to Palestine.[76] The German demand came in reaction to the request made by the War Refugee Board for Immigration to Palestine, with no prior consultation with the British.[77] In the meantime, the Red Cross succeeded in assembling a group of 2,100 Jews for emigration. In September the German Foreign Office informed the Government of Switzerland that these would constitute a trial group who would be permitted to immigrate to British or American territory, but not to Palestine, because the German Government did not want to provoke the Arabs.[78] A paradox then developed: the British now favored immigration to Palestine. This diplomatic ploy was intended as a safeguard against a breach in the solid wall. The Refugee Department of the Foreign Office invited to its meeting Sir Herbert Emerson, James Mann, the representative of the War Refugee Board, and a representative of the US Embassy. Paul Mason, the head of the department, argued that it was not for the Germans to dictate what the emigrants' destination was to be and he suggested that the Swiss inform the Germans that these people would be given a haven in their country. Emerson supported this stand. Mann had but a single aim – removing the rescued individuals – and therefore demanded that the German condition be accepted. The British feared that "he (Mann) would be prepared in the long run to give in to any German stipulation." In effect all that was required was a declaration to provide these emigrants with a haven in one of the countries on the other side of the ocean. But at the close of the meeting Mann retreated from the responsibility of cabling Berne without first taking counsel with Washington.[79] The opportunity was lost. Mann's recommendation to Washington was that it establish a camp for the 2,100 Jews within the United States and this necessitated presidential approval. Mason remarks in his minute that "the President had other things to think about in Quebec" (on summit meeting), and on September 20, he wrote that "the matter is more or less academic and that in practice we should not succeed in geting his party out at all."[80] The plan to save 2,100 souls was shelved. Mason divested himself of all responsibility, placing the blame on Washington.[81]

Against the background of the political activities revolving about the Horthy Offer other efforts were exerted by organizations and individuals on behalf of the Jews of Europe. Brodetsky and Viscount Bearsted, of the leadership of the Anglo-Jewish Association, met with Deputy Foreign Secretary Hall. Along with other matters they raised the suggestion that the interval be exploited by sending to Budapest Dr Gustaw Kuhlmann, Emerson's Swiss deputy, for the purpose of seeking ways and means of giving the Jews some sort of protection, as the Spaniards and Swedes were doing. Hall objected on the grounds that a man working in Britain should not be sent into enemy territory. On the other hand, he admitted, the neutral countries had been promised that Jews would be moved to British territory.[82] On the day after the meeting, Brotman was dispatched to investigate this surprising point, but he could not learn anything further. It was clear that Hall was referring to immigration to Palestine alone.[83] In any event, the Embassy in Washington was requested to clarify the State Department's position *vis-à-vis* a number of governments announcing their readiness to absorb Jews from Hungary. The cable noted that this was a suggestion advanced by the BD.[84] The Jews and their supporters perceived in the new situation a possibility for saving what remained of Hungarian Jewry providing the western powers moved rapidly.[85] And indeed, this time the National Committee for Rescue from Nazi Terror understood that something extraordinary had to be done quickly to move the Foreign Secretary away from his blockade policy. Never before had a Cabinet Minister been confronted with such a large and high-ranking delegation.[86]

On July 26, the delegation was received by Anthony Eden. It was headed by the Archbishop of Canterbury and was composed of representatives of all the churches, the Chief Rabbi, eight Members of Parliament, Herbert Samuel, Selig Brodetsky, Lady Reading, Victor Gollancz, Anthony de Rothschild and others. Eden showed them a copy of the cable confirming that the Horthy Offer had been accepted jointly with the United States. Ostensibly having been transmitted to the Hungarians. Gollancz at once proposed an Anglo-American approach to Horthy "to let as many of these people go as possible, we can take them all." Eden agreed and his word implied that he was assuming an obligation: "that we would be willing to receive anyone let out." At the same time, however, he pointed out that there would be problems of transportation. His deputy, George Hall, gave a modified interpretation of the Foreign Secretary's statement, saying that no negotiations would be conducted with the enemy and no representative would be sent to Budapest. Everything would be conducted in the usual manner through the Protecting Power (Switzerland); in other words, a continuation of the policy instituted in connection with the Brand Mission with one difference: This time Switzerland and the Red Cross would negotiate together in the customary manner.[87]

The delegation left the meeting encouraged by Eden's promise to grant a haven for all. To strengthen the case, Eleanor Rathbone asked in a letter that Britain authorize the Red Cross to act in its name.[88] This letter apparently caused a lively discussion in the organization. Professor Brodetsky and Gollancz understood Eden's statement to mean that the Foreign Office had already informed Hungary via the Red Cross regarding Britain's readiness to absorb all the Jews. Eleanor Rathbone was suspicious and made inquiries at the Foreign Office and discovered that Eden had no basis for his assertions. The Horthy Offer had not as yet been approved. She therefore accused Eden of misleading them and of missing an opportunity to save Jews, as had already happened with the "Adler-Rudel Scheme" to rescue children and bring them into Sweden. Speedy action was essential for rescue and they should not, she insisted, content themselves with the explanation that any action had to be coordinated with the Americans, who were very active in their own right.[89]

Owing to the strong pressures brought to bear, both internally and externally, the British Government was forced to insist that the United States hasten the publication of an affirmative announcement regarding the Horthy Offer[90] The handling of the Horthy Offer was in no way linked to the Gestapo proposal brought by Brand. It would appear that the public was indeed being misled. Brotman met with Mason at the end of August and requested information on the activities on behalf of Hungarian Jewry, but the reply he received was couched in the most general terms. The entire affair irritated the officials, one of whom remarked: "In my opinion a disproportionate amount of the time of the office is being wasted in dealing with these wailing Jews."[91] The cynical remark was entered on September 1. A week later the rescue of the group of 2,000 souls was sabotaged by Mason himself as described. In the latter half of September cables from Riegner reached London about the renewal of the expulsions from Hungary;[92] these were accompanied by reassuring news from Sweden and from the apostolic representative.[93] The BSWJC started another round of activities. Riegner's information was relayed to the World Jewish Congress, New York, to the representative of the War Refugee Board and to the International Red Cross. The BSWJC also turned to the Jewish Anti-Fascist Committee in Moscow although he realized that the latter had no political influence whatsoever. The Committee was asked to try to persuade the Soviet authorities to prevent the final tragedy. Easterman appealed also to the Foreign Office, but the head of the Refugee Department did not hasten to reply. On October 13, he promised to ask the legations in Stockholm and Berne to determine the real situation. And if it was in fact as bad as was being reported, perhaps the British representatives there "may feel able to try to take some steps at Budapest and prevent it."[94]

Two days later Horthy was arrested and the men of the "Arrow Cross" seized power under the protection of the Germans. The death operations were resumed. A cable signed by Silverman and Easterman was dispatched to Eden who was then with Churchill on a visit to Moscow. Eden informed his office that he was discussing with the Soviets ways and means of preventing the resumption of the persecutions.[95] The Anglo-Jewish Association also appealed to the Foreign Office; Brodetsky and Brotman called on Deputy Secretary Hall and requested that Churchill and Eden, while in Moscow, investigate the possibility of issuing another warning.

Hall expressed his conviction that Churchill would make every effort without any special requests from London, but added that the Russians did not tend to be cooperative in matters of this type.[96] The above-mentioned cable from Eden was already in Hall's possession.[97] Weizmann cabled Churchill in Moscow as well. The Foreign Office advised that the reply should read that Churchill promised that his Government and the Government of the USSR would "have in mind" the danger threatening the Jews of Hungary, and nothing more.[98] The non-committal wording does not indicate any joint British-Soviet action: It was indeed phrased by the head of the Refugee Department in London.

At this stage the Foreign Office opposed the resumption of warnings broadcasted to the Hungarians; it released very little information but frequently repeated "We have in mind" statements.[99] The officials decided not to transmit to the Jewish organizations the news issued by Stockholm about the resumption of killing in Budapest. Rescue was to come with the Russian advance.[100] Accordingly, the Foreign Office decided not to react to the letter of the World Jewish Congress concerning the deteriorating situation in Hungary.[101] On November 14, the London office of the Jewish Agency received news of the forced march of 50,000 Jews from Budapest to labor camps in Austria.[102] On December 5, the Jewish Telegraphic Agency published the news of the concentration of Budapest Jews in a ghetto and of increasing incitement against them. The "Arrow Cross" Government threatened to take stringent measures against the Jews who enjoyed Swedish protection if Sweden would not recognize the new regime. In the light of these circumstances the BSJWC asked that new warnings be broadcast to Hungary.[103] Acting on the advice of the Department of Psychological Warfare, the Foreign Office decided to turn down this request. This, they said, would not save the people under Sweden's protection from being thrown into the Danube, as the new regime was threatening, whereas the forced labor campaign "has nothing to do with Jews qua Jews."[104] Another letter, to which were appended descriptions of conditions in Hungary, was sent by the British Section of WJC in January 1945.

The Foreign Office filed the subject under "obsolete"; a reply was sent a month later along the familiar lines: "We have been very interested and the points they raised were of course very much in our minds at the time."[105] On February 23, the British Section voiced its thanks to the Foreign Office for the interest it evinced.[106]

In this manner the Foreign Office wound up its treatment of the problem of the Jews. In April 1945, the Russians captured Hungary.

15

Last-Minute Rescue Attempts

We are of course keeping very clear of any Kuhhandel ("horse-trade") for the release of Jews.

Along with their deep anxiety for the Jews of Hungary, Jewish leaders voiced in government circles in London their concern as to the fate of Jews in other countries in Europe. We have described elsewhere the story of the Mauritius visas on the initiative of Rabbis Herman Hertz and Solomon Schonfeld, the "Adler-Rudel Scheme" for removing children to Sweden, and the food parcel operation for camps and ghettos. The Jewish remnants in occupied Europe teetered between hope and despair. Contributing to this ambivalent mood were the end-of-war feelings, the certainty of an Allied victory, and the confusion prevailing among the Nazis and their cohorts. Events in Hungary did not augur well for the fate of the Jews and violent Nazi reactions against the remnants of Jewry were awaited with great apprehension in the wake of the fast approaching Nazi defeat.[1]

As early as April 1944, the *Jewish Morning Journal* of New York published an item about a joint Gestapo–French Police plan to arrest the remnants of French Jewry on invasion day. Brotman approached the Foreign Office with a proposal to take preventive measures in collaboration with the French underground. The response of the head of the Refugee Department, Randall, was that this would be of no use.[2] In June 1944, immediately following the invasion, Easterman suggested to Hall that the High Command announce that war criminals would be court-marshaled upon capture; a similar suggestion was addressed to the United States Ambassador.[3] On August 4, Easterman was informed that the Joint Chiefs of Staff were prepared to publish a formal warning, despite the fact that the British commander had his doubts as to its effectiveness.[4]

Fear now arose as to the fate of the Jews in the German satellite countries. In the summer of 1944, the Balkan countries were on the verge of surrender and in fear of invasion by the German army, as happened in Hungary. In August, the National Committee for Rescue from Nazi Terror asked the Foreign Secretary for his assurance that in the course of the peace negotiations, whether open or secret, steps would be taken to safeguard the lives of the Jews by evacuating them from the danger zones. The Foreign Office duly noted these suggestions.[5] When in Moscow in October, Eden did not manage to raise this question with his Soviet opposite number. The British letter on this subject elicited no response whatsoever from Moscow.[6] The ambassador was requested to communicate the British Government's annoyance to Molotov, and Lord Halifax was asked to enlist the support of the United States for the British demand.[7] The Russian stand was no doubt caused by differences of opinion *vis-à-vis* the Balkans,[8] whereas the British sought to prevent uprooting of Jews from their countries of residence in line with the declared policy of the Foreign Office.[9] The paucity of source material for the close of 1944 creates the impression that the Jewish organizations in London had despaired of moving the authorities to action in saving the remnants of Jewry. With the war's end already in sight, and intensive rescue operations being conducted in neutral countries, a deintensification of the efforts in London took place. At the end of November, Brodetsky called at the Foreign Office to explore the possibility of requesting the Vatican to protest the killing of Jews in the ovens of Auschwitz and Birkenau. Actually the president of the BD did not voice any specific demand, and indeed his organization was lauded for this: "The Board are a very moderate body, representing the best in British Jewry."[10] In a similar vein, a letter was sent on December 1, 1944 by Harry Goodman of the Agudat Israel to Mason; attached to it was a report from Switzerland about the possibility of assembling Jews in Red Cross camps either against payment or in exchange for German personages (reference was evidently to a possibility of providing them asylum). Goodman neither referred to this information nor demanded that a stand be taken by the Foreign Office. The officials decided to treat this matter like the Brand Mission and determined on this occasion not to transmit information either to the Americans or the Russians.[11]

At the beginning of January 1945 the World Jewish Congress sent Dr A. Leon Kubowitzki (Kubovy) from New York to Europe to observe at close quarters the aid and rescue activities. He revived the efforts of the London section. He seemed not to have expected too much from the Government of Britain and proceeded to establish contact with other bodies in London. He spoke with Mann, representative of the War Refugee Board at the American Embassy, demanding that the Allied forces facilitate the evacuation of Jews in the case of a retreat on the western front. He also asked that the countries which had resumed their war against the Germans demand Red Cross protection for their nationals taken for forced labor, including the Jews.[12]

Accompanied by Lady Reading, Kubowitzki was received by Herbert Emerson for a discussion of the danger threatening the Jews with the

German army's counter-attack. Emerson refused to countenance imposing on the military the task of making special security arrangements for the benefit of a specific sector of the population. In other words, the official in charge of refugees refrained from taking a step that could have saved many lives.[13] Lady Reading and Dr Kubowitzki also approached the Polish Foreign Minister to ask him to request the Pope to enlist Red Cross protection for the Polish Jews interned in German camps.[14] Similar pleas as per the Geneva and Tokyo conventions were directed to other governments as well. The replies were disappointing.[15] Lady Reading and Kubowitzki pinned most of their hopes on the Red Cross, and dispatched a cable to its president, Max Huber, demanding that he declare publicly that the Red Cross extends its protection to the Jews as the conventions stipulated. They thought the Germans would respond to this call as they, too, required extensive services of the Red Cross in the days of defeat.[16]

Lady Reading informed the French Foreign Minister that according to information in her possession the Germans were trying to destroy the surviving remnant of Jewry, among them French fighters, although this was contrary to the Geneva Convention. The French asked the governments of Britain and the United States to address a warning to the Germans.[17] Lady Reading did not approach the British authorities. Sidney Silverman convened a press conference and demanded that warnings be reiterated against anti-Jewish crimes; of the Red Cross he demanded protection for civilian prisoners.[18] There is nothing to indicate any further contact between Silverman and the Government regarding these questions.

Kubowitzki traveled to Switzerland where he met with the president and with the director of the International Red Cross, Prof. Carl Burkhardt, who was about to meet with Himmler to discuss the fate of the civilian prisoners. In Switzerland Kubowitzki learned that the Allies had placed at the disposal of the Red Cross a number of trucks to transport food to prisoners of war in Germany. The Allies did not agree to permit these trucks to carry food to civilian prisoners – Jews – or to bring them to Switzerland on their return trip. This information was conveyed to Lady Reading and Silverman by Riegner via the Foreign Office. Later the trucks were permitted to transport food to the Jews.[19] The World Jewish Congress' failing to approach the Foreign Office was a matter of surprise for the head of the Refugee Department, as may be seen in a minute dated February 26, 1945.[20] Two days later Easterman asked Eden to warn the Germans in his political statement in Parliament against separating Jewish prisoners of war from Poles. As this constituted a clear breach of the Geneva Convention, Silverman had no doubt that the Foreign Office would agree, particularly since Allied military personnel of the Jewish faith were in all likelihood to be found among the victims of the Nazis.[21] Even the heads of the Board of Deputies came to a standstill in their rescue efforts. On February 20, at a meeting with Mason, they raised issues connected with the San Francisco Conference and the state of the Jews as displaced persons in the Allied zones.[22] On January 31, the Foreign Minister of Czechoslovakia addressed to the Government of Britain a demand to institute joint action of all the belligerents for the defense of the deportees and prisoners in Europe. He made it clear that reference was primarily to Jews, among them Czech citizens, and requested a prompt reply. He sent similar letters to the ambassadors of Russia and the United States in London. It was only on February 23 that the Foreign Office at long last dealt with the letter because, as was explained, they had no documentation on file. The discussions continued until March 5, when the Foreign Office decided to cable Washington. They had reached the conclusion that declarations and warnings were of no use as the moderate Nazis seemed to have the upper hand at this stage. Not even at the Yalta Conference did Churchill voice, as planned, the need for a warning concerning the treatment of prisoners of war, let alone of Jewish internees. Nor were declarations by the Red Cross deemed desirable since they might prove detrimental to the FO's efforts on behalf of the war prisoners. And why should the Pope endanger the Catholics in Germany by taking a stand in favor of the Jews?[23] Even during the final month of war, when the noose was being continuously tightened, the victims of the Nazis virtually becoming hostages, the British still tried to play for time. On April 3, Harry Goodman put to Mason the request that government circles issue a call to the German Army to defend the Jews and other refugees against the SS. After delaying for three weeks, actually, almost to end of the hostilities, Mason replied: "We have had this problem in mind," adding that it would be necessary to consult with all the Allied Powers.[24]

Active in Stockholm was Hillel Storch, head of the Swedish Section of the World Jewish Congress. The London Section sent its secretary. L. Zelmanovits and its treasurer, Ben Rubinstein, to assist him. According to a report drawn up by the latter two, Himmler was prepared to release the Jews from Bergen-Belsen whereas Hitler forbade any negotiations whatsoever. In the meantime it was suggested that the British approve the delivery of clothing and blankets to the Germans who had been bombed out of their homes – in exchange for setting Jews free. Soon, it was argued, the British would in any event have to look after these Germans.[25] This plan, like the one of sending truckloads of food from Sweden to Bergen-Belsen, did not win the approval of the Government in London. The War Refugee Board placed at Storch's disposal tens of thousands of food parcels in the Swedish port of Goteborg, some containing kosher food.[26]

The British Minister at Stockholm was not pleased with the two English Jews. After they left Sweden he learned from Storch that they had had talks with Himmler's masseur, a Finn by the name of Felix Kersten. Kersten shuttled between Berlin and Stockholm in connection with the liberation of the Jews and suggested to Storch that he travel to Berlin for talks with Himmler. Storch asked the British Minister to transmit the suggestion to Zelmanovits and Rubinstein so as to receive the approval of the Jewish Agency and of the World Jewish Congress for his trip to Berlin. He further requested a list of candidates for liberation which these organizations had in London.[27] The Foreign Office was of two minds: On the one hand, they were to be accused of causing Jewish deaths by not transmitting the information to the two men; and on the other hand, they did not wish to be involved in negotiations with Himmler lest this become known to the Russians. Eden decided not to transmit the message, thinking initially that he would instruct the minister to intimate to the Swedish Government that it could serve with impunity as liaison between the two sections of the World Jewish Congress.[28] But on this last point Eden reneged; he decided to withdraw from any matter in any way connected with Himmler. At the same time, however, he did not dare assume personal responsibility for this harsh decision and sought Churchill's agreement to run the risk of "an accusation by the Jews that we were blocking a proposal which might result in the saving of Jewish lives – Do you agree?" One month before V-Day Churchill's reply was: "I agree. No truck with Himmler."[29] In the covering memorandum stipulating that the report was not to be made known to the Jews in London, the writer referred to the Prime Minister's decision: "We are of course keeping very clear of any Kuhhandel ('horse-trade') for the release of Jews."[30]

And thus, the British Government remained adamant until the day of victory with regard to its stand and degree of involvement in rescue negotiations.

Notes

Chapter 1 *London Learns of the Final Solution*

1 The letter is in the Archives of the British Section of the World Jewish Congress (BSA). Riegner sent a similar letter to Stephen Wise in New York via the American consul in Geneva. He suspected that it might not reach its destination. Because cables sent from Switzerland were intercepted by the Germans, he asked Silverman to cable Wise from London. Silverman notes in an (undated) memorandum, found in the BSA, to members of Parliament that the US State Department decided not to give the cable to Wise because of what it considered to be the unfounded basis of its information. See also D. Morse, *While Six Million Died*, New York, p. 8. See also Yehuda Bauer, *American Jewry and the Holocaust*, p. 191.

2 BSA.

3 Ibid.

4 Morse. John Morton Blum, *From the Morgenthau Diaries, Years of War 1941–45*, vol. 3, p. 209. David S. Wyman, *Abandonment of the Jews*, pp. 42ff. On the delay in giving Wise the cable, see note 1. On the other hand, after deliberations lasting a number of days the Foreign Office passed the cable to Silverman, Public Records Office, Foreign Office Archives (hereafter FO) 371-30917.

5 Compare Churchill's proposal to mete out corporal punishment to captured German pilots in "retaliation" for the killing of British pilots in Germany, FO 371-42808, Cab. Conclusions 85 (44) July 3, 1944.

6 FO 371-30917, minutes on the Riegner cable and on the letter to Silverman, August 17, 1942.

7 BSA, Perlzweig's letter to Easterman, September 3, 1942.

8 Ibid., Easterman and Barou's cable to Wise and Perlzweig, September 30, 1942.

9 Ibid., Easterman's letter to Benes, November 6, 1942.

10 Ibid., Benes's letter to the WJC London, November 11, 1942.

11 Ibid. The letter was published without comment in World Jewish Congress – The British Section, *Outline of Activities 1936–1946*, p. 13.

12 FO 371-26515, in the discussions held at the Foreign Office on December 23, 1941, doubts were raised about the reputation of the Czechoslovakian secret service and the reliability of Benes's sources. According to the officials, Benes issued many statements and expressed different ideas, thus enabling him *ex*

post facto to "prove" he was right.

13 BSA, received September 4, 1942.

14 Ibid., cable sent by Wise, Goldmann and Perlzweig, September 19, 1942. Perlzweig's cable to Easterman, October 1, 1942: It is necessary to wait because there was a "problem receiving consideration highest authorities whose guidance imperative."

15 Morse, *While Six Million Died*, p. 18.

16 BSA.

17 Ibid., details on the disclosure of the Final Solution order in Silverman's circular letter to members of Parliament before the session of December 9, 1942.

18 Ibid.

19 Henry L. Feingold, *The Politics of Rescue*, pp. 169ff.

Chapter 2 *The Changing Balance of Power in British Jewry*

1 *JC*, November 3, 1939.

2 FO 371-24422, letter from Foreign Office to Information Office, February 8, 1940. According to the Foreign Office, other states viewed the White Paper as one-sided propaganda. The Information Office's reply (March 10, 1940) was: The publication of scientific psychological formulas was preferable to a description of the reality. Andrew Sharf, *The British Press and the Jews under Nazi Rule*, pp. 84ff. Sharf examines the attitude of the British press toward the White Paper. It was published "because of the unscrupulous propaganda Germany was spreading about British treatment of Boer prisoners during the South African war ..."

3 *JC*, November 17, 1939.

4 *JC*, March 15, 1940 and March 29, 1940. See Richard Bolchover, *British Jewry and the Holocaust*, p. 29, note 4. The book deals with the social and ideological image of British Jewry during the Holocaust, not explicitly with external activities.

5 *JC*, January 12, 1940. This was the estimation of BD president Selig Brodetsky.

6 *JC*, January 26, 1940. BD Archives (BDA), file 504: Discussion held on March 12, 1940, with Dr G. L. Schwartz of the London School of Economics, an expert on reparations; Brotman's letter to Schwartz, May 6, 1940: "We feel we ought not to delay very much longer ... " See also World Jewish Congress, *Reports of the World Executive and the British Section*, December 1940, no. 1, pp. 3ff.

7 *JC*, April 4, 1940.

8 *JC*, November 27, 1939; February 23, 1940.

9 Saul Friedlander, *Prelude to Downfall*, pp. 37ff, 65ff.

10 *JC*, December 22, 1939.

11 *JC*, November 24, 1939.

12 CZA, A-82, Bakstansky's letter to Brodetsky, December 8, 1939. See also Chaim Bermant, *The Cousinhood*, pp. 398–9 and Anthony de Rothschild's

memorandum of October 29, 1941 to the Foreign Office advocating mass *aliya* (immigration to Israel) and opposition to a Jewish state. The Foreign Office replied that British policy opposed mass *aliya*. Lord Moyne, the colonial secretary, suggested showing the anti-Zionist memorandum to Churchill, FO 371-27129.

13   Neville Jonas Lasky, *Jewish Rights and Jewish Wrongs*.

14   CZA Z4-302/23, sessions of April 20, 1939 and April 24, 1939.

15   *JC*, November 17, 1939.

16   CZA A-82, circular letter of December 8, 1939. See also Selig Brodetsky, *Memoirs, From Ghetto to Israel*, pp. 194–5.

17   CZA, ibid., Bakstansky's letter to Brodetsky, December 7, 1939.

18   Ibid., handwritten in margin of letter.

19   *JC*, November 17, 1939, complains that only 80 of the 400 deputies, most of them Zionists, attend BD meetings and that their decisions are based on their Zionist political views.

20   *JC*, December 8, 1939: The president "should be par excellence a man of Anglo-Jewry"; *JC*, December 15, 1939; Brodetsky, *Memoirs*, pp. 194–5. On the president's authority see BD Committee Report 1934, p. 4.

21   Brodetsky, *Memoirs*, p. 197. CZA A-82, Bakstansky's letter to Brodetsky, December 7, 1939: Bakstansky's final formulation of Brodetsky's reassuring notification.

22   Brodetsky, *Memoirs*, pp. 208–9.

23   BDA, file Brodetsky, Anthony de Rothschild's letter to Brodetsky, December 16, 1940, Brodetsky's reply of January 16, 1941 and Rothschild's reply to Brodetsky, February 12, 1941, on the issue and the contention that he represented British Jewry.

24   "Anglo-Jewish Association," *Encyclopedia Hebraica* [Hebrew], vol. I, p. 370.

25   Nachum Goldmann, *Zikhronot* [Memoirs], p. 104; Leonard Stein, *The Balfour Declaration*.

26   *BD of British Jews – Annual Report 1939*, p. 49; *The Committee on Administration – Report 1934*, pp. 8–9.

27   Report of the Law and Parliamentary Committee of the BD, June 18, 1940; July 2, 1940.

28   Nachum Goldmann, *Zikhronot*, pp. 173ff, pp. 184ff; *Encyclopedia Hebraica*, vol. 29, p. 377.

29   *The Universal Jewish Encyclopedia*, vol. 8, pp. 459–60.

30   *JC*, October 27, 1939. The BD joined the World Jewish Congress in 1975. See also Nachum Goldmann, *World Jewish Congress and Anglo-Jewry*, London 1954. The BD's Defence Committee allocated considerable sums of money to fight British anti-Semitism. See for example, Report of the Law and Parliamentary Committee, October 10, 1939.

31   World Jewish Congress – The British Section, *Outline of Activities 1936–1946*, p. 4; World Jewish Congress, *Reports of the World Executive and the British Section*, December 1940, no. 1, p. 3.

32   *JC*, July 19, 1940; *JC*, July 26, 1940.

33   AJAA, AJ 37/34, Neville Lasky's letter to Cyrus Adler of Philadelphia, December 29, 1939.

34 Goldmann, *Zikhronot*, pp. 114ff.
35 See for example FO 371-32659, minutes of January 19, 1942, and FO 371-30885, October 18, 1942, for the report of the discussions with Brodetsky, Stein and Brotman where Undersecretary of State Richard Law expressed his opposition to an international Jewish body handling Jewish affairs after the war. Law reports that "they (Brodetsky, Stein and Brotman) were reasonable" and did not seek "a super-national Jewish authority." All the officials involved in the discussion opposed the establishment of an international Jewish organization and said that each state represented its citizens, including the Jews. The same policy was expressed in the correspondence between Law and Major Dugdale, chairman of the Conservative Party, FO 371-32682, Dugdale's letter, December 12, 1942. See also FO 371-36694 for the December 12, 1942 minutes about Hertz's letter.
36 FO 371-23251, MacDonald's letter to Gottler, November 8, 1939.
37 FO 371-42893, Beeley's memorandum, October 14, 1944 and the officials' minutes.
38 See chapters 8 and 14, personal correspondence of Lord Melchett and Lady Reading with Churchill, Eden and Bracken.
39 *JC*, May 17, 1940.
40 FO 371-24228, July 11, 1940, report of the British consul in Chicago on Perlzweig's activities and Butler's remarks in his minutes.
41 Ibid., and FO 371-27125. For Perlzweig's reports see FO 371-25976.
42 Session of December 4, 1940, CZA Z4-302/24 reports that the British asked Chaim Weizmann to help in the establishment of a Jewish Section of the Purchase Commission in the United States.
43 *Report of the World Executive Council and the British Section, London, January to August 1941*. Later a creche was named for Perlzweig: *The Universal Jewish Encyclopedia*, vol. 8, p. 460.
44 FO 371-42877, minutes of August 28, 1944.
45 Eva, Marchioness of Reading, *For the Record, The Memoirs of Eva, Marchioness of Reading*, p. 176, states inexactly that "Dr Perlzweig went on FO Mission to the U.S." For Lord Melchett's political ties to Churchill's inner circle, see N. A. Rose (ed.), *Baffy, The Diaries of Blanche Dugdale 1936-1947*, p. 194. See also David Hakohen, *Et Lesaper* [The Time to Tell], p. 140.
46 BDA, plenum session of January 16, 1944.
47 See, for example, BDA, report of the BD Executive Committee session of December 15, 1943.
48 See, for example, FO 371-42806, minutes of October 20, 1944 on the letter of the colonial secretary: "We should like to please Agudat Israel," and BD Report 1940, p. 41.
49 Brodetsky, *Memoirs*, p. 205.
50 Bernard Homa, *Orthodoxy in Anglo-Jewry*, pp. 28ff.
51 Solomon Schonfeld, *Message to Jewry*, p. 127. Meir Sompolinsky, "The Rescue Policy of the Chief Rabbi's Religious Emergency Council in Britain," *Pedut*, pp. 149ff. An article in the *Jewish Review*, the organ of the religious Zionist Mizrahi Movement, criticizes Schonfeld, but admits that "Dr Schonfeld has a proud record with regard to saving Jews from the continent ... and many thou-

sands who are still alive . . . bear witness to his sacrifice and endeavors . . . "
June 14, 1961, vol. 13, no. 381.

52 Schonfeld, *Message to Jewry*, p. 7. See also Shaul Esh and Shmuel Yehuda Gold
(eds), *Yehudei Britania, Hayeihem Uva'ayoteihem Bedoreinu* [The Jews in
Britain, their Present-Day Life and Problems], p. 55. Chaim Bermant,
Troubled Eden, p. 190.

53 Homa, *Orthodoxy in Anglo-Jewry*, pp. 46–7; Bolchover, *British Jewry and the
Holocaust*, p. 24.

54 Bermant, *Troubled Eden*, pp. 89–90.

55 Esh and Gold, *Yehudei Britania*, p. 22; Salmond S. Levin (ed.), *A Century of
Anglo-Jewish Life*, p. 106.

56 *Jewish Weekly*, September 24, 1943.

57 Bermant, *Troubled Eden*, p. 190.

58 Ibid. According to Homa, *Orthodoxy*, because of the emergency situation
Hertz also acceded to the demand of the Jewish Liberal Movement that its
rabbis be recognized as authorized to perform marriage services, pp. 34–5.

59 Homa, *Orthodoxy*, pp. 18, 29. *The United Synagogue Centenary Exhibition*,
London 1970, pp. 10–11. The electorate is composed of representatives of the
United Synagogue in London, the provincial towns and the Empire
(Commonwealth). According to a chart shown to me by Mr. Moshe Davis, the
chief rabbi's secretary, the chief rabbi's religious authority extends beyond the
electoral bodies.

60 Schonfeld, *Message to Jewry*, pp. 127–42.

61 BDA, file 535. *JC*, March 22, 1940.

62 BDA, ibid., Executive Committee of the BD report, April 15, 1940; JFC
report, April 17, 1940. *JC*, April 19, 1940. See also Brodetsky, *Memoirs*, pp.
197–8.

63 BDA, file 516, report of December 16, 1941.

64 BDA, report of JFC, March 12, 1940. Note for Joint Foreign Committee by
Leonard Stein, January 26, 1943.

65 BDA, file 516, letters of January 31, 1940 and February 1, 1940.

66 *JC*, March 22, 1940.

67 *JC*, April 5, 1940.

68 BDA, file Brodetsky, Barou's letter to Brodetsky, March 28, 1940.

69 BDA, file 516, report of Szwarcbart's meeting with Brodetsky and Stein, July
4, 1940, and exchange of correspondence, June 12, 1940 and August 13, 1940.

70 CZA Z4-302/28, meeting of February 22, 1944, where Brodetsky responded
to Moshe Shertok's criticism of British Jewry for not doing more to save
European Jews.

71 BDA, file 516, A. Axelrod's report of July 10, 1940; Wilfred Israel's letter to
Brotman, August 13, 1940; Brodetsky's letter to Geofrey Le Mander MP,
April 16, 1941. Ibid., Fred Netler's letter from Glasgow to Brotman, May 7,
1941 and Brotman's reply, May 9, 1941. Yad Vashem Archives, Jerusalem
(YVA) M2-486, Szwarcbart's warning about the spread of anti-Semitism in
Scotland in a letter to JFC, April 2, 1941.

72 BDA, file 516, Brotman's letter to B. Benias of Liverpool, September 5, 1940,
expressing concern about Catholic support for Polish anti-Semitism; FO 371-

26737, Foreign Office minute of February 17, 1941. On the attitude of *The Catholic Herald* toward the persecution of Jews see Sharf, *The British Press and the Jews under Nazi Rule,* pp. 18ff, p. 94.

73 BDA, file 516, Szwarcbart's letter to JFC, May 7, 1941.

74 FO 371-26737, letter and minutes of Information Ministry, February 28, 1941. BDA, file 516, Home Office letter to de Rothschild, November 6, 1941. De Rothschild's letter to Brodetsky, November 7, 1941. Report of December 16, 1941.

75 BDA, file 517, report of Brodetsky's meeting with Polish Prime Minister Stanisław Mikołajczyk, April 18, 1944.

76 Ibid., meeting of Brodetsky and Brotman with Mikołayczyk and the Polish interior and foreign ministers and General Kukiel. The JFC session of May 1, 1944 and the Foreign Office also dealt with this serious issue, ibid. In a parallel step the BSWJC met with the Polish prime minister, BSA, letter to Mikołayczyk, May 2, 1944. An Anglo-Jewish Association delegation also met with the Polish foreign minister on the same issue, *The Seventy Second Annual Report of the A.J.A.* 1943/44. To complete the picture, the British Section also met with the heads of the Foreign Office, BSA, report of meeting, February 28, 1944.

77 FO 371-26440, Rathbone's letter to the Foreign Office, November 1, 1941 and minutes. BDA, file 516, letter to Lazarus, July 12, 1940. Letter of the secretary of the Jewish Ex-Service Men's Branch of the British Legion, Glasgow, to Brodetsky about the degradation and threats in the Polish military camps in Scotland, July 21, 1940. Szwarcbart's letter shows that he did not believe the accusations, August 2, 1940. See also *The Times,* April 24, 1944.

78 FO 371-26737; *JC,* March 14, 1941; Hansard April 26, 1944, 747–752.

79 For example *JC,* October 25, 1940. BDA, file 516, Brotman's letter to Stein, September 20, 1940.

80 Ibid., report of Brodetsky and Stein's meeting with Szwarcbart, January 1, 1942.

81 For example, ibid., declaration against anti-Semitism and for equality for Polish Jews at a rally in London on November 3, 1940. Ibid., report of the meeting the Polish minister Kot and the attaché Dr Retinger held with Brodetsky and Stein, September 2, 1940; and Silverman's letter to Brodetsky, June 17, 1941; FO 371-26769, memorandum of June 17, 1941 where the Foreign Office estimates that General Sikorski exaggerated in his declarations to calm the Jews far "too fast for Polish public opinion." BDA, file 516 for the meeting with Sikorski on July 15, 1941.

82 For example, FO 371-26727, August 15, 1941, report given to Anthony Eden by the Polish government on conditions in the Warsaw Ghetto with the remark that the Jews "will probably be a foyer of Communist activity when the German regime collapses in Poland."

83 BDA, file 516, report of July 4, 1940.

84 CZA Z4-302/24, session of July 30, 1940.

85 The heads of the BD concurred with Szwarcbart's opinion that the description of assaults on Jewish soldiers in the Polish army were exaggerated. BDA, file 516, Brotman's letters to the Glasgow Jewish community, August 13, 1940

to Sir Maurice Bloch of Glasgow, August 13, 1940 and to Wilfred Israel, August 14, 1940 against taking any action.

86 Ibid., Brotman's remark to Brodetsky and Stein: In exchange for a budget to be allocated to his office, Szwarcbart will have to supply information. BDA, file 516, Szwarcbart's letter, February 11, 1942.

87 Ibid., Szwarcbart's letter to JFC, July 11, 1940.

88 Ibid., report of Brodetsky and Stein's meeting with Prof. Kot, September 2, 1940. Brodetsky's letter to Szwarcbart, September 11, 1940. Szwarcbart's letter to Brotman, April 10, 1941.

89 YVA M2-462, June 6, 1941, Silverman's letter to Szwarcbart.

90 Ibid., Silverman's letter to Szwarcbart, March 25, 1941. Similar accusations were hurled at Szwarcbart by ultraorthodox Agudat Israel circles in London: Szwarcbart has to demonstrate loyalty to the Polish government, thus he should not be trusted on the issue of the soldiers who deserted. Brotman, who was moderate and compromising, attests that Szwarcbart's status was not secure. BDA, file 516, correspondence with the Joint Orthodox Refugee Jewish Committee December 8, 10, 16, 17, 1940.

91 YVA M1-(1)461, Szwarcbart's December 24, 1940 letter to the BSWJC about the October 15, 1940 meeting of the heads of the BSWJC and the Polish foreign minister; ibid., M2-466, Szwarcbart's letter to the BSWJC, May 5, 1944; Szwarcbart's letter to Dr L. Zelmanovits, October 18, 1944.

92 BSA, Silverman's letter to Szwarcbart, August 30, 1943 and the response of September 1, 1943.

93 YVA M2-466, Ernst Frischer's letter to Nachum Goldmann and Aryeh Tartakower in New York, February 20, 1944; BSWJC letter to Szwarcbart, May 19, 1944. BSA, circular letter, September 26, 1944.

94 *Encyclopedia Hebraica* (Hebrew), vol. 7, pp. 859ff.

95 Berl Locker, *Mikitov ad Yerushalayim* [From Kitov to Jerusalem] pp. 288ff.

96 "Szmuel Mordechai Zygielbojm," *Encyclopedia Hebraica*, vol. 16, p. 740. See also A. S. Stein, *Haver Arthur* [Friend Arthur], pp. 280ff.

97 BDA, file 516, February 16, 1945, Fleischer, in his letter to Brodetsky, asserts that Benes spoke in favor of Zionism in his meetings with Soviet leaders.

98 CZA Z4-302/26, meetings of November 23, 1942. Lord Melchett advocated evacuation and suggested that foreign governments be asked to intervene with the British so that they agree. Locker tried to prevent a discussion of the issue. Benes suggested to Weizmann the emigration of two thirds of the Jews of Czechoslovakia, but admitted that the extent of the annihilation reduced the dimensions of the problem. BDA, file 516, report of the discussion between William Frankel of the BD and Dr Prochazka of the Czech Foreign Ministry, May 11, 1944; the meeting held by Brodetsky, Brotman and Frankel with Dr Ripka, the Czech foreign minister, June 6, 1944.

99 YVA M2-483, report of the April 13–18, 1944 sessions of the BD Foreign Affairs Committee (FAC).

100 BDA, report of FAC sessions of March 18, March 26, and April 11, 1945.

101 BDA, file 510, February 23, 1944, letter from Agudat Israel (signed by Raphael Springer) to Brotman: The Czech Government denied reports of the expulsion of 10,000 Jews from Theresienstadt to the East. Ibid., Frischer, in a letter

to Linton of the Jewish Agency, London, February 24, 1944, rejects the denials of his government. In a July letter (ibid.) to Brodetsky, Frischer cautions against talking about the liquidation of the Theresienstadt ghetto where, he says, conditions were improving. Frischer again accepted the Czech line.

102 BDA, JFC report of August 20, 1940, meeting held by Brodetsky, Stein and Brotman with Benes. BSA, report of discussion Zelmanovits held with Benes on this issue, March 28, 1941. Benes argued that the Zionists wanted a "continuance" of the current situation, but that such "continuance" existed in foreign affairs, not in internal affairs. Representatives of the assimilationists acquiesced to Benes, but Zelmanovits did not. Zelmanovits represented the National Council of Jews from Czechoslovakia, which was basically a Zionist organization. See also CZA Z4-302/24, session of December 4, 1940.

103 BDA, file 510. Report of December 13, 1940, meeting between Victor Bienstock of the Jewish Telegraphic Agency and Jan Masaryk who sought his help in placating the American Zionists who were angry because a Jewish representative was not appointed to the Czechoslovakian National Council. May 24, 1943, copy of a letter from the World Jewish Congress, New York, to Frischer about the meeting Wise and Goldmann held with Benes. They were disappointed, but not surprised at Benes's stand. Moreover, Benes, as was his wont, told Wise and Goldmann that many Jews still survived in Europe in hideouts and small villages!

104 BDA report of JFC, August 28, 1940. Ibid., file 510, report of December 17, 1940 meeting of Czechoslovak refugee organizations initiated by the JFC to reach agreement on the representation issue. Nothing came of this intermediation attempt. BDA, file 510, December 11, 1940: Through Masaryk, Springer succeeded in contacting Benes and an agreement was reached whereby they would meet at the home of Chief Rabbi Hertz. Ibid., correspondence between Dushinsky and the BD, March 8, 1940 to August 12, 1941.

105 Ibid., correspondence with Springer and Goodman, February 15, 19, 23, and March 11, 1943.

106 See report on Theresienstadt, BSA, December 12, 1944.

107 BSA, World Jewish Congress Executive meeting in London, August 16, 1944, and telegram to Wise and Goldmann, August 29, 1944. There were also instances of anti-Semitism in the Czech army stationed in Britain, but they were quashed by Czech leaders. Benes severely criticized the incidents, but nonetheless told British Jewish leaders that they were understandable; BDA, file 510, memorandum sent by Rabbi K. Rosen of Manchester, July 31, 1940. Report of meeting held by Brodetsky, Stein and Brotman with Benes, August 13, 1940. Ibid., file Brodetsky, March 5, 1941, Brodetsky's letter to Brotman: Brodetsky asked if the time had come to raise the issue with the Czechoslovak authorities. The Czechoslovaks did not refrain from sending anti-Jewish reports to the Foreign Office, see for example FO 371-30837. Unlike the Polish case the anti-Semitic ferment among Czechoslovaks in Britain did not elicit a widespread public reaction and thus is not discussed in this study.

108 BDA, file Non-Jewish Cooperation, Brotman's letter to Israel Feldman, September 25, 1940: Allocation of £25. £150 were allocated to this organization in 1941, letter as above of February 12, 1941.

109 Ibid., committee report of March 5, 1941.

110 Ibid., council circular, March 31, 1941.

111 Ibid., Salomon's letter to Simpson, November 4, 1941.

112 Ibid., Salomon's letter to Simpson, September 26, 1941. The BD invested much effort in the issue. On Sabbaths Brodetsky visited East End synagogues and excoriated the black marketeering, in ibid., file Brodetsky, Brotman's letter to Brodetsky, March 12, 1942. The Chief Rabbi published a sermon censuring the practice and a special body, the Trade Advisory Committee, was established by the BD to fight black marketeering among Jews.

113 Ibid., file Brodetsky, Brotman's letter to Brodetsky, November 21, 1941.

114 Ibid., Brotman's letter to Brodetsky, March 11, 1942.

115 Interview with Simpson at his office in London, August 14, 1974.

116 BDA, file Brodetsky, Brotman's letter to Brodetsky, April 16, 1942.

117 Ibid.

118 Ibid., Brotman's letter to Brodetsky, March 12, 1942. Lord Vansittart had an extreme stance concerning punishment of the Germans, see Sharf *The British Press and the Jews under Nazi Rule*, pp. 133, 136.

119 Lord Vansittart said so explicitly. He complained that he had not been informed of the Jewish action against black marketeering, BDA, file Brodetsky, Brotman's letter to Brodetsky, March 12, 1942. A study of the reports of the Defence Committee and the Trade Advisory Board shows their attempts and desire to play down their activities against black marketeering, but in March 1942 they changed their mind, Executive Committee meeting, March 9, 1942. In the meeting held on May 11, 1942, it was decided that Rabbi Hertz would speak against pricegouging on the Festival of Shavu'ot (Pentecost) and that the sermon would be published.

120 Ibid., file the Council of Christians and Jews, report of April 27, 1942 meeting.

121 The Catholic archbishop joined only in September 1942 because he needed the Vatican's approval, ibid., report of September 8, 1942 session.

122 Ibid., report of meetings, April 13, 1942; April 27, 1942.

123 Ibid., report of meeting, June 30, 1942, the Jewish members refused to submit the candidacy of Rabbi Schonfeld.

124 Ibid., report of meeting, April 13, 1942.

125 Ibid., correspondence with Wauchope, October 9, 14, 1942 and January 21, 1943. Wauchope offered to be active in furthering the organization's goals. Later Wauchope asked the Central Council for Jewish Refugees for information on permission for refugees to enter Britain. The answer on January 29, 1943 was that: 1. no entry for adults; 2. government agreement to allow the entry of children ages 2–16 arriving from France, but only to age 14 if they were citizens of an enemy power and on condition that their parents, grandparents, or siblings resided in Britain.

126 Ibid., report of meeting, January 7, 1943.

127 BSA, report of the private House of Commons conference, March 9, 1943. BDA, file 536 for a more detailed report of the meeting.

128 AJAA file, General Correspondence N-R – prior 1948. BDA, file 536, report of committee meeting, March 16, 1943.

Chapter 3 *The British Blockade of European Jewry*

1 CO 733-419/75113. See Norman Bentwich, *They Found Refuge*, p. 115.
2 *JC*, December 8, 1939.
3 A. J. Sherman, *Island Refuge*, p. 264. See also Chaim Shamir, *Beterem Shoah*, pp. 265ff; p. 302; pp. 321ff.
4 Sherman, *Island Refuge*.
5 Ibid., Sir Alexander Cadogan's memorandum (Foreign Office) to Colonial Office, February 21, 1939 and ibid., p. 221; " — the moral dilemma pressed the virtual closing of immigration to Palestine."
6 John Presland, *A Great Adventure, The Story of the Refugee Children's Movement*.
7 Sherman, *Island Refuge*, p. 211. On Weizmann's dramatic discussion with Malcolm MacDonald see N. A. Rose (ed.), *Baffy*, pp. 117–18.
8 Annual Report of the Central British Fund for Jewish Relief and Rehabilitation (CBF) 1972/73.
9 Sherman, *Island Refuge*, p. 196. See also ibid., p. 229 on the Polish Foreign Minister Colonel Beck's demand for Jewish emigration from Poland, expressed during his visit to London in April 1939. Similar pressure was executed by Rumania on the Inter-Governmental Committee for Refugees established by the Evian Conference. Wyman, *Abandonment of the Jews*, pp. 111–12.
10 Sherman, *Island Refuge*, pp. 266–7.
11 Ibid., p. 184. The Lord Baldwin Fund functioned until October 1940. It succeeded to raise £522,000, used for the maintenance of 8000 refugee children.
12 So according to the report of the CBF for the years 1933–9. See also Bentwich, *They Found Refuge*, p. 41. During the war the government agreed to partici-pate in the refugee budget, as the relief funds were not any longer capable to arrange campaigns. On the other hand, the need for funds declined as most refugees recruited to the army and to labor. Sherman, *Island Refuge*, p. 264.
13 So according to Sherman, *Island Refuge*, p. 264. The estimation of CBF Annual Report – *Forty Years On* by H. Oscar Joseph, 1972–3 is 63,000 Jewish refugees. The difference is probably based on the mobility of the refugees. Joseph has his number from the registers of the CBF. Many of the CBF regis-tered might have emigrated.
14 Sherman, *Island Refuge*, pp. 225–6.
15 Joseph, *Forty Years On*. Bentwich, *They Found Refuge*, pp. 102ff.
16 Sherman, *Island Refuge*, p. 235.
17 Ibid., p. 264. Bernard Wasserstein, *Britain and the Jews of Europe*, p. 34.
18 Statement of Policy on Palestine – May 7, 1939 – Cnd. 6019, 2d: 14,1(b). In addition as a contribution toward the solution of the Jewish refugee problem, 25,000 refugees will be admitted as soon as the High Commissioner is satis-fied that the adequate provision for their maintenance is ensured, special consideration being given to refugee children and dependants.
19 FO 371-23251.
20 Ibid. See also Chaim Weizmann, *Yalkut Pirkei Chaim*, p. 299.
21 Ibid., pp. 297–8. FO 371-23239 – on the government's readiness to accept

Jewish help, but without any condition.

22 FO 371-23242 – Zabotinsky's letter to Chamberlain expressing unconditional loyalty. But in his conversation with the colonial secretary he warns of the danger of riots in Palestine organized by Jews.

23 FO 371-23241.

24 FO 371-23242. Foreign Secretary Halifax's letter to Weizmann stressing Weizmann's promise for unconditional Jewish help. Then Weizmann was about to visit the US. One of his tasks was to promote British interests in America. CZA, Z4-302/23, session of the Zionist Executive Committee in London, July 16, 1940. See also *JC*, February 16, 1940: The colonial secretary announces that he is sticking to the White Paper policy, although the Jews of Palestine are supporting Britain. Being so, because Britain is fighting to free their brethren from oppression.

25 *Encyclopedia Hebraica*, vol. 16, pp. 264ff.

26 FO 371-23242.

27 Ibid., thus L. Baggallay from FO recommends to refuse Lord Melchett's proposal to distribute the government's information material in order not to be obliged to the Zionists.

28 Ibid.

29 BDA, file (BD) Law & Parliamentary Committee, sessions of the committee, December 12, 1939; January 16, 1940; February 13, 1940; June 18, 1940: Discussions on this propaganda and the fight against it.

30 *JC*, November 30, 1939; December 22, 1939.

31 Sherman, *Island Refuge*, p. 262. *JC*, April 26, 1940.

32 CO 733-419/75113 – Foreign Office instructions to the British consulates, April 10, 1940.

33 CZA, Z4-302/24, session November 29, 1940. FO 371-25242, Weizmann's cable (November 18, 1940) to David Ben-Gurion, then in USA, not to arouse emotion in connection with the illegal *aliya* as being activated by the Nazis. See also CO 733-429/76021, minute, January 3, 1941. FO 371-25189, minute to report from Madrid, May 21, 1940: Foreign Office doubts about agents among the refugees in Spain and in Scandinavia.

34 CO-733-419/75113.

35 Ibid., Herbert Emerson's meeting with Malcolm MacDonald, February 11, 1940.

36 Ibid.

37 Ibid., Foreign Office memorandum to Colonial Office, February 23, 1940.

38 *JC*, May 17, 1940; May 24, 1940; June 31, 1940; August 2, 1940; February 7, 1941. Bentwich, *They Found Refuge*, p. 115; pp. 118–19. Bolchover, *British Jewry and the Holocaust*, pp. 49ff. Wasserstein, *Britain and the Jews of Europe*, pp. 87ff.

39 CO 733-429/76021, cable from Palestine High Commissioner, September 21, 1940.

40 CO 733-420/75113, Stephen Luke's report, September 24, 1940.

41 CO 733-419/75113, Moshe Shertok's conversation with Colonial Office officials, March 21, 1940.

42 Ibid., Lord Melchett's correspondence with Colonial Office.

43 Ibid., their meeting, January 15, 1940.
44 Ibid., Foreign Office's letter to Colonial Office, January 23, 1940.
45 Ibid., ibid.
46 Ibid.
47 FO 371-25243.
48 FO 371-29170. Bauer, *American Jewry and the Holocaust*, pp. 119ff.
49 CO 733-419/75113. FO 371-25243, Stafford Cripp's cables, December 3, 1940; December 7, 1940.
50 FO 371-24978, minutes, December 18, 1940.
51 CO 733-430/76021.
52 *Sefer Hahagana*, vol. 3, part 1, p. 88.
53 CO 733-430/76021, report March 1940.
54 Bauer, *American Jewry and the Holocaust*, pp. 129ff.
55 CO 733-420/75113, minute, October 9, 1940. Aron Zwergboim, *Parshat Mauritius*, vol. 4, pp. 221–2.
56 CO 733-420/75113, Churchill's minute to Lord Lloyd, November 14, 1940.
57 *Sefer Hamaapilim*, ed. Moshe Basok, pp. 205–6; pp. 216ff; pp. 288–90.
58 CO 733-420/75113. *Sefer Hamaapilim*, p. 214.
59 FO 371-24987, minute, December 18, 1940.
60 Bauer, *American Jewry and the Holocaust*, p. 151.
61 FO 371-25254, letter from British ambassador to Belgium to Lord Halifax, December 17, 1940.
62 Ibid., minute, December 21, 1940. See also Wasserstein, *Britain and the Jews of Europe*, p. 109.
63 FO 371-29221, report from the naval attaché in Madrid, July 22, 1941 and minute of the head of the Refugee Department, August 13, 1941.
64 CO 733-430/76021; FO 371-25241; 25237; 25239.
65 FO 371-32619, minutes to letter of August 14, 1942.
66 On this idea during the war see Premier 4-52/5 – War Cabinet, Jewish Policy, Note by Secretary of State for the Colonies, September 30, 1941. This conception was adopted by the Labour government after the war.
67 R. Meinerzhagen, *Yoman Mizrach Tichoni*, p. 132.
68 BDA, report of the session of BD Executive Committee, June 25, 1940.
69 Ibid., session, February 18, 1941.
70 Ibid., session, September 11, 1940.
71 CZA, Z-4 302/24, sessions, November 12, 1940; November 15, 1940; November 28, 1940. Weizmann opposed the illegal immigration to Palestine from enemy occupied territories, stressing the British officials' arguments and fought against his colleagues in the Political Committee of the Jewish Agency on that issue. Even as late as August 1, 1941 he accepted the plea that enemy agents may appear as immigrants – FO 371-27128. FO 371-26172, report written by Churchill's private secretary John Martin, July 13, 1941: US Treasurer Henry Morgenthau jr. proposed to Weizmann the finance of the *aliya* of 150,000 European Jews within one year. He pressed Weizmann to agree to a joint visit to Roosevelt to move him to advise Churchill to accept this proposal immediately. Weizmann refused, arguing that such undertaking will be a heavy burden on the British-Arab relations. See also *For the Record*,

The Memoirs of Eva, Marchioness of Reading, p. 177, on Weizmann in the days of Yoel Brand's mission. Weizmann concluded: "'There is only one salvation for the Jews and that is the defeat of Hitler. We must do nothing to assist him in the conduct of the war'. It was a hard decision, but a correct one." This conception was common to the government and most British Jews. Hence Bolchover's conclusion.

72   FO 371-32682, letter from Richard Law to Major T. L. Dugdale MP, chairman of the Conservative Party, December 7, 1942. The same view in General Sikorski's letter to BSWJC, May 9, 1942, BSA.

Chapter 4 *Years of Vacillation: The Jewish Leadership, 1939–1942*

1   Brodetsky, *Memoirs*, p. 108
2   *JC*, January 31, 1941.
3   *JC*, October 13, 1939; November 20, 1939. Board of Deputies of British Jews, Report 1940, pp. 25ff.
4   *JC*, October 13, 1939; June 31, 1940; July 26, 1940.
5   BD Report 1940, p. 16 is unsatisfied with the treatment of the matter and expresses its opinion to the authorities. Norman Bentwich, *Wanderer in War*, pp. 21ff. Norman Bentwich, *I Understand the Risk*, p. 32; pp. 66ff. On the cruelty and on the deportation of German Jews from Britain to Canada and Australia see – Martin Rosenbluth, *Go Forth and Serve*, pp. 281–2.
6   *JC*, February 23, 1940. BD Committee on Administration 1934, pp. 6–7. BD Report 1940, p. 16.
7   BDA, file Brodetsky, letter from Stein to Brodetsky, March 12, 1940. Report JFC, March 12, 1940.
8   Ibid., stressing the JFC's independence Brodetsky reports the committee's activity only orally to the BD's Executive Committee.
9   On H. Beeley see chapter 2.
10 BDA, reports on JFC sessions, March 12, 1940 and September 3, 1941.
11 BDA, file 504, letter from Dr Alfred Wiener, May 20, 1940. Ibid., file National Council for Civil Liberties, letter to the council, January 28 1944, stating that Dr Wiener's library is closed to the public and serves only the Foreign Office, the BD and some more authorized organizations. See *Encyclopedia Hebraica*, vol. 16, p. 228, Wiener Alfred.
12 BDA, report JFC February 14, 1940. Three years later Stein became disillusioned. Ibid., Note for JFC, January 26, 1943.
13 He is the author of the comprehensive book, *The Balfour Declaration*. See also Goldmann, *Zichronot*, p. 104.
14 See, for instance, Michael Dov Weissmandel, *Min Hametsar*, p. 194: "Please, deliver this letter to the heads of the three Great Powers that are rendering us help – and to the Pope."
15 *The Autobiography of Nachum Goldmann*, p. 203. Brodetsky, *Memoirs*, p. 208. Norman Bentwich, *My 77 Years*, pp. 191–2. Bentwich was asked to join the JFC in 1942, but resigned after a short time, being disappointed.
16 Goldmann, *Zichronot*, pp. 187–8.

17 BDA, file Refugees, letter from R. N. Carvalho to BD, October 18, 1939 and answer, October 27, 1939.

18 Ibid., correspondence between the lawyer Leslie A. Fawke and Brotman, February 26, 1940; March 5, 1940; March 6, 1940 and correspondence between Mrs. Bund and the Jewish Refugees Committee and BD, March 12, 1940; March 15, 1940; March 18, 1940.

19 Ibid., file Rumania, Lazar Margulies' report to JFC, March 27, 1940.

20 Ibid., "M. D. Mowshowitch" report, March 14, 1940.

21 Ibid., letter from Brotman to Lionel L. Cohen, May 14, 1940 and Cohen's answer, May 19, 1940.

22 Ibid., version of protest, February 26, 1941. *JC*, February 28, 1941. *JC*, February 21, 1941, the British minister, called home from Bucharest, expresses that this information is surely not "Jewish propaganda."

23 BDA, file Rumania, copy of letter from Filderman to Chief Rabbi Herzog, November 11, 1941.

24 Ibid., letter from the Organization of Rumanian "Olim," November 25, 1941. Letter from Rabbi Herzog, December 26, 1941.

25 Ibid., letter from Brodetsky to Lord Litton, January 28, 1942. Litton's answer, February 4, 1942.

26 Letter from Brodetsky to Rothschild, February 3, 1942. Rothschild's answer, February 4, 1942.

27 BDA, file 516, May 6, 1941, report on Szwarcbart's meeting with representatives of the Jewish organizations on the possibility of evacuating parents and children from Vichy France. As to emigration from France it seemed that the British would be flexible. We shall debate this item later in the book.

28 BDA, file Refugees, the case Wincent Silvan, cable, July 31, 1941. Correspondence with Szwarcbart, August 8, 1941; August 10, 1941.

29 Ibid., the case Silberpfenning. Letters, August 8, 1941; August 20, 1941.

30 Ibid., file 516 – letter from Szwarcbart to Brotman, April 10, 1941.

31 YVA – M2-486, letter from JFC to Szwarcbart, July 10, 1941 and answer, July 11, 1941.

32 On political relation between Amery and Dugdale see N. A. Rose (ed.), *Baffy*.

33 BDA, file 516, June 11, 1941, report on unsuccessful conversation in Burma House. Letter from Brotman to Szwarcbart, July 10, 1941. Even Chief Rabbi Herzog's appeal to the Archbishop of Canterbury Dr Cosmo Lang for the *aliya* of *Yeshiva* students had no effect. The Archbishop did not show sympathy to Herzog's worries. In his letter (August 19, 1941) to Lord Moyne, Secretary of the Colonial Office, he writes: "I shall not be in the least surprised if you tell me that you cannot take any action. I merely wish to have the satisfaction of informing the Chief Rabbi that I have communicated with the Government," CO 733-436/75113. Dr William Temple who was soon to take the archbishopric office had strong feelings for the Jewish fate.

34 BDA, file 516, correspondence between the Canadian High Commissioner and Brotman and Szwarcbart, August 29, 1941; August 30, 1941; September 2, 1941; September 10, 1941; September 11, 1941; September 15, 1941.

35 CO 733-436/75113, April 10, 1941.

36 BDA, file Brodetsky, letter from the Chief Rabbi's Emergency Council to

Brodetsky, November 25, 1941. Letter from Brotman to Brodetsky, November 27, 1941. Ibid., file Refugees, letter from Brotman to Brodetsky, same day.

37 BDA, file 510, letter from Frischer to BD, June 15, 1942. Memorandum from Brotman to Brodetsky and Stein, June 17, 1942. Brotman's letter to Captain V. Bulkeley-Johnson of the Rothschild Bank, September 14, 1942.

38 FO 371-29220, letters from Melchett to Eden, October 30, 1941; November 7, 1941. Eden's answers, November 6, 1941; November 21, 1941. An angry minute:
"We, not the Dutch, are defending their Empire," so it is reasonable to demand from the Dutch to render shelter to the Jews who otherwise might try to embark in a British harbour.

39 Sharf, *The British Press and the Jews under Nazi Rule,* pp. 90–1.

40 FO 371-26515, report from the ambassador in Bern, November 19, 1941.

41 FO 371-30898, report from the consul general in Basel, February 18, 1942.

42 BDA, file Refugees, letter from Hans Blum to John Harris, October 30, 1941. Letter from Brotman to Otto Schiff, November 8, 1941. Letter from Schiff to Brotman, November 13, 1941.

43 The text of the declaration in FO 371-30917. See also Report 2 – World Jewish Congress, British Section, London, October 1942.

44 BDA, file Brodetsky, letter from Brotman to Brodetsky, January 9, 1942.

45 The full text of Sikorski's answer in World Jewish Congress, British Section, Outline of Activities 1936–1946, pp. 37–8.

46 FO 371-30917, letter from Sikorski to JFC, May 16, 1942 as answer to JFC's letter, May 5, 1942.

47 Ibid., D.Allen's written remark on Sikorski's letter, August 13, 1942 and G. Lias' minute, July 30, 1942.

48 *Encyclopedia Hebraica,* vol. 16, Welles, H. G., pp. 343–4.

49 Harry Goodman's private archive (GA), letter from Colonial Office to Goodman, October 22, 1942.

50 *JC,* July 24, 1942, Churchill's greeting to the Jewish demonstration in Madison Square Garden, New York.

51 *JC,* December 18, 1942, the day after Eden's declaration on the Final Solution in an editorial: "Answer to the Mass Murderers."

52 See chapter 6 and Bolchover, *British Jewry and the Holocaust,* p. 117.

53 BDA, file 516, letter from "The Council of Polish Jews in Britain," March 6, 1942. Brotman's answer, March 11, 1942. The council's Rabbi Babad's letters to Brotman, March 18, 26, 27, 1942. Brotman's answer, April 14, 1942. Brotman's letter to Stein, April 5, 1942. *JC,* February 27, 1942, Szwarcbart announces that March 27 will be marked as the "Day of the Polish Jewry." There is no sign or report on such a Day in the paper.

54 BSA, cable from Lichtheim, Geneva to Linton, Jewish Agency, London, March 16, 1942. Cable from Riegner, Geneva to BSWJC, March 17, 1942. See Livia Rothkirchen, *Churban Yahaduth Hungaria* (The Destruction of the Hungarian Jewry), pp. 21ff.

55 BDA, file 510, letter from Raphael Springer to BD, April 24, 1942.

56 Ibid., Brotman's answer, same day.

57 Ibid., Brodetsky's letter to Herz, May 24, 1942.
58 Ibid., circular letter from "The Federation of the Czechoslovakian Jews."
59 J. Slavik, *The Persecution of the Jews in Nazi Slovakia.*
60 BDA, file Brodetsky, letter from Brotman to Brodetsky, May 28, 1942.
61 Ibid., letter from Brotman to Brodetsky, June 11, 1942. Letter from Brodetsky to Rabbi Yecheskiel Abramsky, telling that he stays in London Tuesdays, Wednesdays and Thursdays only. The rest of the week he spends in Leeds, July 8, 1941.
62 Ibid., letter from Brotman to Brodetsky, June 11, 1942.
63 *JC*, May 26, 1944.
64 CZA, Z4-302/26, session December 3, 1942, Blanche Dugdale's argumentations.
65 Sharf, *The British Press and the Jews under Nazi Rule*, p. 93.
66 BDA, file Brodetsky, letter from Brotman to Brodetsky, June 25, 1942.
67 BDA, file 504 and file Brodetsky, Brotman's report to Brodetsky and to Stein, June 29, 1942.
68 Ibid., file Brodetsky, letter from Brotman to Brodetsky, October 8, 1942.
69 Ibid., express letter from Brotman to Brodetsky, July 3, 1942.
70 YVA, M-475, circular letter from BSWJC, July 1, 1942.
71 FO 371-30917. BDA, JFC, report of session, July 15, 1942.
72 Ibid., report of session of Executive Committee, BD, July 13, 1942. Ibid., file 510, two letters from Brotman to Masaryk, both dated July 21, 1942.
73 Ibid., report of coversation with Masaryk, July 28, 1942. Letter from Brotman to Masaryk, August 5, 1942.
74 FO 371-30917, minutes and letters on the issue during July and August 1942.
75 BDA, file 510, report of meeting – Stein, Brotman, Dr Frischer and Dr Koebler, June 26, 1942.
76 Ibid., file Brodetsky, Brotman's notes to conversation with Brodetsky, August 26, 1942.
77 Ibid., file JFC, report of session, September 9, 1942. Ibid., file Brodetsky, letter from Brotman to Brodetsky, September 14, 1942.
78 FO 371-30918, minute, September 9, 1942.
79 BDA, file Brodetsky, letter from Brotman to Brodetsky, October 7, 1942.
80 Ibid., reports of BD Executive Committee, September 9 and 15, 1942; October 12 and 19, 1942.
81 CZA, Z-4 302/26, session October 19, 1942. *JC*, November 6, 1942.
82 *JC*, ibid.
83 *JC*, ibid. BDA, session of the Executive Committee, November 9, 1942.
84 BSA, cable from Barou–Easterman to Wise–Perlzweig, June 23, 1942. Answer from New York, June 27, 1942.
85 Ibid., cable from Barou to WJC, New York, July 8, 1942. A. Sharf, "The British Press and the Holocaust," *Yad Vashem Studies*, vol. 5, Jerusalem 1963, pp. 146ff. (Hebrew).
86 BSA, report of the press conference. Cable from Barou–Easterman to WJC, New York, June 30, 1942. *The Times*, June 30, 1942.
87 *The Times*, July 10, 1942. The paper did not quote Szwarcbart and Zygielbojm. BSA, Szwarcbart's circular report, July 10, 1942.

88 Ibid., copy of cable Szwarcbart received from the Polish Ministry for Interior Affairs, July 27, 1942.

Chapter 5 *Attempts to Break the Blockade and the Meager Results*

1 BSA, cable Lichtheim, Jewish Agency, Geneva to Joseph Linton, Jewish Agency, London, March 16, 1942. Cable Riegner, WJC, Geneva to WJC, London, March 17, 1942. Letter from BSWJC to Cardinal Hinsley, March 20, 1942. BDA, file 510, letter from Easterman to Brotman, same date.
2 Ibid., letter from Hertz to Godfrey, March 24, 1942.
3 Ibid., letter from Linton to Brotman. See also S. Rothkirchen, *The Destruction of Slovakian Jewry*, p. 22 and pp. 28ff. As early as March 14, 1942 the Pope sent a note of protest to the Slovakian government.
4 BDA, report of the session of the Executive Committee of BD, March 9, 1942.
5 CZA Z-4 302/25, sessions, March 26, 1942; April 15, 1942; April 29, 1942; May 4, 1942; May 5, 1942.
6 BDA, report of BD Executive Committee sessions, March 30, 1942; April 27, 1942; May 11, 1942.
7 FO 37-32663, minute, March 31, 1942.
8 CZA Z4-302/25, session, April 15, 1942.
9 Ibid., sessions April 29, 1942; May 4, 1942.
10 Ibid., sessions May 14, 1942; May 18, 1942; May 19, 1942; May 22, 1942.
11 Ibid., session, May 22 1942.
12 FO 371-32667, October 16, 1942, minute on politics toward the Jews in general and those in Turkey in particular.
13 FO 371-32665. CZA Z4 302/25, sessions, July 16, 1942; July 21, 1942.
14 *An Account of the Work of the Friends Committee for Refugees and Aliens 1933–1950*, London 1954, pp. 112ff.
15 FO 371-32667, minute, October 3, 1942.
16 N. A. Rose (ed.), *Baffy*, pp. 194ff. Aryeh L. Avneri, *From "Velos" to "Taurus,"* pp. 317ff.
17 CZA Z4-302/25, session, March 25, 1942. Robert S. Sherwood, *Roosevelt and Hopkins*, p. 717.
18 CZA Z4-302/25, session, September 28, 1942.
19 BSA, Lachs's document, August 13, 1942. Letter from BSWJC to Lachs, August 25, 1942.
20 *JC*, September 11, 1942.
21 CAB 66/29, sessions, September 23, 1942; September 28, 1942.
22 CO 733-436/75113. USA allocated 5000 visas for children in France. According to CZA Z-4 302/26, session, December 24, 1942, absorption facilities for 9000 children were available.
23 BD Annual Report 1942, p. 18. CZA 302/26, sessions, February 16, 1943; February 17, 1943; February 18, 1943. All three sessions were dedicated to the desperate efforts to evacuate from France.
24 See chapter 11.

Chapter 6 *The Declaration of December 17, 1942*

1 BDA, report JFC, February 19, 1941.
2 Ibid., file 510, report of conversation Brotman–Springer, September 7, 1942.
3 Springer discovered to me that the government censor counseled with Goodman on Jewish topics.
4 BDA, file without mark, Brotman's report to Brodetsky on his conversation over the telephone with Goodman, September 23, 1942.
5 Ibid., letter from Brodetsky to Brotman, October 5, 1942.
6 S. Brodetsky, Anglo-Jewry 5703, *Zionist Review*, September 11, 1942.
7 CZA 302/25, session, March 31, 1942.
8 BDA, file without mark, letter from Brodetsky to Brotman, October 5, 1942.
9 CZA 302/25, session, September 17, 1942.
10 BDA, JFC report, November 2, 1942.
11 BSA, letter from Easterman to Berl Locker, November 24, 1942.
12 BDA, JFC report, November 30, 1942.
13 *JC*, December 18, 1942.
14 A. Sharf, "The British Press and the Holocaust," *Yad Vashem Studies*, vol. 5, Jerusalem 1963, pp. 146ff.
15 Ibid., p. 150. BSA, December 5, 1942, the message arrived from WJC, New York and was circulated to heads of organizations, political parties, churches, ministers and to the press.
16 FO 371-30924, letter from British ambassador to the Polish exile government to Eden, December 3, 1942 and FO's answer, December 9, 1942. *JC*, December 11, 1942.
17 *JC*, ibid., interview with Sir Henry Morris-Jones MP.
18 Hansard, House of Commons, vol. 385, no. 17, December 17, 1942, pp. 2082–7.
19 BSA, letter from Easterman to Richard Law, December 14, 1942 and Law to Easterman, December 16, 1942.
20 The October 1943 Moscow Summit denounced the atrocities against the people in the occupied countries, but the Jews were not mentioned especially.
21 *JC*, December 25, 1942, the full text of the Declaration.
22 FO 371-34361, minute January 14, 1943. The same source reports that the Polish demanded retaliatory measures such as heavy bombing of German cities. This demand was refused with the interesting explanation: "We have told General Sikorski that reprisals are not acceptable and wait his view on our compromise proposal" (January 15, 1943). The compromise proposal is not described. A month earlier the BSWJC proposed some reprisals; the Foreign Office rejected them with the argument that Roosevelt would not admit that hundreds of thousands of prisoners of war are in the hands of the Wehrmacht. Silverman too pressed the American ambassador to favor reprisals. BSA, Easterman's letter to Silverman, December 26, 1942. Silverman's letter to Easterman, December 17, 1942.
23 *JC*, December 25, 1942.
24 Ibid., December 4, 1942.
25 FO 371-34361. See note 22.

26   *JC*, December 25, 1942.

27   Ibid.

28   Ibid.

29   *JC*, November 20, 1942; December 11, 1942.

30   BSA, this anxiety was expressed by Easterman in his cable to WJC, New York, December 23, 1942.

31   FO 371-30885, report of meeting, October 1, 1942.

32   BSA, long cable from Easterman and Barou to Wise and Perlzweig, WJC, New York on the Declaration and demonstration in the House of Commons and cited in a circular to friends and leaders, December 18, 1942. *JC*, March 5, 1943, against this appearance of boast.

33   Wyman, *Abandonment of the Jews*, pp. 73–4.

34   FO 371-36649, letter from Dr W. Temple to Churchill, January 8, 1943 and from Eden to Temple, January 16, 1943.

35   BSA, December 22, 1942, Easterman's complaining letter to Brodetsky. The final passage sounds: "The JTA also reports you as saying, 'This Joint Committee was working well'. Well, Well!!" See also *JC*, December 25, 1942, report from the plenary session of the BD. BSA, December 9, 1942, letter from Perlzweig, New York to Easterman. See also *JC*, November 11, 1942, p. 8: Brotman's complaints against WJC enthusiasts in London.

36   *JC* November 27, 1942.

37   *JC* December 25, 1942.

36   *JC* November 27, 1942, the editorial.

37   *JC* December 25, 1942.

38   BSA, cable no. 2 from Barou and Easterman to Wise, December 23, 1942. CZA Z-4-302/26, session, December 21, 1942.

39   FO 371-32682, letter from Rothschild to J. Martin, Churchill's secretary, December 16, 1942. In October Brodetsky asked Rothschild to arrange an appointment with Eden. He refused to do so. CZA Z4-302/26, session November 30, 1942. FO 371-32682, letter from Martin to Lawford, December 18, 1942.

40   CZA Z-4-302/26, session December 7, 1942. In conversations Weizmann had later with Churchill he did not present the rescue problem as urgent. He pressed for a change of the White Paper policy or for its cancelation. This might be the result of the impression a disappointed Weizmann brought from his visit to the USA that the Free Nations will not invest efforts in rescuing Jews. Ibid., session January 1, 1943. See also CZA Z-4-302/27, sessions, February 23, 1943; March 1, 1943; March 8, 1943.

41   Martin Kingsley, *Harold Laski*, pp. 154–5.

42   CZA Z-4-302/26, session, January 18, 1943. Hansard vol. 426, no. 189, col. 1258. Attempt to defend Churchill by Oskar Rabinovitz, *Sir Winston Churchill and Israel* in *The Jewish Historical Society of England*, vol. XXII, pp. 72ff.

43   CZA Z-4-302/26, sessions, December 17, 1942; December 21, 1942; December 22, 1942.

44   Ibid., session December 17, 1942. FO 371-32682, summary, December 23, 1942.

45 BDA, Annual Report of BD 1943, p. 39.

46 BSA, cable from Easterman–Barou to Wise–Perlzweig, New York, December 31, 1942. The members of the WJC, New York were strongly impressed by the successes in London, excusing their lack of achievements being compelled to wait for official guidance, whereas the European authorities are responding fast. Ibid., cable from Perlzweig–Miller, December 20, 1942.

47 FO 371-32682, letter from Rothschild to Eden, December 24, 1942 and Eden's answer, January 5, 1943.

48 Ibid., minute, December 16, 1942. Minute Law to Eden, December 23, 1942.

49 FO 371-32681, summary of session, October 28, 1942. FO 371-36649, Eden's letter to Temple, January 16, 1943; the Archbishop doubted whether he could help in rescuing the children.

50 CZA, Z4-302/26, sessions, January 18, 1943; February 15, 1943. FO 371-32682, minute, December 16, 1942.

51 FO 371-36648, Memorandum by the Secretary of State for Foreign Affairs, January 9, 1943.

52 The archive of The Chief Rabbi's Religious Emergency Council (RECA), Hertz's letter to Brodetsky, January 15, 1943. See also *Manchester Guardian*'s article in *JC*, January 8, 1943 and Report – Board of Deputies for the Year 1943, p. 39.

53 *JC*, January 29, 1943, the resolution in favor of an "Open Door Policy" in Britain, Palestine and the colonies taken by the Liberal Party and mailed to the Prime Minister and the Home Secretary. In the same day's *JC* a report of a dispute in the House between Miss Rathbone and Home Secretary Herbert Morrison on absorption of refugees in Britain. The Home Secretary got furious and insulted Rathbone so heavily that he had to apologize.

54 *JC*, December 25, 1943.

55 RECA, Brodetsky's letter to Hertz, January 11, 1943 and Hertz's letter to Brodetsky, January 15, 1943.

56 Ibid., Brodetsky's letter to Hertz.

57 BDA, report of JFC sessions, January 18, 1943; February 15, 1943.

58 RECA, Hertz's letter to Hill, February 18, 1943.

59 See chapter 11 and RECA, Schonfeld's letter to Isaac Wolfson, March 18, 1943.

60 CZA, Z4-302/26, session, January 21, 1943. RECA, Schonfeld's letter to Hertz, February 5, 1943.

61 Ibid., Schonfeld's letters to the editors of *John Bull* and *Sunday Chronicle*, both February 12, 1943.

62 *JC*, January 29, 1943.

63 CZA, Z4-302/26, session, January 21, 1943.

64 Print of the cable published by NCRNT.

65 RECA, Schonfeld's letter to Hertz, February 5, 1943. CZA Z4-302/26, sessions, December 21, 1942; January 25, 1943. CZA Z4-302/27, session, February 1, 1943. BDA, Brodetsky admitted that Schonfeld initiated the resolution signed by 280 members of Parliament to be tabled, according to the shorthand report of the plenar meeting of BD, March 23, 1943, but the rabbi's name is omitted in the official report of the meeting. RECA, Schonfeld's letter to Brotman, January 22, 1943. Brodetsky's letter to Hertz, January 11, 1943.

Lord Wedgewood supported Schonfeld because of the urgency, letter in *JC*, February 12, 1943.

66 Reprint in RECA.
67 Ibid., Schonfeld's letter to Hertz, February 5, 1943.
68 *JC*, January 29, 1943; February 5, 1943.
69 RECA, Brodetsky's letter to Hertz, February 3, 1943.
70 Ibid., letter from Agudat Israel to Brotman, February 9, 1943.
71 Ibid., letter from the Bishop of Chichester to Schonfeld, February 15, 1943.
72 Ibid., Schonfeld's letter to Wolfson, March 18, 1943. *JC*, March 26, 1943. RECA, Schonfeld's letter to Hertz, February 5, 1943. Schonfeld in *Zionist Review*, March 5, 1943.
73 RECA, letter from Foreign Office to Schonfeld, February 14, 1943. Schonfeld's letter to Foreign Office, February 18, 1943. FO 371-36711, the letter with minute. RECA, Randall's letter to Schonfeld, April 15, 1943. FO 371-36711, Schonfeld's memorandum. RECA, letter from Foreign Office to Schonfeld, April 15, 1943.
74 Ibid., letters from Foreign Office to Schonfeld, April 13, 1943; April 15, 1943. Schonfeld's letter to Wolfson, March 18, 1943. Wolfson, who was in conflict with Brodetsky, offered Schonfeld pecuniary assistance for his political work. This offer was rejected. Schonfeld, however, proposed Wolfson to assist to maintain the Jews who will succeed in arriving at Mauritius.

Chapter 7 *Before and After Bermuda Conference*

1 BDA, file 536, Suggested Steps for Saving Jews in Nazi-Occupied Europe, January 19, 1943.
2 Ibid., sessions, March 9, 1943; March 16, 1943.
3 Ibid., session, March 25, 1943. Copy of cable and signatures edited by NCRNT. (No date).
4 BSA, cable from Riegner, March 10, 1943. Letter to Law, March 21, 1943.
5 Robert E. Sherwood, *Roosevelt and Hopkins*, p. 717.
6 FO 371-36648. CZA Z-4-302/27, session, June 3, 1944. Rabbi Erving Miller from USA reported on his conversation with Attlee. The Deputy Prime Minister expressed his weariness of hearing that the Jews are suffering more than others and his desire to limit the entrance of Jews into Palestine, the fatherland of the Arabs.
7 BSA, resolutions, December 11, 1942; December 15, 1942. FO 371-32682, letter from Major T. L. Dugdale MP to Law, November 24, 1942. CO 733-436/75113, memorandum, October 28, 1942.
8 The Jewish delegation in the meeting with Eden asked for permits for immediate entrance to Britain for 10,000 refugees. This fact was mentioned in the margin, but not in the official report of the meeting. The ministers expressed that they feared more the possible American reaction than the delegation, FO 371-32682.
9 FO 371-36648, Memorandum by the Secretary of State, December 30, 1942.
10 Premier 4/52/5, part 2, 5820, War Cabinet Meeting, December 30, 1942.

11 BDA, report JFC session, April 7, 1943. Viscount Cranborne's speech in the House of Lords as the Archbishop of Canterbury tabled a resolution to save Jews, March 23, 1943. (Shonfeld's initiative).

12 Ibid., file refugees, report of the conversation, January 12, 1943.

13 This answer was far from being exact, as the speaker was probably well aware of Emerson's report to the Foreign Office that the destruction was being speeded up and that was the reason Emerson proposed to send food to Switzerland and to permit Joint to transfer larger sums to Switzerland for the absorbtion of 10,000 more refugees, the United Nations guaranteeing their later removal. He stressed that Switzerland has returned refugees to occupied territories. The British military attaché in Bern reported on August 16, 1942 that the Swiss authorities is giving haven to POW, desertees and political refugees, but not to Jews trying to escape from Belgium and the Netherlands. Being racial victims there is no juridical obligation to give them refuge. The Belgian ambassador in London sent complaints, FO 371-32660.

14 FO 371-36694, memorandum on the points for discussion, December 30, 1942. Brodesky's letter, January 5, 1943. Minute on the meeting.

15 FO 371-36648, Easterman's letter to Law, January 6, 1943 with enclosures. Law's report of the meeting, January 7, 1943 and minutes.

16 *JC*, January 22, 1943.

17 BDA, report of plenar meeting, January 19, 1943.

18 BSA, Churchill's letter to Lady Reading with enclosure, February 21, 1943.

19 Ibid., BSWJC's letter to Eden, February 18, 1943.

20 *Jerusalem Post*, October 29, 1963 published this information from a secret memorandum, year 1943, sent by the Washington ambassador to Foreign Office.

21 FO 371-36648, cable from Eden to Halifax, Washington, January 1943.

22 CAB 95/15 (J.R.43), session January 7, 1943. See also chapter 10.

23 Ibid., session January 27, 1943. BDA, file Refugees, Rathbone's letter to Home Office, January 8, 1943.

24 CAB 95/15 (J.R.43), session, February 19, 1943.

25 FO 371-36694, minute, January 28, 1943.

26 FO 371-36676, Eden's cable to Halifax, February 26, 1943. Distributed to War Cabinet members.

27 FO 371-36653, Rathbone's letter to Randall, February 27, 1943. Rathbone's and Randall's memoranda, and minutes, March 8, 1943; March 15, 1943.

28 BSA, The Parliamentary Committee's resolution toward the establishment of NCRNT, March 8, 1943.

29 Eleanor Rathbone, *Rescue the Perishing*, pp. 6ff.

30 Ibid., p. 9. BDA, file 536, report of BD session, March 9, 1943.

31 Rathbone, *Rescue the Perishing*, p. 10. Mary D. Stocks, *Eleanor Rathbone*, pp. 300–1.

32 Victor Gollancz, *Let My People Go*, p. 7. BSA, report of the BSWJC's Executive Committee, April 7, 1943.

33 Sharf, *The British Press and the Jews under Nazi Rule*, p. 139. Perhaps we have here the key to understanding Gollancz's later approach of forgiveness toward the Nazis, which reached its peak in demanding not to execute Adolph

Eichman. On Gollancz's activities during the war see also B. Loker, *Mikitov Ad Jerushalayim*, pp. 191ff.

34 Gollancz, *Let My People Go*, pp. 2ff.; pp. 8ff.
35 Kingsley Martin in *New Statesman*, February 17, 1967. This author found in Gollancz's behavior techniques from Catholic monasticism. On Gollancz's propensity to Christianity see Loker, *Mikitov Ad Jerushalayim*, pp. 205–6 and *JC*, August 31, 1962.
36 Rathbone, *Rescue the Perishing*, pp. 18ff.
37 Oswald Mosley, *My Life*, pp. 410ff, claims that he was freed from arrest because he suffered from phlebitis. Home Secretary Morrison ordered Mosley's release after consultation on a high level. How can the release of his followers be explained? On anti-Semitism and the release of the British Fascists see *Civil Liberties*, March 1944, p. 1.
38 BDA, file National Council for Civil Liberties, letter from Sidney Salomon to the Council, February 2, 1943. See also *Civil Liberties*, February 1943.
39 BDA, reports of Law & Parliamentary Committee session, April 4, 1943 and sessions of Executive Committee, April 8, 1943; May 5, 1943. YVA M2-490, report of the Central Committee of the Information Department of the Jewish Agency, London, February 16, 1943. Brodetsky states that when discussing rescue issues, black market problems are being put on the agenda.
40 CAB 95/15 (J.R.43), session, February 19, 1943.
41 *JC*, March 26, 1943.
42 BSA, report of meeting Law–Silverman, April 2, 1943.
43 FO 371-36659, cable to embassy, Washington, April 6, 1943. Minute, April 14, 1943.
44 Ibid., memorandum from JFC, April 15, 1943 and Eden's order to dispatch it to the British delegation, April 21, 1943.
45 BDA, report of the plenar sessions, April 18, 1943; March 23, 1943.
46 CZA, Z4-302/27, session, April 19, 1943.
47 BSA, report of meeting Law–Silverman, April 2, 1943.
48 Rathbone, *Rescue the Perishing*, p. 15.
49 CAB 95/15 (J.R.43), session, April 1, 1943.
50 Bauer, *American Jewry and the Holocaust*, p. 401.
51 Rathbone, *Rescue the Perishing*, p. 15.
52 Ibid., pp. 15ff.
53 CAB 95/15 (J.R.43), session, May 3, 1943.
54 Mark Wischnitzer, *To Dwell in Safety*, p. 246.
55 Feingold, *The Politics of Rescue*, pp 167ff.
56 The British did not absolutely avoid negotiations with the Germans. The negotiations were not limited to POW and exchange of civilians, but included also the feeding of the population of Greece. See Rathbone, p. 16.
57 *JC*, May 21, 1943. BDA, file Refugees, interpretation of the House of Commons' session, May 21, 1943. See also Reports of the World Jewish Congress (B.S.), no. 5, July 1943 – "A Note on Bermuda and After."
58 BDA, file 536.
59 *JC*, May 28, 1943.
60 BDA, Executive Committee of BD, session, June 1, 1943. Characteristic words

from Brodetsky to the critical Dr J. M. Machover stating that the Bermuda Conference touched the problems only superficially, but what the government decided to do will be implemented with energy and with awareness. Ibid., file Refugees, Brodetsky's letter to Machover, July 16, 1943.

61 BSA, Declaration of May 31, 1943. Cable to WJC, New York, same date. Cable from Perlzweig, WJC, New York, May 24, 1943.
62 Ibid., Ben Rubinstein's letter to Lady Reading, June 18, 1943.
63 Ibid., Melchett's letter to his sister, Lady Reading, May 13, 1943.
64 Ibid., report of the meeting.
65 *JC*, June 4, 1943, Brodetsky's address to Jews in East End.
66 JTA, Stein's address to AJA assembly, June 4, 1943. BSA, Brodetsky's letter to BSWJC, May 10, 1943.
67 Ibid., letter from BSWJC, June 17, 1943.
68 Ibid., Lord Melchett's letter to Lord Nathan of Churt, June 11, 1943.
69 BDA, report of BD plenar session, July 4, 1943.
70 Ibid., file 536, letter from NCRNT, May 10, 1943.
71 Ibid., Notes for Press Conference. No date, probably from the middle of May 1943. Also FO 371-36660.
72 FO 371-36679, minute and letter to Ministry of Shipping, May 4, 1943.
73 BDA, report of BD Executive Committee meeting, June 1, 1943. BSA, report of NCRNT meeting, June 18, 1943.
74 JTA, June 4, 1943.
75 See also chapters 4 and 8.
76 BSA, Perlzweig's letter to Easterman, May 24, 1943.

Chapter 8 *The Bermuda Policy and its Opponents*

1 AJAA, memorandum 37/43, August 8, 1943.
2 Board of Deputies Annual Report 1943.
3 BDA, reports of BD plenar meetings, September 12, 1943; March 19, 1944.
4 The historians are S. A. Cohen, G. Shimoni, B. Wasserstein and R. Bolchover. See Bolchover, *British Jewry and the Holocaust*, p. 54 and W. Laqueur, *Israel-Arab Reader*, pp. 77ff.
5 The Seventy-Second Annual Report of the Anglo-Jewish Association 43/44. AJAA, letter to Foreign Secretary, October 29, 1943. Answer in the name of acting Foreign Secretary W. Churchill, November 6, 1943. Ibid., Stein's memorandum 37/43, August 8, 1943.
6 Ibid., report of session of AJA General Purpose and Foreign Committee (GPFC), September 27, 1943.
7 Ibid., ibid. See also *Jewish Weekly*, September 17, 1943. YVA M2-487, report of AJA Council meeting, August 30, 1943.
8 Thus in the delegation to Eden, December 24, 1942.
9 *Jewish Weekly*, September 24, 1943.
10 BDA, reports of FAC (BD) sessions, September 7, 1943; November 9, 1943.
11 AJAA, report of GPFC, September 27, 1943; December 18, 1943; December 22, 1943. We learn from these reports of quite ridiculous negotiations with

Zog, King of Albania, earlier left by Brotman.

12 AJAA 37/34, letters to American Jewish Committee (AJC), December 6, 1943; March 8, 1944; March 14, 1944.

13 BSA, report of BS Council, December 13, 1943. AJAA 37/34, letter from Temkin to Gottschalk, AJC, March 8, 1944. GPFC's resolution, November 11, 1943.

14 The Seventy-Second Annual Report of the AJA 43/44.

15 BSA, report of BS Council, December 13, 1943.

16 BDA, correspondence with AJA in the reports of BD Executive Committee sessions between July 5, 1943 and September 3, 1943 and of sessions, September 27, 1943; November 2, 1943. AJAA, reports of GPFC sessions, September 27, 1943; October 18, 1943.

17 See chapter 2.

18 BDA, report of BD Executive Committee sesions in March 1944. See also N. Goldmann, *Jewish Observer and Middle East*, February 5, 1954. YVA, M-470, report of BS Council meeting, April 18, 1944.

19 YVA, M-470, report of BS Council meeting, April 18, 1944.

20 AJAA, the full text of the agreement, March 9, 1944.

21 BSA, letters from Easterman to Brotman, May 18, 1944; May 30, 1944; June 5, 1944. Letters from Brotman to Easterman, June 2, 1944; June 7, 1944; June 9, 1944. Easterman's letter to Lady Reading, June 9, 1944.

22 AJAA, summary undated.

23 BDA, report of FAC session, February 8, 1944: Summary of Brodetsky's talks with Undersecretary George Hall MP.

24 Ibid., report of FAC session, November 22, 1943.

25 AJAA, report of "Joint Meeting Re Contact with Inter-Governmental Committee," November 23, 1943. BDA, file 527, report of session of Central Council for Jewish Refugees, October 4, 1943.

26 BDA, reports of BD plenary meetings, July 4, 1943; October 17, 1943. YVA, M2-482, invitations to BD plenary meetings, November 11, 1943; December 9, 1943. BDA, report of BD plenary meeting, December 19, 1943.

27 BDA, report of BD plenary meeting, February 20, 1944.

28 Ibid., report of BD plenary meeting, June 18, 1944.

29 Ibid., file 536, reports of sessions of NCRNT, June 3, 1943; June 28, 1943; July 1, 1943.

30 Ibid., NCRNT session, September 23, 1943.

31 Ibid., Note by Rathbone, October 1, 1943.

32 Ibid., Note by Rathbone, October 12, 1943. NCRNT Memorandum, November 1943. On March 7, 1944 NCRNT concluded that they could not start any public campaign, because the money would be dedicated to secret work and account could not be rendered.

33 Ibid., NCRNT meetings, November 4, 1943; November 9, 1943; December 7, 1943.

34 Ibid., Rathbone's letter to Hall, November 25, 1943. FO 371-36669, Rathbone's letter to Law, November 18, 1943.

35 FO 371-36669, Rathbone's letter to Hall, November 26, 1943 and minutes. FO 371-42751, Note on the Proposed Declaration of the United Nations and the

Published Statement of the British and the U.S. Governments, by E. F. Rathbone, December 13, 1943.

36 BDA, Rathbone's notes toward the meeting with Eden, January 11, 1944. Date of the notes December 20, 1943. Report of NCRNT session, February 10, 1944. FO 371-42751, report of the meeting and minutes.

37 Ten Points Programme, London, January 1944.

38 FO 371-42751, minute, February 24, 1944.

39 BDA, report of JFC meetings, April–June 1943.

40 BSA, report of Barou's and Easterman's talks with Benes, July 23, 1943. Report of Silverman's and Easterman's talks with Law, July 7, 1943.

41 Ibid., Frischer's letter to Easterman, August 5, 1943. On July 28, 1943 Frischer delivered a message he got from Riegner to Easterman. Easterman's letter to Law, August 18, 1943.

42 Ibid., report of Easterman's meeting with Paul Grey, Foreign Office, August 27, 1943. Summary of telephone conversation Easterman–Grey, August 30, 1943.

43 Ibid., Easterman's letter to Law, September 9, 1943. Foreign Office's letter to Easterman, October 25, 1943.

44 Ibid., summary of talks Easterman–Maiski, September 8, 1943. Maiski rejected the proposal that the Red Cross shall render help to refugees in Soviet countries. Easterman's letter to Maiski, September 9, 1943.

45 Ibid., Masaryk's letter to Easterman, October 6, 1943. Similar answer from the Polish Foreign Ministry, September 29, 1943.

46 Ibid., Easterman's letter to Masaryk, October 11, 1943.

47 FO 371-34374, Easterman's letter to Foreign Office, October 11, 1943 and answer, October 25, 1943 and minutes. Prem 4/52/5, draft of letter from Greenway to Sole, October 1943.

48 BSA, Easterman's letter to Brograve Beauchamp, December 17, 1943.

49 Ibid., summary of talks Easterman–Gusev, December 23, 1943.

50 Feingold, *The Politics of Rescue*, p. 305.

51 FO 371-42775, Lady Reading's letter to Bracken, February 22, 1944 and answer, February 29, 1944. Reading is hinting at WRB's activity. BSA, cable to WJC, New York, February 23, 1944.

52 FO 371-42775, Melchett's letter to Eden, February 22, 1944 and answer, March 1, 1944. Goldmann, Silverman and Easterman visited Law on March 2, 1944 and exhibited the same items. Randall's report, same date.

53 Feingold, *The Politics of Rescue*, p. 252.

54 FO 371-42728, minutes to Halifax's cable no. 982. Foreign Secretary's note to Cabinet Committee on Refugees, March 10, 1944 and minutes. Cables to Halifax, Washington, March 10, 1944; March 20, 1944.

55 Ibid., letter from Eden to British ambassadors to the exile governments with annex, April 1, 1944. Halifax expressed Britain's dissatisfaction with the version of Roosevelt's declaration, because it included promises and threads that were impossible to implement, in his opinion. Cable from Halifax, March 21, 1944. On the last minute mention of the Jews see Randall's minute, March 25, 1944. FO 371-42723, Halifax's cable to Foreign Office, March 28, 1944 and Foreign Office cable to Halifax, April 1, 1944.

56 BSA, report of Easterman's talk with an official at the Soviet Embassy, April 4, 1944. Easterman's letter to Soviet Ambassador, April 10, 1944 and answer, April 11, 1944.

57 FO 371-42728, minutes to cable no. 845 from embassy, Moscow.

58 BSA, circular letter issued by Easterman, April 3, 1944.

59 FO 371-34365, Robertson's letter to Eden, March 11, 1943 and answer from Foreign Office, March 22, 1943.

60 BSA, Frischer's letter to Easterman, March 26, 1943 and answer, March 30, 1943.

61 FO 371-36672, Easterman's letter to Undersecretary George Hall MP, October 10, 1943. BSA, Easterman's letter to Foreign Office, October 20, 1943 and answer, October 26, 1943. Easterman's letter to Paul Grey, October 29, 1943. Two further letters to Grey sent on December 7, 1943.

62 FO 371-36672, Easterman's letter to Donald Hall, December 16, 1943. Foreign Office answers to Joseph Linton, Jewish Agency and to Easterman and minutes, January 4, 1944. Hall's letter to Easterman, January 18, 1944.

63 BSA, Easterman's letter to the Archbishop, January 14, 1944.

64 FO 371-42755, Easterman's letters to Foreign Office, January 13, 1944; January 21, 1944. Hall's letter to Easterman, January 19, 1944. Minute, February 1, 1944.

65 BSA, the Archbishop's letter to Easterman, April 7, 1944. Easterman's letter to Law, March 31, 1944.

66 FO 371-36666, Easterman's letter to Law, September 1, 1943. Foreign Office answer, September 9, 1943 and minutes.

67 FO 371-42755, S. Weissman's letter from Lisbon to Barlas, Istanbul, December 20, 1943. Easterman's letter to Hall, January 11, 1944.

68 FO 371-42757, Emerson's secret memorandum on refugee children in France, March 1, 1944. Jewish children are not mentioned in the five pages long memorandum. Letter from Georges Boris, Free French Committee, to Albert Cohen, BSWJC, March 16, 1944. Easterman's letter to D. Hall, March 13, 1944. Hall's answer, April 24, 1944. Randall's letter to Easterman, May 23, 1944, and minutes. BSA, Weissman's report, March 10, 1943. Report of Easterman's meetings with Hall, April 13, 1944; April 14, 1944. On the fight against the Jews' escape routes see Survey of Activities of H.M.G. on behalf of Refugees, June 1944, FO 3712-42730. See also FO 371-42807, minutes to Hall's talk with Silverman and Easterman, July 5, 1944. Warning to Rathbone that fleeing Jews endanger the escape routes of RAF crews, February 22, 1944, FO 371-42727.

69 BDA, file 514, Randall's letter to Brotman, June 30, 1943. Szwarcbart's letter to Brotman, July 21, 1943.

70 Ibid., file 514, report of the meeting of Brodetsky–Brotman with Law–Randall, August 5, 1943.

71 FO 371-36694, Jewish Agency's report, January 28, 1943 and minutes. FO 371-36676, cable from Halifax, February 19, 1943 and Foreign Office answer, February 26, 1943.

72 FO 371-36669, Easterman's letter to Hall, November 16, 1943. Foreign Office answer, December 2, 1943. BSA, report of Easterman's meeting with Hall,

November 11, 1943. BDA, file Rumania, letter from Foreign Office to Brotman, November 24, 1943. Brotman also demanded warning to Rumania. Foreign Office wanted time to look into the matter.

73 FO 371-42772, Easterman's letter to Hall, March 10, 1944. Hall's answer, March 16, 1944 and minute.

74 Ibid., Randall's letter to R. Eastwood, Colonial Office, February 19, 1944. See also CZA, Z4-302/28, sessions, April 4, 1944; April 17, 1944 on the Colonial Office's purpose to delay the immigration to Palestine, still possible in the frame of the White Paper.

75 FO 371-42721, minute on the visit of Shertok and Linton to the Foreign Office, March 2, 1944. FO 371-42762, letter from Gater, Colonial Office to Jewish Agency, April 5, 1944.

76 BSA, report of meeting with Benes, March 21, 1944.

77 Ibid., Easterman's letter to Rathbone, March 20, 1944. Easterman's letter to Gusev, March 27, 1944.

78 YVA, M2-472, letter from Brotman to Easterman, June 9, 1944, being part of continued dispute between the two organizations on their agreement. Both initiated meetings with the Soviet Ambassador. On Brodetsky's meeting with Gusev see BDA, file FAC, report of the talk with Gusev, May 5, 1944.

79 BSA, report of council meeting, December 13, 1943.

80 Ibid., Easterman's letter to Reading, December 20, 1943.

81 FO 371-42775, Randall's report on talk with Szwarcbart, January 7, 1944 and minutes. Randall's letters to Playfair and Bliss, January 13, 1944.

82 Ibid., Bliss' letter to Randall, January 26, 1944. Mynors' letter to Randall, February 3, 1944.

83 Ibid., Lady Reading's letter to Bracken, February 22, 1944 and answer, February 29, 1944. Melchett's letter to Eden, February 22, 1944 and answer March 1, 1944.

84 Ibid., unsigned memorandum from Washington Embassy, received on June 1, 1944 and minutes.

85 FO 371-42757, Emerson's memorandum, Rescue, Concealment and Preservation of Refugees in the Occupied and Satellite Countries of Europe – March 1, 1944.

86 FO 371-39524, letter from IGCR to Foreign Office, September 28, 1944 and minutes.

87 FO 371-42762, letter from Colonial Office to Jewish Agency, April 5, 1944 , summary on this policy with its limitations.

88 FO 371-36666, letter from G. Walker-Smith to Foreign Secretary's secretary, September 17, 1943 and answer September 25, 1943. A. Walker's minute.

89 FO 371-42762, letter from Ministry for Foreign Affairs, Bern to the British Legation, February 4, 1944.

90 Ibid., Walker's minute.

91 Ibid., Randall's letter to Home Office, March 3, 1944 and Home Office answer, April 1, 1944 and minutes.

92 Feingold, *The Politics of Rescue,* pp. 241ff. Wyman, *Abandonment of the Jews,* pp. 209ff.

93 FO 371-42727, letter from Randall to Emerson, January 5, 1944.

94 Ibid., minute to article in *New York Times*, December 31, 1943. Minute to cable from Washington Embassy, January 26, 1944. Minute sent from Refugee Department to Eastern Department (East Europe), January 31, 1944. Eden's memorandum to War Cabinet Committee for Refugees, February 1, 1944.

95 BSA, Easterman's letter to Law, January 30, 1944. Report of Easterman's meeting with Donald Hall, February 28, 1944. BDA, file Refugees, report of Brodetsky's meeting with Hall and Randall, February 1, 1944.

96 For instance, *Manchester Guardian*, January 29, 1944; February 12, 1944.

97 FO 371-42727, the wording of Eden's answer to Lipson MP. Hansard, February 9, 1944.

98 FO 371-42727, cable from Foreign Office to embassy in Washington, February 4, 1944. Letter from Washington Embassy to Foreign Office, February 11, 1944. Letter from Randall to A. J. Newling, February 21, 1944.

99 Ibid., cable from Foreign Office to Washington Embassy, February 4, 1944. Out of prudence it was decided not to reject the 10 million dollar proposal, but only to express reservation. See chapter 12. It was decided to agree to a smaller American allocation: $100,000 of Joint's means to distribute food to Jews in Hungary and Rumania with the help of the Red Cross. See letter from Randall to MEW, February 15, 1944.

100 FO 371-42728, note by Secretary of State for Foreign Affairs to Cabinet Committee for Refugees, March 10, 1944.

101 FO 371-42729, the minster of MEW in the refugee committee meeting, March 14, 1944.

102 FO 371-42728, cable from ambassador, Washington to Foreign Office, March 12, 1944 and answer, March 22, 1944. Emerson admitted that the American system is more advantageous for the persecuted – thus his words in the cabinet refugee committee, CAB 95/15, March 14, 1944. As a matter of fact, the overwhelming part of WRB's budget was granted by Joint – $15 million. The orthodox Waad Hazala contributed one million dollar and WJC $300,000. The US Government allocated less than half a million dollars to its WRB. See Final Summary Report of the Executive Director, War Refugee Board, Washington, September 15, 1945, p. 13.

103 FO 371-42730, minutes, May 7, 1944; May 15, 1944.

104 FO 371-42724, letter from embassy, Ankara to D. E. Howard, Foreign Office, April 3, 1944 and Howard's answer, April 24, 1944. No doubt the American amplitude was propitious and helpful. But it did not cause a revolutionary turn. The WRB activity started late, too late. See Menachem Bader, *Shlichuyot Azuvot*, pp. 70ff. John Mortom Blum, *From the Morgenthau Diaries – Years of War,* p. 207ff; pp. 223ff. Wyman, *Abandonment of the Jews,* p. 216ff.

105 FO 371-42731, letter from Winterton to Eden, February 17, 1944.

106 Ibid., letter from Emersom to Haccius, February 21, 1944.

107 FO 371-42727, minutes refering to meeting with Law, February 28, 1944.

108 *JC*, March 3, 1944.

Chapter 9 *Aid and Rescue Efforts to Comfort the Seablocked*

1 See Saul Friedlander, *Prelude to Downfall*, p. 100. FO 837-1223, minutes of January 9, 1941. The prefix FO 837 indicates documents of the Ministry of Economic Warfare (MEW). The letters FO (Foreign Office) were affixed to them after the Foreign Office dismantled MEW after the war. The documents of this archive are not listed in the Foreign Office index.

2 On Hoover and his humanitarian projects see D. Hinshaw, *Herbert Hoover American Quaker*; Wyman, *Abandonment of the Jews*, p. 281; Bauer, *American Jewry and the Holocaust*, p. 329.

3 FO 837-1213, Lord Halifax's cable to Foreign Office, October 15, 1942. Foreign Office cables to Washington, November 12 and 16, 1942. Cable from Washington to the Foreign Office, December 13, 1942. FO 837-1214, February 24, 1943, *Note on Blockade Respecting Relief*, is a general survey of developments on the issue (hereafter *Note on Blockade*). FO 837-1215, Selborne's memorandum to Eden, April 13, 1943.

4 FO 837-1215, MEW letter to Washington, November 17, 1943.

5 FO 837-1214, Foreign Office letter to MEW, February 16, 1943. MEW letter to the embassy in Washington, February 16, 1943. Embassy letter to Foreign Office, March 8, 1943: Fear that the Americans will ship part of the supplies destined for Britain to European populations. Selborne's memorandum to Eden, April 13, 1943 before Herbert Lehman's London visit.

6 Ibid., minutes of April 9, 1943.

7 *Report of the World Jewish Congress (British Section)* no. 5, July 1943, *A Note On Bermuda and After*, p. 8.

8 *Note on Blockade*.

9 FO 371-28833, Agudat Israel letter to embassy in Washington, October 24, 1941. Wise's letter to embassy, October 24, 1941. Perlzweig's letter to embassy, October 28, 1941. Washington Embassy letter to Foreign Office, November 8, 1941.

10 YVA M2-486, Szwarcbart's letters to JFC, February 4, 5, and 11, 1942.

11 BDA, file Brodetsky, Agudat Israel's letter, February 4, 1942.

12 Ibid., Brotman's letter to Brodetsky, February 5, 1942.

13 FO 837-1223, minutes of March 17, 1942. Wyman, *Abandonment of the Jews*. Bauer, *American Jewry and the Holocaust*.

14 BDA, report of JFC meeting, May 4, 1942.

15 BSA, report of Szwarcbart and Frischer. YVA M2-464, report on negotiations, July 3, 1942.

16 BSA, Perlzweig's cable to Easterman, September 4, 1942. The information on the agreement came as a surprise to the British Section which also wanted to join the parcels program. The information came from New York.

17 *Note on Blockade*.

18 BSA, Perlzweig's letter to Easterman, October 1, 1942.

19 Ibid., Frischer's letter to Easterman, December 23, 1942. BDA, file 538, report of Brotman's meeting with a MEW official, January 18, 1943.

20 *Note on Blockade*. See also FO 371-28833, de Gaulle's letter to Churchill, November 28, 1941.

21 BDA, file 438, letter from the Polish Jewish Council in Great Britain to Brotman, December 28, 1942.

22 Ibid., January 12, 1943. On MEW's anger at the publicizing of the program learned from private letters opened by the censor, February 3, 1943; February 6, 1943. Ibid., report of plenum meeting, January 13, 1943.

23 Ibid., cables to Schwartz, January 3 and 15, 1943.

24 Ibid., letter from Dr Stanisław Schimitzek, the official in charge of the parcels shipment at the Polish Legation in Lisbon, February 3, 1943. Schwartz's cable, January 23, 1943.

25 Ibid., Brotman's letter to M. Stephany, January 19, 1943.

26 Ibid., Frischer's report, January 1943.

27 YVA M2-479, Szwarcbart's letter to BD, February 12, 1943. This information about Warsaw was inaccurate because the Warsaw Ghetto Uprising broke out only in April.

28 BDA, file 538, council letter to the BD, February 15, 1943; Brotman's cable to Joint in Lisbon, February 18, 1943; Joint cable, March 5, 1943.

29 Ibid., Joint cables, April 2 and 7, 1943; Joint report, June 26, 1943.

30 Ibid., Schimitzek's report, June 1, 1943.

31 Ibid., Brotman's letter to MEW, June 1, 1943.

32 Ibid., Trading with the Enemy Department letter to BD, July 6, 1943. Apparently the Quaker program was discovered by the postal censor.

33 Ibid., Trading with the Enemy Department letter, January 11, 1944.

34 Ibid., report of meeting at the Polish Welfare Ministry, August 11, 1943.

35 Ibid., Joint's letters to the BD, August 16 and 21, 1943 and BD's reply, September 6, 1943. Polish Welfare Ministry letter, September 2, 1943.

36 BSA, Frischer's letter to Easterman, December 23, 1942. BDA, file 538, report of Brotman's meeting with MEW official, January 18, 1943. MEW letter to Brotman, January 19, 1943 and Brotman's reply, January 22, 1943.

37 BSA, Frischer's letters, January 27, June 17, 1943.

38 BDA, file 538, Frischer's letter to Brotman, March 5, 1943. Ibid., April 12, 1943.

39 Ibid., Frischer's letters to Brodetsky, August 21, September 17, 1943; Brotman's letter to MEW, September 21, 1943; Brotman's letter to Frischer, January 14, 1944; Frischer's letters to Brotman, June 17, September 17, October 16, November 10, 1943 and January 6, 1944.

40 Ibid., confirmation of receipt signed by W. Kopp, camp commandant, for the prisoners, who according to the commandant were forbidden to write. Report of discussion of the heads of the BD with Joseph Schwartz, November 5, 1943. Brotman's letter to Szwarcbart, November 26, 1943. The above confirmations are in the file, ibid. On Dr Michael Weichert see Bauer, *American Jewry and the Holocaust*, pp. 85–92, 318–22, 333. BDA, ibid., Schimitzek's notices to Joint in letter from Joint, January 11, 1944, Schwartz's cable, January 20, 1944, and his letter to BD, February 9, 1944.

41 Ibid., MEW letter to Brotman, February 2, 1944, and Frischer's letter to Brotman, January 6, 1944. Frischer requested aid for Birkenau prisoners, referring to it as a new camp for about 35,000 Jews.

42 FO 371-36669, MEW letter to Foreign Office, November 22, 1943, and

Foreign Office minutes, November 30, 1943. FO 371-42731, MEW letter to BD, February 2, 1944.

43 BDA, file 538, Brotman's letter to Frischer, February 21, 1944. Frischer's letters, March 6, 17, 1944.

44 Ibid., Schwartz's cable, March 22, 1944, and report of the negotiations with MEW.

45 Ibid., Frischer's letters to Brotman, March 17, April 24, 1944; Brotman's letter to Frischer, March 20, 1944.

46 Ibid., file 510, Frischer's letter to Brotman, September 14, 1944.

47 Ibid., the reports are attached to Frischer's letter of May 1, 1944. Other detailed reports from January–March 1944, and June 2, 1944.

48 Ibid., MEW's letter to Brotman, May 30, 1944. On the suspicions against Weichert see Bauer, *American Jewry and the Holocaust*, p. 85.

49 Ibid., Schwartz's cable, May 9, 1944. Schwartz's letter, May 9, 1944. Schimitzek's report to the Welfare Ministry, May 11, 1944.

50 Ibid., Frischer's letter to Brodetsky, May 31, 1944.

51 Ibid., Brodetsky's letter to Frischer, June 13, 1944. Letter of the Central Council for Jewish Refugees to Brotman, May 26, 1944, and Brotman's letter to Schonfeld, June 8, 1944. At the time the relations between the BD and the Anglo-Jewish Association were strained. The latter had a great influence in the Jewish Colonisation Association.

52 Ibid., report of meeting, July 21, 1944.

53 Ibid., Polish Welfare Ministry letter to Brotman, September 12, 1944.

54 Ibid., Polish Welfare Ministry letter to Brotman, March 17, 1945. BD letters to the Central British Fund for Jewish Relief and Rehabilitation (CBF), April 1 and 6, 1944.

55 BDA, file 538, Brotman's letter to Schonfeld, June 2, 1944. Brotman's letter to Emerson, June 8, 1944. Brotman's letter to MEW, June 19, 1944.

56 Ibid., file 538, Brotman's letter to Schonfeld, July 12, 1944. MEW letter to Brotman, July 18, 1944.

57 Ibid., report of meeting with Welfare Minister Stanczyk, July 21, 1944. During the meeting with Stanczyk, Brotman suggested that Poland instruct its diplomatic representatives in Hungary to grant certificates of protection to Polish refugees in Hungary and Hungarians of Polish origin. Welfare Ministry letter to BD, September 5, 1944. Correspondence between the Polish Welfare Ministry and MEW, August 7 and 11, 1944, and Foreign Office letter to Brotman, August 12, 1944. Ibid., Brotman's letter to Schonfeld, August 8, 1944. Schonfeld's letter to Brotman, August 15, 1944; Brotman's reply, August 17, 1944, and Polish Welfare Ministry letter to Brotman, August 7, 1944.

58 Ibid., Schimitzek's letter, October 13, 1944. Polish Welfare Ministry's letter to BD, November 8, 1944.

59 Ibid., South African Jewish BD letter to BD, November 22, 1945. Brotman's letter to the South African Jewish BD, November 28, 1945.

60 CZA Z4-302/26, meeting of January 1, 1943.

61 FO 371-36711, Joseph Linton's letter to Foreign Office, January 5, 1943. Lewis Namir's memorandum to Foreign Office, January 20, 1943. S. Adler-Rudel, *A Chronicle of Rescue Efforts*, p. 218.

62   Adler-Rudel, *A Chronicle of Rescue Efforts,* p. 225. See also Leni Yahil, *Hatzalat Yehudei Denya,* p. 233.

63   Adler-Rudel, *A Chronicle of Rescue Efforts,* pp. 222–3; pp. 225ff.

64   FO 371-36659, cable from consul in Stockholm to Foreign Office, April 21, 1944. Minutes of discussion held by Namier, Adler-Rudel and Linton with the head of the Foreign Office Refugee Department, April 30, 1943. FO 371-36660, Adler-Rudel's letter to Emerson, May 5, 1943. Adler-Rudel's article shows that this is not the way the Swedes presented the last two conditions to him. FRUS, Dipl. Papers, 1943, vol. 1, pp. 305.

65   FO 371-36711, minutes on Brotman and Stein's meeting with Law, March 10, 1943.

66   FO 371-36659, A. Walker's minutes, April 30, 1943.

67   FO 371-36660, "Summary of the Main Reasons for the Continuation of the Food Blockade."

68   FO 371-42816, C. Cheetham's minutes, August 17, 1944.

69   FO 837-1213, cable from Washington to MEW, October 16, 1942. FO 837-1214, cables from Washington to MEW, February 6, 16, 19, 1943: Lehman is dangerous because he is both intimate with the president and influenced by Hoover. FO 371 -36510, letter from Washington to MEW, March 12, 1943. FO 371-36512, MEW cable to Washington, February 20, 1943. Cable from Washington to MEW, March 30, 1943. Eden's cable to Washington, April 24, 1943. Cable to Law from Bermuda, April 25, 1943. FO 371-36513, cable from Washington to Foreign Office, April 30, 1943. See also *Report of the World Jewish Congress (British Section),* no. 5, July 1943, p. 8.

70   FO 371-36660, Emerson's letter to Randall, May 7, 1943.

71   FO 371-36659, Foreign Office cable to minister in Stockholm, May 13, 1943. FRUS, Dipl. Papers – 1943, vol. 1, pp. 304–5.

72   FO 371-36659, Foreign Office cable to Washington and Stockholm, July 27, 1943. CZA Z4-302/27, July 22, 1943 meeting.

73   FO 371-36515, Washington Embassy letter to MEW, August 13, 1943. FO 371-36666, MEW letter to the Foreign Office, August 28, 1943. Foreign Office letter to Stockholm, minutes, September 8, 1943.

74   BDA, file 527, report of CBF meeting, May 10, 1943. CZA Z4-302/27, meeting of April 29, 1943.

75   From my interview with Mr. Adler-Rudel, and indeed no publication mentions his scheme.

76   FO 371-36666, Note by E. F. Rathbone, October 1, 1943, and Rescue Measures for Victims of Nazi Persecution, Enclosure 2 to Miss Rathbone's letter, October 2, 1943.

77   FO 837-1215, the ambassador's cables to MEW, December 21, 29, 1943.

78   FO 371-42367, Anglo-American letter to the Swedish Minister in London, December 20, 1943. Cable from Washington to MEW, December 30, 1943. MEW letter to Emerson, December 30, 1943.

79   Ibid., MEW letter to Emerson, December 30, 1943; MEW letter to the Washington Embassy, January 23, 1944.

80   FO 837-1216, MEW cable to Washington, January 12, 1944. According to Halifax's report of January 6, 1944 about the "Feed Europe Now!" movement

around which Roosevelt's opponents, Hoover's Quaker associates, church officials, separatists, and *The New York Times* coalesced. All of them considered Churchill to be the representative of the British hard line.

81 BDA, report of BD Foreign Affairs Committee meeting, December 28, 1944.

82 FO 837-1217, cable from Washington to Foreign Office, June 30, 1944.

83 FO 371-43476, report of discussions with the Swedish Legation in London, June 26, 1944.

84 FO 371-42816, C. Cheetham's minutes about the "Horthy Offer," August 17, 1944.

85 Adler-Rudel, *A Chronicle of Rescue Efforts,* pp. 234–5.

Chapter 10 *The Search for Refugee Havens*

1 CAB 95/15 (J.R. 43), sessions of December 31, 1942 and January 7, 1943.

2 Ibid., session of January 27, 1943.

3 BSA, Easterman's reports of his discussions with Maisky, January 27, February 4, 1943.

4 Ibid., Rubenstein's letters to Melchett, February 2, 3 and 4, 1943.

5 Ibid., Rubenstein's cable to Haccius, March 11, 1943.

6 Ibid., Rubenstein's questionnaire letter to Dr Diringer, March 12, 1943.

7 Ibid., Easterman's letter to Lord Melchett, March 19, 1943; Rubenstein's letter to Lady Reading, March 18, 1943. A British officer, whose opinion Melchett solicited, concluded that Eritrea was suitable as a temporary refuge, but not as a permanent settlement, Melchett's letter to Rubenstein, April 28, 1943.

8 FO 371-36720, Silverman's note and memorandum and minutes there.

9 Ibid., note of April 1, 1943.

10 Ibid., Foreign Office letter to the deputy minister of war, April 14, 1943. Foreign Office letter to Silverman, May 3, 1943.

11 Premier 4-52/5 – Prime Minister's personal minute April 27, 1943. Note by the Prime Minister. War Cabinet. Palestine, April 28, 1943.

12 Ibid. See Nathaniel Katzburg, *Medini'ut Bemavokh,* pp. 98ff on the development of the issue from the British view and its context within Palestine policy. According to Katzburg, *Medini'ut Bemavokh,* p. 74, Churchill saw the establishment of Jewish colonies in Africa as compensation for the partition of Palestine.

13 FO 371-36720, minutes on Jewish settlement in the Italian colonies, June–July 1943.

14 CAB 95/14, Foreign Office Memorandum, October 21, 1943; Secretary of State for the Middle East Memorandum, November 1, 1943.

15 BDA, file Refugees, memorandum of November 10, 1939. *JC,* November 10, 1939.

16 *Jewish Affairs,* I/4, London, November 1941, pp. 6–7. Rabbi Perlzweig strongly rejected Mussolini's proposal.

17 BSA, Rubenstein's report of March 1, 1943 meeting. Letter to Lady Reading of March 9, 1943.

18 Ibid., memorandum of March 12, 1943.

19   FO 371-36628, report of the British Consul in Addis Ababa, March 25, 1943 and a profuse correspondence on the issue.
20   Documents of the Chief Rabbi's Religious Emergency Council, in Schonfeld's archive. Note on Consultation with the Royal Ethiopian Legation, May 7, 1943. Schonfeld might have been approached by an organization founded in the US, the Council for an Autonomous Jewish Province in Harrar, which according to the Foreign Office was based on economic fraud, FO 371-40141.
21   BSA, Rubenstein's report of his meeting with the Ethiopian Consul, August 17, 1943. Rubenstein noted with satisfaction that despite the suspicion of foreigners, the consul trusted him. Rubenstein promised to arrange a meeting between the consul and Weizmann because Rubenstein spoke of deepening the understanding between the Jews of Palestine and the Ethiopians against the Arabs. Incidentally, Weizmann was opposed to these territorial solutions: FO 371-35034, letter from Isaiah Berlin, who served as attaché for public opinion at the British Embassy in Washington, to the Foreign Office, May 18, 1943.
22   FO 371-35040, letter from the minister in Addis Ababa, October 25, 1943, and Randall's minutes. CAB 95/14, Secretary of State for the Middle East Memorandum, November 1, 1943, p. 3.

Chapter 11   *The Rescue Efforts of the Chief Rabbi's Religious Emergency Council*

1   CO 323-1846-7031/44. This file is named "Rabbis to Mauritius." Summary on the activities of The Chief Rabbi's Religious Emergency Council (REC) in minute, September 3, 1942. No mention of the council's work inside Britain.
2   Ibid., letter from Hertz to Cranborne, September 3, 1942 and Cranborne's answer, September 8, 1942 and Hertz's memorandum, September 11, 1942.
3   Ibid., minute, September 3, 1942.
4   Ibid., minute written by Cranborne, September 19, 1942. Marginal note by an official that the colonies have done their utmost in absorbing refugees. Who would now be able to give shelter to those rabbis?
5   Ibid., report of Hertz's talk with Cranborne, September 29, 1942.
6   Ibid., minute, October 6, 1942.
7   Ibid., letter to Randall, October 13, 1942 and minute. Minute, October 15, 1942.
8   Ibid., letter from J. B. Sidebotham to Randall, October 5, 1942. Randall's answer, October 9, 1942. Cranborne's letter to Hertz.
9   Ibid., Hertz's letter to Cranborne, October 30, 1942. FO 371-32681, FO's letter and minute, October 30, 1942.
10   CO 323-1846-7031/44, Cranborne's letter to Hertz, November 11, 1942.
11   Ibid., Hertz's letter to Cranborne, November 25, 1942 and Cranborne's answer, December 7, 1942. Schonfeld's letter to Oliver Stanley, November 11, 1942 and Stanley's answer, December 4, 1942.
12   Author of *Min Hametsar*. On Weissmandel, see indexes in Rotkirchen and Bauer. Schonfeld was Weissmandel's close friend from the years they studied together in the *yeshiva* in Slovakia. Weissmandel smuggled a letter from Slovakia to his friend in London in the summer of 1942 asking for rescue

money and shipment of food to Slovakia and to Poland "like the shipments to Greece." He begged Rabbi Schonfeld to burn the letter after the reading and not to mention it at all. The letter is published in *Min Hametsar*, p. 103. FO 371-32682, Stanley's letter to Schonfeld, December 9, 1942, enclosed a list of European rabbis.

13 FO 371-36711, Schonfeld's letter to FO, February 18, 1943 and minute. Randall's letters to Schonfeld, March 6, 1943; March 15, 1943 and Schonfeld's answer, March 17, 1943. Cable from embassy, Ankara, March 23, 1943. Letter from Joseph Linton, Jewish Agency, to FO, March 3, 1943. RECA, Schonfeld's letter to Randall, April 17, 1943.

14 CO 323-1846-7031/44, Randall's letter to J. B. Sidebotham, February 5, 1943. Stanley's letter to Schonfeld, February 23, 1943. Schonfeld's letter to Stanley, February 26, 1943, and minute. Schonfeld's letter to Stanley, March 9, 1943 and minute, March 12, 1943.

15 FO 371-36707, FO's cable to embassy, Ankara, February 16, 1943.

16 CO 323-1846-7031/44, CO's letter to FO, March 1, 1943, Schonfeld's letter to Stanley, May 5, 1943.

17 Ibid., letter from Czechoslovakian Deputy Foreign Minister S. Ripke to FO, April 5, 1943. Letter from Poland's ambassador to FO, April 13, 1943. CO's letter to FO, May 21, 1943.

18 Ibid., Schonfeld's letter to CO, May 19, 1943 and minute, May 31, 1943.

19 Ibid., Hertz's letter to Stanley, May 30, 1943.

20 Ibid., CO's cables to governors of colonies, June 3, 1943.

21 Ibid., cable from the governor of Kenya, June 10, 1943.

22 Ibid., cable from the governor of the Seychelles Islands, June 11, 1943.

23 Ibid., cable from the governor of Cyprus, June 7, 1943.

24 Ibid., cable from the governor of Mauritius, June 10, 1943. Stanley's letter to Hertz, June 18, 1943. Hertz's answer, June 21, 1943. Minutes to this correspondence in FO 371-36735.

25 Thus Rabbi Schonfeld admitted on January 21, 1975 when I interviewed him. CO 323-1845-7031/44, minute, June 21, 1943.

26 FO 371, 36735, CO's letter to FO, June 26, 1943.

27 CO 323-1846-7031/44, CO's letter to FO, June 26, 1943 and Randall's answer, July 13, 1943 on negotiations with the enemy about the rabbis. Prem 4/52/5, Churchill asked to clarify whether negotiations with the enemy are taking place, as he had knowledge about the transfer of a list of 625 candidates for *aliya* from Germany by the Swiss government. He strongly opposed any negotiations of this kind. Eden reassured the Prime Minister stating that the list was handed over without negotiation. Eden promised not to accept any German condition for the exchange of these Jews. Personal Minute of Prime Minister, June 22, 1943. Eden's letter to Churchill, June 27, 1943. FO 371-36735, Schonfeld's letters to Randall, July 23, 1943; August 6, 1943. FO's instructions to the envoys in these countries, August 11, 1943. FO's letter to the embassy, Lisbon, August 19, 1943.

28 Ibid., cable from the governor of Maritius to CO, July 23, 1943.

29 FO 371-36704, letter from Ripke to British Ambassador to Czechoslovakia, July 3, 1943. CO 323-1846-7031/44, minute, July 20, 1943.

30   FO 371-36735, Schonfeld's letter to Stanley, July 21, 1943.

31   *Encyclopedia Hebraica*, vol. 6, p. 559.

32   CO 323-1846-7031/44, minute, July 28, 1943.

33   FO 371-36735, CO's cable to the governor of Mauritius, August 5, 1943. The governor's answer, August 11, 1943. CO's letter to Hertz, August 14, 1943.

34   CO 323-1846-7031/44, Eastwood's minute, August 28, 1943.

35   Ibid., CO's letter to FO, August 24, 1943. FO 371-36735, FO's letter to CO, September 2, 1943 and minute. FO's letter to Schonfeld, September 11, 1943.

36   Ibid., the letter dated September 9, 1943. FO 371-42777, list transmitted to the Turkish Foreign Ministry by the British Envoy, December 28, 1943.

37   Ibid., FO's cable to Ankara, January 20, 1944. Letter from British Embassy to Turkish Foreign Ministry, January 26, 1944 including a further list of rabbis. FO's letter to Schonfeld, January 27, 1944.

38   Ibid., Schonfeld's letter to Randall, February 4, 1944.

39   Ibid., CO's letter to I. L. Henderson of FO, February 17, 1944.

40   Ibid., Schonfeld's letter to FO, March 3, 1944. Hertz's letter to Eden, March 6, 1944. Eden's answer, March 25, 1944.

41   Ibid., Schonfeld's letter to Randall, April 19, 1944. Randall's answer, May 4, 1944.

42   FO 371-42777, Schonfeld's letter to Randall, April 26, 1944. Hertz's letter to Stanley, May 4, 1944. FO's cable to Ankara, June 5, 1944.

43   Ibid., Eastwood's letter to Randall, May 22, 1944. Randall's answer, May 31, 1944. FO 371-42858, cable from governor of Mauritius to Colonial Secretary, June 29, 1944. FO 371-42859, Stanley's letter to Hertz, July 19, 1944.

44   Solomon Schonfeld, *Message to Jewry*: "We obtained 340 Mauritius visas and the necessary transit visas from Turkey, Spain and Portugal, which saved the lives of many ... " Schonfeld continues: "At a later stage, we did much to facilitate the transfer of the Mauritius Refugees to Palestine." To whom and to what did Rabbi Schonfeld refer? None of his candidates ever reached Mauritius. In my interview with him he could not single out a single person who was saved by his visa campaign. The Mauritius Refugees (all "illegals") were handled exclusively by the Jewish Agency. These facts do not diminish the estimation of his and Rabbi Hertz's intensive efforts to construct an avenue of rescue. Maybe the author mixed the facts. He is credited for the rescue of many European Jews on the eve of the war. Evaluating his activities, the Council of London named a Plaza after him.

45   FO 371-42858, Schonfeld's letters to Randall, July 24, 1944; August 1, 1944. FO's cable to envoy, Bern, August 30, 1944.

46   Ibid., Schonfeld's letter to Randall, August 25, 1944. Randall's answer, September 6, 1944.

47   Ibid., Schonfeld's letter to Randall, July 24, 1944. List of rabbis, September 28, 1944.

48   FO 371-42859, Schonfeld's letters to Randall, October 4, 1944; October 25, 1944; November 21, 1944. Randall's letters to Schonfeld, October 17, 1944; November 11, 1944.

49   See Nathan Ek, *Yad Vashem Studies*, vol. 1, pp. 93ff. Yonas Turkow, *Sofan shel Ashlayoth*, pp. 54ff. Also in London a fight for the verification of these

documents took place. Schonfeld was informed about the issue and the fate of these internees. See FO 371-42889, Schonfeld's letter to FO, October 23, 1944 on the transfer of these Jews from the exchange camp to Auschwitz.

50   FO 371-42889, Schonfeld's letter to CO, November 21, 1944. FO's cable to envoy, Bern, December 9, 1944.

51   Ibid., letter from Jewish Agency to FO, September 12, 1944. FO's answer, September 25, 1944.

52   See Rotkirchen, *Churban Yahaduth Hungaria*, pp. 37ff; pp. 40ff.

53   FO 371-42859, Masaryk's letter to the British Ambassador, September 12, 1944 and FO's minute, September 28, 1944.

54   FO 371-42889, Schonfeld's letter to Paul Mason, new head of FO's Refugee Department, October 16, 1944. Reference to Hertz's letter to Eden on the same topic.

55   Ibid., FO's letter to CO, October 17, 1944. Mason's letter to Schonfeld, October 17, 1943. L. Cheetham's minute to CO's letter to FO, November 13, 1944, mentioning Hertz's effort to obtain British protection for the Hungarian Jews. See also FO 317-42859, Schonfeld's letter to FO, November 21, 1944, and chapter 14.

56   FO 371-51146, letter from British Legation, Stockholm to the Swedish Government, December 24, 1944. FO 371-42889, minute, November 13, 1944. FO's cable to legation, Stockholm, December 21, 1944.

57   FO 371-51146, cable from legation, Stockholm to FO, February 23, 1945.

58   Ibid., minute, April 17, 1945. Schonfeld's letters to FO, June 8, 1945; June 11, 1945. Henderson's answer, June 23, 1945.

59   We shall later learn about Harry Goodman's efforts to save Rabbi Ungar.

60   FO 371-51146, CO's letter to Schonfeld, December 11, 1944. CO's letter to FO, December 13, 1944.

61   Ibid., FO's letter to Schonfeld, March 14, 1945. Schonfeld's answer, March 21, 1945. FO's letter to envoy, Bern, April 4, 1945.

62   See Rotkirchen, *Churban Yahaduth Hungaria*, p. 242: Weissmandel's letter to Hechalutz's office in Geneva asking his friend Rabbi Schonfeld to visit Lambeth Palace (the residence of the Archbishop of Canterbury) to beg for help.

63   FO 371-51146, Weissmandel's letter from December 1, 1944 was handed over to FO on January 5, 1945 in a meeting with Henderson. Report of the meeting, January 8, 1945. FO's letter to Schonfeld, January 15, 1945.

64   Bauer, *American Jewry and the Holocaust*, p. 449.

65   Meier Sompolinsky, "Jewish Institutions in the World and the Yishuv as Reflected in the Holocaust Historiography of the Ultra-Orthodox," in *The Historiography of the Holocaust Period*, pp. 612ff.

66   FO 371-42777, Schonfeld's letter to Randall, February 4, 1944 and minute. Ambassador's cable, Ankara, March 10, 1944.

67   Ibid., Schonfeld's letter to FO, March 3, 1944 and negative answer, March 25, 1944. MEW's letter to FO, March 20, 1944.

68   FO 371-42752, FO's letter to Bank of England, January 25, 1944. Schonfeld's letter to Randall, February 8, 1944. Randall's letter to the Treasury, February 15, 1944. Treasury's answer, February 18, 1944. Randall's letter to Schonfeld,

March 6, 1944. FO 317-42777, Hertz's letter to Eden, March 9, 1944. Minute, March 20, 1944. Randall's letter to the Treasury, May 9, 1944. MEW's letter to FO, May 12, 1944. Eden's answer to Hertz, May 22, 1944. Hertz's letter to Eden, June 4, 1944.

69   FO 371-42889, letter from IGCR to FO, October 11, 1944. FO's cables to legation, Bern, October 26, 1944, November 9, 1944. Cables from legation, October 28, 1944; November 10, 1944. FO's letter to IGCR, November 14, 1944.

70   Weissmandel's letters published in *Min Hametsar*. See also Rotkirchen, *Churban Yahaduth Hungaria*, p. 236; p. 240.

71   BSA, report of meeting Schonfeld–Zelmanowitz, April 17, 1944.

72   Schonfeld's letter in *The Times*, June 6, 1961.

73   FO 371-51175, Schonfeld's letter to Ernest Bevin and Mason's answer, October 17, 1945. In December 1944 some Italian Jews fostered the idea to establish a Jewish state in the German province of Brandenburg, proposing Albert Einstein to become its president. Perhaps Schonfeld was influenced by these people. They distributed printed material on the proposal, trying to promote their idea. Sir William Beveridge preceded them, as he in the beginning of 1943 in a lecture stressed such an idea which frightened the Zionist headquarter. See CZA, Z4-302/27, session February 1, 1943. Most probably, the Beveridge vision encouraged the anti-Zionist rabbi.

Chapter 12 *The Ten Million Dollar Illusion*

1   FO 371-42731 .

2   John Morton Blum, *From the Morgenthau Diaries, Years of War, 1941–1945*, p. 218: "Well, Morgenthau replied, 'Breck . . . we might be a little frank. The impression is all around (that) you, particularly, are anti-Semitic'." See also ibid., pp. 211–12, 220–2. Feingold, *The Politics of Rescue*, pp. 115ff.

3   BSA, Nahum Goldmann suggested two million dollars from private Jewish sources – thus Easterman in talk with the American vice director of IGCR Patrick Malin, October 5, 1943 and in letter to the same, December 22, 1943.

4   Ibid., circular letter December 27, 1943. The idea was first launched in Easterman's letter to Haccius on July 30, 1943 and cabled to WJC office in New York on September 3, 1943 for implementation.

5   Ibid., Easterman's letter to Brotman, January 18, 1944.

6   BDA, file Refugees, report of meeting Brotman–George Randall, January 14, 1944. Easterman revealed the proposal to Soviet Ambassador Maisky on September 8, 1943, who strongly opposed considering it a threat to the blockade on Germany. BSA, report on the conversation.

7   FO 371-42752, letter from Randall to Emerson, December 22, 1943.

8   Ibid., letter from Emerson to Randall, December 24, 1943. The same advice from Lord Winterton, chairman of IGCR to Deputy Foreign Secretary George Hall, December 29, 1943.

9   FO 371-42731, Randall's minute, January 3, 1944, and Hall's answer to Winterton, January 4, 1944.

10 Ibid., letter from International Red Cross, Geneva, to its London office, December 3, 1944.
11 BSA, summary letter from Tartakower to Haccius, January 12, 1944.
12 FO 371-42752, Camps' letter to Foreign Office, January 28, 1944.
13 Ibid., letter from Playfair of the Treasury to Randall, February 2, 1944 and Randall's answer, February 6, 1944.
14 FO 371-42727, cable to ambassador in Washington, February 23, 1944. Due to importance copies were distributed to War Cabinet members.
15 FO 371-42751, minute on meeting with Goldmann, March 2, 1944.
16 FO 371-42811, Lady Reading's letter to Eden, July 26, 1944 and Eden's answer, August 11, 1944. Henderson's minute, August 6, 1944.
17 BSA, report of Kubowitski's meeting with Gustav Kuhlmann, IGCR, January 17, 1945.
18 FO 371-42811, minute, December 21, 1944.
19 BSA, report of Reading's and Kubowitski's talk with Emerson, Kuhlmann and Malin, January 8, 1945. Kubowitski's cable to Goldmann, January 9, 1945. Report of Kubowitski's meeting with Kuhlmann on January 17, 1945; the latter explained that only limited means for rendering help were available to the President of the US. So loans were rendered to the Red Cross. Large sums had to be approved by Congress and therefore secrecy could not be maintained.

Chapter 13 *Ireland and the Jews of Europe*

1   Dermot Keogh, *Ireland and Europe 1919–1948*, p. 118.
2   Ibid., p. 115.
3   Ibid., p. 128.
4   Robert Briscoe, *For the Life of Mine*, p. 284.
5   Keogh, *Ireland and Europe 1919–1948*, pp. 191ff.
6   Ibid., p. 199. *The Times*, May 14, 1945.
7   National Archives of Ireland (NAI), Department of Foreign Affairs (DFA), P90 25344, March 3, 1944; March 27, 1944.
8   Ibid., 202/63, Charles Bewley to Secretary of External Affairs, Confidential Report, December 12, 1938. Keogh, *Ireland and Europe 1919–1948,* pp. 100ff.
9   Ibid., pp. 103ff.
10 Ibid., p. 111.
11 NAI, The Taoiseach's Office, SPO S11007A, September 24, 1945.
12 Keogh, *Ireland and Europe 1919–1948*, p. 206.
13 Ibid., p. 110.
14 Ibid., pp. 108ff.
15 On the close relations between Briscoe and de Valera see the former's book *For the Life of Mine.*
16 Keogh, *Ireland and Europe 1919–1948*, p. 110.
17 Ibid., p. 227, note 32.
18 Ibid., p. 111.
19 Ibid., pp. 182–3.

20   *The Times*, December 22, 1942, letter from Sir Neil Malcolm.

21   BSA, letter from Richard Law, Foreign Office, to Easterman, January 20, 1943.

22   Goodman's private archive (GA), letter from Goodman to J. H. W. Dulanty, April 8, 1943.

23   Ibid., Goodman's memorandum to Joseph P. Walshe, May 5, 1943.

24   Ibid., Goodman's written summary to Dulanty, May 5, 1943 and his summary to the heads of BD, May 16, 1943.

25   Ibid., Goodman's summary to JFC, same date.

26   Ibid., Goodman's letter to Walshe, May 5, 1943. The Irish Red Cross' letter to Goodman, May 14, 1943.

27   Ibid., Goodman's letter to Dulanty, May 20, 1943.

28   Ibid., Points for Discussion with Mr. Randall, July 7, 1943. Report of interview with Randall, July 9, 1943. Other issues were also discussed at this meeting such as immigration to Palestine and exchanges, parallel to meetings with BD, BSWJC etc.

29   Ibid., Goodman's letter to Dulanty, July 19, 1943. Goodman's letter to J. A. Belton, the Irish High Commissioner's secretary, July 23, 1943.

30   Ibid., Goodman's letter to Walshe, August 9, 1943.

31   Ibid., Goodman's letters to the Irish High Commissioner, September 6, 17, 24, 1943. High Commissioner's letter to Goodman, September 9, 1943.

32   Ibid., Goodman's letter to the High Commissioner, October 20, 1943.

33   Ibid., Goodman's letter to the High Commissioner, November 9, 1943.

34   Ibid., Goodman's letter to Walshe, November 24, 1943.

35   Ibid., Goodman's letter to Dr Paschal Robinson, the Nuncio in Dublin, November 24, 1943. Robinson's letter to Goodman, December 1, 1943.

36   Ibid., Goodman's letter to the High Commissioner, December 29, 1943.

37   Ibid., the High Commissioner's letter to Goodman, December 30, 1943. Goodman's letters to the High Commissioner, March 17, 1944 and to Walshe, March 31, 1944.

38   NAI DFA 2/12, *aide-memoire* to Das Auswartiges Amt, Berlin, January 6, 1944.

39   Ibid., 2/12-48/1, Irish Minister in Berlin Cornelius Cremin to Department of External Affairs, March 24, 1944. GA, Goodman's cable to Walshe, April 16, 1944. Walshe's cable to Goodman, April 19, 1944.

40   NAI DFA 2/12, Cremin, Berlin to Walshe, May 12, 1944. GA, Walshe's cable to Goodman, May 16, 1944.

41   Yonas Turkow, *Sofan shel Ashlayoth*, pp. 174–5. Natan Ek, *Yad Vashem Studies*, vol. 1, Jerusalem 1957, pp. 109ff.

42   GA, Goodman's letter to Walshe, May 22, 1944. Cable from Goodman to Walshe, May 27, 1944 and letter, June 12, 1944.

43   Ibid., Goodman's letter to Walshe, June 26, 1944. Zaidman's letter to Goodman (no date) with a list of names, being attached to Goodman's letter to the Foreign Office – FO 371-42872, July 4, 1944. Zaidman writes, "225 Pers. Juden Sud-Amerikaner mit Konsularpasse wurden 18.4.44 von Vittel via Drancy – in unbekanter Richtung deportiert . . . " The letter, written on linen and smuggled to London, is in the possession of the Goodman family. Zaidman survived. He has been the archivist of the Warsaw Ghetto Jewish

Community. He published *The Diary of the Warsaw Ghetto*.

44 GA, Walshe's cable to Goodman, August 28, 1944. Goodman's letter to Walshe, September 6, 1944.

45 Ibid., Goodman's cable to Walshe, July 7, 1944 and letter, same date. Walshe's cable to Goodman, July 10, 1944.

46 Ibid., Goodman's letter to the High Commissioner, July 31, 1944 and cable to Walshe, August 8, 1944.

47 FO 371-42815, Deputy Secretary, Dominion Office to Foreign Office, Statement of August 18, 1944.

48 Ibid., Mac Lennan's letter to Ian Leslie Henderson, August 22, 1944.

49 GA, Springer's letter to the High Commissioner and to the Irish Red Cross, August 12, 1944. The London US Embassy's letter to Agudat Israel, August 29, 1944.

50 FO 371-42817, US Embassy's letter to Foreign Office, Sepember 9, 1944.

51 Ibid., Foreign Office's letter to US Embassy, September 21, 1944.

52 GA, Goodman's letter to Walshe, September 29, 1944 and cable, October 4, 1944. Walshe's letter to Goodman, October 5, 1944.

53 Ibid., Goodman's summary on negotiations in Dublin, October 25, 1944. See *Jewish Weekly* (Agudat Israel's paper), November 3, 1944 and *JC*, same date.

54 GA, Walshe's letter to Goodman, November 29, 1944.

55 Ibid., Goodman's letter to Walshe, May 16, 1945. Walshe's letter to Goodman, June 4, 1945. Goodman's letter to Walshe, June 7, 1945. Walshe's cable to Goodman, August 14, 1945.

56 Ibid., the British Foreign Office's letter to Goodman, November 11, 1944.

57 FO 371-51146, Agudat Israel's letter to Foreign Office, January 9, 1945. Foreign Office's letter to Goodman, January 27, 1945.

58 NAI DFA 2/12/48/12, cable from Cremin, Berlin to Foreign Affairs Department, Dublin, October 10, 1944.

59 GA, Walshe's letter to Goodman, November 29, 1944. Goodman's answer, December 19, 1944.

60 NAI DFA 2/12/48/12, Cremin, Berlin to Foreign Affairs Department, Dublin, October 22, 1944.

61 Ibid., DFA 48/12/48/23/2/12, Foreign Affairs Department, Dublin to Cremin, Berlin, December 8, 1944 and Cremin's answer, December 13, 1944.

62 Ibid., DFA 2/12/48/12/44/48, Cremin to Dublin, December 21, 1944.

63 Ibid., Cremin to Dublin, December 23, 1944.

64 GA, Walshe's letter to Goodman, February 9, 1945.

Chapter 14 *Reactions to the Crisis of Hungarian Jewry*

1 Feingold, *The Politics of Rescue*, pp. 244ff.

2 BDA, file 543, report of emergency meeting, March 2, 1944.

3 Ibid., Mowshowitz report to Brodetsky, March 22, 1944.

4 Ibid.

5 Ibid., cable from Ben-Zvi to Brodetsky, July 11, 1944. Cable from Brodetsky to Ben-Zvi, July 11, 1944.

6   Ibid., report of Mowshowitz's meeting with Brodetsky, March 22, 1944; BSA, report of Easterman's talk with Donald Hall, March 21, 1944.

7   FO 371-42723, letter from Brodetsky to Eden, March 22, 1944 with minutes; Randall's report on meeting of Jewish delegation with Henderson, March 28, 1944; report on this by Brotman.

8   Ibid., Easterman's letter to Donald Hall, March 28, 1944.

9   CZA-302/28, session, March 28, 1944.

10 FO 371-42723, cable from the Foreign Office to the British attaché to Yugoslavia in Cairo, April 10, 1944. See also Martin's reply to Weizmann, April 24, 1944.

11 BDA, file 543, report of talk of William Frankel, the new secretary of the Foreign Affairs Committee of the Board of Deputies, with Walker and Randall, May 5, 1944.

12 FO 371-42723, Easterman's letter to Law, March 31, 1944.

13 BDA. file 543, Easterman's letters to Law, March 31, 1944 and April 10, 1944; letter from Law to Easterman, April 4, 1944.

14 BDA, file 543, Temkin's report to Brotman, April 3, 1944.

15 Ibid., Simpson's letter to Brotman, April 6, 1944; Easterman's letter to Brotman, April 14, 1944.

16 FO 371-42724, letter from the BD (Brotman) to Foreign Office, April 11, 1944; report of Easterman's talk with Donald Hall, April 13, 1944; Hall's letter to Easterman, May 2, 1944, with minutes; report of Frankel's talk with Walker and Randall on May 5, 1944; FO 371-42725, Hall's letter to Easterman, May 2, 1944; Easterman's letter to Donald Hall on May 16, 1944 and his reply on May 24, 1944. See also the article of Bela Vago "The British Government and the Fate of Hungarian Jewry in 1944," in *Rescue Attempts During the Holocaust*, pp. 205–33.

17 Ibid., letter from Linton of Jewish Agency to Foreign Office, May 12, 1944; reply of Foreign Office, May 31, 1944.

18 FO 371-42723, letter from Rathbone to Randall, March 24, 1944; letter from Rathbone to Brigadier Harvey Watt, March 24, 1944.

19 Ibid., letter from Rathbone to Randall, April 1, 1944; Randall's reply on May 15, 1944. The minute says that leaflets were dropped from the air. Due to top secrecy she was not informed. No indication of where dropped or of contents.

20 FO 371-42725, report of talk with American officials on April 12, 1944; cable from British Ambassador to Government of Yugoslavia in Cairo, April 26, 1944.

21 BSA, memorandum from May 24, 1944.

22 Ibid., Reading's letter to Easterman, May 28, 1944.

23 CAB. 95/12, cable from High Commissioner, Jerusalem, to Colonial Secretary, May 26, 1944.

24 See Chaim Barlas, *Rescue in the Days of the Holocaust*, p. 74 and p. 103. He may have referred to financial assistance sent to the Jewish underground in Warsaw which did not arrive in time.

25 BDA, report of plenary session, June 18, 1944. See also brochure: Nazi Extermination of the Jews, Speeches by Prof. S. Brodetsky and Dr Chaim Weizmann, and Resolution Adopted by the Board of Deputies of British Jews.

London, June 18, 1944.

26 BSA, cable from Easterman to Goldmann, June 2, 1944.

27 FO 371-42725, report of meeting at Foreign Office with American officials, April 12, 1944; FO 371-40621, see also minutes in this spirit following visit by Goldmann and Easterman at Foreign Office, regarding defense of Jews in case of cease-fire with Germans on March 2, 1944; FO 371-41129, see also minutes of June 27, 1944 and June 28, 1944.

28 BSA, report of Easterman's talk with George Hall, May 1, 1944; talk of Silverman and Easterman with Eden, May 3, 1944.

29 FO 371-42798, minute on Easterman's letter on April 19, 1944.

30 FO 371-2808, Eden's remark, July 25, 1944.

31 FO 371-42877, Silverman's letter to Eden and minutes, July 28, 1944.

32 Ibid., Mason's letter to Easterman, October 19, 1944; see also Easterman's letters to Foreign Office, August 30, 1944 and September 13, 1944 and minutes; cable from Foreign Office to Lord Halifax on November 17, 1944. Eden refused to send greetings to the Conference despite pressure from Lady Reading and Lord Melchett; see letter from Lady Reading to Law on November 3, 1944; see Lord Melchett's letter to Eden on November 7, 1944.

33 FO 371-42807, report of talk with Silverman, July 4, 1944; ibid., reprint of debates in Parliament, July 5, 1944.

34 BSA, report of Silverman's talk with Hall, July 20, 1944, the day the leak was published; see John Conway, *Between Apprehension and Indifference*, Wiener Library Bulletin, vol. XXVII, 1973/1974, p. 44; ibid., Conway was mistaken when he said that Washington had leaked the news, presumably hoping to change British attitudes. The truth was different. The Germans were right in assuming that this was a British release, note 30, p. 48. See also David Hadar, *The Attitude of the Great Powers to the Mission of Joel Brand Molad*, p. 124.

35 FO 371-42808, Melchett's letter to Churchill, July 1, 1944.

36 BDA, file 543, Easterman's letter to Brotman, July 7, 1944; FO 371-42807, the letter of the Archbishop of Canterbury to the Foreign Office, July 28, 1944. In his letter he pressed for a repeated number of broadcasts of his plea to the Hungarian people, even if this effort "would save only one soul."

37 FO 371-42809, Churchill's letters to the Archbishop, July 13, 1944 and to Lord Melchett, July 13, 1944.

38 Ibid., the Prime Minister's personal minute, July 11, 1944. See also W. S. Churchill, *The Second World War*, vol. VI, Appendices, p. 541.

39 FO 371-42807, Eden's minute to the Prime Minister on July 3, 1944.

40 Ibid., Churchill's minute to the Foreign Secretary, June 29, 1944 and Eden's to Churchill, July 3, 1944.

41 FO 371-42808, Rathbone's letter to Eden, July 6, 1944; Eden's reply, July 7, 1944.

42 FO 371-42809, Eden's minute to the Prime Minister, July 6, 1944.

43 Ibid., personal minutes of the Prime Minister to Eden, July 7, 1944 and July 8, 1944.

44 FO 371-42808, Cab. Conclusion 85 (44), July 3, 1944.

45 FO 371-42809, cable from Foreign Office to the embassy in Moscow, July 13, 1944.

46   FO 371-42810, Randall's talk with Rathbone, July 18, 1944; FO 371-42815, personal announcement by Molotov to Eden, August 16, 1944.

47   BDA, file 543, Easterman's letter to Brotman, July 7, 1944 – the initiative came from the British Section.

48   Cab. 95/15, letter from Hertz to Churchill, May 8, 1944. The idea did not originate with Hertz. On July 26, 1933 the Conservative MP, Commander Oliver Locker-Lampson, tabled a bill that would enable Jews residing outside the Empire – meaning the Jews of Germany – to obtain British citizenship, or at least to broaden the Palestinian citizenship to extend to all persecuted Jews. He added that Britain had accepted the mandate "to fulfill the Messianic miracle there." A minute of the Foreign Office reads: "The House was greatly moved by Commander L.-L.'s oration." His bill reached only a first reading. See Sherman, *Island Refuge*, p. 39.

49   FO 371-42725, minute of the Refugee Department, May 10, 1944.

50   This point may have arisen because Rabbi Hertz mentioned the Balfour Declaration in his letter as a basis for this request; it is doubtful that this reminder was wise.

51   FO 371-42725, summary of discussions in Note for the Secretary of State, June 9, 1944.

52   Ibid., letter from Mason to Martin, May 16, 1944.

53   Cab. 65/42 47, decision, June 12, 1944.

54   Cab. 95/15, letter from Eden to Hertz, June 28, 1944.

55   FO 371-42726, minute, June 26, 1944.

56   FO 371-42808, letter from Eastwood, the Colonial Office to Randall, July 11, 1944 and minute.

57   FO 371-42810, cable from the High Commissioner to the Colonial Office, July 19, 1944.

58   FO 371-42811, letter from Colonial Office to Foreign Office, July 28, 1944. See Chaim Barlas, *Rescue in the Days of the Holocaust*, pp. 35–6 – the formulation of the approval; according to Barlas, these approvals saved some 50,000 souls in Hungary, and the idea came from rescue workers in Geneva.

59   FO 371 42810, Bentwich's proposal and minute, July 19, 1944.

60   Ibid., memorandum of a talk between the NCRNT and the Foreign Office, July 26, 1944.

61   FO 371-42880, Hall's letter to Squadron-Leader Fleming, July 28, 1944.

62   FO 371-42897, memorandums of Heathcote-Smith, October 24, 1944 and November 9, 1944; Emerson's letter to Winterton, October 24, 1944; Malin's letter to Mason, November 6, 1944; Mason's reply, December 6, 1944.

63   FO 371-42808, Morrison's letter to Eden, July 1, 1944.

64   FO 371-42810, Shertok, who was in London in connection with the Brand mission, feared that rejecting the transaction might harm the attitude to the Horthy Offer; see Shertok's letter to Randall, July 20, 1944.

65   Cab. 95/15, cable from legation in Berne to Foreign Office, August 1, 1944; meeting of the Cabinet's Committee on Refugees, August 8, 1944; FO 371-42812, cable from Foreign Office to Legation in Berne, August 6, 1944.

66   FO 371-42814, memorandum from the Foreign Secretary to the War Cabinet, August 8, 1944, – "Hungarian Offer to Allow Jews to Leave Hungary."

67 FO 371-42814, Premier 4-52/5-8.8.44, wording of the declaration of acceptance of the "Horthy Offer," August 22, 1944.

68 FO 371-42815, War Cab. Concl. 107/44, August 16, 1944.

69 FO 371-42816, minute of Colonial Office, August 24, 1944.

70 Ibid., cable from Lord Moyne, August 26, 1944 and minute.

71 Ibid., letter from London office of the Red Cross to the Foreign Office, August 31, 1944 and minute.

72 FO 371-42819, letter from Colonial Office to Foreign Office, October 12, 1944. Reply from Foreign Office, October 17, 1944 and minutes.

73 Ibid., cables from legation in Stockholm, October 10 and 12, 1944.

74 FO 371-42816, Brotman's letter to the Foreign Office, August 29, 1944 and minutes.

75 FO 371-42817, report of Shertok's and Linton's talk at the Foreign Office, September 5, 1944 and minute; cable from Foreign Office to Embassy in Ankara, September 15, 1944.

76 FO 371-42815, letter from Political Department of Foreign Office to the British Minister in Berne, August 5, 1944; see Barlas, *Rescue in the Days of the Holocaust*, pp. 193–4; see Jonas Turkov, *Sofan shel Ashlayot*, pp. 160–1.

77 Ibid., minute, C. Cheetham, August 24, 1944.

78 Ibid., cable from legation in Berne, September 8, 1944.

79 Ibid., Mason's minute, September 12, 1944.

80 Ibid., cable from legation in Berne on September 15, 1944; Mason's minutes, September 20, 1944 and October 10, 1944.

81 FO 371-42817, letter from Mason to Kuhlmann, September 18, 1944; FO 371-42818, Mason's minute, October 10, 1944.

82 FO 371-42810, report of Brodetsky's and Bearstead's talk with George Hall, July 18, 1944.

83 Ibid., Brotman's questions, July 19, 1944 and Henderson's minute, July 24, 1944.

84 Ibid., cable from Foreign Office to embassy in Washington, August 1, 1944.

85 FO 371-42810, Shertok's letter to Randall, April 20, 1944; FO 371-42811, letter from D. R. Grenfell MP, Chairman of the National Committee for Rescue from Nazi Terror, to Eden, July 20, 1944.

86 Ibid., Grenfell's letter.

87 FO371-42812, report of meeting between Foreign Secretary and a delegation of the NCRNT, July 26, 1944.

88 Ibid., Rathbone's letter to Eden, July 27, 1944.

89 Ibid., Rathbone's letter to Eden, July 31, 1944.

90 FO 371-42815, Rathbone's letter to Eden on August 9, 1944; FO 371-42814, note for the Secretary of State, August 14, 1944; ibid., report of talk between Rathbone, Lady Reading, Gollancz and Locker with Hall, August 9, 1944.

91 FO 371-42817, report of Brotman's talk with Mason, August 31, 1944 and Allan Walker's minute, September 1, 1944.

92 BSA, cables from Riegner to the British Section of WJC on September 20, 1944 and September 21, 1944.

93 Ibid., cable from BSWJC to Riegner, September 25, 1944.

94 Ibid., Easterman's letter to Paul Mason on September 25, 1944; Mason's reply

on October 13, 1944.

95 FO 371-42820, Foreign Secretary's cable to his office, October 16, 1944; Mason's letter to Easterman, October 23, 1944, and minutes. In his cable Eden agrees to delaying the advance of the Red Army toward Budapest so as to enable the Hungarian Army to get organized. This caused concern in the Refugee Department for the fate of the Jews.

96 BDA, file 543 and FO 371-42820, report of meeting of Brodetsky and Brotman with Hall, October 18, 1944.

97 Ibid., Mason's minute to Hall, October 18, 1944.

98 FO 371-42821, Mason's letter to Martin, October 30, 1944.

99 Ibid., Mason's letter to K. E. Robinson, Colonial Office, November 13, 1944.

100 FO 371-42820, cables from legation in Stockholm, October 20, 1944 and October 28, 1944, and minutes.

101 FO 37-42821, letter from Zelmanovits to Foreign Office, November 2, 1944, and minutes.

102 BDA, file 543, cable from Lichtheim, Geneva, to Linton on November 14.

103 FO 371-42824, letter from Zelmanovits to Mason, December 5, 1944.

104 Ibid., Mason's letter to Zelmanovits on January 4, 1945, and minutes.

105 FO 371-51111, letter from Zelmanovits to Foreign Office, January 16, 1945; Foreign Office's reply, February 19, 1945 and minutes.

106 Ibid., letter from Zelmanovits to Foreign Office, February 23, 1945.

Chapter 15 *Last-Minute Rescue Attempts*

1 See Livia Rothkirchen, "The Final Solution in Its Last Stages," *Yad Vashem Studies* VIII, pp. 7ff.

2 FO 371-42755, Randall's minute to Charles Peake, April 17, 1944.

3 FO 371-42726, Easterman's letter to Hall, June 26, 1944; BSA, Easterman's letter to US Ambassador, June 28, 1944; BDA, file 543, Easterman's letter to Brotman, July 7, 1944.

4 FO 371-4276, letter from Army General Staff to Foreign Office, August 4, 1944.

5 FO 371-42815, letter from National Committee for Rescue from Nazi Terror to Eden, August 19, 1944; reply from Foreign Office, August 31, 1944. To emphasize its importance, the letter is signed by the Archbishop of Canterbury and members of Parliament.

6 FO 371-42820, cable from Foreign Office to ambassador in Moscow, October 16, 1944 and minute, November 7, 1944.

7 Ibid., cables to Embassies in Moscow and Washington, November 14, 1944.

8 See W. S. Churchill, *The Second World War*, vol. VI, pp. 190ff.

9 FO 371-42817, Mason's memorandum, September 9, 1944, especially the paragraph: D. Armistice Terms.

10 FO 371-42824, report of talk between Brodetsky and Mason, November 30, 1944; letter from Foreign Office to Brodetsky, December 14, 1944, and minute.

11 FO 371-42823, letter from Goodman to Mason, December 1, 1944; reply from

Foreign Office, December 14, 1944 and minutes.

12 BSA, letter from World Jewish Congress to Mann, January 9, 1945.

13 Ibid., report of talk by Reading and Kubowitzki with Emerson, January 8, 1945.

14 Ibid., cable from Reading and Kubowitzki to Polish Foreign Secretary, January 18, 1945.

15 Ibid., copies of letters to governments of Czechoslovakia, Holland, Belgium, and Luxembourg and their replies.

16 Ibid., cable from Reading and Kubowitzki to Huber, January 18, 1945. Even the Red Cross officials had that opinion as their staffs rendered relief to German bombed-out civilians. Thus Monsieur Haccius to Zelmanovits, in Zelmanovits' memorandum, February 15, 1945.

17 BSA, cable from Reading to the Foreign Secretary of France in Paris, February 2, 1945; reply from the French Ambassador in London, February 12, 1945.

18 Ibid., report of Silverman's press conference, February 1, 1945.

19 Ibid., cable from Riegner, March 5, 1945. According to Kubowitzki at a press conference in London, March 15, 1945.

20 FO 371-51172, Mason's minute, February 26, 1945.

21 BSA, Easterman's letters to Eden and to the ambassadors of the USA and USSR, February 28, 1945. Information about ghettos in Polish prisoner-of-war camps was published, February 27, 1945 in the London newspaper, *The Polish Daily*. Szwarcbart demanded the Polish Government to carry out retaliation against German captives.

22 BDA, file-Refugees, report of talk by Brodetsky and Brotman with Mason, February 20, 1945.

23 FO 371 51172, Ripka's letter to Nichols, January 31, 1945 and minutes.

24 FO 371-51115, Goodman's letter to Mason, April 3, 1945; Mason's reply, April 23, 1945.

25 BSA, the plan sounds like a deal of Jews in exchange for clothes, analogous to the Brand transaction. Hence the proposal was formulated in a different manner in a cable to Goldmann which was sent via the USA Embassy. See cable, March 28, 1945.

26 BSA, Zelmanovits' report on his visit to Stockholm, March 28, 1945. Finally, the War Refugee Board instructed its representative in Stockholm not to place the parcels at the disposal of Storch but rather of the Swedish Red Cross or of the Young Men's Christian Association.

27 FO 371-51194, cable from Mallet to Foreign Office, March 25, 1945. Finally Norbert Masur went to Himmler. See Norbert Masur, *En Jude Talar med Himmler*.

28 FO 371-51194, minutes on above cable.

29 Ibid., Prem 4/52/5 I/786, detailed memorandum from Eden to the Prime Minister and the Premier's minute, April 5, 1945.

30 FO 371-51115, minute, April 7, 1945.

Bibliography

Adler-Rudel, S., *A Chronicle of Rescue Efforts*, Leo Back Institute Year Book XI, 1966.

Avneri, Aryeh L., *From "Velos" to "Taurus"* (Hebrew), Tel-Aviv, 1985.

Barlas, Chaim, *Rescue in the Days of the Holocaust* (Hebrew), Tel-Aviv, 1975.

Basok, Moshe (ed.), *Sefer Hamaapilim* (Hebrew), Jerusalem, 1947.

Bauer, Yehuda, *American Jewry and the Holocaust*, Detroit, 1982.

Baumel, Esther Judith Tydor, *The Jewish Refugee Children in Great Britain*, Ramat-Gan, 1981.

Bentwich, Norman, *Wanderer in War*, London, 1946.

——, *I Understood the Risk*, London, 1950.

——, *They Found Refugee*, London, 1956.

——, *My 77 Years*, Philadelphia, 1961.

Bermant, Chaim, *Troubled Eden*, London, 1969.

——, *The Cousinhood*, London, 1972.

Blum, John Morton, *From the Morgenthau Diaries, Years of War*, Boston, 1967.

Bolchover, Richard, *British Jewry and the Holocaust*, Cambridge, 1993.

Briscoe, Robert, *For the Life of Mine*, London, 1958.

Brodetsky, Selig, *Memoirs, From Ghetto to Israel*, London, 1959.

Conway, John, "Between Apprehension and Indifference," *Wiener Library Bulletin,* vol. XXVII, 1973/4.

Encyclopedia Hebraica, Jerusalem.

Esh S. and Gold Y. (eds), *Yehudi Britannia, Hayehaim, Uba'ayotehem Bedoreinu* (Hebrew) [The Jews in Britain, Their Present-Day Life and Problems], Jerusalem, 1966.

Eva, Marchioness of Reading, *For the Record*, London, 1972.

Feingold, Henry L., *The Politics of Rescue*, New Brunswick, 1970.

Friedlander, Saul, *Prelude to Dawnfall*, New York, 1967.

Goldmann, Nachum, *World Jewish Congress and Anglo-Jewry*, London, 1954.

——, *The Autobiography of Nachum Goldmann*, New York, 1961.

——, *Zikhronot* [Memoirs] (Hebrew), Jerusalem, 1972.

Gollancz, Victor, *Let My People Go*, London, 1943.

Hadar, David, *The Attitude of the Great Powers to the Mission of Yoel Brand*, Jerusalem, 1971.

Hakohen, David, *Et Lesaper* [Time to Tell] (Hebrew), Tel-Aviv, 1974.

Hinshaw, D., *Herbert Hoover, American Quaker*, New York, 1950.

Homa, Bernard, *Orthodoxy in Anglo-Jewry*, London, 1969.

Joseph, H. Oscar, *CBF Annual Report – Forty Years On*, London, 1972–3.

Katzburg, Nathaniel, *Medini'ut Bemavokh* (Hebrew), Jerusalem, 1972.

Keogh, Dermot, *Ireland and Europe 1919–1948*, Dublin, 1989.

Kingsley, Martin, *Harold Lasky*, London, 1953.

Lasky, Neville Jonas, *Jewish Rights and Jewish Wrongs*, London, 1939.

Levin, Salmond, S. (ed.), *A Century of Anglo-Jewish Life*, London, 1970.

Locker, Berl, *Mikitov ad Yerushalayim* (Hebrew), Jerusalem, 1970.

Masur, Norbert, *En Jude Taler med Himmler* (Swedish), Stockholm, 1945.

Morse, Arthur D., *While Ten Million Died*, New York, 1967.

Mosley, Oswald, *My Life*, London, 1968.

Presland, John, *A Great Adventure, The Story of the Refugee Children's Movement*, London, 1944.

Rabinowitz, Oskar, *Sir Winston Churchill and Israel*, The Jewish Historical Society of England, London, 1970.

Rathbone, Eleanor, *Rescue the Perishing*, London, 1943.

Rose, N. A. (ed.), *Baffy, The Diaries of Blanche Dugdale, 1934–1947*, London, 1973.

Rosenbluth, Martin, *Go Forth and Serve*, New York, 1961.

Rothkirchen, Livia, *Churban Yahaduth Hungaria* (Hebrew), Jerusalem, 1961.

——, *The Final Solution in its Last Stages*, Yad Vashem Studies, Jerusalem, 1971.

Schonfeld, Solomon, *Message to Jewry*, London, no date.

Sefer Toldoth Hahagana (Hebrew), Tel-Aviv, 1971–2.

Shamir, Chaim, *Beterem Shoah* (Hebrew), Tel-Aviv, 1974.

Sharf, Andrew, *The British Press and the Jews under Nazi Rule*, London, 1964.

Sherman, A. J., *Island Refuge*, London, 1973.

Sherwood, Robert S., *Roosevelt and Hopkins*, New York, 1948.

Slavik, J., *The Persecution of the Jews in Nazi Slovakia*, London, 1942.

Sompolinsky, Meier, "The Rescue Policy of the Chief Rabbi's Religious Emergency Council" (Hebrew), in *Pedut*, Ramat-Gan, 1984.

——, "Jewish Institution in the World and the Yishuv as Reflected in the Holocaust Historiography of the Ultra-Orthodox," in *The Historiography of the Holocaust Period*, Yad Vashem, Jerusalem, 1988.

Stein, A. S., *Haver Arthur* [Friend Arthur] (Hebrew), Tel-Aviv, 1953.

Stein, Leonard, *The Balfour Declaration*, London, 1961.

Stock, Mary D., *Eleanor Rathbone*, London, 1950.

Turkow, Yonas, *Sofan shel Ashlayot* [End of Illusions] (Hebrew), Tel-Aviv, 1973.

United Synagogue – Centenary Exhibition, London, 1970.

Universal Jewish Encyclopedia, New York, 1948.

Vago, Bela, "The British Government and the Fate of Hungarian Jewry in 1944," in *Rescue Attempts During the Holocaust*, Jerusalem, 1972.

Wasserstein, Bernard, *Britain and the Jews of Europe*, London, 1979.

Weissmandel, Michael Dov, *Min Hametsar* (Hebrew), New York, 1952.

Weizmann, Chamim, *Yalkut Pirkei Chaim* (Hebrew), Jerusalem, 1966.

Wischnitzer, Mark, *To Dwell in Safety*, Philadelphia, 1948.

Wyman, David S., *Abandonment of the Jews*, New York, 1984.

Yahil, Leni, *Hatzalat Yehudei Denyia* (Hebrew), Jerusalem, 1967.
Zwergboim, Aron, *Parshat Mauritius* (Hebrew), Yad Vashem Studies, Jerusalem, 1960.

Index